Secondary Curriculum

Secondary Curriculum

Theory and Development

Daniel Tanner
Rutgers University

The Macmillan Company, New York
Collier-Macmillan Limited, London

In Memory of
My Mother and Father

Foreword

After almost two decades of curricular ferment and reform in secondary schools, there is mounting criticism by youth and adults of the whole educational establishment. This is, therefore, a most appropriate time to assess the curriculum of secondary schools to determine its present status, to discover the alternate curricular practices that have been tried or considered, and to clarify the unfinished business facing those concerned with curricular improvement.

Professor Tanner approaches the curricular scene by examining in depth the major threads and emphases of the reform movement, *viz.*, reorganization within discrete disciplines and inquiry and discovery methods. He illustrates the forms that these emphases take in a range of specific programs. He then analyzes and criticizes these developments; he views them in historical perspective and makes clear the antecedents. The similarities and differences among the positions taken by various influential leaders are interpreted and fundamental assumptions are challenged. The areas that have or that lack research support are noted. Exaggerated claims are laid bare. Confusions between slogans and fundamental reforms are bluntly identified.

Professor Tanner reviews in bold and direct fashion many of the most persistent curricular issues. He traces them historically, and views them in the context of current conditions and demands. Thus, the continuing struggle between the influences toward both specialization and integration are portrayed, and their consequences examined. The problems inherent in building interrelationships among disciplines and in helping the learner to a meaningful synthesis are sharply delineated. The dilemmas involved in achieving a balance of emphases in the curriculum are faced openly and constructively.

In addition to treating overall or general curricular conditions and developments, Professor Tanner reports major advances in each of the subject areas in the secondary school. The broader social setting in which innovations are taking place is revealed, and the backgrounds for these innovations are used to help explain and interpret them. Thus, an up-to-date review and criticism of both general and specific subject-based curricular problems are presented.

Throughout the volume Professor Tanner provides a forward thrust. He not only opens for inspection many of our current "hang-ups," but also suggests frontiers and possible and promising next steps. The task of changing the curriculum as well as alternate approaches and viewpoints relative to this task are reviewed.

Daniel Tanner has provided a volume characterized by currency, criticism, and perspective. These qualities commend it to both the newcomer in the curricular arena and the concerned practitioner who seeks involvement and action in the next advances in the secondary school curriculum.

Gordon N. Mackenzie
Professor of Education
Teachers College, Columbia University

Preface

A few years ago, at an annual meeting of the American Association for the Advancement of Science, I attended a general session that featured an address calling for a national experimental cities program to solve the urban ills of our nation. The speaker unveiled the preliminary plans for a prototype city, drawn up with the aid of funds from various departments of the federal government and several leading industrial firms. I was excited at the prospect of sharing a vision of the future created by a group of our leading university and industrial specialists in urban planning. It did not bother me that we would need to construct fifty new cities every three years, each with a quarter of a million inhabitants, just to keep pace with our population growth—not to mention the urban reconstruction necessary to clear the vast slums of our existing cities. After all, our society has the resources and intelligence to reallocate its priorities whether by choice or necessity.

The speaker proceeded to describe how the controlled city of a quarter of a million people would be designed to utilize the most advanced techniques of construction, transportation, communications, waste removal, and city planning. Buildings would be assembled, disassembled, and reassembled through techniques like those employed in using an erector set so as to allow for changing requirements for housing, industry, and public services. Inflatable buildings, which can be instantly deflated, also would be used, along with precast and even prefurnished units put together like building blocks and rearranged to whatever patterns might be desired in the future. Sections of the experimental city would be domed and completely climate controlled. Where the activities in expanding and changing conventional cities take place above the ground, the technology of the experimental city would allow for physical growth and change through underground facilities. Transportation would be provided by moving sidewalks and computer-controlled pods. Wastes would not be wasted, but would be processed for recycling within the controlled city's closed-earth system. The speaker described how the controlled city would be run like a gigantic public utility. Factories, businesses, homes, and schools would be built in modular complexes to minimize problems of transportation, waste recycling, police surveillance, and other services.

How would the controlled city be populated? Acknowledging that it might be difficult to find voluntary inhabitants, the planning group reasoned that since our society manages to push people around under conditions of war, highway construction, slum clearance, and other wrongly directed activities, why should it not be legal to require people to move in the "right" direction?

How paradoxical that the very experts who conceived this Utopian vision of man's future urban life should assume that people would not be willing to inhabit such a community! It occurred to me that the experts had designed a technological system in which people function both as integral parts of the machinery and as objects to be processed through that machinery. In essence, a technological system is created in which human beings are engaged in activities to serve the system and to keep it functioning smoothly and perpetually. Left out of the system are the very qualities that make us human. Where the technological experts had accounted for all of the elemental questions and needs, they had failed to deal with the larger questions of ecology, beauty, and human relationships. They had created a dehumanized community. Nothing in the plan called for birds, trees, and saloons in the controlled city. Perhaps if people could not be expected to inhabit such a city voluntarily, one could not expect birds to do so.

I was both surprised and disappointed by the proposal because I found it so unlike the planned city in Tapiola, Finland, and the planned communities outside Stockholm which I had visited some years earlier. These communities appeared to be designed for people and not the other way around. Why had our own experts dreamed up such a colorlessly efficient and unappealing system of machinery to be served by people for people-processing? I do not know for certain. But it seems to me that if cities are to be planned from the ground up, it is necessary for the planners to know at least as much about people as they do about technology.

To a considerable extent, the curriculum reforms of the 1950's and 1960's were undertaken in a manner remarkably similar to the strategies of the technologists who were responsible for drawing up the plans for our controlled city. The learner, like the prospective inhabitant of the controlled city, was to be transformed so as to improve the efficiency of the system. Special areas of the curriculum were favored in order to meet our new national priorities in the era of the cold war and the age of nuclear weaponry and space exploration. The overriding goal was to exploit our nation's intellectual resources in order to meet the crises of the times. Instead of examining and reconstructing the curriculum in a total ecological framework, the curriculum was dissected into component parts, and priorities were given to the specialized areas of science, mathematics, and modern foreign languages. Almost forgotten for the time being in our pursuit of academic excellence were the needs of our youth and the problems of our people. The academic disciplines were no longer conceived to meet our needs for general education in a free society, but to discover and develop the talents of prospective scientists, engineers, and linguists who would be necessary to our nation's pursuit of world leadership. When we began to become aware of the dangers of curriculum imbalance and fragmentation, the resultant strategy was to create reform projects in the component disciplines of the social studies and English in a manner imitative of the reform efforts in the sciences. The result was the further fragmentation of the curriculum. Moreover, vocational studies, the arts, and various other subjects were regarded as curriculum frills.

Quite suddenly and explosively, educators in our schools and colleges found themselves confronted by student demands for a life-relevant curriculum. The U.S. Riot Commission Report of 1968 noted that the curriculum of our secondary schools had been largely irrelevant to the life experiences of disadvantaged youth. Our great armies of unemployed youth caused our leaders to seek a more recognized place for vocational education in our secondary schools. Characteristically, however, we were responding to crises through emergency and piecemeal measures. Nonschool educative agencies and programs were created to deal with the new crises in a manner not dissimilar to the action taken during the 1930's. Many of these efforts have had limited impact. Emergency priorities of the past have left us with an imbalanced and fragmented curriculum ill-suited to the needs of a large proportion of our youth.

Throughout this textbook I have attempted to show the need for developing a balanced and coherent curriculum. The curriculum is more than the sum total of the separate disciplines that comprise the course of study. Reconstruction in a given discipline or area of the curriculum, whether it be in mathematics or vocational education, cannot be undertaken without eventually affecting other disciplines and curriculum areas. Furthermore, we can no longer establish curriculum priorities and directions in our elementary and secondary schools solely to suit the interests of university scholars as set against the nature and needs of children and youth and the problems of contemporary life in our society at large. Old dichotomies, conflicts, and vested interests must be recognized for what they are if educators are to avoid an imbalanced and disjointed curriculum that is irrelevant to the lives of students.

Part I of this textbook explores the long struggle on the part of educators to reconstruct the teaching-learning process so that the traditional emphasis on memorization and regurgitation of information is discarded in favor of understanding. In this connection, the case is made for viewing the learner realistically as a developing human being and not as a miniature adult scholar. In Chapter 2, the focus is on reconciling the conflict between general education and specialism, between disciplinarity and interdisciplinarity, and between the needs of the college-bound and those who will be entering the world of work directly from high school. Through a coherent and life-relevant program of general education in the setting of the comprehensive high school, the common needs of a cosmopolitan student population can be met while, at the same time, opportunities are provided through diversified studies for meeting the special needs, talents, and interests of all of our youth.

Part II examines curriculum reform efforts in the various disciplines and subject fields. The treatment is not merely descriptive, but analytical and critical. Although separate chapters are devoted to the various curriculum areas, an attempt is made to view each area in terms of the total school curriculum. The doctrine of structure and disciplinarity is examined critically along with the sweeping claims made for many of the new curriculum packages. The need for careful and objective evaluation is stressed, rather than reliance on the testimonials of our university scholar-specialists who are charged with the responsibility of assessing their own works. Ironically, in curriculum evaluation, many of these scholar-specialists have scrupulously avoided the very scientific spirit of inquiry that they have so vigorously promoted as the organizing principle for their respective subject matters. Various promising aspects of the curriculum reform movement also are explored in terms of the total curriculum framework of the school. Theoretical bases of curriculum construction are examined along with the sociopolitical forces that have led to curriculum change and reform.

Finally, Part III presents a critical review of various curriculum innovations in terms of their prospects for improving the teaching-learning process. The curriculum change process is explored and various sources of influence are discussed. The need to utilize the new technology for humanistic goals is emphasized.

Each chapter has a summary statement, which is intended not only to highlight principal points and conclusions but to examine briefly some important implications of the material presented in the chapter. The problems for study and discussion at the end of each chapter are designed to stimulate the further analysis of the material and to lead the student to explore additional sources.

In conclusion, we have witnessed the many adjustments in the curriculum reform movement in recent years. There is growing recognition of the dangers of curriculum imbalance in schools that must serve a diverse pupil population. Efforts are once again being made to take into account the nature and needs of children and youth, as well as the problems of contemporary social life. Young people are demanding such changes. Whether all this signals a new humanitarian motive remains to be seen. Nevertheless, educators now are spending a diminishing portion of their time in debating such issues as mass education versus quality education, intellectual studies versus utilitarian studies, essential subjects versus nonessential subjects, curriculum uniformity versus curriculum diversity, and so on. The act of opening educational opportunities to all the youth in our society has enhanced the possibilities for hidden talents to be discovered and potentials to be realized. The need to develop diversified curricula to serve the goals of many youths who will end their formal education in high school is gaining new recognition.

But the problem of meeting the general education needs of a heterogeneous population in the setting of the comprehensive high school remains sadly neglected. The focus of the curriculum reform movement has been primarily on the academic disciplines as college preparatory studies. Relatively little has been done to develop problem-centered and interdisciplinary studies for purposes of general education. In view of the growing social awareness on the part of our youth, it seems likely that educators will turn once again to the problem of general education in our secondary schools.

According to Mark Twain's Law of Periodical Repetition, everything that has happened once must happen again and again and again—and not capriciously, but at regular periods, and each thing in its own period. While the humanitarian-progressivist vision of the 1930's is not likely to guide our curriculum reform efforts in the 1970's, the resurgent humanitarian motive will require a new reconstruction to meet the new demands of changing social conditions.

I am indebted to Gordon N. Mackenzie of Teachers College, Columbia University, for his careful review of the manuscript and for his many valuable suggestions during the preparation of this textbook.

Over the years I have been influenced, directly and indirectly, by many educators. I am grateful to Harold B. Alberty of The Ohio State University for his many exciting ideas on general education. Ralph Bender, also of The Ohio State University, has given me a real appreciation of the place of vocational education in our comprehensive secondary schools. Roald F. Campbell of the University of Chicago has stimulated my interests concerning various nationalizing influences on the curriculum. The late Hilda Taba shared many valuable ideas with me when I was on the faculty at San Francisco State College. J. Paul Leonard, former President of San Francisco State College, has contributed greatly to my perspective of the curriculum in secondary and higher education. Through many discussions with my friend and colleague Aaron S. Carton of the State University of New York at Stony Brook I have gained valuable insights into important problems in the teaching-learning process.

For their generosity in providing me with various materials, I wish to acknowledge my appreciation to Jerry P. Becker, Arnold B. Grobman, Josephine B. Pane, and Carl J. Schaefer, all of Rutgers University. I owe special thanks to Marion Ann Keller for her careful typing of the manuscript, and to Mary Ellen Matthews for her assistance in proof-reading the manuscript.

Finally, I am grateful to my wife, Laurel, for her constant encouragement.

D. T.

Contents

Part II   Disciplinarity and Curriculum Reform

Part III   Patterns and Prospects

Part I

Curriculum Synthesis and Perspective

*The solution which I am urging
is to eradicate the fatal disconnection of subjects
which kills the vitality of our modern curriculum.*

—ALFRED NORTH WHITEHEAD

Chapter 1

Inquiry-Discovery as Educational Process

The recent resurgence of activity in curriculum revision and reform has been marked by attempts (1) to develop content through structural schemes derived within the discrete disciplines and (2) to develop instructional processes through inquiry-discovery modes. The search for structure and the concern for inquiry and discovery are not new. They have their antecedents in a wide variety of approaches to organizing curriculum content and instructional processes through unit teaching, the project method, problem solving, critical thinking, and various other attempts to deal with subject matter through higher cognitive levels or styles. However, the events of recent history have produced unparalleled demands and activities in reformulating subject matter to represent the conceptual and methodological approaches of the scholar-specialist seeking new knowledge. While such efforts may seem long overdue, they do not solve the problems relating to curriculum priorities and imbalance, separation versus integration, and specialization versus diversification. Although it is claimed that the inquiry-discovery mode is becoming the new unifying theme among the disciplines, there is reason to suspect that inquiry-discovery is often being used as an attractive label or slogan rather than as a style of learning. In this chapter we shall examine some of the issues connected with inquiry-discovery as an educational process.

THE EXPANSION OF KNOWLEDGE: CURRICULUM PRIORITIES AND HIERARCHIES

The accelerating expansion of knowledge multiplies the areas of specialization through which new knowledge is sought and utilized. Coupled with the universalization of secondary education in our society and the opening of college gates to an increasing proportion of our population, new pressures and demands are created for the diversification of the

3

curriculum and the adding of new courses in our schools and colleges. Outmoded knowledge and time-life limits point to the futility and folly of additive approaches to curriculum building. This does not mean that the curriculum should not be expanded and diversified to meet the specialized needs of wider populations. However, this kind of expansion and diversification does not solve the problem of outmoded knowledge. Nor does it meet the need for determining curriculum priorities in a society where wise citizenship is desired of all members.

The Discrete Disciplines and the Total Curriculum

Recent attempts at course-content improvement have been confined largely to the discrete disciplines. This not only creates problems in building interrelationships among the disciplines and developing meaningful syntheses for the learner, but raises the danger that curriculum specialists in certain areas of knowledge will seek to imitate the strategies and modes of those disciplines that occupy the highest positions in the new curriculum hierarchy. In recent years, our national policy has favored curriculum revision in the sciences and mathematics over revision in other curriculum fields. This has been in response to the growing scientific and technological competition with the Soviets. In vying to regain a respectable position in the curriculum hierarchy, we now find the social scientists and even the language arts specialists attempting to develop their curricula in the image of the sciences—as structural entities and discrete disciplines. Curriculum developers in the social studies, who once were concerned with having the student explore broad social problems through interdisciplinary approaches, are now concentrating their efforts on parceling the social studies into discrete domains of specialization.

Undoubtedly, the inquiry-discovery mode in the teaching-learning process and the development of content through structural schemes have contributed significantly to curriculum improvement. But, as in all reform efforts, there are dangers of overemphasis and misuse which derive from exaggerated claims. In viewing the current scene and in looking to the immediate future, curriculum workers will need to consider a number of questions: Is subject matter being forced to fit artificially into a "structural schema"? Is the learner merely being required to imitate the advanced scholar who is in the forefront of the search for new knowledge? Are the major programs of curriculum revision and reform creating problems of specialization and compartmentalization through the options taken in organizing knowledge into discrete disciplines?

SOME ANTECEDENTS TO INQUIRY-DISCOVERY

Discovery as Self-expression

The laissez-faire pedagogy of Rousseau's *Emile,* published in 1762, advised the reader to capitalize on the natural curiosity of the learner and to frame problems that will enable the student to learn by discovery: "Put the problems before him and let him solve them himself. Let him know nothing because you have told him, but because he has learnt it for himself. Let him not be taught science, let him discover it." [1] Rousseau's romanticism, however, abhorred any systematic approach to the process of inquiry-discovery and the organization of knowledge. Contemporary adherents of romantic naturalism see inquiry-discovery as the natural and spontaneous expression of the learner in interaction with his environment. This approach should not be confused with Dewey's progressivism or experimentalism, which places great store in reflective thinking as developed through the problem method.

The Problem Method and Reflective Thinking

The twentieth-century orchestrator of discovery as method was John Dewey. In attacking the passivity of the traditional type of education in which knowledge is treated as mere subject-matter information to be absorbed and regurgitated by the learner, Dewey viewed method as being identical with the process of reflection:

> While we may speak, without error, of the method of thought, the important thing is that thinking is the method of an educative experience. The essentials of methods are therefore identical with the essentials of reflection. They are first that the pupil have a genuine situation of experience—that there be a continuous activity in which he is interested for its own sake; secondly, that a genuine problem develop within this situation as a stimulus to thought; third, that he possess the information and make the observations needed to deal with it; fourth, that suggested solutions occur to him which he shall be responsible for developing in an orderly way; fifth, that he have opportunity and occasion to test his ideas by application, to make their meaning clear and to discover for himself their validity.[2]

Dewey did not regard trial-and-error behavior as reflective experience. Reflection, according to Dewey, "is the accurate and deliberate instituting of what is done and its consequences." [3] He did not propose a singular

---

[1] Jean Jacques Rousseau, *Emile* (London: J. M. Dent & Sons, Ltd., 1911), p. 131.

[2] John Dewey, *Democracy and Education* (New York: The Macmillan Company, 1916), p. 192.

[3] *Ibid.*, p. 177.

and immutable problem method, but described reflective experience in a variety of ways while identifying certain general features of this method:

> They are (1) perplexity, confusion, doubt, due to the fact that one is implicated in an incomplete situation whose full character is not yet determined; (2) a conjectural anticipation—a tentative interpretation of the given elements, attributing to them a tendency to effect certain consequences; (3) a careful survey (examination, inspection, exploration, analysis) of all attainable consideration which will define and clarify the problem in hand; (4) a consequent elaboration of the tentative hypothesis to make it more precise and more consistent . . . ; (5) taking one stand upon the projected hypothesis as a plan of action which is applied to the existing state of affairs: doing something overtly to bring about the anticipated result, and thereby testing the hypothesis.[4]

According to Dewey, this is what makes thinking itself an *educative* experience. While Dewey championed the inquiry-discovery approach, he did not see the learner as a miniature scientist who must follow the same pathways of original discovery that have produced existing bodies of knowledge. "No one expects the young to make original discoveries of just the same facts and principles as are embodied in the sciences of nature and man. But it is not unreasonable to expect that learning may take place under such conditions that from the standpoint of the learner there is genuine discovery." [5] He repeatedly cautioned against modeling the teaching-learning process after adult scholarship, in that "the method of organization of material of achieved scholarship differs from that of the beginner." [6]

Dewey regarded knowledge not as an end in itself, but as "the working capital, the indispensable resources, of further inquiry; of finding out, or learning, more things." [7] He observed that a stupendous bulk of subject matter had been created and that man had allowed himself to regard this bulk as genuine knowledge. According to Dewey, knowledge is "an outcome of inquiry and a resource in further inquiry." [8] When man regards the bulk of information and subject matter as an end of instruction, he has allowed the mind to be "taken captive by the spoils of its prior victories," and thus "the spoils, not the weapons and the acts of waging the battle against the unknown, are used to fix the meaning of knowledge, of fact, and truth." [9]

Unfortunately, the problem method has been used inaccurately in

---

4 *Ibid.*, p. 176.
5 *Ibid.*, p. 354.
6 *Ibid.*, p. 216.
7 *Ibid.*, p. 186.
8 *Ibid.*, p. 220.
9 *Ibid.*

relation to the routine and mechanical operations that the student learns to perform after having first mastered the procedures necessary for the solution of a model problem. Under such circumstances the student is not engaged in the higher cognitive processes necessary to problem solving in the real sense, such as formulating the problem, casting hypotheses, designing procedures and techniques for testing the hypotheses, discriminating between relevant and irrelevant data, reaching tentative conclusions, and so on. The rather mechanical use of a model problem with model procedures is little more than a set of exercises to be followed by the learner. Little or no application is made toward relating these specific exercises to problems of broader implication.

The Project Method

As early as 1911 the project method was used in agriculture classes in the high school. An outgrowth of Dewey's conception of knowledge as the power to do and his belief in learning by doing, the project method gained wide practice in agricultural education. And it remains a significant method in high school classes in vocational agriculture to this day. Instead of merely following the race experience (i.e., the practices of his father on the farm in growing crops and raising livestock), the student attempts to apply the latest approved practices that he has learned at school to an actual life situation. Thus in growing a crop he must learn the best practices relative to soil conditions, growing season, plant varieties and their characteristics, disease prevention and treatment, nutrition, weed control, insect control, harvesting, storage, marketing, bookkeeping, and so on. Organized knowledge (i.e., genetics, pathology, entomology, etc.) is valuable not as an end in itself, but as a means of implementing approved practices and in preventing and solving problems in the context of a life experience. In this way, the life experience becomes educative and the school experience is related to life.

William Heard Kilpatrick (1871–1965), professor at Columbia's Teachers' College, viewed the project method as an application of Dewey's problem method. He conceived of the project method as integral to the curriculum through a variety of manifestations: to embody some idea in external form (such as producing a play or constructing some object or apparatus), to straighten out some intellectual difficulty (to solve a problem), to obtain some item or degree of skill or knowledge, and to develop aesthetic experience.[10] He advised teachers of the importance of "concomitant" learnings in which the subject matter to be learned is not the only thing at stake, but the student's attitudes (positive or negative)

---

[10] William Heard Kilpatrick, "The Project Method," *Teachers College Record*, Vol. 19 (September, 1918), pp. 319–335.

are also regarded as the product of the learning experience. The student who is learning arithmetic may at the same time be learning to like or dislike the subject. Thus the learner functions as a complete organism with attitudes and feelings that bear directly on his learning.

In his analysis of the project method, Alberty identified the conditions or stages through which the project method is practically synonymous with Dewey's analysis of the complete act of thought and thereby becomes merged with the problem method: (1) a situation calling for adjustment, (2) defining a purpose to adjust the situation, (3) casting about for solutions, (4) carrying out plans toward the solution of problems, (5) judging success or failure, and (6) feeling satisfied or dissatisfied.[11]

While the project method originated as an attempt to deal with concrete activities and problems within their natural or ecological setting, it often came to be applied to instructional procedures confined to the classroom. The fallacy of assuming that the higher cognitive processes are to be derived automatically from practical activities was matched by the fallacy that verbal abstractions through prefabricated didactic instruction will shape behavior in the absence of practical activity. Efforts to link both worlds often were far from successful because of a lack of appropriate curriculum materials and teacher know-how.

Although Kilpatrick gained a wide following, even some progressive educators, such as Boyd H. Bode (1873–1953) of The Ohio State University, argued that the project method, as originally conceived, suffered from certain obvious defects and limitations. According to Bode, "it takes no account of either logical organization or 'social insight.' Its spirit is the spirit of an exclusive vocationalism. . . . Learning that is limited to this method is too discontinuous, too random and haphazard, too immediate in its function . . . it does not fully meet the demand for a kind of education that is not tied up so closely with immediate demands." [12]

While the project method never became a really dominant method in the various areas of the curriculum, it continues to retain a significant place in agricultural education, the industrial arts, the graphic arts and, to some extent, in the sciences, where it serves to complement laboratory work. In the adult world of work, the project approach is commonly used where teams of specialists must work together toward a common goal. Thus the project method has been used for a wide variety of purposes, such as the development of the first atom bomb through the Manhattan Project of World War II, the building of the first supersonic aircraft, the achievement of the first organ transplants in humans, and the design

---

11 Harold B. Alberty, *A Study of the Project Method in Education* (Columbus, Ohio: Ohio State University Press, 1927), p. 73.

12 Boyd H. Bode, *Modern Educational Theories* (New York: The Macmillan Company, 1927), pp. 150–151.

and construction of new cities. The project approach also has been employed with considerable success in recent years in developing new curricula through such groups as the Physical Science Study Committee, the School Mathematics Study Group, the Biological Sciences Curriculum Study, Project English, Project Social Studies, and others.

The growth of independent study programs in the high school during the 1960's has been accompanied by some renewed interest and activity in the project method. To be successful, independent study requires competent faculty guidance. In an increasing number of schools having independent-study programs, students are involved in projects which they may pursue in the laboratory, library, or resource centers. However, many programs of independent study have been developed with the primary goal of utilizing faculty personnel more efficiently, rather than improving the learning process.

The Laboratory Method

Despite the enormously growing influence of science on society during the nineteenth century, the laboratory sciences did not gain a firm foothold in the secondary schools and colleges until the twentieth century. Two great exponents of introducing more scientific studies into the curriculum in England during the latter part of the nineteenth century were Herbert Spencer (1820–1903) and Thomas Henry Huxley (1825–1895). Spencer and Huxley had a sizable following in the United States, where the grip of the classical studies on school and college curricula was being seriously questioned. Spencer had countered the mental-discipline rationale of the classicists with the argument that the sciences, rather than the classical subjects, were without peer as intellective disciplines. The expansion of scientific knowledge and the growing demands for utilitarian studies led to greater diversification of curricula in secondary schools and colleges at the turn of the century. Laboratories designed for instruction were appearing in larger numbers. However, the instructional laboratory was limited largely to techniques and exercises that had a limited relationship to modes of scientific inquiry.

Although Dewey was one of the great champions of the laboratory method, he deplored the tendency for school laboratory work to become obsessed with mere measurement, manipulation of apparatus, and acquisition of information in the absence of contact with problems for purposes of discovery.[13] Dewey viewed the laboratory method as the means through which man inquires in order to alter conditions and whereby he becomes intellectually fruitful:

---

[13] Dewey, *op. cit.*, p. 233.

The most direct blow at the traditional separation of doing and knowing and at the traditional prestige of purely "intellectual" studies, however, has been given by the progress of experimental science. . . . Men have to *do* something to the things when they wish to find out something; they have to alter conditions. This is the lesson of the laboratory method, and the lesson which all education has to learn. The laboratory is a discovery of the conditions under which *labor* may become intellectually fruitful and not merely externally productive. If, in too many cases at present, it results only in the acquisition of an additional mode of technical skill, that is because it still remains too largely but an isolated resource, not resorted to until pupils are mostly too old to get the full advantage of it, and even then is surrounded by other studies where traditional methods isolate intellect from activity.[14]

As laboratory work developed in the secondary schools, it largely failed to capture the spirit of scientific inquiry and instead tended to become a series of representative exercises which the student followed, step by step, through a laboratory manual. Traditional laboratory work failed to provide stimulation for further inquiry. The success of the student was determined by his ability to follow the instructions of the laboratory teacher and the laboratory manual. Few laboratory activities were truly experimental and students in the laboratory were merely required to repeat well-worn procedures. Bentley Glass, a scientist who played a leading role in high school biology curriculum reform, criticized the prevalent laboratory work where students know "in advance, from textbook and discussion, exactly what they were supposed to discern and conclude. It has been sheer cookbookery, a ritual of recipes. Small wonder that interest was often deadened." [15]

Curriculum reform efforts in the sciences during the late 1950's and through the 1960's have been marked by attempts to completely reconstruct laboratory experiences along the lines of inquiry through hypothesis testing. Scientists responsible for curriculum reform have attempted to view the teaching laboratory as a center for genuine inquiry. "For the first time, I think, education in the natural sciences, at least at the secondary school level, has assigned the acquisition of scientific information and concepts a place of lesser importance than the understanding of the very nature of scientific inquiry and of the scientific enterprise in which modern man is embarked." [16] Similar statements are to be found in descriptions of laboratory work developed by the Physical Science Study Committee where "the student is expected to wrestle with a line (or con-

14 *Ibid.*, pp. 321–322.

15 Bentley Glass, "Renascent Biology: A Report on the AIBS Biological Sciences Curriculum Study," in *New Curricula,* Robert W. Heath (ed.) (New York: Harper & Row, Publishers, 1964), p. 106.

16 *Ibid.*, p. 117.

verging lines) of inquiry, including his own laboratory investigations, that leads to basic ideas. . . . The student's laboratory guidebook keeps specific instructions to a minimum. . . . The student is responsible for thinking out the nature and the meaning of what he is to do." [17]

Statements by scholars concerning the nature and objectives of laboratory work in the new science curricula are remarkably similar to Dewey's conceptions of the laboratory method and the problem method which he had propounded more than half a century earlier. Dewey's essentials of reflection are clearly embodied in modern statements on curriculum reform, which advocate that pupils "must learn to ask the right questions . . . to frame testable hypotheses. They must learn to draw valid conclusions from their data and to determine the significance of their findings. They must learn that science frequently advances through the correction of the errors and inadequacies of earlier science. And all of this takes time." [18]

Although many of the new curriculum projects in the sciences have attempted to utilize laboratory experiences as a means of leading the student into new realms of inquiry, rather than merely serving to demonstrate the material encountered in the classroom and textbook, relatively little research has been conducted on the effects of such laboratory experiences.

INTEGRATED KNOWLEDGE AND THE DISCIPLINES

The Logical and the Psychological: An Untenable Dualism

Traditional approaches to subject matter organization have tended to represent a logical accounting and inventorying of man's knowledge in given fields. Unfortunately, such approaches in organizing and presenting the subject matter often are devoid of any substantial treatment of how the "discipline" came about and how it serves as a system for discovering and interpreting new knowledge.

The doctrine of mental discipline provided only temporary justification for organizing and presenting subject matter as a mere accounting of information in given fields. The argument that the strengthening of the mind is enhanced through mental exercises, just as one strengthens the muscles of the body by calisthenics, supported the notion that the curriculum need not be relevant to reasoning in life situations; instead,

[17] Gilbert C. Finlay, "The Physical Science Study Committee," in *Curriculum Improvement and Innovation: A Partnership of Students, School Teachers, and Research Scholars,* W. T. Martin and Dan C. Pinck (eds.) (Cambridge, Mass.: Robert Bentley, Inc., 1966), pp. 68–69.

[18] Glass, *op. cit.,* p. 107.

the mind would be strengthened best through difficult and tedious mental gyrations and memoriter tasks. Interests, attitudes, and feelings of the learner could be ignored. A logical ordering of the curriculum content was compatible with this rationale. The traditional subjects, such as Latin and geometry, were particularly valued for their alleged superiority in developing the mental powers. The pedagogical formula was simply to have the student exercise his mind; the more difficult the material, and the more the student would be made to work hard in suffering through his studies, the greater the likelihood that the mind would be strengthened.

As the doctrine of mental discipline began to be demolished, the prefabrication of the curriculum into logically organized bodies of information came to be challenged along with the hierarchical position of the traditional studies. Not only were the traditional approaches to curriculum organization deemed inadequate for preparing the future scholar, whether scientist, mathematician, or historian, but it was recognized that such approaches perpetrated a distorted conception of knowledge, yielding little meaning and carry-over for the demands of real life. Dewey repeatedly condemned the old curriculum in warning that when knowledge is organized and presented to the learner in ready-made fashion, when it is emasculated of the inquiry which produced it, its really thought-provoking character and organizing function disappear:

> This is the contradiction: the child gets the advantage neither of the adult logical formulation, nor of his own native competence of apprehension and response. Hence the logic of the child is hampered and mortified, and we are almost fortunate if he does not get actual non-science, flat and commonplace residua of what was gaining scientific vitality a generation or two ago—degenerate reminiscence of what someone else once formulated on the basis of the experience that some further person had, once upon a time, experienced.[19]

Ideally, knowledge should be so selected and organized in the curriculum that there is no discernible dichotomy between the "logical" and "psychological" ordering of subject matter. Although many of the new curriculum projects are intended to eliminate this distinction by interpreting the disciplines as systems by which man discovers and develops new knowledge, the subject matter often represents the world of the mature scholar and not that of the child or adolescent. During the 1960's it became fashionable to hold that there is no distinction between the mature scholar and the schoolboy in styles of inquiry. As "intellectual

---

[19] John Dewey, *The Child and the Curriculum* (Chicago: The University of Chicago Press, 1902), p. 34.

activity anywhere is the same," [20] the new curriculum projects were required merely to select and organize the subject matter in the interests of mature scholars. While this approach may produce a curriculum that is an effective expression of the discipline as the mature scholar deals with it, the suitability of the subject matter for the schoolboy is open to serious question. This issue is discussed in greater detail later in this chapter.

Curriculum Integration

The first half of the twentieth century was marked by notable attempts at restructuring the curriculum in the secondary schools and colleges, particularly for general education purposes, by merging subjects that previously were separated by departmental domain. It had become increasingly evident that students could not be expected to synthesize and transfer their learnings when the curriculum consisted of subjects organized as separate and insulated entities. After all, subject matter was man's creation in order to record race experience and to organize knowledge for purposes of gaining new knowledge. Such systems of organizing subject matter were not created by nature. The inevitable problem which gained new recognition during this period was that the greater the specialization of knowledge, the less was the likelihood that the learner would be able to resynthesize his studies for application to the broader problems of life.

Many schools and colleges attempted to improve curriculum articulation through various integrated approaches to subject matter. These included correlated, fused, and broad-field types of organization. Some secondary schools attempted to develop their programs of general education through a core curriculum that was virtually free of all traditional subject boundaries. One type of core curriculum might be based upon the perceived problems, needs, and interests of adolescents within a framework of problem areas, while another might be developed as teacher-student planned activities without reference to any formal design.[21] Nevertheless, key elements in such core programs were student inquiry and self-direction. The problems of implementing such core programs were many, including the need for teachers with unusual skills, the development of appropriate resource materials in the absence of traditional textbooks, the breaking down of departmental lines, and the willingness

---

[20] Jerome S. Bruner, *The Process of Education* (Cambridge, Mass.: Harvard University Press, 1960), p. 14.

[21] Harold B. and Elsie J. Alberty, *Reorganizing the High School Curriculum*, 3rd ed. (New York: The Macmillan Company, 1962), pp. 216–225.

to allow students to investigate and to encounter topics and problems of controversy considerably beyond what would be permitted in the traditional classroom. The powerful influences of specialism, which gained renewed vigor with the advent of nuclear weaponry, the cold war, and Sputnik, served to diminish these efforts toward integrating the curriculum of the secondary school.

Student-Centered Vs. Subject-Centered Approaches

The reaction against rigid and catechismlike treatment of subject matter led some educators, in the name of progressivism, to promote and adopt practices that were excessively student-centered. Boyd H. Bode, a contemporary of Dewey and a fellow progressive, wrote in 1927, "We hear a great deal . . . about 'child purposing' and about individual differences, without a sufficiently counterbalancing emphasis upon the need of developing and directing the activities of pupils toward a preconceived end." [22] Even as early as 1902, Dewey himself warned of the danger of expecting the learner to function effectively in the absence of the requisite environing conditions that stimulate and guide thought:

> If, once more, the "old education" tended to ignore the dynamic quality, the developing force inherent in the child's present experience, . . . the "new education" is in danger of taking the idea of development in altogether too formal and empty a way. The child is expected to "develop" this or that fact or truth out of his own mind. He is told to think things out, or work things out for himself, without being supplied any of the environing conditions which are requisite to start and guide thought. Nothing can be developed from nothing . . . and this is what surely happens when we throw the child back upon his achieved self as finality, and invite him to spin new truths. . . .[23]

The Great Depression of the 1930's gave impetus to pupil-centered approaches as a reaction to the lack of relevance between the traditional curriculum and the problems of youth in a society beset with social and economic dislocations. At a time when the survival of democracy was at stake, a number of progressive educators viewed the school as a key agency for correcting social ills. Progressive secondary schools attempted to reformulate the curriculum according to youth needs and the broader problems of society. In these schools, democratic teaching methods were fostered in an attempt to connect educational means with the society goal of the democratic ideal. The aim was to develop the school as an institution for humanizing a society that was torn by a new industrial

---

22 Bode, *op. cit.*, p. 33.
23 Dewey, *The Child and the Curriculum, op. cit.*, pp. 23–24.

turmoil. As mentioned earlier, the core curriculum, with its attempt to resynthesize subject matter in terms of youth problems and the problems of society, was one approach that gained considerable attention.

The problem of resynthesizing the subject matter for these purposes was never solved, however, and many teachers floundered without an adequately defined structural and organizational framework for their pupil-centered approaches. Moreover, despite the great interest generated by the progressives, only a very small proportion of our secondary schools were engaged concertedly in these experimental practices.

NATIONAL NEEDS AND THE DISCIPLINES

Dewey's conception of inquiry as the key to the process of education came to be badly interpreted by both his disciples and critics. A dichotomy was established leading to conflicting camps: those advocating a learner-centered curriculum versus those favoring a subject-centered curriculum. The Deweyan concept of subject matter as an outcome of inquiry and as a resource for further inquiry became lost in a welter of fusillades between those who viewed the learned as the key source of data in structuring the curriculum, and those who saw subject matter as either sacred unto itself or as the means of serving national needs.

The emergence of the United States from the Great Depression and World War II witnessed a new national emergency. The cold war and Sputnik gave critics of progressive education new recognition. Where the progressive educators viewed education as the chief means of individual enlightenment for social reconstruction and the growth of democracy, the new essentialists saw education as the machinery for regaining our clear-cut techno-military-political leadership in the era of the cold war. With the new national emergency, the "soft pedagogy" of the progressives yielded to the "tough pedagogy" of the essentialists. Through the National Defense Education Act of 1958 and the efforts of the National Science Foundation (established by act of Congress in 1950), new curriculum priorities were identified and a new curriculum hierarchy emerged. The sciences, mathematics, and modern foreign languages were singled out for federal support at all educational levels.

Priorities and Imbalance

Where one of the key emphases of the 1930's and 1940's was on improving curriculum articulation in the secondary school and college through correlated, fused, broad fields, and core frameworks for balanced and integrated studies, the focal point of the 1950's and 1960's was on subject matter as discrete disciplines. A host of federally financed and foundation-supported projects and programs concerned with course-content development and revision gained national prominence—the Physical Science Study Committee (PSSC), the Biological Sciences Curriculum Study (BSCS), the Chemical Education Materials Study (CHEM Study), the Chemical Bond Approach Project (CBA), the School Mathematics Study Group (SMSG), the University of Illinois Committee on School Mathematics (UICSM), the MLA Foreign Language Program, the Foreign Languages in the Elementary School Program (FLES), and others. The new curriculum priorities had created a new imbalance.

In 1964 Goodlad was unable to report any substantial curriculum rejuvenation in English, the social sciences, and the arts.[24] However, a modest program was launched in 1962 by the U.S. Office of Education to improve curricula and instruction in English and the social studies. This program, identified as Project English and Project Social Studies, led to the establishment of curriculum centers at various universities. A considerable number of similar projects have subsequently been sponsored by professional organizations, particularly in the social sciences. Nevertheless, in 1966 Goodlad described the curriculum-building activity in the social studies as being "in flux and confused."[25] With regard to the humanities, Goodlad observed that "at times it seems as though certain forces and factors in modern America are conspiring against a greater emphasis on the humanities in elementary and secondary education."[26] Goodlad also warned that the continuing heavy support for curriculum programs in the sciences and mathematics, in marked contrast to the modest support levels for projects in the social studies, English, and the arts, would probably create an ever-widening gap.[27]

Lack of Functional Relationships

Curriculum reform in the sciences and mathematics during the 1950's and 1960's was marked by a host of well-supported, independently operated projects. Little effort was made to correlate different projects or to relate various branches of science as an integrated curriculum for the secondary school. As mentioned earlier, the chief focus was on the discrete disciplines. Only recently has the problem of articulation received some attention. The efforts in the social studies and English have tended to follow the pattern established by the sciences—with each project following a course of its own. Thus, for the most part, projects in literature

---

[24] John I. Goodlad, *School Curriculum Reform in the United States* (New York: The Fund for the Advancement of Education), 1964.

[25] John I. Goodlad, *The Changing School Curriculum* (New York: The Fund for the Advancement of Education, 1966), p. 56.

[26] *Ibid.,* p. 71.

[27] *Ibid.*

have operated independently of other projects in English. Moreover, most of the projects in the social studies have been concerned with curriculum development in the discrete subjects such as anthropology, economics, geography, history, political science, and sociology. Relatively few of these projects have been designed to integrate the social sciences at the secondary level, and none of them were being related to any of the literature projects.

THE NEW UNIFYING THEME: INQUIRY-DISCOVERY

A Curriculum Manifesto

The key document that marked the turning point for curriculum theory and development in the post-Sputnik era was *The Process of Education,* published in 1960 as the result of a 1959 conference sponsored by a group of governmental agencies, scientific bodies, and the Carnegie Corporation.[28] Chaired by the Harvard psychologist Jerome Bruner, the conference was comprised mainly of scientists, mathematicians, and psychologists. Many of the conference participants were university professors working on programs of course-content improvement in the sciences and mathematics at the elementary and secondary levels under the auspices of the National Science Foundation and private foundations.

As a product of the "profound scientific revolution" and the impending "long-range crisis in national security," [29] *The Process of Education* represented an attempt to translate into psychological modalities certain key principles from leading curriculum projects in the sciences and mathematics. Nevertheless, the major themes of the book soon became a veritable manifesto for curriculum workers not only in the sciences and mathematics but also in the social sciences and humanities. Where Conant's *The American High School Today* had exerted unprecedented influence in shaping policies and practices for our secondary schools, it neglected to deal with the rationales for selecting and organizing learning experiences.[30] The Conant Report was primarily a prescription of necessary courses, credits, and systems of processing students for academic potential within the "democratizing" comprehensive high school. In contrast, the Bruner Report focused on several psychophilosophical themes which, at the time, were emerging from certain major curriculum projects. Both reports grew out of the crisis of the cold war and Sputnik.

---

[28] Jerome Bruner, *The Process of Education, op. cit.*

[29] *Ibid.,* p. 1.

[30] James Bryant Conant, *The American High School Today* (New York: McGraw-Hill Book Company, Inc., 1959).

Inquiry-Discovery and Intellectual Development

The several psychophilosophic themes of the Bruner Report were derived from a central hypothetical proposition: "that intellectual activity anywhere is the same, whether at the frontier of knowledge or in the third-grade classroom" [31] and, therefore, "any subject can be taught effectively in some intellectually honest form to any child at any stage of development." [32] In 1910 Dewey had written in the preface of his first edition of *How We Think* that "this book represents the conviction . . . that the native and unspoiled attitude of childhood, marked by ardent curiosity, fertile imagination, and love of experimental inquiry, is near, very near, to the attitude of the scientific mind." [33] Although Dewey's statement concerning the child's attitude of learning was made more than half a century earlier than Bruner's, there is an obvious similarity between the two. But where Dewey viewed the child's attitude of learning as being very near that of the scientific mind, Bruner took the position that intellectual activity is the same at any level.

Reflection As Developmental Stage. The thesis that intellectual development occurs through developmental stages was supported by the mathematician-philosopher, Alfred North Whitehead.[34] Whitehead criticized conventional schooling for assuming that the learner's progress is to be conceived as a steady advance through subject matter. He maintained that intellectual development occurs through cyclical or recurring stages which can be said to represent the rhythm of education. The stage of *romance* represents the learner's first apprehension of a phenomenon or problem in terms of the import of unexplored relationships. According to Whitehead, in this stage knowledge is not dominated by systematic procedure and dissection. The second stage is that of *precision,* in which the width of relationship is subordinated to exactness of formulation. Without the previous stage of romance, the stage of precision is barren and devoid of further relevance. It is through the stage of romance that ideas with possibilities of wide significance are opened to the learner. Then, through precision, systematic progress is made in analyzing data and in reaching new disclosures. The final stage, according to Whitehead, is that of *generalization,* which represents a synthesis of knowledge and a return to romanticism with the added advantage of systematized understandings and techniques relevant to wider learning. Although Whitehead conceived of these stages as cyclical, recurring repeatedly at all ages,

---

[31] Bruner, *op. cit.,* p. 14.

[32] *Ibid.,* p. 32.

[33] John Dewey, *How We Think* (Boston: D. C. Heath and Company, 1910), p. 111.

[34] Alfred North Whitehead, *The Aims of Education and Other Essays* (New York: The Macmillan Company, 1929).

he held that maturational levels must be taken into account. For example, early adolescence is a period in which the stage of romance can flourish and can set the stage for greater precision and generalization. The stages are not distinctly separate, but are interwoven in a harmony of patterns that enables the learner to seek fruition and begin afresh in the cyclic process of education.

Some years earlier, Dewey had advanced the thesis of reflection as a developmental stage. Dewey viewed the power of reflective thinking as a developmental stage rather than as something that is manifest in the early stages of childhood curiosity. According to Dewey, the first stage (in earliest childhood) is a vital overflow, an expression of an abundant organic energy, a physiological uneasiness that leads a child to get into everything and to handle objects until they cease to yield new qualities. While such activities are far from reflective or intellectual, they are essential to intellectual development.[35]

The second stage develops under the influence of social stimuli as "the child learns that he can appeal to others to eke out his store of experience. . . . His *why* is not a demand for scientific explanation. . . . The search is not for a law or principle, but only for another, a bigger fact. Yet there is more than a desire to accumulate just information or heap up disconnected items." [36] It is during the second or social stage that the child begins to realize that factual descriptions of whatever it is that directly meets the senses are not the whole story, and herein lies the germ of intellectual curiosity.

Dewey's third stage becomes manifest as curiosity rises above the organic and social level. No longer is curiosity discharged by receiving immediate answers to spontaneous questions. No longer is the child more interested in merely asking questions and receiving answers without seeking more remote relationships and ends. Reflective thinking occurs during the third stage as "a distant end controls a sequence of inquiries and observations and binds them together as means to an end." [37] In a lecture given in April, 1899, at the University of Chicago Elementary School, Dewey stated that the young child is unable to distinguish in modes of thought between experimental science and carpentry and that "such work as they can do in physics or chemistry is not for the purpose of making technical generalizations or even arriving at abstract truths." [38]

There is a remarkable similarity between Dewey's three stages of curiosity in childhood and Piaget's four stages of intellectual growth in

---

[35] Dewey, *How We Think, op. cit.,* pp. 31–32.

[36] *Ibid.,* p. 32.

[37] John Dewey, *How We Think,* rev. ed. (Boston: D. C. Heath and Company, 1933), p. 39.

[38] John Dewey, *The School and Society* (Chicago: The University of Chicago Press, 1915), p. 44.

childhood. But where Dewey did not attempt to affix the stages to specific age levels, Piaget dated the appearance of these stages by chronological age. The developmental-stage schema of Dewey and Piaget appears to conflict with Bruner's notion of intellectual activity being the same whether at the frontier of knowledge or in the third-grade classroom. According to Piaget, the stage of *formal operations,* where the individual develops hypothetical reasoning and the capability to perform controlled experimentation, is not usually established until the period between late childhood and early adolescence.[39] Before an individual reaches the stage of formal operations, he progresses through three essential stages: first, a *sensory-motor* stage (first two years), in which the child learns to control perception and motor responses in dealing with objects and language; second, a *preoperational* or *representational* stage (to about age six or seven), in which the child learns to extract concepts from experience and, at the latter phases of this stage, learns to make perceptual and intuitive judgments; third, a stage of *concrete operations* (between seven and eleven years), in which the youngster learns to solve physical problems by anticipating consequences perceptually. Although it may be possible to accelerate somewhat these developmental stages, Piaget believes that these stages evolve as optimal periods for the individual and, consequently, great pressure to accelerate these stages would be of dubious value.

Abilities and Priorities. If, as Piaget maintains, the stage of formal operations is not reached until the period between late childhood (age eleven or twelve) and early adolescence (age fifteen), Bruner's thesis of intellectual activity would be vastly misleading as a basis for designing curricular content and process. But even if Bruner's proposition should be found valid, it fails to answer the question of whether a given subject should indeed be taught to a particular group of students at a given grade level. For example, the fact that certain principles and operations in probability and statistics can be learned by a ten-year-old does not require that such material be part of the curriculum of the ten-year-old. Yet many educators jump to this conclusion and, following Bruner, stress the urgency for schools and society to take advantage of these capabilities. The secretary of the now defunct Educational Policies Commission of the NEA put it this way:

> I have seen elementary school children working in probability theory, which is usually taught at the college level or above. . . . I know a ten-year-old who can translate from binary to decimal numbers and back as easily as I can translate words from one language to another.

---

[39] Jean Piaget, *The Psychology of Intelligence* (New York: Harcourt, Brace & World, Inc., 1950), pp. 87–158.

As we go into the abstract future we are bound to need to take advantage of these capabilities.[40]

Why the urgency? Why the "need to take advantage of these capabilities"? As cited earlier, Bruner observed in 1960 that "the new spirit perhaps reflects the profound scientific revolution of our times. . . . The trend is accentuated by what is almost certain to be a long-range crisis in national security." [41] Many other educators in the ensuing years have given similar warnings in support of the hard line in education. Even the secretary of the NEA's Educational Policies Commission, an organization once noted for its balanced and progressive stance on educational problems, threatened that "we live with the uncertain and shifting spectacle of the cold war, the race for space, and the harnessing of the atom." [42] Therefore, in order to survive, we will need to make adaptations in our traditional views concerning educational ends and means:

> Some levels of education—higher and graduate—have traditionally aimed at developing the ability to handle abstractions abstractly, but this goal has been sought infrequently at the secondary level and rarely in the elementary school. It is necessary to make this goal the central purpose in all of education.
>
> To achieve this end we will have to make adaptations in many of our traditional views. We will need to make it our main objective to develop the abstract rational powers. . . . The alternative is to condemn a significant share of the American people to drudgery, or slavery, or both.[43]

In 1933 Dewey warned that abstract thinking should not be regarded as a substitute for thinking on practical matters, nor should it be regarded as a higher form of thinking:

> Educators should also note the very great individual differences that exist; they should not try to force one pattern and model upon all. . . . While education should strive to make men who . . . partake of the spirit of the scholar, philosopher, and scientist, no good reason appears why education should esteem the one mental habit inherently superior to the other and deliberately try to transform the type from concrete to abstract. Have not our schools been one-sidedly devoted to the more abstract type of thinking, thus doing injustice to the majority of pupils? [44]

Dewey's conception of reflective thinking allowed for the development of both abstract and practical powers. "Every human being has both capa-

---

40 James E. Russell, *Change and Challenge in American Education* (Boston: Houghton-Mifflin Company, 1965), pp. 55–56.

41 Bruner, *op. cit.,* p. 1.

42 Russell, *op. cit.,* p. 15.

43 *Ibid.,* p. 24.

44 Dewey, *How We Think,* rev. ed., 1933, *op. cit.,* p. 228.

bilities, and every individual will be more effective and happier if both powers are developed in easy and close interaction with each other. Otherwise the abstract becomes identical with the academic and pedantic." [45]

According to Bruner, "We might ask as a criterion for any subject taught in primary school, whether, when fully developed, it is worth an adult's knowing, and whether having known it as a child makes a person a better adult." [46] But the child is not a miniature adult and consequently this may be an unsuitable criterion. A more appropriate criterion might be whether the subject matter is worth a child's knowing. Does it make him a better person here and now?

INQUIRY-DISCOVERY:
MORE PROBLEMS AND CRITICISMS

The romantic notion that the young child and the mature scholar share alike the learning mode of inquiry-discovery has been embraced by many scholars in the various disciplines who have been active in elementary and secondary course-content improvement projects. We have seen how this notion conflicts with the thesis of reflection as a developmental stage, as advanced by Dewey and Piaget. But even if the inquiry-discovery mode, as exemplified by hypothesis testing and investigative styles characteristic of the mature scholar, were not stressed until the learner entered what Piaget calls "the stage of formal operations," there would still be serious reasons for challenging this as a dominant principle for curriculum reform.

Scholar and Schoolboy

Some of the chief reasons for questioning inquiry-discovery as a primary mode of organizing instruction are enumerated as follows: First, it is a debatable point whether the learning style of the adolescent is virtually identical to that of the mature scholar. It is one thing to be learning something for the first time as an adolescent, and quite another thing to be a mature scholar who is in the forefront of his field in discovering new knowledge. Second, whereas the mature scholar tends to confine his activity to a specialized area of inquiry, the adolescent in school is expected to deal with what is virtually a total spectrum of race experience through a multiplicity of courses that represent the various disciplines. The orchestral man is an exceedingly rare individual, even among the mature scholars who win Nobel prizes. Third, where the mature scholar

---

[45] *Ibid.*, p. 229.
[46] Bruner, *op. cit.*, p. 52.

has long been committed to his vocational choice and area of inquiry, the adolescent is at the early stages of such commitment. But even if an adolescent has made a decision to become a sociologist, for example, can we fairly assume that in the physics class "it is easier for him to learn physics behaving like a physicist than doing something else"? [47] Fourth, effective learning occurs through a wide variety of activities and not merely through inquiry-discovery. It is not merely a problem of economy of time that makes inquiry-discovery unfeasible as a dominant mode of learning, but rather the fact that people learn many things effectively through other approaches. Even the mature scholar benefits from attending lectures given by his colleagues, observing demonstrations, viewing didactic films, reading reports in the journals, and participating in conferences and discussions. And, fifth, where it is necessary for the adolescent to learn how to relate knowledge and to synthesize his learnings from many disparate fields, the inquiry-discovery mode of the mature scholar is limited professionally to a small part of a single discipline, which may or may not relate to another discipline. The editor of *Science*, official journal of the American Association for the Advancement of Science, warns his colleagues against the bigotry produced by narrowness of specialization:

> One of the most astonishing characteristics of scientists is that some of them are plain old-fashioned bigots. Their zeal has a fanatical, egocentric quality characterized by disdain and intolerance for anyone or any value not associated with a special area of intellectual activity.
> . . . One must be able to specialize but one must be able to escape the web of his own rationalizations. Many have not the will or wit to do this. Thus they are cut off from the rest of the evolving fund of knowledge. . . .
> Avoidance of bigotry carries with it important bonuses. If one is tolerant and willing to admit quality in others, the world can be a great teacher.[48]

Although the worlds of the scholar-researcher and the schoolboy are necessarily very different, this does not mean that the scholar-researcher should not be engaged in course-content development and reform for elementary and secondary schools. As discussed throughout this text, scholar-researchers have made and are making unparalleled contributions in developing new textbooks and other curriculum materials that reject the arbitrary and dogmatic representations of knowledge that have placed a premium on rote learning and regurgitation. They have rejected the traditional approaches of treating subject matter as a corpus of inert and unchallengeable factual matter to be passively absorbed for the

---

[47] Bruner, *op. cit.*, p. 14.

[48] Philip H. Abelson, "Bigotry in Science," *Science*, Vol. 144 (April 24, 1964), p. 371.

examination. They have sought to develop the subject matter through principles that undergird the discipline and represent the thinking of real people. And they have worked in teams to produce learning materials that represent the thinking of scholars in interaction.

But while such activities have produced new courses that help to deepen the understandings and competencies of the student within the disciplines, the relationship between the discipline and other areas of knowledge, both in the curriculum and in society, is weakened. The discipline-oriented scholar is concerned with generating and codifying knowledge within his discipline. He seeks purity, not social problem solving. When curriculum reform in the secondary school is confined primarily to making the discipline more discrete, the curriculum becomes more relevant to the discipline-oriented scholar who produced the new course, and less relevant to the task of solving pervading problems in society. Under such circumstances, the high school is made to serve merely as an imitation of the discipline-oriented graduate school.

Research and Evaluation

Unfortunately, the enthusiasm accompanying many of the new projects has produced many exaggerated and unwarranted claims. As discussed in the coming chapters, a considerable portion of the material in the new programs does not follow the inquiry-discovery mode as originally purported. And many of the leaders of these new projects, who originally set out to show how the new courses would prove far superior to traditional courses as measured by pupil achievement, have tended to back away from comparative studies when the findings fail to support their hypotheses. In succumbing to parental affection for their pet projects, they have unscientifically substituted a ruling theory for what were originally working hypotheses. Getzels offers this criticism of these newer courses of study and the claims made for them:

> There has recently been a stir in education for a "new kind of teaching." Numerous articles and books have appeared arguing that present methods no longer meet the challenge of the new age. The call is for instructional methods (and materials) emphasizing the ability to see generalizations in specifics, to discover, to ask fruitful questions. . . . The newer teaching guides abound in such terms as insight, problem-solving, discovery, inquiry, originality, creativity.
>
> In many ways this trend is to the good. But the new materials and methods are like those they are supposed to supersede in that they are based more on exhortation and testimonial than on empirical demonstration that *this* curriculum and *this* teaching method does indeed make *this* difference. While the new curriculum-makers and methodologists are exhorting the experimental approach to knowledge, they are

not to any great extent submitting their own exhortations to experiment.[49]

Needed Research. In reviewing the research on learning by discovery, Wittrock concluded that although many strong claims are made for discovery methods, almost none of the claims have been empirically substantiated. He cautioned that in assessing the effectiveness of discovery methods it is necessary to take into account the objectives of the teaching-learning situation and the particular types of discovery methods employed. Thus the discovery treatment may involve a wide repertoire of teacher-induced strategies and/or learner-induced strategies for given situations. Wittrock speculates that "as a way to learn a few specific associations, discovery may be inferior to more highly directed procedures. . . . If the criteria are transferred to new concepts, originality, and learning by discovery, learning by discovery as a treatment may fare well." [50]

Cronbach also observes that there are many claims and endorsements but little substantiated knowledge concerning the conditions under which discovery methods are advantageous. He recommends that researchers put aside the polemic question as to whether teaching through discovery is better than didactic teaching. Instead, in framing research studies attention should be given to exploring a fivefold interaction of criteria: (1) the subject matter in the classroom setting, (2) the type and amount of instruction and/or guidance provided, (3) the type and amount of discovery or inductive experience, (4) the pattern of learning outcomes, and (5) the level of development of the pupils. Concerning the assessment of learning outcomes, Cronbach notes that too many studies are limited to the amount or rate of learning despite the preachments in the general literature that learning has many outcomes. The need is to appraise educational development multidimensionally if we are to really assess the outcomes that spokesmen claim for discovery methods. Consequently, data must be collected on such outcomes as theoretical understanding, aptitude, heuristics (ability to solve diverse and new problems through general search and information-processing behaviors), valuation (interest, desire, and appreciation for learning in a given field), epistemology (concept of logic and criteria of truth in a field), and creative urge. In this way, we may find that inductive teaching has value in virtually every area of the curriculum, though its function may be limited.[51]

---

[49] J. W. Getzels, "Creative Thinking, Problem-Solving, and Instruction," in *Theories of Learning and Instruction,* Sixty-third Yearbook, Part I, National Society for the Study of Education (Chicago: The University of Chicago Press, 1964), pp. 257–258.

[50] M. C. Wittrock, "The Learning by Discovery Hypothesis," Chapter IV in *Learning by Discovery: A Critical Appraisal,* Lee S. Shulman and Evan R. Keislar (eds.) (Chicago: Rand McNally & Company, 1966), p. 73.

[51] Lee J. Cronbach, "The Logic of Experiments on Discovery," Chapter V in Shulman and Keislar, *ibid.,* pp. 76–92.

The importance of the common motive among children and adults to maximize similarity to human models must not be overlooked in teaching by discovery. Thus the desire to emulate the attractive features of human models can be a critical factor in school performance and in developing inquiry methods.

Other Claims and Findings. Kagan claims four advantages for the discovery method: (1) it requires greater involvement on the part of the learner, and the more active the involvement the greater the likelihood of learning; (2) it requires extra intellectual effort which, in turn, increases the value of the task; (3) it increases the learner's expectancy of being able to solve different problems autonomously; and (4) it provides the latitude and freedom necessary to release the learner from the submissive posture that may otherwise develop between teacher and student. Kagan acknowledges that the method of discovery may not be as appropriate for children of low motivation and cognitive ability and it may place the impulsive learner at a disadvantage. He regards the discovery method as more appropriate for older learners (age nine or above).[52]

In interpreting the research on the varieties of learning in relation to discovery, Gagné concludes that discovery can be identified widely in classroom situations. While principle learning can occur with or without discovery, there is evidence that the learned principle may be better retained and more readily transferable when discovery is introduced as a requirement. According to Gagné, problem solving requires discovery because the learner must generate a novel combination of previously learned principles. If discovery is to take place, however, the prerequisite capabilities of the learner must be established, because discovery is dependent upon internal events generated within the learner.[53]

Bloom and Broder found that there were several bases for discriminating between successful and unsuccessful behavior in problem solving: (1) the successful student exhibited an understanding of the nature of the problem and its key elements, while the unsuccessful student often was unable to interpret directions or to select key elements for solving the problem; (2) the successful student was able to transfer his own background of knowledge to the particular problem, whereas the unsuccessful student seemed unaware of the possibilities for recognizing the relevance between one's own background of knowledge and the ideas contained in the problem; (3) the successful student tended to approach the problem as a situation requiring systematic analysis and perseverance, while the unsuccessful student would either probe no further if he was

---

[52] Jerome Kagan, "Learning, Attention, and the Issue of Discovery," Chapter XI in Shulman and Keislar, *ibid.*, pp. 154, 158–161.

[53] Robert M. Gagné, "Varieties of Learning and the Concept of Discovery," Chapter X in Shulman and Keislar, *ibid.*, p. 150.

unable to find the pat solution, or would allow himself to be distracted or to digress into extraneous considerations; and (4) the successful student showed self-confidence and displayed an attitude toward the solution of the problem that valued reasoning and avoided personal bias, while the unsuccessful student had the attitude that one either knows the solution or does not, tended to allow his own biases to interfere with his reasoning, and showed less self-confidence.[54]

In reviewing the research on problem solving in the classroom, Hudgins observed that although the studies on discovery methods versus other approaches are conflicting, the classroom climate must permit pupils to vary their approaches in seeking solutions if the inhibiting effects of stereotypy are to be avoided. He also noted that individuals often will conform to group pressures even when the individual's solution is right and the majority solution is wrong, although creative individuals are less prone to the conforming pressures of the group; moreover, minority members of a group can contribute significantly in improving group performance in solving problems. Hudgins concluded that the transfer of general training in reasoning to solving specific problems appears to be well supported by the research.[55]

Receptive Vs. Discovery Learning. Ausubel has noted the widespread confusion in distinguishing between discovery learning and other cognitive styles. He points out that it is erroneous to conceive of receptive learning as invariably rote and discovery learning as invariably meaningful. "Both kinds of learning can either be rote *or* meaningful depending on the conditions under which the learning occurs." [56] Obviously, where such confusions exist, it would be virtually impossible to anticipate meaningful findings from controlled research comparing the "discovery method" with the "didactic" or "receptive method."

Ausubel also challenges Bruner's thesis that mastery of the heuristics of discovery (development of general search and information-processing behaviors in solving diverse problems within a discipline) will enable one to inquire fruitfully in other disciplines. Aside from the countless studies that fail to show such transfer, Ausubel points to the "laughable errors of logic and judgment committed by distinguished scientists and scholars who wander outside their own disciplines." [57] He disputes the

---

[54] Benjamin S. Bloom and L. J. Broder, *Problem-Solving Processes of College Students: An Exploratory Investigation,* Supplementary Educational Monographs, No. 73 (Chicago: The University of Chicago Press, 1950).

[55] Bryce B. Hudgins, *Problem Solving in the Classroom* (New York: The Macmillan Company, 1966).

[56] David P. Ausubel, "Learning by Discovery: Rationale and Mystique," *Bulletin of the National Association of Secondary School Principals,* Vol. 45 (December, 1961), p. 28.

[57] David P. Ausubel, *Educational Psychology: A Cognitive View* (New York: Holt, Rinehart and Winston, Inc., 1968), p. 488.

notion of discovery proponents, especially Bruner, that the goals of the mature researcher and the student are identical, and maintains that the level of abstraction, generality, and sophistication between the two may involve qualitative as well as quantitative differences.[58]

The Research Void.   Research on discovery methods leaves much to be desired. Aside from the aforementioned problem of lumping too many things under the discovery banner, there is the tendency to assess learning outcomes through instruments, such as paper-and-pencil tests, which measure rate and amount of learning more faithfully than they measure the behavior of the learner in discovery situations. While the discovery process is complex and multidimensional, this provides no excuse for using it as a convenient label or slogan just to be in fashion with the times. Most of the major curriculum reform projects have made sweeping claims concerning their discovery approaches in the absence of controlled research.

> Despite their frequent espousal of discovery principles, the various curriculum reform projects have failed thus far to yield any research evidence in support of the discovery method. . . . For one thing, the sponsors of some of these projects have not been particularly concerned about *proving* the superior efficacy of their programs, since they have been thoroughly convinced of this from the outset.[59]

Because most of the major curriculum projects in science and mathematics are dependent on grants from such agencies as the National Science Foundation, their proponents' reluctance to expose them to controlled research may reflect the desire to "demonstrate" their worth without jeopardizing their source of funds. Another complicating factor is that, despite their claims of adherence to "discovery" principles and the "structure of the discipline," most of the projects employ a wide variety of approaches in organizing the subject matter and in designating instructional methods. Moreover, authorities within given disciplines are not in general agreement as to what should properly constitute the program of instruction at various grade levels. In the absence of careful and objective research, the schools will continue to make decisions concerning the adoption of curriculum projects according to the weight of authority, testimonials, and teacher preferences.

The bankruptcy of psychological theory in dealing with the assessment of discovery methods in the classroom is attributed by some investigators to the tendency of psychologists, historically, to confine their work to the safety of clean laboratory techniques while ignoring those questions that

---

[58] *Ibid.*, p. 489.
[59] *Ibid.*, p. 498.

are most critical to society.[60] Instead of confining research activities to the laboratory, or limiting studies to the manipulations of a given variable within a classroom period of fifty minutes, the assessment of discovery requires research into the ecology of the classroom and the school.

Inductive and Deductive Modes

Many of the leaders responsible for developing the new discovery approach courses claim to embrace the *inductive* mode or process through which the learner induces generalizations from specific information and observations. In contrast, the *deductive* mode or process starts with a generalization through which the learner derives specific information, answers, or even further generalizations.

In attempting to embrace the inductive mode, many curriculum developers have equated induction with inquiry. They contrast the inductive process with traditional teaching methods through which the teacher didactically presents generalizations, rules, and ready-made explanations to the students for purposes of memorization and mechanical application in finding specific answers to questions or problems. Obviously, the former approach emphasizes inquiry-discovery, while the latter encourages rote learning within a sphere of narrow application. But the latter is not the only alternative to induction. Inquiry and discovery also can occur where the teacher and students start with an explanation of the generalization or principle and then seek to inquire into and discover the variety of specific conditions, phenomena, applications, interpretations, and conclusions for which the generalization is indeed valid. Thus, both inductive and deductive strategies may involve inquiry and discovery, though the strategies are essentially different. Too many proponents of the inductive approach claim that it has an exclusive identity with inquiry and discovery.[61]

It is inaccurate and misleading to use induction and discovery as synonymous terms. And it is equally inaccurate and misleading to regard deductive and didactic teaching as synonymous approaches. Research comparing inductive and deductive methods has been most inadequate and one cannot conclude from the existing evidence that one approach is superior to the other. At this stage it would appear that both modes of learning are valuable for different purposes. The limited body of existing research has tended to contrast inductive methods with rote or didactic approaches, rather than with deductive strategies. This has led many curriculum developers to assume that the inductive approach is

---

[60] Shulman and Keislar, *op. cit.,* pp. 166–167.

[61] An example is Edwin Fenton, *Teaching the New Social Studies: An Inductive Approach* (New York: Holt, Rinehart and Winston, Inc., 1966).

the proper singular banner under which their programs are to be represented. Both processes are essential to critical thinking and discovery,
according to Dewey:

> The inductive movement is toward *discovery* of a binding principle;
> the deductive toward its *testing*—confirming, refuting, modifying it on
> the basis of its capacity to interpret isolated details into a unified ex-
> perience. So far as we conduct each of these processes in the light of
> the other, we get valid discovery or verified critical thinking.[62]

Two Modes of Thought. Conant has described the world of science
as functioning through two definable, though not necessarily exclusive
modes of thought: the theoretical-deductive mode and the empirical-
inductive mode. The man who creates a theory, an imaginative and
sweeping conceptualization that outstrips the existing factual knowledge, is following the theoretical-deductive method of inquiry. Most
of the striking advances in science are attributed to this mode of thought.
On the other hand, the classifiers, observers, experimenters, and those
concerned with the application of theoretical knowledge in solving practical problems may be said to be following the empirical-inductive tradition.

> Often it happens in the history of science that the inventor of the
> wide generalization (which must at the start be an hypothesis) is not the
> man who explores the consequences in the laboratory or in the field
> . . . those with a preference for the theoretical-deductive mode of
> thought are the constructors of the theories. The classifiers, the ob-
> servers, the experimenters are in the empirical-inductive tradition. Yet
> . . . the two categories are not necessarily mutually exclusive. The
> greatest scientists can and have used both modes of thought; the empiri-
> cal-inductive is by itself insufficient to generate advances in scientific
> theory.[63]

Conant sees both modes of thought as essential to society. "Just as a
man needs two legs to walk on, the social sciences need two types of
thinkers if the advance is, as it should be, to meet the needs of a free and
highly industrialized society." [64]

The assumption made by many leaders in developing new curricula,
that scholar-researchers confine their activities to one mode of thought
(commonly termed the "inductive approach" in the new curricula), would
appear to be grossly inadequate and misleading according to Conant's
views.

---

[62] John Dewey, *How We Think,* 1910 ed., *op. cit.,* p. 82.
[63] James Bryant Conant, *Two Modes of Thought* (New York: Trident Press, 1964),
pp. 30–31.
[64] *Ibid.,* p. 95.

Intuitive and Analytic Thinking

An important theme of *The Process of Education,* and integral to Bruner's concept of inquiry-discovery, deals with the nature and importance of intuition. Intuition is seen as "the intellectual technique of arriving at plausible but tentative formulations without going through the analytic steps by which such formulations would be found to be valid or invalid . . . the shrewd guess, the fertile hypothesis, the courageous leap to a tentative conclusion—these are the most valuable coin of the thinker at work." [65] Yet Bruner acknowledges that little is known concerning intuitive thinking or the variables that influence it in the teaching-learning process. And while he advocates the cultivation of intuitive thinking in the young learner on the one hand, he cites on the other hand the importance of having a high degree of mastery of the subject in order to function effectively through intuition. He also stresses the importance of having students check intuitive solutions with analytic methods wherever possible.[66]

The role of intuition in research has been widely discussed, although research on intuition has been given very little attention. A research professor of mathematics discusses the role and importance of intuition in making creative breakthroughs in problems that had remained unsolved for many years and had become "classic." He attempts to explain why new and fresh solutions often are produced by the more youthful scholars:

> The experienced individuals may have stopped working on them, having found their efforts at solution frustrated, and therefore have gone on to problems promising quicker results. I believe that what happens here is that the collective intuition in the field of a particular problem continues to grow, being passed on by the older workers to the younger. Ultimately, due to a combination of a more mature collective intuition (which has been growing unnoticed), new methods, and individual genius, someone (usually a younger mathematician, relatively new in the field, and possessing a fresh individual intuition) is able to solve the problem. That feeling of awe, which I am sure many older creative mathematicians get regarding the powers of the younger generation of creative workers, has a firm basis. The younger man has not only come into the particular field without having to clutter up his brain with concepts and methods which served their purpose and are now discarded, but using new concepts and methods he has built up an individual intuition which forms a platform from which he can regard his field of research with an eye undimmed by the recollection of earlier

---

[65] Bruner, *The Process of Education, op. cit.,* pp. 13–14.
[66] *Ibid.,* pp. 55–58.

and faulty intuitions. . . . It is almost a truism that without intuition, there is no creativity in mathematics.[67]

The current use of the term *intuition* by Bruner and others closely resembles Dewey's conception of the term *inference*, as illustrated in the following passage:

> Every inference, just because it goes beyond ascertained and known facts . . . involves a *jump from the known into the unknown*. It involves a leap beyond what is given and already established. . . .[68]
>
> It proceeds by anticipation, supposition, conjecture, imagination. All foresight, prediction, planning, as well as theorizing and speculation, are characterized by excursion from the actual into the possible.[69]

Dewey regarded inference as essential to reflective activity and, consequently, involving not only a leap to a suggested conclusion, but also the testing of the suggestion "to determine its agreement with the requirements of the situation." [70]

Inferential and intuitive thinking processes have not been clearly differentiated in the psychological literature. However, where the term *inference* is often used to describe a process of deriving a conclusion or assumption from limited information or data, the term *intuition* tends to be used to describe an insightful process of apprehending a solution that is not analytically derivable from the given information or data. Thus the latter term often is connected with a less predictable and more creative act of thought.

In the traditional classroom, emphasis is given to eliciting the correct answers to questions and problems, while guessing and the testing of hunches tend to be discouraged. Students are reluctant to propose solutions unless they are quite certain that their answers are correct. After all, a wrong answer may reveal the student's ignorance to the teacher and his classmates. Thus, hypothetical thinking based upon intuition is discouraged and the learner fails to develop the self-confidence and daring necessary in proposing novel solutions that transcend the available data. Moreover, in the intuitive process, it is not possible for the learner to verbalize analytically just how he arrived at his proposed solution. Under conventional classroom conditions, this inability is considered a weakness rather than a normal condition of intuitive reasoning.

In recent years the term *intuition* has received considerable attention in various curriculum development projects. Some of the new projects in course-content improvement are seeking to develop a favorable climate

---

[67] R. L. Wilder, "The Role of Intuition," *Science,* Vol. 156 (May 5, 1967), p. 608.
[68] Dewey, *How We Think,* rev. ed., 1933, *op. cit.,* p. 96.
[69] *Ibid.,* p. 104.
[70] *Ibid.,* p. 98.

for intuitive thinking by exposing students to problems that have yet to be solved by scholar-researchers in the given discipline. And most of the new projects are attempting to stimulate the intuitive powers of young-sters by exposing them to problems for which the methods and answers are indeed known but are not given to the learner. Instead, the student is encouraged to make intelligent guesses, to hypothesize, and to test out his possible solutions. However, the extent to which these approaches are successful in developing intuitive abilities has yet to be determined.

Evolution of Terminology

At the beginning of this chapter, we discussed how Dewey's concern for inquiry as an educative process was embodied in his conception of reflective thinking. In 1910 Dewey described reflective thinking as "judg-ment suspended during further inquiry." [71] Reflection involves not sim-ply a sequence of ideas, but a *con*-sequence. . . .[72] To maintain the state of doubt and to carry on systematic and protracted inquiry—these are the essentials of thinking." [73] Throughout the 1930's and early 1940's progres-sive educators experimented with a variety of instructional modes and curriculum designs that were conceived to foster reflective thinking. A number of attempts were made to identify and evaluate specific aspects of reflective thinking in the teaching-learning process during the late 1940's and throughout the 1950's. These efforts were marked by the em-ployment of a wide variety of terms to describe elements in the process of reflective thinking. Perhaps the use of varied terminology reflected the enormous complexity and magnitude of the task. Or perhaps it was symptomatic of efforts to avoid identification with a term that was so directly connected with progressive education. At any rate, at one point reflective thinking was encompassed in the literature under the general term of *higher mental process;* [74] at yet another point, the term *critical thinking* was used in describing a variety of functions related to reflective thinking.[75] And, with the 1960's, we find most of the curriculum projects claiming "inquiry" and "discovery" as the "new" instructional strategy. Whether or not this represents a curriculum revolution depends on whether it is used authentically as an instructional process or whether it is used as a mere slogan in promoting a packaged curriculum product.

---

[71] John Dewey, *How We Think,* 1910 ed., *op. cit.,* p. 13.

[72] *Ibid.,* p. 2.

[73] *Ibid.,* p. 13.

[74] See The National Society for the Study of Education, *The Measurement of Under-standing,* Forty-fifth Yearbook, Part I (Chicago: The University of Chicago Press, 1946), p. 1.

[75] See Paul L. Dressel and Lewis B. Mayhew, *General Education: Explorations in Evaluation* (Washington, D.C.: American Council on Education, 1954).

In the absence of controlled research on inquiry-discovery as method, the term may lack authentic meaning and application.

SUMMARY

The emphasis on inquiry-discovery in teaching and learning has come to be associated with the new programs of course-content improvement. However, inquiry-discovery as a mode of teaching and learning has antecedents in unit teaching, the project method, problem solving, reflective thinking, and critical thinking.

Most of the new projects have sought to reformulate the subject matter, materials, and techniques within given disciplines in such a way as to represent the manner through which the scholar-specialist seeks new knowledge. These attempts are reflected in the Brunerian notion that "intellectual activity anywhere is the same, whether at the frontier of knowledge or in a third-grade classroom." This premise appears to conflict with the thesis, advanced by Dewey early in this century and more recently by Piaget, that levels of intellectual activity are outgrowths of developmental stages. In this connection, for example, the development of hypothetical reasoning and the ability to perform controlled experimentation cannot ordinarily be anticipated until late childhood or early adolescence. This conflict has profound implications for curriculum workers and until it is settled considerable confusion can be expected among those who are responsible for shaping the curriculum.

It can be argued, moreover, that inquiry-discovery should not be the dominant mode of organizing instruction on the grounds that (1) the learning style of the adolescent is not identical to that of the mature scholar, (2) the mature scholar tends to be concerned with a specialized area of knowledge and the search for new knowledge in his discipline, while the adolescent in school is expected to concern himself with a multiplicity of areas of knowledge or disciplines, (3) the adolescent is, at best, only at the beginning stages of commitment to a vocational choice in a particular discipline or field, whereas the mature scholar has long been committed to his discipline, (4) effective learning is a product of a wide variety of activities and is not limited to inquiry-discovery, and (5) the adolescent must learn to relate knowledge and synthesize his learnings from many disparate fields, while the inquiry-discovery mode of the mature scholar is limited professionally to a small part of a single discipline which may or may not be connected with other disciplines.

Nevertheless, the emphasis on inquiry-discovery in reformulating subject matter and revitalizing teaching-learning methods comes as a rejection of traditional approaches that conceive of knowledge as bodies of information to be arbitrarily and dogmatically handed down to students from a higher authority. Over the years this conception of subject matter has given undue emphasis to rote learning and has provided students with a false impression of what knowledge and schooling are all about.

While many claims are being made for learning by discovery, these claims have yet to be substantiated by empirical research. This may be attributed not to inherent inadequacies of discovery methods per se, but to the tendency for many curriculum developers and researchers to lump too many things under the attractive banner of inquiry-discovery. Inquiry-discovery is a complex and multidimensional function in teaching and learning and its effectiveness would appear to hinge not only on the specific inquiry-discovery strategies being employed, but also on such factors as (1) the nature of the subject matter, (2) the nature of the learner, (3) the nature of the teacher, (4) interaction processes between and among the aforementioned, (5) the specific learning outcomes desired, and (6) the validity of instruments and procedures for measuring the outcomes of inquiry-discovery treatments. Too many tests and studies have been limited to measuring and comparing the amount and rate of learning subject matter. Learning has many outcomes, and the multidimensionality of inquiry-discovery requires more sophisticated treatments.

Considerable attention has been given to reformulating the subject matter, materials, and techniques of given disciplines so that the emerging pattern can be said to represent the scholar-researcher's conceptual and methodological framework. Little attention, however, has been given to the importance of the human model for emulation. Yet the desire to emulate desirable features of the human model can be a powerful factor in developing attitudes and styles of learning. Similarly, insufficient attention has been given to peer interaction in inquiry-discovery processes.

It is claimed for many of the new courses that an inductive approach is followed. Induction has been equated with inquiry-discovery. But inquiry-discovery can also take place through deductive methods where the teacher and students may search for conditions, phenomena, applications, interpretations, and conclusions after starting from a generalization or principle. Although deduction is essentially different from induction, it is erroneous to assume that the former is synonymous with didactic teaching while the latter is synonymous with inquiry.

Another issue concerns the trend of introducing certain subject matter at earlier levels of schooling. The past decade has been marked by many attempts to demonstrate how young children are capable of dealing with abstract knowledge. But simply because it can be demonstrated that youngsters at a given age are able to learn a particular subject matter, it does not necessarily follow that such material should be made part of the curriculum for that age level. For example, while kindergarten pupils are indeed capable of learning oral communication in Mandarin, Russian, and Swahili, this does not mean that these languages should be taught in the kindergarten. Yet a number of scholar-specialists have sought to introduce economics, anthropology, probability, foreign languages, and other subjects in the primary grades. Although there is a paucity of developmental studies on the effects of introducing such studies at earlier ages, the existing research fails to show any significant advantages in these practices.

The frantic activity in course-content improvement through a multiplicity of federally financed projects during the decade of the 1960's has been a product of the long-range crisis in national security. The consequence has been that priorities have been given to certain areas of the curriculum, particularly the sciences, mathematics, and modern foreign languages. This has not only created a problem of curriculum hierarchy and imbalance, but has caused many curriculum workers in the less favored fields, such as social studies and English, to imitate the strategies of the higher-status projects, particularly those in the sciences. Thus virtually every group has been searching for the "structure of the discipline" and seeking to pattern the new courses in the style of the scholar-researcher who is on the forefront in discovering new knowledge. Moreover, the activity of most projects tends to be confined to a specific discipline. Virtually no attention is being given to the problem of curriculum integration. The schools have been subjected to increasing pressures to adopt more new programs, to introduce new subjects earlier, and to accelerate learning—in the absence of hard evidence that students will benefit from such innovations.

During the 1960's inquiry-discovery had become a slogan in curriculum reform, not for purposes of individual enlightenment or social harmony but for purposes of meeting national needs in an age of international peril.

PROBLEMS FOR STUDY AND DISCUSSION

1. Below is a statement made by John Dewey in 1902 concerning intellectual activity of the teacher in the schoolroom, as contrasted with the world of the professional scholar at the frontier of knowledge. Do you agree or disagree with the statement? Why?

    Every study or subject . . . has two aspects: one for the scientist as a scientist; the other for the teacher as a teacher. These two aspects are in no sense opposed or conflicting. But neither are they immediately identical. For the scientist, the subject-matter represents simply a given body of truth to be employed in locating new problems, instituting new researches, and carrying them through to a verified outcome. To him the subject-matter or the science is self-contained. . . . He is not, as a scientist, called upon to travel outside its particular bounds; if he does, it is only to get more facts of the same general sort. The problem of the teacher is a different one. . . . He is concerned with the subject-matter of the science *as representing a given stage and phase of the development of experience.* . . . He is concerned, not with the subject-matter as such, but with the subject-matter as a related factor in a total and growing experience. Thus to see it is to psychologize it.

It is the failure to keep in mind the double aspect of subject-matter which causes the curriculum and child to be set over against each other. . . . [John Dewey, *The Child and the Curriculum* (Chicago: The University of Chicago Press, 1902), pp. 29–30.]

2. Taking Dewey's statement a step further, would you agree that every study or subject has *three* aspects: one for the scientist as a scientist, one for the teacher as a teacher, and one for the pupil as a pupil? Why?

3. What are some of the possible sources of conflict in classroom practice between Dewey's position in problem 1 above and Bruner's statement below?

   . . . intellectual activity anywhere is the same, whether at the frontier of knowledge or in a third-grade classroom. . . . The schoolboy learning physics is a physicist, and it is easier for him to learn physics behaving like a physicist than doing something else. [Jerome S. Bruner, *The Process of Education* (Cambridge, Mass.: Harvard University Press, 1960), p. 14.]

4. What is the basic source of conflict between Piaget's theory of intellectual development and Bruner's thesis as stated above? What are the implications of Piaget's theory of intellectual development for educators who seek to articulate the curriculum of the elementary school with that of the middle school or junior high school?

5. What are some of the possible reasons why the research comparing inquiry-discovery methods with other approaches has failed to substantiate the many claims made for inquiry-discovery?

6. Conant has stated that "one may speak of induction as the process of going from particulars to the general and deduction as the reverse procedure." [James Bryant Conant, *Two Modes of Thought* (New York: Trident Press, 1964), p. 1.] In much of the literature from the new curriculum projects one finds that the term *induction* has been equated with *inquiry*. Illustrate how inquiry processes might be developed through *deductive* methods of teaching.

7. Why does curriculum development require not only the addition of new subject matter and revision of the old within existing disciplines, but also (a) new approaches to organization and treatment of the subject matter within each discipline, and (b) new designs for the resynthesis and integration of the various disciplines into the frame-

work of a total school curriculum? How do you account for the tendency during the 1960's to neglect the problem of curriculum synthesis and integration?

SELECTED REFERENCES

Aschner, Mary Jane, and Charles E. Bish (eds.). *Productive Thinking in Education*. Washington, D.C.: National Education Association, 1965.

Ausubel, David P. *Educational Psychology: A Cognitive View*. New York: Holt, Rinehart and Winston, Inc., 1968. Ch. 14.

Bode, Boyd H. *Modern Educational Theories*. New York: The Macmillan Company, 1927.

Broudy, Harry S., B. Othanel Smith, and Joe R. Burnett. *Democracy and Excellence in American Secondary Education*. Chicago: Rand McNally & Company, 1964. Chs. 12, 14.

Broudy, Harry S., and John R. Palmer. *Exemplars of Teaching Method*. Chicago: Rand McNally & Company, 1965. Ch. 11.

Bruner, Jerome S. *The Process of Education*. Cambridge, Mass.: Harvard University Press, 1960.

———— *Toward a Theory of Instruction*. Cambridge, Mass.: Harvard University Press, 1966.

———— (ed.). *Learning About Learning*. Washington, D.C.: Office of Education, U.S. Department of Health, Education, and Welfare, 1966.

Conant, James Bryant. *Two Modes of Thought*. New York: Trident Press, 1964.

Dewey, John. *The School and Society*. Chicago: The University of Chicago Press, 1900.

———— *The Child and the Curriculum*. Chicago: The University of Chicago Press, 1902.

———— *How We Think*. Boston: D. C. Heath & Company, 1910, and rev. ed., 1933.

———— *Experience and Education*. New York: The Macmillan Company, 1938.

———— *Logic—The Theory of Inquiry*. New York: Holt, Rinehart and Winston, Inc., 1938.

Flavell, John H. *The Developmental Psychology of Jean Piaget*. Princeton, N.J.: D. Van Nostrand Company, 1963.

Goodlad, John I. *The Changing School Curriculum*. New York: The Fund for the Advancement of Education, 1966.

Heath, Robert W. (ed.). *New Curricula*. New York: Harper & Row, Publishers, 1964.

Hudgins, Bruce B. *Problem Solving in the Classroom*. New York: The Macmillan Company, 1966.

Hullfish, H. Gordon, and Philip G. Smith. *Reflective Thinking: The Method of Education*. New York: Dodd, Mead & Company, 1961.

Peters, R. S. (ed.). *The Concept of Education*. New York: The Humanities Press, 1967.

Piaget, Jean, and B. Inhelder. *The Growth of Logical Thinking from Childhood to Adolescence.* New York: Basic Books, 1958.

Russell, James E. *Change and Challenge in American Education.* Boston: Houghton Mifflin Company, 1965.

Shulman, Lee S., and Evan R. Keislar (eds.). *Learning by Discovery: A Critical Appraisal.* Chicago: Rand McNally & Company, 1966.

Smith, B. Othanel, and Robert H. Ennis (eds.). *Language and Concepts in Education.* Chicago: Rand McNally & Company, 1961.

Taba, Hilda. *Curriculum Development: Theory and Practice.* New York: Harcourt, Brace & World, Inc., 1962. Chs. 8, 9, 11, 14, 17, 19.

Thelen, Herbert A. *Education and the Human Quest.* New York: Harper & Row, Publishers, Inc., 1960.

Whitehead, Alfred North. *The Aims of Education and Other Essays.* New York: The Macmillan Company, 1929.

Chapter 2

General Education and Curriculum Integration

"Education," wrote Plato, "is the first and fairest thing that the best of men can ever have, and which, though liable to take a wrong direction, is capable of reformation. And this work of reformation is the great business of every man while he lives." [1] The historic conflict between general education and specialized knowledge has not been a creation of the schools. This conflict reflects changes that have occurred in our social and material world, to which our schools have been expected to respond through constant readjustment and reformation of the curriculum. At times, our society has looked to the schools to develop a harmony of curriculum to counterbalance the lack of harmony in our lives. At other times, our society has demanded that the schools change their curriculum priorities to meet the need for specialized knowledge.

Yet the schools of a free society are expected to provide the kind of general education that seeks to enable all citizens to exercise independent judgment while sharing in the responsibility for acting in the common good. However, the trend toward the specialization of knowledge has created a problem of curriculum fragmentation. Knowledge becomes compartmentalized into separate domains. In the name of scholarships, knowledge is treated as an end unto itself, with a resulting neglect of human problems and concerns. Along with the explosion of knowledge, we have an incessant multiplication of studies. Each specialized domain has its adherents who seek for their discipline a recognized place in the curriculum.

Nevertheless, the attempt to control the multiplication of studies by arbitrarily eliminating areas of knowledge will not, in itself, redirect our

---

1 Plato, *Laws*, Book I.

energies toward the human condition. A more promising and constructive alternative is to develop new interrelationships of knowledge for purposes of finding solutions to man's pervasive problems. Disciplinarity need not destroy the possibilities for interdisciplinarity. "The body of knowledge is indeed one," wrote Dewey; "it is a spiritual organism. To attempt to chop off a member here and amputate an organ there is the veriest impossibility. The problem is not one of elimination, but of organization; of simplification not through denial and rejection, but through harmony." [2]

DILEMMAS OF DISCIPLINARITY

As discussed in Chapter 1, one of the theses of the curriculum reform movement of the 1960's was that the schoolboy engaged in an area of intellectual activity for the first time is not unlike the mature scholar in the forefront of his discipline.[3] A second thesis, which also became a guiding doctrine of the new discipline-centered curriculum reforms, was that through the efforts of the best minds in any particular discipline the fundamental structure of that discipline can be developed, thereby bringing the fruits of scholarship and wisdom to the student just beginning his studies.[4] Although Part II of this book is devoted to a critical assessment of the currriculum reform efforts within the various disciplines and areas of subject matter, in this chapter we are concerned with the implications of these discipline-centered efforts for general education in the secondary school.

The Narrow Vision

Bruner stated his ideas as premises. Yet many educators came to embrace them as dogma. The long-standing dilemma of whether the curriculum should be subject-centered, or based upon the nature, needs, and interests of the learner, or derived from the demands of contemporary life could now be resolved. Subject-centeredness caused its own bankruptcy, because virtually anything could become a subject in the school curriculum. On the other hand, a discipline possesses the virtues of purity, specialism, and authority. What could be more imposing than the credentials of the discipline-oriented university scholars in pointing the way to curriculum salvation? Moreover, in an atmosphere of missile gaps, who could say that the discipline-focused curriculum is unresponsive to the

---

2 John Dewey, *The Educational Situation* (Chicago: The University of Chicago Press, 1902), p. 89.

3 Jerome S. Bruner, *The Process of Education* (Cambridge, Mass.: Harvard University Press, 1960), pp. 19–20.

4 *Ibid.,* p. 14.

demands of contemporary life? And aren't the disciplines the most efficient pathways toward new knowledge in an age of increasing specialization? Finally, as discussed in Chapter 1, if the mature scholar and the
immature schoolboy are essentially alike in their processes of inquiry,
then problems connected with the learner's nature, needs, and interests
become irrelevant in the new discipline-focused curriculum.

> The curriculum should consist entirely of knowledge which comes
> from the disciplines, for the reason that the disciplines reveal knowl-
> edge in its teachable forms. . . . Education should be conceived as a
> guided *recapitulation of the processes of inquiry which gave rise to the
> fruitful bodies of organized knowledge comprising the established dis-
> ciplines.*
>   . . . There is no place in the curriculum for ideas which are re-
> garded as suitable for teaching because of the supposed nature, needs,
> and interests of the learner, but which do not belong within the regu-
> lar structure of the disciplines, for the disciplines are in their essential
> nature bodies of knowledge organized for the most effective instruction.[5]

In a later work, Phenix contends that the first principle in determining
curriculum content is that such content should be derived entirely from
the domains of disciplined inquiry, because "the richness of culture and
the level of understanding achieved in advanced civilization are due almost entirely to the labors of individual men of genius and of organized
communities of specialists." [6] However, if the "regular structure of the
disciplines" is appropriate for individual men of genius and organized
communities of specialists, is it also appropriate for the common man or
citizen? Furthermore, the increasing specialization of knowledge has
created a heightened interdependence in man. And, moreover, not only
does the criterion of disciplinarity eliminate vocational education from
the curriculum, but it creates a variety of serious problems in general
education—the education that is relevant to our lives as responsible citizens in a free society.

Disciplinarity and Life Relevance

If the curriculum is to be organized according to the disciplines of inquiry, does this mean that each subject must be identified as a discipline
or part of a discipline? [7] Under such requirements, the problem of a
growing multiplicity of subjects or courses, characteristic of the tradi-

---

5 Philip H. Phenix in A. Harry Passow (ed.), *Curriculum Crossroads* (New York:
Teachers College Press, 1962), p. 64.

6 Philip H. Phenix, *Realms of Meaning* (New York: McGraw-Hill Book Company,
1964), p. 10.

7 Jane R. Martin, "The Disciplines and the Curriculum," *Educational Philosophy and
Theory*, Vol. 1, 1969, p. 24.

tional subject curriculum, remains unsolved because the incessant expansion of knowledge leads to the creation of new disciplines and branches of disciplines. In the social sciences we have such recognized areas of knowledge as anthropology, economics, geography, history, government, psychology, and sociology. The biological sciences also are a conglomerate of specialized areas of knowledge. And, for example, what about ecology —an area of knowledge that not only is identified with biology but with the social sciences, while also deriving important applications from the physical sciences. As will be discussed in Part II of this book, the new curriculum projects have failed to demonstrate the validity of "structure of the discipline" as a unifying principle.

Second, the premise that the curriculum should consist entirely of knowledge that derives from the disciplines also eliminates many legitimate studies such as literature and the fine and performing arts. To seek to reconstruct these aspects of human experience along the lines of the so-called established disciplines will surely rob literature and the arts of their vitality and authenticity.

Third, many fields of knowledge are multidisciplinary in nature. This fact applies not only to the biological and social sciences but also to the physical sciences. Consequently, the principle of "structure of the discipline" must be modified considerably when subjects in the curriculum are organized as fields of knowledge.

Fourth, the multidisciplinary characteristics of many fields require cross-disciplinary and interdisciplinary approaches in order to discover new knowledge and to solve problems as they occur in man and his universe.

Fifth, many significant problems and problem areas of society are not within the exclusive domain of any one discipline. We have already mentioned how problems in ecology are not confined to a singular discipline or domain of knowledge. Moreover, when society makes demands such as that the schools provide instruction concerning the dangers of narcotics, for example, we are left with the problem of determining in which discipline or domain of knowledge such a problem belongs—biology, health education, sociology? Or should the problem be treated within each of these domains? If so, how is the subject matter parceled out? And then, after it is parceled out, how is it put together again so that it becomes relevant to the life of the learner in a manner that meets society's demands that it be placed in the school curriculum? Or do we avoid this dilemma simply by adding a course on narcotics to the overcrowded curriculum?

The same dilemma applies to the question of black studies.

Under such circumstances, do we avoid these studies because they do not fit the criterion of disciplinarity? This is not likely because the schools, as instruments of society, have been unable to ignore the demands and expectations of society. As Martin observes, "Given a world which does not cooperate with the disciplines or, perhaps, disciplines which do not keep up with the world, our Discipline Principle advocate is saying 'So much the worse for the world' whereas he should be saying 'So much the worse for the disciplines.' " [8]

One notes an increasing concern, even on the part of research specialists, about the failure of the puristic discipline principle to have relevance and application to problems of the real world. For example, a nuclear physicist points out that the university's orientation toward disciplinarity has made its goals remote from those of society, and even serves to divert society from its real goals.

> the pervasiveness of the university's influence on the society and the fragmentation and concern for disciplinary purity of the university . . . divert society from its real goals. Our society is not a university; the goals of our society are not the same as the goals of the fragmented and discipline-oriented university. It is hardly acceptable for the university to persuade the society that at this stage in history the university's own intellectual goals and aspirations—remote, pure, and fragmented—deserve the highest place among the goals of the society.[9]

In recent years, the university scholar-specialists have succeeded in imposing their disciplinary purity on the elementary and secondary schools. But before discussing further the implications of imposing the discipline principle of the university on the lower levels of schooling, let us examine briefly some principal sources of educational objectives and curricular influences.

SOURCES OF EDUCATIONAL OBJECTIVES

Curriculum development throughout the twentieth century has reflected recurring shifts of emphasis and focus in response to changing sociopolitical forces. History is never repeated exactly, however, because each epoch creates its own particular demands and responses. While it is easy to call for a balance in emphasis and focus, the school, as an institution of society, has been compelled to respond to the larger social forces and pressures, particularly during periods of crisis. Yet a simplified analysis of the major sources of educational objectives is not only useful in gaining perspective but is essential to an understanding of the influences at work.

---

8 *Ibid.,* p. 30.

9 Alvin M. Weinberg, *Reflections on Big Science* (Cambridge, Mass.: The M.I.T. Press, 1967), pp. 159–160.

The Learner, Contemporary Life, and Subject Matter

A statement of rationale for analyzing and developing any curriculum, formulated by Tyler in 1950, remains relevant to education today.[10] According to Tyler, there are four fundamental questions that must be answered in the development of a curriculum:

1. What educational purposes should the school seek to attain?
2. What educational experiences can be provided that are likely to attain these purposes?
3. How can these educational experiences be effectively organized?
4. How can we determine whether these purposes are being attained? [11]

On the question of objectives, Tyler identifies three principal sources, while taking the view that "no single source of information is adequate to provide a basis for wise and comprehensive decisions about the objectives of the school." [12] The three sources identified by Tyler are (1) studies of the learners themselves, (2) studies of contemporary life, and (3) suggestions from subject specialists. In discussing the historic inadequacy of the subject specialists as a source of objectives, Tyler notes that they have been asked the wrong question: "What should be the elementary instruction for students who are later to carry on much more advanced work in the field?" Instead, according to Tyler, the question should be: "What can your subject contribute to the education of young people who are not going to be specialists in your field; what can your subject contribute to the layman . . . the citizen?" [13]

By relying primarily on the scholar-specialists as the source of educational objectives during the late 1950's and the decade of the sixties, we have often obtained the right answers to the wrong question. The scholar-specialists have followed the discipline doctrine in formulating curriculum objectives, selecting curriculum experiences, organizing curriculum experiences, and evaluating their own handiwork. During this era, curriculum reform decisions have been based on the assumption that the learner is simply an intellectual resource to be developed, and that the priority of contemporary life is national supremacy.

In recent years, students have been demanding that the school and college curriculum be made relevant to the problems of contemporary life. The student protest movement also reflects the low priority we have given to the felt needs of the learner in an age when nations seek to

---

10 Herbert M. Kliebard, "The Tyler Rationale," *School Review*, Vol. 78 (February, 1970), pp. 259–272.

11 Ralph W. Tyler, *Basic Principles of Curriculum and Instruction* (Chicago: The University of Chicago Press, 1950), pp. 1–2.

12 *Ibid.*, p. 4.

13 *Ibid.*, p. 17.

exploit their intellectual resources in the pursuit of excellence. By ignoring two of the three principal sources of curriculum objectives, as outlined by Tyler more than two decades ago, we have served the interests of the mature scholar at the expense of the immature learner, and we have suffered the consequences of curriculum imbalance and fragmentation.

During an earlier epoch, some educators not only sought a better understanding of the learner, but looked to the learner as the principal source of educational objectives while all but ignoring the nature of knowledge and the race experience in developing and utilizing knowledge. This also led to curriculum imbalance and confusion.

Turning to Tyler's second source of educational objectives—studies of contemporary life—it is one thing to attempt to make a curriculum relevant to contemporary life, and quite another to allow the curriculum to bend to whichever sociopolitical demand of the day is most powerful. Thus we have the NEA's Project on Instruction responding to the national pursuit of excellence with the declaration that "it is appropriate in our society to consider education as a demand upon the individual. . . . Progress and happiness can both be served, it is conceded, when adults get behind the child and push." [14] Educators have not often been very successful in resisting sociopolitical demands and pressures.

Tyler's sources of educational objectives bear a remarkable resemblance to Bode's identification in 1931 of three points of view or determinants of the curriculum: (1) the standpoint of the subject-matter specialist whose business it is to extend the domain of knowledge in his chosen field; (2) the standpoint of the practical man who views knowledge as a means to an end; and (3) the standpoint of the interests of the learner.[15] However, Bode warned of the inadequacies, conflicts, and dangers inherent in these determinants in the absence of reflective consideration of what constitutes a good life in a good society. Thus, education should be primarily a means for acquiring an outlook on life rather than receiving a ready-made outlook. According to Bode, the schools in a democracy cannot impose a scheme of living or an official creed upon the learner. The task of education is to enable learners to develop a philosophy of life or social outlook through genuine educative participation if they are to become effective participants in the life of a democratic community.

In the absence of reflective consideration of what constitutes a good life in a good society, schooling can be made to serve any master.

---

14 Project on Instruction, *Schools for the Sixties* (New York: McGraw-Hill Book Company, Inc., 1963), p. 11.

15 Boyd H. Bode, "Education at the Crossroads: What Principles Should Determine the Curriculum?" *Progressive Education*, Vol. 8 (November, 1931), pp. 543–549.

Relationship of Learning Processes to Needs, Developmental Tasks, and the Learning Environment

It is often argued that the primary and distinctive responsibility of the school is to promote intellectual growth and the assimilation of knowledge. While most educators agree that the central focus of the curriculum is the development of cognitive capabilities, there has been a long-standing disagreement concerning the extent to which noncognitive processes, needs, and developmental tasks should be taken into account in designing the curriculum.

Table 2-1 presents summary listings of some knowledge components, cognitive processes, affective processes, need processes, and developmental tasks. A cursory examination of the listings reveals that several of the items in the various categories are closely related. For example, the task of developing intellectual skills and the need for knowing and understanding are directly connected with the cognitive goals of the school. If students have poor attitudes toward learning (affective processes), interference with the cognitive processes will result. Thus, cognitive development is inseparably linked to the affective processes and to certain needs and developmental tasks. If one of the activities in a social studies class is to examine all sides of a controversial issue, then an implicit goal of the activity is to foster openmindedness. Students who have closed or prejudiced minds are simply not going to see all sides of the issue. If a student learns to dislike mathematics in school, it is unlikely that he will become a mathematician. If a student is lacking in self-esteem, or if he is not desirous of achieving socially responsible behavior in the classroom, serious problems in cognitive learning can be anticipated. Many high school dropouts have left school because they could see no connection between the cognitive goals of the school and their developmental task of preparing for an occupation.

The social situation of the classroom and school appears to have an important bearing on achievement. Coleman reports these findings in his national study on the effects of segregated schooling:

> Finally, it appears that a pupil's achievement is strongly related to the educational backgrounds and aspirations of the other students in the school . . . children from a given family background, when put in schools of different social composition, will achieve at quite different levels . . . if a white pupil from a home that is strongly and effectively supportive of education is put in a school where most pupils do not come from such homes, his achievement will be little different than if he were in a school composed of others like himself. But if a minority pupil from a home without much educational strength is put with schoolmates with strong educational backgrounds, his achievement is likely to increase.
> . . . A pupil attitude factor, which appears to have a stronger rela-

Table 2-1. Constellations of Selected Biosocial, Cognitive, and Affective Processes

Knowledge Components	Cognitive Processes [1]	Affective Processes [2]	Need Processes [3]	Developmental Tasks [4] (Adolescence)
Concept	Recall	Receiving	Physiological	Developing intellectual skills necessary for civic competence
Fact	Comprehension	Responding	Safety	Desiring and achieving socially responsible behavior
Problem	Translation	Valuing	Belonging	Achieving emotional independence of parents and other adults
Issue	Interpretation		Self-esteem	Accepting one's physique and using the body effectively
Solution	Extrapolation		Self-actualization	Achieving a masculine or feminine social role
Generalization	Application		Knowing and understanding	Achieving new and more mature relations with age-mates of both sexes
Theory	Analysis			Acquiring a set of values and an ethical system as a guide to behavior
	Synthesis			Achieving assurance of economic independence
	Evaluation			Selecting and preparing for an occupation
	Creativeness *			Preparing for marriage and family life

[1] Benjamin S. Bloom (ed.), Taxonomy of Educational Objectives, Handbook I: Cognitive Domain (New York: David McKay Company, Inc., 1956).
[2] David R. Krathwohl, Benjamin S. Bloom, and Bertram S. Masia, Taxonomy of Educational Objectives, Handbook II: Affective Domain (New York: David McKay Company, Inc., 1964).
[3] Abraham H. Maslow, "A Theory of Human Motivation," Psychological Review, Vol. 50 (July, 1943), pp. 370–396.
[4] Robert J. Havighurst, Developmental Tasks and Education, 2nd ed. (New York: Longmans, Green & Co., 1952).
* Added by author.

tionship to achievement than do all the "school" factors together, is the extent to which an individual feels that he has some control over his own destiny.[16]

If a school and its curriculum are to be relevant to life, the cognitive goals cannot be separated from the various biosocial processes and inter-actions that affect human behavior. By taking these relationships into account, educators can seek to provide the adolescent with the learning experiences that are essential to the development of his standards of judgment and the understanding of his values and motivations. The curriculum must fit together for the learner in a coherent relationship if the school and society are themselves to be coherent.

CURRICULUM VENTURES AND CHANGING SOCIAL FORCES

Brief mention was made in Chapter 1 of how the social dislocations of the 1930's, coupled with the rise of experimentalism, led many schools and colleges to examine and reconstruct their curricula in terms of the nature and needs of the learner and the problems of society. Secondary schools, particularly those encompassing the junior high grades, experi-mented with core curricula that were student-centered and life-focused. Because the high schools, historically, served a predominantly college-preparatory function, the prevailing question was whether they could undertake fundamental reconstruction of the curriculum without sacrific-ing the level of learning required by the colleges.

The Eight-Year Study

In 1930 the Progressive Education Association established the Com-mission on the Relation of School and College to study the possibilities for allowing secondary schools freedom to attempt fundamental recon-struction. After studying the problems, the commission proposed that an experiment be undertaken in which a number of public and private secondary schools throughout the nation would embark on curriculum reform consonant with the general views of the commission.

> We are trying to develop students who regard education as an en-during quest for meanings rather than credit accumulation; who desire to investigate, to follow the leadings of a subject, to explore new fields of thought; knowing how to budget time, to read well, to use sources of knowledge effectively and who are experienced in fulfilling obliga-

---

16 James S. Coleman, *Equality of Educational Opportunity* (Washington, D.C.: U.S. Government Printing Office, 1966), pp. 22–23.

tions which come with membership in the school or college community.[17]

Thirty schools were invited to participate, and more than three hundred colleges and universities agreed to allow these schools to ignore the
usual college entrance requirements. Each school was free to develop its
own experimental curriculum. According to Aikin, some college professors felt that "progressive education now had enough rope to hang itself." [18]

Findings and Evaluation.   The longitudinal study covered the period
from 1932 to 1940. The evaluation of the Eight-Year Study was under the
direction of Ralph W. Tyler of the University of Chicago. The evaluation procedure was to match each of 1,475 graduates of the experimental
schools who had entered college with graduates of other secondary schools
who were also in college. The pairs were matched according to similarities in socioeconomic background, aptitude, interests, age, race, sex, and
other variables.

At the close of the study, the evaluation report revealed that the
graduates of the experimental schools had performed as follows:

1. earned a slightly higher total grade average;
2. earned higher grade averages in all subject fields except foreign
   languages;
3. received slightly more academic honors each year;
4. were more often judged to possess a high degree of intellectual
   curiosity and drive;
5. were more often judged to be precise, systematic, and objective in
   their thinking;
6. were more often judged to have developed clear or well-formu-
   lated ideas concerning the meaning of education;
7. more often demonstrated a high degree of resourcefulness in meeting new situations;
8. had about the same problems of adjustment as the comparison
   group, but approached their solution with greater effectiveness;
9. participated somewhat more frequently in student groups;
10. earned a higher percentage of nonacademic honors (officerships,
    athletic awards, etc.);
11. had a somewhat better orientation toward the choice of a vocation;
12. demonstrated a more active concern for what was going on in the
    world.[19]

A further finding of the study was that the graduates of the more experimental schools attained strikingly higher levels of performance in

---

[17] Wilford M. Aikin, *The Story of the Eight-Year Study* (New York: McGraw-Hill
Book Company, Inc., 1942), p. 144.

[18] *Ibid.*, p. 24.

[19] *Ibid.*, p. 144.

the areas listed above. Reporting to the Association of American Colleges in 1940, the dean of Columbia College observed that "it looks as if the stimulus and the initiative which the less conventional approach to secondary school education affords sends on to college better human materials than we have obtained in the past." [20]

Implications.   Unfortunately, the five volumes of the report of the Eight-Year Study were released in 1942—at a time when our nation's interests were overwhelmingly directed upon the crises of World War II. Cremin comments that "it is a pity they [the volumes of the report] appeared in the middle of a war, for they have never received the attention they deserve; even after two decades the challenge and excitement of the venture are apparent to the most casual reader." [21]

Although the schools differed widely in their degree of curriculum experimentation, the more venturesome schools reorganized their curricula around the needs and interests of students, and related their curricula to community problems. Traditional subject-matter divisions and barriers were broken and contemporary materials were utilized.

No comparable study has been undertaken in the years since the Eight-Year Study. Much of the curriculum evaluation today is not of the longitudinal type and is directed primarily at achievement in specific subject fields. The Eight-Year Study can be criticized on a number of methodological and procedural grounds, but it has never been demonstrated that more rigid controls over certain variables would have negated the findings. Moreover, subsequent studies have shown that experimental curricula do not penalize students with regard to academic learning.[22] And while some researchers, such as Wallen and Travers, have raised questions regarding the possible "Hawthorne Effect on the students from the experimental schools," [23] it is exceedingly doubtful that a novelty effect could be extended over a period of the years of high school and college. If such a long-range effect were possible, it would not be a novelty effect, but rather an effect of the experimental conditions.

Other questions can be raised concerning possible differences between the parent groups, although socioeconomic and other home and family criteria were used in matching the two student populations. It would appear likely that parents who choose to send their children to experimental secondary schools are somewhat different from those whose children attend conventional schools. Yet it would be virtually impossible to perfectly equate two such parent populations.

---

20 *Ibid.*, pp. 147–150.

21 Lawrence A. Cremin, *The Transformation of the School* (New York: Alfred A. Knopf, Inc., 1961), p. 254.

22 Norman E. Wallen and Robert M. W. Travers, "Analysis and Investigation of Teaching Methods," Chapter 10 in N. L. Gage (ed.), *Handbook of Research on Teaching* (Chicago: Rand McNally & Company, 1963), p. 473.

23 *Ibid.*, p. 473.

Regardless of the questions raised over the decades following the Eight-Year Study, it is unfortunate that our secondary schools have not caught the spirit of experimentation. The curriculum reform era of the late 1950's and the decade of the 1960's was led not by the schools, but by university specialists in the disciplines whose efforts were directed at curriculum uniformity, not diversity.

Renewed Focus on General Education

The Harvard Report.   With the end of World War II, various groups of educators looked optimistically to the postwar years as an era of extended educational opportunity and regeneration of general education in school and college. The Harvard Report of 1945 looked to general education as the means of developing the understandings that all citizens of a free society must havè in common despite their differences in gifts and destinies.[24] Accordingly, "Education must look to the whole man. It has been wisely said that education aims at the good man, the good citizen, and the useful man." [25] The Harvard Report went on to discuss the necessary relationships between general and vocational education in a society where all men must be free citizens and all men must be productively engaged in work.

Educational Policies Commission.   Perhaps the most comprehensive and progressive document concerned with youth education for the postwar era was produced by the NEA's Educational Policies Commission in 1944 under the title, *Education for ALL American Youth.* A revised edition appeared in 1952 while James B. Conant was serving as chairman of the commission. In this document, the commission described the mission of the comprehensive high school in a democratic society.

> Schools should be dedicated to the proposition that every youth in these United States—regardless of sex, economic status, geographic location, or race—should experience a broad and balanced education which will (1) equip him to enter an occupation suited to his abilities and offering reasonable opportunity for personal growth and social usefulness; (2) prepare him to assume the full responsibilities of American citizenship; (3) give him a fair chance to exercise his right to the pursuit of happiness through the attainment and preservation of mental and physical health; (4) stimulate intellectual curiosity, engender satisfaction in intellectual achievement, and cultivate the ability to think rationally; and (5) help him to develop an appreciation of the ethical values

---

[24] Report of the Harvard Committee, *General Education in a Free Society* (Cambridge, Mass.: Harvard University Press, 1945), p. 94.

[25] *Ibid.,* p. 74.

which should undergird all life in a democratic society. It is the duty of a democratic society to provide opportunities for such education through its schools.[26]

Throughout the years of high school, all students would participate in an integrated common-learnings course where they would devote a block of time daily to studies designed to meet their needs for "competence as citizens of the community and the nation; in understanding of economic processes and of their roles as producers and consumers; in living together in family, school, and community; in appreciation of literature and the arts; and in the use of the English language." [27] The content and activities in the common-learnings course would consist of a number of preplanned problems in areas closely related to the present problems and needs of youth. Conventional subject boundaries would be crossed or dissolved depending upon the particular problem under study. In addition, students would pursue specialized academic and vocational studies, and courses to meet their individual interests.

Education for ALL American Youth was vigorously attacked by the essentialists. Referring to this document, Bestor noted that "concern with the personal problems of adolescents has grown so excessive as to push into the background what should be the school's central concern, the intellectual development of its students." [28] According to Bestor, "the stage of integration or synthesis arrives—for the mature man and for the student alike—after, and only after, he has marshaled the array of separate intellectual powers that he knows are required," [29] and it is through the disciplines of science, mathematics, history, English, and foreign languages that these powers are developed.[30]

The Colleges.   During the immediate post-World War II years, many colleges and universities were seeking to develop integrated programs in general education, some of which were designed with student needs in mind. As an illustration, let us examine briefly some developments at a large state college. Beginning in 1947, following an extensive faculty study of student needs, the faculty at San Francisco State College, under the leadership of the college's president, J. Paul Leonard, engaged in a series of annual conferences devoted to the development of a new general education program. Emerging from these efforts were the following general education objectives: (1) recognition and satisfaction of the basic indi-

---

26 Educational Policies Commission, *Education for ALL American Youth—A Further Look* (Washington, D.C.: National Education Association, 1952), pp. 32–33.

27 *Ibid.*, p. 233.

28 Arthur Bestor, *The Restoration of Learning* (New York: Alfred A. Knopf, Inc., 1956), p. 120.

29 *Ibid.*, p. 60.

30 *Ibid.*, p. 40.

vidual needs of the student as a person; (2) development of the student as a citizen aware of his responsibilities to his college, his community, his state, his nation, and the world; (3) development of the student's ability to adjust to the problems of home and family life; (4) recognition of the need to offer the student guidance in the choice of a vocation through the exploration of many fields of learning; (5) recognition of the student's need to equip himself with the basic skills required for success in any field of human endeavor.[31]

The titles of various courses in general education offered during the 1950's indicate the experimental nature of the curriculum. A two-semester course was titled "Personal, Social, and Occupational Development"; one of the three required courses in the natural sciences was "Mathematics in Human Affairs"; and a two-semester course in the humanities bore the title, "A Study of Life Values." Among other required courses in general education were "Creative Arts Exploration," and "International and Intercultural Relations." [32]

One of the faculty who participated in the development of the curriculum in general education at San Francisco State College gives this account of the program's demise:

> As the literature on the San Francisco State College general education program in the early fifties shows, the philosophy of the program was then very much oriented to the concept of "student needs." Indeed the structure of the program and the shape of the early courses were based on an extensive faculty study of these "student needs."
>
> While the concept of student needs as the organizing principle was not completely understood by all of the faculty involved in the development of courses during the early period of the general education program, it is important nevertheless to emphasize that this philosophy was dominant; failures to comply with it were primarily due to inadequacies on the part of the faculty rather than to disagreements with the philosophic framework. By the late fifties, however, this general agreement among the faculty no longer held. Because the college had begun to carry on a great deal of graduate work and had brought to the faculty a large number of excellent specialists—faculty who were expert in their own fields of specialization but who were not themselves broadly educated—the philosophy of the program underwent a change. Of course this change affected the basic goals of the general education program.
>
> It became a more traditional program, with emphasis on subject matter coverage. . . . As I look back now, I would say that the program originally developed at San Francisco State College no longer existed around 1958.[33]

---

[31] Russell Thomas, *The Search for a Common Learning: General Education, 1800–1960* (New York: McGraw-Hill Book Company, Inc., 1962), p. 254.

[32] *Ibid.*, pp. 255–256.

[33] Letter to the author, dated March 5, 1965.

By the late 1950's the accelerating trend toward academic specialism had caused many college faculties to turn their interests away from integrated and student-centered approaches in general education. The situation in the secondary schools, as discussed later in this chapter, was marked by unprecedented curriculum reform efforts led by university specialists in the established disciplines.

THE SEARCH FOR RELEVANCE AND COHERENCE THROUGH THE SUBJECT CURRICULUM

General education can be said to represent a search for curriculum relevance and coherence in an epoch of exploding knowledge and growing academic specialism. We have discussed the concern of the experimentalists during the 1930's and 1940's to reconstruct the curriculum of the secondary school so as to make it relevant to the common problems, needs and interests of youth. However, such fundamental reconstruction has taken place in only a very small fraction of our secondary schools.

In response to the growing proliferation of courses, the failure of students to relate the subject matter from one course to another, and the growing concern for providing all youth with a common base of studies, various modifications of the traditional subject curriculum have been attempted in our secondary schools.

Correlation

One approach has been to correlate two or more subjects. This can be done within a given field, such as correlating history and geography, or between fields, such as correlating history and literature or science and mathematics. Correlation may be developed by an individual teacher who is responsible for the different courses, or by two or more teachers seeking common relationships between or among their separate courses. Sometimes these relationships are little more than the chronological sequencing of subject matter. A more difficult and sophisticated approach is to correlate the subjects according to common themes, concepts, or values. For example, the theme of "self-identity in a mass society" might be one of many correlational links between the subjects of U.S. history and American literature.

Typically the correlated courses remain intact and are scheduled separately, although some middle schools and junior high schools provide a time block of two periods in which an individual teacher will be expected to correlate the language arts and the social studies. Other schools provide for combined classes in a time block of two periods so that two teachers may work together as a team in correlating two subjects or subject fields. However, not all block-time teaching is designed for curriculum correlation. In his report on the junior high school, Conant recommended that a block of time be scheduled in grade 7, in which one teacher would have the same group of pupils for two or more periods, generally in English and the social studies.[34] Nevertheless, Conant's purpose in advocating block-time scheduling in the seventh grade is to enable the teacher to know his pupils better because he is working with fewer of them for a longer time period daily. Conant made it clear that in recommending block-time classes he was not advocating the breaking down of subject matter lines.

Although correlation presents opportunities for providing for the crossing of subject boundaries, thereby improving the possibilities of articulating the work in two or more different subjects, the subjects continue to retain their own identities. The subject matter is not reformulated to meet the problems of the learner or of society.

Fusion

The merger of related subjects into a new course is often referred to as fusion. A common example is the merger of botany and zoology into biology. Fusion is intended to produce a new synthesis of subject matter. Areas of knowledge previously taught as separate and even unrelated subjects are fused into a singular subject in which new relationships are made possible. The fused course should not be merely a combination of separate components that were formerly separate subjects. Thus the biology course might be developed around such unifying threads of thought as evolution, genetic continuity, complementarity of organism and environment, adaptation to change, and so on.

Less commonly, there is fusion between different fields of knowledge. For example, Reed College has fused literature and political science into a course called political literature. At the university level one finds such courses as mathematical sociology in which the concepts and tools from one field of knowledge are used to solve problems or gain perspectives and understandings in another discipline.

Broad Fields

A further step toward the integration of subject matter within the context of the subject curriculum is to bring together an entire branch of knowledge into a common unity. This is known as the broad fields approach. Examples of the broad fields are general science, social studies, and English. Although the intent is to synthesize an entire branch of

---

[34] James B. Conant, *Education in the Junior High School Years* (Princeton, N.J.: Educational Testing Service, 1960), pp. 22–23.

knowledge into a unified and organic relationship, the subject matter often is organized in piecemeal fashion and the result is a conglomeration of unrelated studies. Thus one may find a course in social studies that is a haphazard mixture of material drawn from different disciplines with no effort made to develop a unified synthesis of this broad field of knowledge. In English, one may find composition, literature, and grammar taught as separate and unrelated subject matters. The course in general science also may be a mixture of separate topics and concepts drawn from physics, chemistry, botany, zoology, geology, and astronomy with no concerted effort made to develop an organic synthesis of the subject matter. Such failures are not inherent weaknesses of the broad fields approach, but rather represent teaching inadequacies, the lack of appropriate curriculum materials, or the lack of commitment to the integrative principle. As discussed in later chapters, the discipline-centered curriculum reform efforts of recent years have represented a movement toward specialization and away from correlation and integration. For example, the National Council of Teachers of English, once strongly in favor of correlated and integrated curriculum designs,[35] more recently expressed opposition to such approaches because they undermine the discipline principle.[36]

The broad fields approach presents opportunities for developing a comprehensive unity from a branch of knowledge that otherwise would be incomprehensible to the learner. Students cannot pursue even a representative sampling of the great multiplicity of specialized subjects that are derived from the many disciplines comprising each major branch of knowledge. Consequently, through thematic and conceptual frames of reference, the subject matter can be integrated in meaningful ways by the broad fields approach.

Many colleges and universities have followed the broad fields approach for purposes of general education. For example, Michigan State University requires that all students take a three-term sequence in each of several broad fields courses such as natural science, social science, and American thought and language. The course in natural science integrates, thematically and conceptually, material from the physical and biological sciences. The course in social science is organized around broad interdisciplinary problems and themes, such as the nature of social change, the individual in society and culture, problems of equalizing opportunity (economic, educational, associational, political), problems of deprivation, problems of political control and change, problems of reconciling national self-interest with needs for world peace, and others. In the broad

---

[35] National Council of Teachers of English, *A Correlated Curriculum* (New York: Appleton-Century-Crofts, 1936).

[36] See John J. DeBoer, "The New English," *The Educational Forum*, Vol. 32 (May, 1968), pp. 393–402.

fields course in American thought and language, students read selected American documents, historical and contemporary, and express themselves in writing on significant ideas, problems, and issues relating to these documents.

Although the broad fields approach, properly organized within a synthesizing framework, can enable the learner to appreciate the interdependence of knowledge, it is not based upon the problems, needs, and interests of the learner. Instead, it is an attempt to integrate concepts, skills, and generalizations from several disciplines or areas of study within a branch of knowledge. Consequently, the broad fields approach does not require a radical modification of the subject curriculum.

Other Approaches to Integration:
The Humanities in the Subject Curriculum

Partly as a reaction to the priority accorded the sciences and mathematics in the curriculum reform movement, an increasing number of high schools established courses in the humanities during the 1960's. Many high schools also were attracted to the idea of offering one or more courses in the humanities because such courses are commonly offered in the colleges and they carry an aura of prestige consonant with our national pursuit of excellence. Consequently, despite the fact that the humanities course provides opportunities for integrating several fields of knowledge, it is usually designed for the college-bound and academically able student. Under such circumstances, it serves merely as another college preparatory subject and not as a part of the general education program of the high school. Yet, at the college level, the humanities course is commonly offered as part of the general education sequence.

The humanities course typically is focused on Western culture as developed in social and political institutions and in artistic, literary, philosophical, and religious expression. Thus it cuts across the subject boundaries of history, literature, music, and the visual arts. It thereby seeks an integration of these areas of knowledge and expression in ways not possible through separate and fragmented subjects.

Organization.   The most traditional organization of the humanities course is the historical-cultural approach. In this approach, the material is arranged chronologically according to major themes or movements. The historical-cultural approach often turns into a survey course and bears the limitation of not relating the subject matter directly to the lives of the learner.

A second approach is to focus on the great works or cultural exemplars of mankind. The "great works" approach is intended to develop the student's critical abilities in evaluating and appreciating the art object qua art object. Nevertheless, the treatment often is to arrange the "great works" into a chronological sequence and schema of representational movements (classicism, romanticism, realism, impressionism, postimpressionism, etc.). In many courses that follow this approach, the learner is expected to judge the exemplars according to the generally accepted standards of the expert critic and connoisseur.

A third approach is to organize the material into "great issues" through the use of original documents. While this approach is often historically and philosophically oriented, some courses are organized to relate contemporary issues to the cultural heritage. The "great issues" approach is more commonly found in the college than in the high school.

Appreciation and Performance. The humanities course, regardless of the approach followed in organizing the material, tends to treat the subject matter as academic knowledge. Actual performance on the part of the student is not integral to the aesthetic goals of the humanities course, and such performance experience is deprecatingly left to the elective "frill" subjects in art and music, or to cocurricular activities. Thus, Broudy, Smith, and Burnett advocate studying the exemplars with emphasis on developing analytic skills and aesthetic tastes characteristic of the critic and connoisseur, while holding the view that any performance course, for people without talent, "rapidly reaches the point of diminishing returns, except on a hobby basis." [37] This issue is discussed further in Chapter 8.

General Education. While the humanities course presents promising opportunities for unifying learning experiences that otherwise are fragmented among several subject fields, in most high schools where it is offered it is not really designed to meet the general education needs of the student body. In the sense that the humanities course is restricted to the college-bound and academically able student, in the sense that it deprecates artistic performance by adolescents, in the sense that it carries an aura of snob appeal, the humanities are not very humane.

THE SEARCH FOR RELEVANCE AND COHERENCE THROUGH THE INTEGRATED CORE APPROACH

Recognizing the limitations of the subject curriculum in providing learning experiences that deal directly with problems demanding social action, or with problems based on the personal-social needs of youth, many secondary schools instituted core programs during the 1930's. The

---

[37] Harry S. Broudy, B. Othanel Smith, and Joe R. Burnett, *Democracy and Excellence in American Secondary Education* (Chicago: Rand McNally & Company, 1964), p. 228.

core approach gained popularity particularly in the junior high school, where it was found useful in enabling students to make a smoother transition from the self-contained elementary classroom to the departmentalized secondary school.

Before discussing the nature and function of the more integrated types of core programs, it should be noted that the term *core curriculum* has been defined and applied in a variety of ways. Some educators apply the term even to that part of the subject curriculum that is common to all youth in the secondary school for purposes of general education. Thus this would include (1) separate subjects required of all students, (2) correlated subjects required of all students, and (3) fused subjects required of all students.[38]

However, for our purposes, the core approach will be treated as an advanced form of curriculum integration which is essentially different from the subject curriculum in focus and framework.

Rationale of the Core Approach

As the concerns of adolescents and the problems of life do not limit themselves to any particular subject, discipline, or subject field, the core approach is intended to enable the adolescent to study problems that demand personal and social action in the contemporary world. Required of all students in the school, the core curriculum is intended to serve the general education needs of youth in a manner not possible through the traditional subject curriculum. Because the most advantageous treatment of such personal and social problems is in the context of the values of our society, classroom activities are intended to reflect the democratic value system while also serving to illuminate the conflicts and contradictions of contemporary social reality.

> The core curriculum . . . places considerable emphasis upon the deliberate study of the moral content of the culture—especially as this content bears upon the resolution of the social issues that divide the people and thereby prevent effective social action.
>
> . . . It is customary to think of social problems as being capable of solution by means of facts and descriptive principles without explicit reference to the values involved. The core curriculum rejects this view and instead makes the value content of a social problem, along with facts and descriptive principles, the object of study. . . . It is the chief characteristic of the core curriculum, as a pure type, that the democratic value system is not only taught as a standard of judgment but that it

---

[38] Harold B. and Elsie J. Alberty, *Reorganizing the High School Curriculum,* 3rd ed. (New York: The Macmillan Company, 1962), pp. 204–216.

is also deliberately criticized and reconstructed so as to bring it into line with the social realities of today.[39]

Some of the early efforts in developing core approaches for general education were designed to transform the multiplicity of separate subjects into a comprehensive and unified organization of studies without any particular focus on personal and social needs and problems. In other words, the intent was to integrate various subjects into a coherent framework of learnings that could and should be shared by all, but no special emphasis was to be given to personal and social problems over other kinds of common learning. However, core approaches later emerged that had a central focus on contemporary social problems, the rationale for them being that the core should be that part of education which all citizens of an interdependent culture must share. Thus many core approaches became more closely related to the social studies than to any other field of knowledge.

Types of Core Approaches

Alberty and Alberty describe two types of learner-centered core approaches. One type is based upon common problems, needs, and interests of adolescents within a framework of societal problem areas.[40] Although this approach draws heavily from various sources of organized subject matter, the purpose is to use material from all pertinent areas of knowledge to solve common and persistent life problems. Teachers often work together in teams to develop one or more resource units for each problem area. Because teachers and students cannot rely on the textbook, carefully developed resource units and a rich variety of appropriate library materials are necessary to the success of this core approach. Obviously, the resource units require considerable cooperative effort on the part of the faculty and must be kept current.

The problem areas are preplanned by the core faculty, grade level by grade level, in an articulated sequence. Nevertheless, in some schools, teachers and students are allowed to add problem areas of their own immediate choosing. And they may also modify or eliminate certain preplanned problem areas at their own discretion. The problem areas may relate to personal and community health, conservation of natural resources, war and peace, intercultural relations, aesthetic values, community planning, consumer economics, and others. An example of this type of core approach is the common learnings program in the visionary

---

[39] B. Othanel Smith, William O. Stanley, and J. Harlan Shores, *Fundamentals of Curriculum Development,* rev. ed. (New York: Harcourt, Brace & World, Inc., 1957), p. 315.

[40] Alberty and Alberty, *op. cit.,* pp. 216–222.

proposal of the Educational Policies Commission for education in the post-World War II years.[41] A number of the experimental schools in the Eight-Year Study followed this type of core approach.

A second type of core approach is based upon teacher-student planned activities without reference to any formal structure.[42] In some cases the students and teacher formulate the problem areas cooperatively. The problem areas, in turn, serve to establish the nature of the learning units to be developed by the class. In comparison to the first type of core, in which the problem areas and resource units are preplanned for the students, the second type of core leaves the teacher and students free to determine the problem areas and learning activities they choose to engage in. While both core types require highly resourceful teachers, the second type is particularly demanding because the teacher cannot rely on any predetermined problem areas. And although it can be argued that a core approach based upon teacher-student planned activities without reference to any formal structure allows the class great freedom and flexibility in determining the learning activities, the lack of a predetermined design can leave wide gaps in the scope and sequence of the general education program. Without highly resourceful teachers, and in the absence of an unusually rich collection of learning materials in a wide variety of problem areas, a laissez-faire situation may result. Relatively few schools have attempted this type of core approach.

Other Characteristics and Functions of the Core Curriculum

Core classes are commonly organized on a block-time basis, allowing each teacher to devote more time to fewer students each day than is otherwise possible under the traditional subject curriculum. Homeroom activities are often combined with the core classes and the core teacher engages in individual and group guidance. Because the focus of study is on problem areas, emphasis is given to the development of problem-solving skills and inquiry learning. Although inquiry learning has been a central focus of the discipline-centered curriculum projects in the recent curriculum reform movement, disciplinarity has no monopoly on inquiry. Inquiry into pervading social problems has been a chief emphasis of the more advanced types of core curricula. Emphasis on problem solving and critical thinking is found in much of the literature on the core curriculum.

Democratic values are encouraged as teachers and students engage in cooperative planning and group activity. Moreover, the units of study within each problem area in the core curriculum are sufficiently com-

---

41 *Education for ALL American Youth, op. cit.*
42 *Ibid.*, pp. 222–225.

prehensive to allow for a wide range of pupil differences in ability and achievement. Since ability and achievement are related to socioeconomic opportunity, grouping practices according to ability and achievement tend to segregate students by socioeconomic level. Such practices are commonly found in the traditional subject curriculum. On the other hand, the core approach allows for considerable pupil diversity and makes it unnecessary to section pupils according to different status levels. Consequently, the core brings together students representative of the total school community. Moreover, through its focus on life-relevant problems, the core approach provides considerable opportunity in a workshop atmosphere for using the community as a learning resource.

In the setting of the comprehensive high school, the core class, heterogeneously grouped, will be representative of the total student population at the grade level for which it is intended. In other words, a ninth-grade core class will be made up of students representing the full range of aptitudes, achievement levels, interests, and aspirations found in the total ninth-grade student body of the school. Whether preparing for college or a vocation, students will be members of the same core class. In an era of segregating students through grouping and tracking, the core class, heterogeneously grouped, presents opportunities for all to share ideas in investigating universal problems of youth and society. Some schools group students in core classes according to aptitude and achievement measures, but this practice defeats the social-integrative functions of the core curriculum in the comprehensive secondary school.

The Core and Total Curriculum Design

We have discussed how the core approaches that are student-centered and that provide for the investigation of broad problem areas (either preplanned, or determined by the pupils and the teacher) are intended to meet the general education needs of all youth. Most schools, however, supplement the core with required courses in specific disciplines or areas of knowledge, such as mathematics, which are offered for purposes of general education but in the context of the subject curriculum. In addition to the core studies and any other subjects which comprise the general education program, the students pursue *specialized* studies in academic or vocational areas, and *exploratory* studies through elective courses.

A simple schematic representation of the relationship of the core to other studies within the total curriculum framework is presented in Figure 2-1. The distribution is hypothetical and is not intended to represent a model arrangement. The day is divided into 10 modules, although the schedule may include more modules. (An additional module, not shown in Figure 2-1, is scheduled each day for lunch.) A flexible schedule may be provided within this framework so that the distribution of time

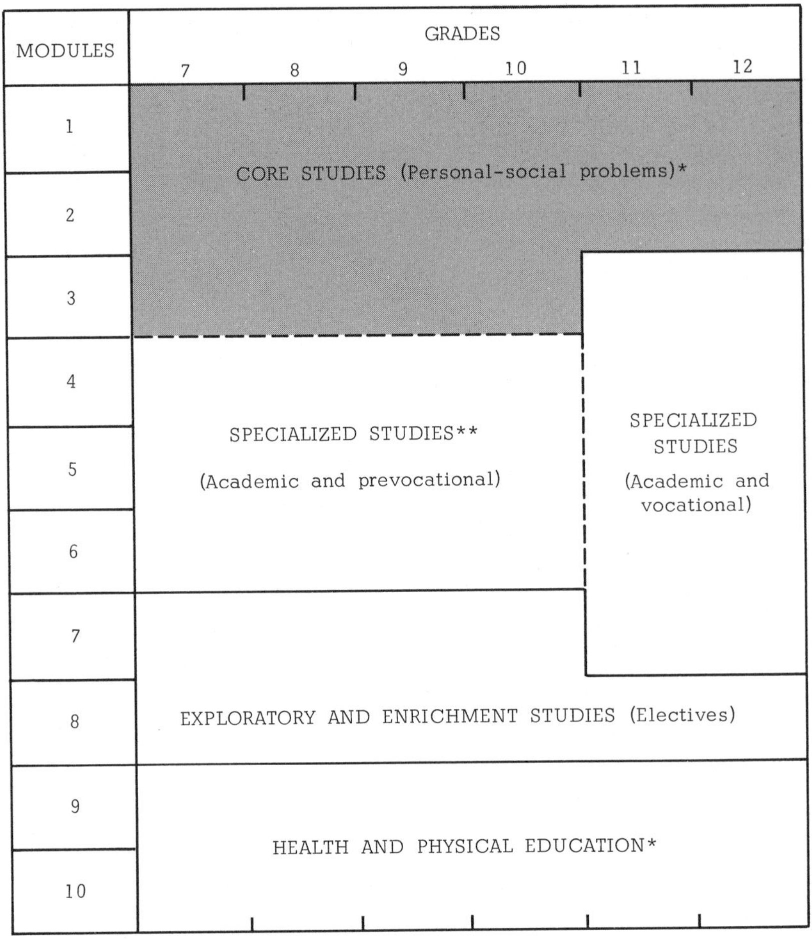

*General education

**Includes general-education studies in subject fields such as mathematics

Figure 2-1. Relationship of Core Studies to the Total Curriculum Design

devoted to the various studies is not identical each day of the week. For example, physical education and laboratory sciences may be offered three days per week in larger time blocks.

Within the curriculum framework outlined in Figure 2-1, some of the specialized and exploratory studies could be discipline-centered, while others might be organized as broad fields. Thus, within the total curriculum framework, it is possible to combine several modes of subject-matter organization. For example, in addition to core studies that are organized according to personal-social problems, a high school student might take discipline-centered courses in advanced algebra and chemistry (as part of his specialized academic studies), along with a discipline-centered course in sociology and an interdisciplinary course in the humanities (as part of his exploratory and enrichment studies). The teacher of sociology might want to correlate some of the work in his discipline with the core studies (horizontal articulation), while also building on the learnings derived from a U.S. history course taken by all students during the preceding school year (vertical and horizontal articulation). Similarly, the chemistry teacher would draw upon the students' learnings from course work taken previously in biology, general science, and algebra.

When combining several modes of subject-matter organization within the total curriculum framework, the results need not be eclectic if the program of studies is articulated as a coherent whole. Here, the entire faculty may be committed to the fullest possible vertical and horizontal articulation of the curriculum within the particular requirements of a program of studies that consists of several different modes of subject-matter organization. A further vehicle for enhancing the consistency and coherence of such a curriculum might be a commitment on the part of the total faculty for employing inquiry-discovery or problem solving as a common and unifying methodology, as opposed to didactic teaching and rote learning.

Our secondary schools rarely give adequate attention to overall curriculum design. The curriculum reform movement, with its task force and packaged approach to curriculum construction, requires that educators devote more attention to the problem of how such packages should fit into the total curriculum framework of the school. No matter how well conceived and synthesized such packages may be, their self-contained and discipline-centered qualities add to the problem of curriculum fragmentation. Yet many secondary school administrators have been content to adopt various curriculum packages while giving little or no attention to how such packages fit into the design of the total curriculum. Under such circumstances, curriculum development is simply a process of replacing old courses with new packages and adding new packages to existing course offerings. The process has been one of course substitution and accretion. At a time when more attention should be given to the overall design of the curriculum and the structure and function of general education, the focus has been on the piecemeal adoption of curriculum packages.

THE CORE STRUGGLE

A national survey conducted by the U.S. Office of Education in 1957 revealed that almost one fifth of the separately organized junior high schools and secondary schools with junior high grades were offering block-time courses. Of the schools with block-time classes, 20 per cent offered courses in which two or more subjects were fused or unified around a central theme, or units of work, or problems.[43] Only 12 per cent of the schools with block-time classes were found to be offering a core consisting of either predetermined problem areas based upon the personal-social needs of adolescents, or no predetermined content, thereby leaving the teacher and pupils free to select the problems for study. Although a number of subsequent studies on a smaller scale have been undertaken since Wright's study, the findings have revealed no marked changes or trends. If anything, the emphasis on disciplinarity during the 1960's has strengthened the subject curriculum through packaged programs from various curriculum projects, while the proportion of schools with student-centered core programs has declined somewhat.

In view of the early enthusiasm for the integrated types of core, why do we find only a small proportion of the junior high schools following such core approaches? In this section some of the principal difficulties and obstacles are reviewed briefly.

Teacher Competence and Commitment

Undoubtedly the decline in the proportion of schools offering learner-centered types of core may be partially attributed to the difficulties in finding teachers who were committed to such approaches and who were sufficiently resourceful in working with adolescents on life problems. Teachers and curriculum workers also have tended to be oriented toward subject fields and textbooks. Relatively few teachers were prepared to deal with the broad problem areas of the core curriculum. Undoubtedly, team teaching arrangements would have been helpful, but few schools were ready or able to implement team teaching in their core curricula.

Yet another possible difficulty, which was never properly researched and documented, was the reluctance of many teachers to broach highly controversial social problems and issues. Lacking adequate community and administrative support in an era of McCarthyism, the core problems and themes tended to be safe, lackluster, and even insignificant.

Space Age Pressures and Nationalizing Influences

Essentialist Opposition. Powerful external forces were at work during the 1950's and 1960's calling for a return to the academic essentials or disciplines in answer to the pressures of the cold war and the space age. In the wake of Sputnik I, an essentialist critic, in an interview featured

---

[43] Grace S. Wright, *Block-time Classes and the Core Program* (Washington, D.C.: Office of Education, U.S. Department of Health, Education, and Welfare, 1958).

on the cover of a leading business magazine, presented the readers with a list of questions to be addressed to school administrators:

> Let the citizens ask the following questions of the principal or the superintendent:
>
> 1. How many graduates of the local high school last spring had completed five years of physics?
> 2. How many had completed four years of chemistry?
> 3. How many had taken one year of astronomy?
> 4. How many had taken five years of biology?
> 5. How many had completed ten years of mathematics through trigonometry?
> 6. How many had completed five years of a foreign language?
> 7. How many had completed all these things?
>
> Citizens have a right to the answers. I hope they will permit no evasions by those to whom they have entrusted the running of their schools.[44]

Science and Politics. Also in January of 1958, testifying before a committee of the United States Senate, the German-educated missile expert, Wernher von Braun, after acknowledging that "I have never been an educator, so I have no experience in the field of education," advocated that we rid our schools of their ballast (sic) by adopting the European system of education.

> There is a lot more ruthlessness over there in just washing out the less competent. It is, you might say, a survival-of-the-fittest type of training: whoever does not live up to the standards is simply eliminated . . . the less able will be dropped with a lot less regard to their own personal interests.
> Thus the European school systems . . . are loaded with much less ballast [sic]. . . . As a result, the teachers of these schools need not bother with the less gifted.[45]

Von Braun then offered this reminiscence of his own education in Germany, contrasting his own required studies against those in American schools:

> I do not remember that I ever attended any classes in Europe (Germany) on "family life" or "human relations," or subjects like "boy-girl relations at college." We just learned reading, writing, and arithmetic in the lower schools. Later on they taught us technical and scientific subjects, but nothing else.

---

[44] Arthur Bestor, "What Went Wrong With U.S. Schools," *U.S. News & World Report*, Vol. 44 (January 24, 1958), p. 71.

[45] Hearings Before the Committee on Labor and Public Welfare, United States Senate, Eighty-Fifth Congress, *Science and Education for National Defense* (Washington, D.C.: U.S. Government Printing Office, 1958), p. 65.

This whole area of "social adjustment to life," which plays such an important role in American education, is given very little attention in Europe.[46]

Finally, von Braun expressed his support of Admiral Rickover's proposal for the creation of a governmental commission to serve as an "inspection agency, to establish standards of educational requirements for graduates of high schools." [47]

Testifying before the same committee on the same day was Lee Du-Bridge, then president of the California Institute of Technology. After recommending that the curriculum areas of science and mathematics be singled out for special federal support, DuBridge cited the need for the teacher to "be able to recognize and encourage special talent, special interest, special curiosity on the part of students; he must be an effective friend and counselor to students and especially to those who are unusually gifted and ambitious." [48] Then DuBridge turned to the problem of what to do with the less able student, with this comment: "The right of a student to an education is a right which persists as far as his intellectual capacities and his ambition should take him. This might be to the sixth grade, in the case of the unfortunate individual, and it might be through the doctor of philosophy for those who are better favored by genetics or environment." [49]

Unfortunately, the senators did not ask DuBridge or von Braun what society should do with those unfortunate individuals who are dropped from school when they reach the sixth grade because they are less favored by genetics or environment. Even if our schools were able to unload their "ballast," to use von Braun's expression, we must ask not only what will society do with these youngsters, but what will they do to society.

While DuBridge and von Braun unhesitatingly blamed the schools for our nation's alleged missile gap, they found no fault with America's scientific-industrial-military complex.

Other witnesses called for national testing programs to assess achievement and to ferret out our talented youth. Inserted in the official report of the Senate hearings was a five-thousand-word essay by John W. Gardner entitled "The Great Talent Hunt." [50] Gardner's essay exhorted our schools to continue in the great talent hunt, but made no mention of the disadvantaged.

Pursuit of Excellence. The national priorities in the era of the cold war and the space age had created new priorities in the curriculum. The academic disciplines, particularly the sciences and mathematics, held the

---

46 *Ibid.*, p. 67.
47 *Ibid.*
48 *Ibid.*, p. 39.
49 *Ibid.*, p. 54.
50 *Ibid.*, pp. 1447–1454.

key to our nation's salvation. The goal was no longer general education, but the pursuit of excellence—the development and utilization of our nation's intellectual resources. Curricula concerned with the personal-social needs of adolescents were labeled as "anti-intellectual" studies.[51] Our nation's political leaders and intellectuals were blind to the conditions that were to give rise to the great social conflicts and upheavals of the late 1960's and early 1970's.

Heralded by the discipline-centered projects supported by the National Science Foundation, a new era of curriculum reform emerged. As discussed throughout this chapter, the prevailing doctrine of the curriculum reform movement was "structure of the disciplines."

In 1952, as chairman of the Educational Policies Commission, Conant had endorsed the progressive document, *Education for ALL American Youth—A Further Look,* which advocated a learner-centered core approach. But in 1959 Conant's vision of general education in the comprehensive high school was this list of subjects to be required of all students: "four years of English, three or four years of social studies —including two years of history (one of which should be American history) and a senior course in American problems or American government —one year of mathematics in the ninth grade (algebra or general mathematics), and at least one year of science in the ninth or tenth grade, which might well be biology or general physical science." [52]

In Conant's 1960 report on the junior high school, discussed earlier, his recommendation for block-time teaching in grade 7 was aimed at reducing teacher load and not at breaking down subject-matter lines through core approaches. His proposal called for a departmentalized organization of subject matter in the junior high school.

DISCIPLINARITY AND GENERAL EDUCATION

General education, according to the Harvard Report, indicates "that part of a student's whole education which looks first of all to his life as a responsible human being and citizen." [53] The principle of the "structure of the disciplines," on the other hand, is concerned first and foremost with the student as a specialized scholar and not as a citizen. Thus, for example, the biologist's view of ecology may be quite different from that of the politician or of the conservation-minded citizen. Similarly, the scholar's understanding of racial inequality, as viewed within the structural framework of his specialized discipline (whether it be anthropology, history, political science, or sociology) is essentially different from the

[51] Richard Hofstadter, *Anti-intellectualism in American Life* (New York: Alfred A. Knopf, Inc., 1963), p. 347.

[52] James B. Conant, *The American High School Today* (New York: McGraw-Hill Book Company, Inc., 1959), p. 47.

[53] Report of the Harvard Committee, *op. cit.,* p. 51.

concerns of the citizen whose life is directly affected by social inequity.

While the disciplines and the principle of structure have a legitimate and valuable function in the school curriculum, the problems of man as a responsible human being and citizen require a wider vision of curriculum. As Martin puts it, "No matter how much value one places on the disciplines and their modes of inquiry, they are not the whole of life nor ought they to be the whole of education." [54]

Disciplinarity, Interdisciplinarity, and the Application of Knowledge

The contemporary dilemma will not be solved by seeking to do away with disciplinarity. In an age of specialism such efforts not only are likely to meet with failure, but may yield undesirable consequences. The problem is how to use the discipline principle so that the curriculum is made relevant to the learner and to life problems. In other words, while the discipline principle has served the world of the mature scholar-researcher quite well, it has not served the general education needs of youth.

Limitation of Disciplinarity. Unfortunately, in the contemporary curriculum reform movement, the discipline principle has become the discipline doctrine. The concern for the production of knowledge within the structural confines of the discipline takes precedence over the application of knowledge. When practical problems are approached, they are studied only from the vantage point of a particular discipline. Moreover, the learner is required to be engaged in the problem as a scholar and not as a citizen who is a direct participant in the problem.

The limitations of the university-generated discipline principle must be clearly recognized by those responsible for curriculum development at the elementary and secondary levels of schooling. University specialists who are engaged in curriculum projects for the schools must come to see the learner as a citizen and not as merely a budding research scholar. Even at the university level of scholarship the validity of the discipline principle is challenged because it fails to recognize and attack problems of an interdisciplinary and applied nature.

> They [the scholar-specialist-practitioners] impose upon the elementary curriculum their narrow disciplinary points of view, which place greater value on the frontiers of a field than on its tradition, and they try to put across what seems important to them, not what is important when viewed in a larger perspective. The practitioners have no taste for application or even for interdisciplinarity since this takes them away from their own universe.

---

[54] Martin, *op. cit.,* p. 35.

In the first place, the university must accord the generalist of broad outlook the status and prestige it now confers solely upon the specialist of narrow outlook; and in the second place, the university must rededicate itself to education. . . . I realize that the first of these measures is viewed with suspicion by the university. Specialization is "blessed" in the sense that only the specialist knows *what* he is talking about; yet, if only the specialist knows what he is talking about, only the generalist knows *why* he should talk at all.[55]

The nature of advanced scholarship has been such that university scholars prefer to reduce problems to abstractions and prefer to study problems as ends in themselves, rather than to apply knowledge toward needed practical solutions. Weinberg illustrates this condition by relating how a study by leading scientists, commissioned by the National Academy of Sciences to make recommendations for the control of world population growth, managed to recommend that more support be given for research while avoiding any mention of how existing knowledge might be applied to the problem.[56]

Secondary School and University. In the universities, scholarly reputations are built on specialization and, as one becomes more highly specialized in his discipline, one is likely to encounter fewer scholars who are in direct competition. But this situation is not true of the secondary school. Yet secondary school teachers, as products of the universities, easily fall prey to the university mentality and readily accept the discipline-centered curriculum packages developed for their youngsters by university scholars. Because the university scholar is himself devoted to a particular discipline, or even to a particular specialty within a discipline, he naturally seeks to impose his own disciplinarity on the secondary school.

Although the rationale of disciplinarity may serve the purpose of advancing the discipline, as well as the interests of the scholar-specialists, its validity in terms of what constitutes good education goes untested. Furthermore, the school is left to grope not only with the problem of establishing priorities and balance from among the competing specialties, but with that of relating the specialized material to other fields. A university administrator puts it this way:

What is questionable about these undertakings is that for the most part they have been a matter of each discipline for itself; the effort has been not merely to improve the quality of teaching materials but also to stake out a new or enlarged claim for each discipline in the limited time-budget of the secondary school. In the assertion of these claims

---

[55] Weinberg, *op. cit.*, pp. 160–161.
[56] *Ibid.*, p. 157.

little or nothing is asked or said about their proper relations with cog-
nate disciplines. Reconciliation tends to be left to chance, to bargaining,
or to the peculiar qualifications of professional curriculum makers.[57]

The commitment to disciplinarity and specialism on the part of university scholars places the academic disciplines above the integrative, aesthetic, practical, and vocational studies. Their interests and commitments,
and the nature of the reward system, lead them to avoid the broadly
integrative freshman courses, or even undergraduate courses altogether,
in favor of the advanced specialized courses.

When their less renowned colleagues turn to curriculum reform at
the elementary and secondary levels of schooling, they too embrace the
discipline principle. At the secondary level, many teachers, as products
of the universities, have learned to hold the academic disciplines above
the integrative, aesthetic, and vocational studies in the hierarchy of educational priority and prestige.

Even among those university educators who favor more synthesized
and life-relevant studies in general education in higher education, one
finds a tendency to regard the secondary school curriculum as a set of
"tooling-up" studies in preparation for college. Bell sees the mission of
the secondary school as concentrating on facts and skills whereas the
undergraduate curriculum of the colleges should be concerned with the
interrelations of disciplines, and the application of these disciplines to
general problems.[58] In contrast to the years of secondary schooling, Bell
regards the college years as "the testing years—the testing of one's self
and one's values; the exploration of different fields before settling in to
a single one." [59]

What of the student who does not go on to college? Is he to be denied
the learning experiences that are essential to the development of one's
standards of judgment, the testing of one's self and one's values, and the
exploration of diverse fields in determining what one wants to do with
his life? And what about the student who is college bound? Can he
postpone until college those learning experiences that deal with the problems and standards of judgment that will form one's values and guide
one's behaviors in the context of real life?

By denying the majority of adolescents who are not college bound the
opportunity to relate the curriculum to life problems, it is likely that two
divided and conflicting populations in society will be created. Indeed,
there are obvious signs today of mounting conflict between the blue-
collar laboring groups and our college populations.

57 David B. Truman, "The Social Sciences and Public Policy," *Science,* Vol. 120 (May
3, 1968), p. 512.
58 Daniel Bell, *The Reforming of General Education* (Garden City, N.Y.: Doubleday & Company, Anchor Books, 1968), p. 185.
59 *Ibid.,* p. 185.

Adolescents in secondary schools are no less concerned with values, aspirations, and personal-social problems than are college youth. The fragmented, discipline-centered curriculum is just as meaningless and irrelevant to the high school adolescent as it is to the college student. If anything, adolescence in its early stages, because it is marked by more rapid psychobiological change, is an even more crucial period of life and education than the college years. Consequently, the curriculum of the secondary school must be no less relevant to life than the curriculum of the college. We cannot expect the adolescent to make coherent a curriculum that is incoherent.

Curriculum Coherence and Perspective

The explosion of knowledge has led to the creation of new disciplines and subdisciplines. While scholars seek to protect the distinctive elements and features that give dimension and boundaries to their areas of specialization, they also must recognize that division can lead to distortion. In attacking many problems, not only does it become necessary for the specialist to use the tools and concepts of other disciplines, but cross-disciplinary and interdisciplinary approaches are required.

For those concerned with curriculum construction in general education, the problem of developing meaningful synthesis and perspective becomes increasingly necessary and increasingly difficult with the creation of new knowledge and new specialties. In an effort to view the curriculum in general education in a coherent perspective, some curriculum theorists have proposed that the various areas of knowledge be grouped according to certain common properties. For example, Phenix classifies the areas of knowledge into several "realms of meaning." [60] One realm, designated as "symbolics," is seen to encompass ordinary language, mathematics, and various nondiscursive forms of expression such as gestures and rituals. Under the realm of "empirics" are the physical and biological sciences. To the realm of "esthetics" belong the various arts and literature. Areas that are comprehensively integrative, such as history and philosophy, are classified under the realm of "synoptics." Phenix also designates realms, such as "ethics," for those experiences that are beyond the province of given academic disciplines.

Unfortunately, such proposals fail to give us the coherence and perspective needed in curriculum construction because their classificatory limits are artificial and misleading. Can aesthetics be ascribed exclusively to the arts and literature, and not to the sciences? Are the sciences simply a matter of empirics? Creative acts in the sciences are not devoid of aesthetic and emotive experience, and great theories are not the creations

---

[60] Phenix, *Realms of Meaning, op. cit.,* pp. 4–14.

of empirical data. "We now realize," observed Einstein, "how much in error are those theorists who believe that theory comes inductively from experience." [61] While the freedom of choice in science is not the same as that of the writer of fiction, it nevertheless requires levels of inquiry "which are no longer directly connected with complexes of sense experience." [62]

The thesis that the realm of "symbolics" is separate from the realm of "empirics" also is of doubtful validity and serves to confuse rather than to clarify the task of the curriculum maker in developing a coherent perspective of the curriculum in general education. Moreover, it is misleading to consider "symbolics" apart from science, not merely because science makes use of mathematics and ordinary symbolic language, but because science utilizes concepts and language of a supernational character. [63]

For similar reasons, the proposal of Broudy, Smith, and Burnett—reducing the curriculum in such a way that aesthetics, symbolics, sciences, and so on are classified as separate domains—is of doubtful validity. [64] However, their inclusion of "molar problems" in the curriculum presents opportunities for interrelated and integrated studies that are indeed life-relevant. Such studies can give coherence and perspective to a curriculum in general education that would otherwise be fragmented and discipline-centered. Unfortunately, many students would be denied such experiences because the proposal places these problem-solving studies at the end of secondary schooling. The authors admit that

> these problem-solving courses will come late in the school life of the pupil. This means, of course, that early dropouts may miss them altogether. This is regrettable, but then one regrets all dropouts if they occur before their learning potential is exploited to the full. There seems to be little point in giving problem-solving instruction to those who have not been sufficiently motivated to master the other parts of the curriculum by which intelligent encounters with problems are made possible. [65]

The authors then go on to identify a variety of problem areas from which molar problems would be derived, such as racial integration, mass media, and the emerging nations.

The notion that the study of such molar problems must be placed near the very end of the high school years can be challenged on at least three grounds. First, there is no evidence that such problems cannot be studied

---

61 Albert Einstein, *Out of My Later Years* (New York: Philosophical Library, 1950), p. 72.

62 *Ibid.*, pp. 63–64.

63 *Ibid.*, pp. 112–113.

64 Broudy, Smith, and Burnett, *op. cit.*, pp. 83, 247.

65 *Ibid.*, p. 272.

intelligently without having first "mastered" the component elements of such problems, provided that one has attained a reasonably normal level of skill development in reading and writing. Moreover, the very failure to "master" the component elements in the first place may well be a result of the lack of relevance that conventionally packaged subject matters have for the learner. In other words, such material might be far more meaningful when studied from the vantage point of life-relevant problems. Second, many students who drop out of school do so for reasons that are not connected with intelligence. And third, the dropout, as a citizen of society, will be expected to evaluate arguments and make judgments in dealing with many molar problems and issues, ranging from race relations to international relations.

The record of democratic nations, indeed, of all nations, fails to reveal that the intellectual elite have a monopoly on wisdom and can be counted on to use their intelligence in the best interests of the human race. There are leading biologists, chemists, and physicists who have used their intelligence for creating biological, chemical, and nuclear weapons —just as there are leading scientists who have been engaged in tasks to improve man's condition. To deny a large proportion of our youth the opportunity to investigate life-relevant problems in school is to deny them their rights as citizens.

The Discipline Doctrine and the Coherent Curriculum

Discussed in Part II are some of the efforts being made in an increasing number of curriculum projects to modify the discipline doctrine. Such efforts are being undertaken partly in the realization that the principle of structure is invalid for many realms of knowledge, partly as a result of the failure of a number of projects to produce the learning outcomes that were claimed for them, and partly in the recognition that an array of specialized and independent projects does not make for a coherent and comprehensive school curriculum. The enrollment decline in high school physics since the advent of the highly theoretical course developed by the Physical Science Study Committee (PSSC) has led to the production of alternative courses that give recognition to the applications of knowledge. The demand that the curriculum be relevant to problems of social significance has resulted in a number of projects in the social studies that are conceived to focus on problems, issues, or broad themes that transcend any single discipline.

Nevertheless, the promising possibilities of utilizing the discipline principle for cross-disciplinary, multidisciplinary, and interdisciplinary studies are yet to be exploited effectively in making the curriculum relevant to the learner and the problems of the wider society. At times, the curriculum content drawn from various disciplines will have to be resynthesized into new interdisciplinary combinations. At other times, the integrity of each discipline will be maintained, but cross-disciplinary and multidisciplinary approaches will need to be followed in the course of study. In any case, a reorganization of both the content and the framework of the curriculum will be required if fragmentation is to be avoided and if coherence and balance are to be attained.

In viewing the total curriculum of the secondary school, it would be possible for a student to pursue certain specialized and discipline-oriented studies, for example, in mathematics, while simultaneously engaging in general education studies that are problem-centered and that draw on material from several disciplines or areas of knowledge. In the latter case, the treatment may be interdisciplinary or life-centered, depending upon the nature of the problem, the nature of the learners, and the resources of the school and community.

Such strategies of curriculum reconstruction present promising possibilities for a life-relevant curriculum in general education while also meeting the specialized educational needs of each learner. And educators need not pursue these strategies in the spirit of compromise or in the tone of eclecticism.

The Renewed Search for Life Relevance

There is a renewed realization that a school curriculum cannot be thought of simply as a collection of compartmentalized discipline-centered courses if it is to be relevant to the lives of adolescents and the problems of society. While holding that important educational contributions are to be made through the disciplines, Foshay points to the failure of the discipline-dominated curriculum to allow students to come to grips with the great public problems:

> the disciplines proposal does not deal directly with the relationship between education and life—what we call "relevance." One of the oldest questions in education is how education is to be related to real life. The disciplines proposal . . . does not deal, of itself, with the kinds of life problems the core curriculum used to be concerned with, problems which do not come in packaged disciplines. . . .To the degree that we allow the school curriculum to be dominated by the disciplines proposal, we fail to offer students the opportunity to become more than superficially acquainted with great public problems.[66]

Undoubtedly, much can be learned by looking back at the earlier efforts to make the curriculum life-relevant. But this does not mean that for-

---

[66] Arthur W. Foshay, "How Fare the Disciplines?" *The Phi Delta Kappan,* Vol. 51 (March, 1970), p. 351.

mulas of the past will be entirely appropriate for the contemporary dilemma.

> The questions of the integration of knowledge and the relevance of knowledge to the real world will not be denied. They demand a response from the school curriculum, one way or another. If the discipline-oriented curricula cannot respond effectively to these questions, then other responses will be found. It is predictable that we will reinvent the core curriculum, perhaps with some modifications, that a substantial incursion into the regular school day will be made by what were formerly thought of as co-curricular activities, and that students will increasingly refuse to undertake the discipline-oriented subjects. . . .
>
> Over the long run, it is quite possible that some new version of what a school is and ought to become will be developed. The task is mind-boggling. Without sacrificing the intellectual quality (but at the same time changing its spirit) of the best of the new curricula, we have to find ways of allowing the real problems of the external world to come under searching examination in school. Our secondary school students are . . . challenging the concept of adolescence itself. They want to see themselves as participants in the world they live in, not as apprentices for it. They want the world to be in the school and the school in the world.[67]

Addressing the same problem, Bellack sees promise in "a general education program that would include basic instruction in the major fields . . . the natural sciences, the social sciences, mathematics, and the humanities, together with a coordinating seminar in which students deal with problems 'in the round' and in which special effort is made to show the intimate relationships between the fields of study as concepts from these fields are brought to bear on these problems." [68]

Examining the college curriculum in an era of student protest, Schwab also proposes that in addition to the mode of disciplinarity, the college student should have some opportunity in a mode that illuminates the relationships that exist or that can be induced among the otherwise divorced subject areas.[69]

In searching for curriculum relevance and coherence, the spirit must be one of reconstruction. Patchwork repairs are not likely to solve the problem. If history is not to be a recycling of errors, educators will need to search for solutions and not compromises.

However well intentioned the pioneers behind the core curriculum

---

[67] *Ibid.*, p. 352.

[68] Arno A. Bellack, "What Knowledge Is of Most Worth?" *The High School Journal*, Vol. 48 (February, 1965), p. 331.

[69] Joseph J. Schwab, *College Curriculum and Student Protest* (Chicago: The University of Chicago Press, 1969), pp. 238–241.

may have been, the conditions were not ripe for success. Perhaps the core curriculum was victimized by accidents of history. The spirit of social reconstruction of the Great Depression called for a reconstructed curriculum. World War II and the subsequent cold war and space age placed quite different demands upon the schools. In an era of McCarthyism, social problems and issues—the very spirit of the core—became unsafe for the brave as well as the timid. No longer were core teachers able or willing to distinguish between problems of great significance and activities that, at best, must be regarded as trite.

"In summary," writes Taba, "one could say that the unified or core program design has not yet received a fair test." [70] It is not likely that the core, as it was originally constituted, will ever receive a fair test. But the new generation, unlike the old, is demanding a truly life-relevant curriculum. For the first time, the demand for curriculum reconstruction is coming from the young—not from the philosophers, the scientists, or the politicians. The challenge to the educators is to enable the new generation to become familiar with curriculum approaches that allow for the investigation of pervading social problems and that do not conform to the orthodoxies of the established disciplines. But this time the schools and their teachers must see to it that all possible sources of data and resources of wisdom are made available to the new generation in their quest for life relevance. Under such circumstances, these educators need not worry too much about convincing their opponents. The real challenge is the new generation.

The physicist Max Planck remarked in his autobiography, published in 1937, that "a new scientific truth does not triumph by convincing its opponents and making them see the light, but rather because its opponents eventually die, and a new generation grows up that is familiar with it." [71]

SUMMARY

The great curriculum reform movement in the secondary schools has reflected the trend in our universities toward curricular specialism. Led by university scholars in the various disciplines, the focus of the reform movement has been on "each discipline for itself." Because these university scholars tend to be mainly concerned with the frontiers of knowledge in their particular disciplines, little attention has been given to interdisciplinarity and application.

---

[70] Hilda Taba, *Curriculum Development: Theory and Practice* (New York: Harcourt, Brace & World, Inc., 1962), p. 412.

[71] Max Planck, *Scientific Autobiography and Other Papers,* translated by F. Gaynor (New York: Philosophical Library, 1949), pp. 33–34.

Although the trend toward specialism of knowledge has created greater interdependence among men, the curriculum reforms have neglected interdisciplinarity. The result has been an increasing fragmentation in school and college studies.

From the period of the Great Depression to the immediate post-World War II years, many educators looked to general education as the means of providing an integrative focus to school and college studies. In the more experimental secondary schools, efforts were made to develop core or common-learnings classes that would be relevant to the problems of the learner and society. Many colleges developed interdisciplinary studies for purposes of general education. The goal was to create a coherent curriculum in an era of great social change, growing diversity of the school population, and increasing specialization of knowledge. While leading educators envisioned the post-World War II years as a period of curriculum reconstruction directed at the concerns that all citizens of a free society share in common, the pressures of the cold war and the space age led to curriculum development in other directions. Instead of a new unity and coherence in the curriculum, the outgrowth was disciplinarity and fragmentation. The colleges turned from interdisciplinary studies in general education to distribution requirements in which students proceeded to choose courses from separate disciplines and various departments. The secondary schools adopted packaged programs in the different disciplines developed by scholar-specialists in the universities.

The great federally supported curriculum projects reflected the national pursuit of excellence. The principal task of the schools was to develop our nation's intellectual resources. The curriculum was to be reconstructed according to the world of advanced scholarship. The personal-social problems of youth had no place in a curriculum designed to meet the new national priority of scientific and technological advancement. Our federal government and the great philanthropic foundations provided funds on an unprecedented scale to aid in the search for and development of academic talent. Virtually ignored were the needs of the ordinary student and the disadvantaged.

The late 1960's were marked by student protest, particularly in the colleges, against the inequities of our society and the allocation of our nation's resources toward military and technological ends rather than toward social reconstruction. But the new cry also was for a life-relevant curriculum in school and college. Perhaps for the first time, the demand for curriculum reconstruction was coming from youth and not from the educators, philosophers, scientists, industrialists, or politicians.

In response to the demand for curriculum relevance, many schools and colleges made piecemeal adjustments—such as adding courses in black studies and urban studies—while the fundamental curriculum remained essentially unchanged. More recently, educators have shown concern for reassessing the doctrines of disciplinarity and specialism which have governed the curriculum reform movement during the decades of the 1950's and 1960's. Renewed interest is being directed at the nature of the learner and the needs of society as sources of curriculum construction, and not just the nature of knowledge as an end in itself.

Some proposals have called for compromise and patchwork solutions. But if curriculum anarchy is to be avoided, a new reconstruction will be necessary. Disciplinarity can be made to contribute to interdisciplinarity, particularly for purposes of general education. Opportunities to investigate life-relevant problems in general education classes in the comprehensive secondary school need to be provided. Such classes can draw their subject matter from the organized bodies of knowledge as well as from the community, but the outcomes will be synthesis, application, and the development of learning skills—and not the mere acquisition of specialized information. These classes, by bringing together students of different backgrounds and aspirations, can serve to relate differences in outlook to the problems that all citizens in society must face.

If the adolescent is to grow as a responsible human being and citizen, a wider and more coherent vision of curriculum will be necessary.

PROBLEMS FOR STUDY AND DISCUSSION

1. Do you agree with this statement? "There is no place in the curriculum for ideas which are regarded as suitable for teaching because of the supposed nature, needs, and interests of the learner, but which do not belong within the regular structure of the disciplines." [Philip H. Phenix in A. Harry Passow (ed.), *Curriculum Crossroads* (New York: Teachers College Press, 1962), p. 64.] Support your position.

2. A university professor has maintained that where the function of the secondary school is "concentrating on facts and skills," the college is the place where students can "deal with the interrelations of disciplines, and . . . apply these disciplines to general problems. . . . It should be the testing years—the testing of one's self and one's values; the exploration of different fields before settling in to a single one; and the experience of belonging to a common intellectual community in which diverse fields of knowledge are commingled." [Daniel Bell, *The Reforming of General Education* (Garden City, N.Y.: Doubleday & Company, Inc., Anchor Books, 1968), p. 185.] Do you agree with this position? Why or why not?

3. Compare the general education requirements (courses required of all students) in several junior and senior high schools with the re-

quirements recommended by Conant. What similarities and differences do you find?

4. According to a 1967 report of the U.S. Commission on Civil Rights, "when disadvantaged Negro students are in class with similarly situated whites, their average performance is improved by more than a full grade level. When they are in class with more advantaged white students, their performance is improved by more than two grade levels." [U.S. Commission on Civil Rights, *Racial Isolation in the Public Schools* (Washington, D.C.: Superintendent of Documents, 1967), p. 91.] What implications does this finding have for grouping students according to aptitude and achievement measures in required (general education) courses in a racially heterogeneous comprehensive secondary school?

5. In a racially heterogeneous school where students are grouped by aptitude and/or achievement measures, make a count of the proportion of nonwhite students in various general education class sections, such as ninth-grade English. Do the grouping practices tend to foster racial isolation?

6. A government leader has observed that "several generations ago, we turned to the schools to introduce new immigrants to the American way. We turned to the schools when we woke up one morning a decade ago to find a Russian satellite circling the globe. And we always turn to the schools when we need trained persons to fill our manpower needs." [Robert H. Finch, "That Question of Relevancy," in *The School and the Democratic Environment,* report of a conference sponsored by the Danforth Foundation and the Ford Foundation (New York: Columbia University Press, 1970), p. 18.] How have the changing sociopolitical pressures affected the general education programs of the comprehensive secondary school during the era of the cold war and the space age? In what ways, if any, do you believe that the secondary schools will change their programs in general education in response to the contemporary demands for curriculum relevance?

7. In 1899 Dewey wrote: "A society is a number of people held together because they are working along common lines, in a common spirit, and with reference to common aims. The common needs and aims demand a growing interchange of thought and growing unity of sympathetic feeling." [John Dewey, *The School and Society,* rev. ed. (Chicago: The University of Chicago Press, 1915), p. 14.] Do you believe that the same principle should hold true of the general education curriculum in the comprehensive secondary school? Why or why not?

8. What limitations and pitfalls, if any, do you see in efforts to use the community as a learning "laboratory" for general education classes?

9. Draw up a list of some problems based upon the common needs and interests of adolescents, which might be investigated in a core class. How might these problems draw on organized subject matter from the various disciplines?

10. Many educators have pointed to the tendency of teachers to stress the lower cognitive processes of recall, while giving inadequate attention to interpretation, application, analysis, and synthesis. Examine some teacher-made tests and, using Bloom's *Taxonomy of Educational Objectives, Handbook I: Cognitive Domain,* classify the various items according to cognitive levels. Do any of the items deal with the "affective domain"?

SELECTED REFERENCES

Alberty, Harold B., and Elsie J. Alberty. *Reorganizing the High School Curriculum,* 3rd ed. New York: The Macmillan Company, 1962.

Aikin, Wilford M. *The Story of the Eight-Year Study.* New York: McGraw-Hill Book Company, Inc., 1942.

Association for Supervision and Curriculum Development. *Life Skills in School and Society.* 1969 Yearbook. Washington, D.C.: National Education Association, 1969.

———. *To Nurture Humaneness.* 1970 Yearbook. Washington, D.C.: National Education Association, 1970.

———. *Youth Education.* 1968 Yearbook. Washington, D.C.: National Education Association, 1968.

Bell, Daniel. *The Reforming of General Education.* New York: Columbia University Press, 1966.

Berman, Louise M. *New Priorities in the Curriculum.* Columbus, Ohio: Charles E. Merrill Books, Inc., 1968.

——— (ed.). *The Humanities and the Curriculum.* Washington, D.C.: Association for Supervision and Curriculum Development, NEA, 1967.

Bestor, Arthur. *The Restoration of Learning.* New York: Alfred A. Knopf, Inc., 1956.

Bloom, Benjamin S. (ed.). *Taxonomy of Educational Objectives, Handbook I: Cognitive Domain.* New York: David McKay Company, Inc., 1956.

Broudy, Harry S., B. Othanel Smith, and Joe R. Burnett. *Democracy and Excellence in American Secondary Education.* Chicago: Rand McNally & Company, 1964.

Bruner, Jerome S. *The Process of Education.* Cambridge, Mass.: Harvard University Press, 1960.

Conant, James B. *The American High School Today.* New York: McGraw-Hill Book Company, Inc., 1959.

————. *Education in the Junior High School Years.* Princeton, N.J.: Educational Testing Service, 1960.

Crary, Ryland W. *Humanizing the School.* New York: Alfred A. Knopf, Inc., 1969.

Cremin, Lawrence A. *The Transformation of the School.* New York: Alfred A. Knopf, Inc., 1961.

Educational Policies Commission. *Education for ALL American Youth— A Further Look.* Washington, D.C.: National Education Association, 1952.

Gwynn, J. Minor, and John B. Chase, Jr. *Curriculum Principles and Social Trends,* 4th ed. New York: The Macmillan Company, 1969.

Hofstadter, Richard. *Anti-intellectualism in American Life.* New York: Alfred A. Knopf, Inc., 1963. Chs. 12, 13, 14.

Huebner, Dwayne (ed.). *A Reassessment of the Curriculum.* New York: Teachers College Press, 1964.

King, Arthur R., Jr., and John A. Brownell. *The Curriculum and the Disciplines of Knowledge.* New York: John Wiley & Sons, Inc., 1966.

Krug, Edward A. *The Secondary School Curriculum.* New York: Harper & Row, Publishers, 1960. Chs. 7, 8.

National Society for the Study of Education. *General Education.* Fifty-first Yearbook, Part I. Chicago: The University of Chicago Press, 1952.

————. *The Integration of Educational Experiences.* Fifty-seventh Yearbook, Part III. Chicago: The University of Chicago Press, 1958.

Passow, A. Harry (ed.). *Curriculum Crossroads.* New York: Teachers College Press, 1962.

Phenix, Philip H. *Realms of Meaning.* New York: McGraw-Hill Book Company, Inc., 1964.

Report of the Harvard Committee. *General Education in a Free Society.* Cambridge, Mass.: Harvard University Press, 1945.

Schwab, Joseph J. *College Curriculum and Student Protest.* Chicago: The University of Chicago Press, 1969.

Smith, B. Othanel, William O. Stanley, and J. Harlan Shores. *Fundamentals of Curriculum Development,* rev. ed. Harcourt, Brace & World, Inc., 1957.

Taba, Hilda. *Curriculum Development: Theory and Practice.* New York: Harcourt, Brace & World, Inc., 1962.

Tanner, Daniel. *Schools for Youth—Change and Challenge in Secondary Education.* New York: The Macmillan Company, 1965. Chs. 6, 7, 8.

Thomas, Russell. *The Search for a Common Learning: General Education, 1800–1960.* New York: McGraw-Hill Book Company, Inc., 1962.

Tyler, Ralph W. *Basic Principles of Curriculum and Instruction.* Chicago: The University of Chicago Press, 1950.

Vars, Gordon F. (ed.). *Common Learnings: Core and Interdisciplinary Team Approaches.* Scranton, Penna.: International Textbook Company, 1969.

Weinberg, Alvin. *Reflections on Big Science.* Cambridge, Mass.: The M.I.T. Press, 1967.

Williams, Aston R. *General Education in Higher Education.* New York: Teachers College Press, 1968.

Part II

Disciplinarity and Curriculum Reform

There is no end to this spiral process:
foreign subject matter transformed through thinking
into a familiar possession
becomes a resource for judging and assimilating
additional foreign subject matter.

—JOHN DEWEY

Chapter 3

Curriculum Change in the Sciences

Curriculum reform during the 1960's was characterized by (1) attempts to accelerate teaching and learning by having children and youth deal with advanced levels of subject matter at earlier ages and grade levels, (2) enlistment of university scholars as principal agents in reformulating the content and processes of instruction within each of the major disciplines at both the elementary and secondary levels, (3) efforts to apply the mode of inquiry-discovery, or the style of the scholar, to each discipline for virtually every age and grade level, and (4) endeavors to reformulate the subject matter for the various disciplines around key principles, concepts, and generalizations that presumably comprise the structure of knowledge within each discipline.

A significant aspect of the new projects in course-content improvement is the rejection of the traditional textbook, with its additive and encyclopedic treatment of knowledge, in favor of instructional materials in which knowledge is treated as the system of inquiry in a discipline. The didactic and receptive methods of instruction, characteristic of the traditional classroom, are also rejected in favor of methods that purportedly represent the inquiry-discovery styles of the scholar-researcher at work. In this chapter a variety of these new curriculum projects are examined in terms of the problems and issues that must be faced when any significant attempts are being made to change the curriculum.

THE NEW HIGH SCHOOL PHYSICS

Physical Science—Archetype for Curriculum Reform?

As discussed in Chapter 1, underlying much of the effort to improve course content during the 1960's was the premise that "the schoolboy learning physics *is* a physicist, and it is easier for him to learn physics like a physicist than doing something else."[1] This proposition, which has served as a key doctrine for the new high school physics (Physical Science Study Committee), came to be adopted as a basic premise in the development of courses in other fields of science and even in the social studies.

The appearance in 1960 of the new high school physics course prepared by the Physical Science Study Committee under the leadership of Professor Jerrold R. Zacharias of MIT attracted the interest of educators in many fields because it represented the first and most complete attempt at course-content improvement at the high school level during the cold war era. Prepared under the leadership of university physics professors in cooperation with science educators, high school teachers, and supervisors, the PSSC course was financed through grants from the prestigious National Science Foundation and contributions from the Ford and Sloan Foundations. Not only has the work of the Physical Science Study Committee served as a source of emulation for programs of course-content revision in other fields, but its umbrella organization, Education Development Center (formerly Educational Services Incorporated), has become engaged in curriculum development in other sciences, mathematics, social studies, and engineering sciences—from the primary grades through college. Most of EDC's multimillion-dollar budget is derived from the National Science Foundation and other federal agencies. Since 1966 it has also been functioning as one of the Regional Educational Laboratories through Title IV of the Elementary and Secondary Education Act of 1965.

Although the Physical Science Study Committee originally contemplated the development of an integrated two-year course in physics and chemistry, it finally chose the route of creating a one-year course in physics. According to Zacharias, this decision was made reluctantly but of necessity in view of the organizational elements of the high school.[2] The problem of gaining the cooperation of physicists and chemists in creating an integrated course in physical science must have been an equally pervading factor in making this decision. The difficulty of getting physicists and chemists to join together in developing integrated courses in physical science at the introductory level in college is reflected also in efforts to develop new high school courses.

---

[1] Jerome S. Bruner, *The Process of Education* (Cambridge, Mass.: Harvard University Press, 1960), p. 14.

[2] Jerrold R. Zacharias and Stephen White, "The Requirements for Major Curriculum Revision," Chapter 5 in *New Curricula*, Robert W. Heath (ed.) (New York: Harper & Row, Publishers, 1964), p. 70.

Rationale and Objectives

The work of the Physical Science Study Committee began with the rejection of the conventional high school physics course and its treatment of physics as an assertion of the main developments and ideas of modern technology. An account of how Zacharias first became interested in reforming the teaching of physics reveals his concern that MIT students, even after two years of study at one of the leading institutions of its kind, were accepting material on authority without questioning it: "He still found them as juniors blandly accepting physics as handed down by their instructors, what Zacharias calls 'physics theology,' instead of questioning, doubting, and probing behind established doctrine in search of real understanding." [3] No account is given as to why Zacharias chose to focus his main efforts on high school physics instead of college physics. However, the decade of the 1950's was a period in which the schools were being subjected to severe criticism by many college professors in certain disciplines.[4] "There was, for example, a great deal of talk in the country, even before Sputnik, about the superiority of Russian science." [5] Some college professors, notably Arthur Bestor of the University of Illinois, blamed the soft pedagogy of the schools for the allegedly small enrollments in high school science courses. The time seemed ripe for moving into the high school, and Zacharias was able to obtain support from the National Science Foundation in carrying out this task.

When the first edition of the new textbook in high school physics appeared in 1960, it was described as "the heart of the PSSC course, in which physics is presented not as a mere body of facts but basically as a continuing process by which men seek to understand the nature of the physical world." [6] The rationale and objectives of the new PSSC course are described as follows:

> The committee chose to plan a course dealing with physics as an explanatory system, a system that extends from the domain inside the atom to the distant galaxies. The course tells a unified story. . . . The aim was to present a view of physics that would bring a student close to the nature of modern physics and to the nature of physical inquiry. Finally, the committee sought to transmit the human character of the story of physics, not simply an up-to-date codification of the findings.

---

3 Education Development Center, *Annual Report* (Newton, Mass.: The Center, 1967), p. 24.

4 See Arthur Bestor, *Educational Wastelands* (Champaign, Ill.: University of Illinois Press, 1953) and, by the same author, *The Restoration of Learning* (New York: Alfred A. Knopf, Inc., 1956).

5 Educational Development Center, *op. cit.*, p. 24.

6 James R. Killian, Jr., "Preface to the First Edition" in *Physics*, 2nd ed., by the Physical Science Study Committee (Boston: D. C. Heath and Company, 1965), p. vi.

The student should see physics as an unfinished and continuing activity. He should experience something of the satisfaction and challenge felt by the scientist when he reaches vantage points from which he can contemplate both charted and uncharted vistas.

. . . This deeper development meant carrying key concepts to higher levels than have been ordinarily reached in secondary-school courses. Deeper development also meant a more extensive exploration of the substructure of experiment and thought that underlies the basic physical principles.

. . . The course materials do not assert the ideas of physics, then illustrate their utility by exemplifying them in problems and in laboratory exercises. Instead, the student is expected to wrestle with a line (or convergent lines) of inquiry, including his own laboratory investigations, that leads to basic ideas.[7]

A more recent statement of objectives for the PSSC course emphasizes that the committee "set out to create a course that would accomplish a number of things not then possible with the available teaching materials." [8] Thus the following specific objectives for the new course in high school physics were formulated on the grounds that the conventional courses were inadequate in meeting these aims:

1. To present physics as a unified but living and ever-changing subject.
2. To demonstrate the interplay between experiment and theory in the development of physics.
3. To lead students to recapitulate the process by which knowledge is gained in the first place, rather than merely absorbing what they were told by books and teachers; to learn to observe nature closely and to interrogate it, thus learning not only the laws and principles of physics but the evidence upon which they are based and their limitations.
4. To extend the capacity of students to read critically, to distinguish between the essential and the peripheral, to make defensible generalizations from particular facts.
5. To provide a foundation for those students who went on to further study in science and technology.[9]

To carry out the above objectives, the PSSC course includes in addition to the textbook, a laboratory guide, a series of films, laboratory apparatus, achievement tests, and many paperbacks that contain biographical as well as topical material. A teacher's guide and resource book also have been developed. All of these materials are designed to form a complete cur-

---

[7] Gilbert C. Finlay, "The Physical Science Study Committee," in *Curriculum Improvement and Innovation: A Partnership of Students, School Teachers, and Research Scholars,* W. T. Martin and Dan C. Pinck (eds.) (Cambridge, Mass.: Robert Bentley, Inc., 1966), pp. 67–68.

[8] Education Development Center, *Annual Report, op. cit.,* p. 25.

[9] *Ibid.*

riculum package. Laboratory materials are intended to foster inquiry and experimental style, rather than consisting of mere exercises. PSSC summer and in-service institutes, supported by the National Science Foundation, have been offered at colleges and universities throughout the nation to acquaint high school teachers with the course and to improve their backgrounds in physics.

ASSESSMENT: RESEARCH, OPINIONS, AND PROBLEMS

Evaluation of the PSSC Course

Many advantages are claimed for the new high school physics. Some of these are enumerated as follows:

1. Gives real knowledge of science, less technology.
2. Stimulates class discussion, creative thinking, and shows the unity of physics, not its separate classical divisions. Facts are related, not isolated.
3. Gives the best possible background for terminal students and also aids in adjustment to college work.
4. Leads from experimental information to logical conclusions and does away with pure memory work.
5. Appeals to girls as well as boys.
6. Deletes much trivial material and integrates all important topics from modern physics.
7. Allows for open-end experiments that challenge the ingenuity of students.[10]

Testimonials Vs. Research. Virtually all of the advantages cited for the PSSC course are derived primarily from the testimonials of the project staff and from certain teachers who are using the materials, and not from controlled research. Soon after the PSSC course was implemented, a number of comparisons were made of student achievement in conventional and PSSC classes. Many of these studies revealed that when achievement was measured on existing standardized tests, students in the conventional classes tended to make significantly higher scores. For example, Hipsher found that the high school students in the conventional physics course did significantly better than the PSSC students on the Cooperative Physics Test.[11] During the early stages of its efforts in developing and assessing the new physics course, the Physical Science Study Committee found that on the Physics Achievement Test of the College Entrance Examination Board, the PSSC students performed poorly on

---

[10] *Ibid.,* pp. 75–76.
[11] Warren L. Hipsher, "Study of High School Physics Achievement," *The Science Teacher,* Vol. 28 (October, 1961), pp. 36–37.

the material that is included in conventional courses but not in the PSSC course.[12] Consequently, the committee maintained that "any attempt to evaluate the PSSC course, or any other course, will be realistic only if the nature and objectives of the course are taken into account." [13] A later statement asserts that "the committee's own evaluations are directed toward the improvement of the course, not comparisons with other courses." [14]

As the result of the findings concerning the performance of PSSC students on the College Board Physics Achievement Test, the board made an unprecedented decision to develop a special test specifically suited to the content of the PSSC course. However, the special test was abandoned after two years in favor of a single test that was designed to include items representative of the conventional physics courses and the PSSC course. Scores on this test show no significant differences between PSSC students and students having taken conventional high school physics courses. Moreover, comparisons between the two groups in grades obtained in college physics courses reveal that PSSC students do not obtain higher grades.[15, 16] In the belief that most college physics courses represent conventional approaches to physics, the Physical Science Study Committee produced in 1968 a textbook for the first course in college physics which is designed as an extension of the rationale and subject matter treatment of the high school PSSC course.

Avoidance of Controlled Research.   To summarize the dilemma, we find the Physical Science Study Committee maintaining that the PSSC course is superior to the conventional high school physics on any number of grounds, while asserting at the same time that controlled comparison studies are inappropriate because the objectives and content of the courses are so different. It is, of course, legitimate to argue that thus-and-such a test is not an adequate criterion measure for comparing the worth of two different courses. But this does not mean that adequate instruments cannot be developed to evaluate various outcomes from different high school physics courses in an appropriate experimental design. Until such measures are taken, we will continue to find statements like this: "In any case, the 'effectiveness' of the PSSC high school physics course can scarcely be

---

12 Francis L. Friedman, Jerrold R. Zacharias, Walter Michels, and Fred Ferris, "The Relation of the PSSC Physics Course to Conventional High School Courses," *The Science Teacher*, Vol. 29 (February, 1962), pp. 49–55.

13 *Ibid.*, p. 49.

14 Finlay, *op. cit.*, pp. 75–76.

15 J. Stanley Marshall, "Implementation of Curriculum Change in the Sciences: A Case Study," Chapter 8 in *New Curricula*, Robert W. Heath (ed.), *op. cit.*, pp. 130–131.

16 Albert C. Braden, "Study of Success in College Physics," *Science Education*, Vol. 51 (December, 1967), pp. 461–463.

questioned. A sizable percentage of high school physics teachers and professional physicists throughout the country consider the course a challenging and rewarding experience for students, an opinion which I personally share." [17]

According to Zacharias and White, "The entire program must be looked upon as an experiment, and until solutions to any given program have withstood the test of use, they must be looked upon as hypotheses. In the end, it will be the students and the teachers who must decide upon the soundness of these hypotheses." [18] These are indeed strange research procedures and conditions for the testing of hypotheses, especially when one considers that they are prescribed by physicists. Ironically, the work of the Physical Science Study Committee is often cited as a model for course development through critically evaluated experimentation:

> What holds real promise for the future is the application of *systematic* research to the question, the attempt to develop *systematically* new methods and new curricula. What I mean by research here is *experimentation* in which new patterns are devised, their results evaluated, and the patterns revised in accordance with the results until general conclusions based on a sufficient body of critically evaluated experiments are possible. As a model for such an attempt I have in mind the efforts of the Physical Science Study Committee.[19]

Unfortunately, the evaluation of the PSSC course has been clouded by conflicts between the curriculum goals established by the committee and the evaluation goals of independent researchers. Inadequacies in experimental design and criterion measures have produced considerable debate and confusion. The Physical Science Study Committee has taken the position that controlled experimentation comparing PSSC classes with conventional high school physics classes is improper because the courses are completely different in scope and process. But this is not an adequate justification for avoiding controlled experimentation. The solution is to develop valid criterion measures and methodological approaches for experimental design. In the absence of such research, the developers of new courses become its proponents and are tempted to claim too much for their efforts, while problems are either oversimplified or ignored. Mere propositions come to be accepted as gospel. Paradoxically, such a stance in developing new courses in science is antithetical to the very spirit of science.

---

17 Frederick L. Ferris, Jr., "Testing in the New Curriculums: Numerology, 'Tyranny,' or Common Sense?", *The School Review*, Vol. 70 (Spring, 1962), p. 118.

18 Zacharias and White, *op. cit.*, p. 77.

19 Donald F. Hornig, "On Science Education in the United States," in *ESI Quarterly Report,* Summer–Fall, 1965 (Newton, Mass.: Education Development Center, Inc., 1965), p. 80.

The Mature Researcher Vs. the Schoolboy. Despite the fact that PSSC has served as an archetype for course construction in many different fields, it must be evaluated critically on a number of grounds. For example, it remains to be shown that it is indeed easier for the schoolboy to learn physics like a physicist than by other means. Relatively few high school students of physics are aspiring physicists. And even the schoolboy who is an aspiring physicist may not need to approach all of the subject matter as though it were being discovered for the very first time. Not only might such an approach sacrifice breadth for depth, but it could well ignore some of the principal didactic means by which scientists actually communicate with each other—through the learned journals, lectures and symposia at meetings of professional societies, and books. Furthermore, the basis of culture is that fundamental knowledge need not be rediscovered by each new generation.

When curriculum experiences for youth are modeled in the image and style of the mature scholar, there is the tendency for the new physics to become the physicist's physics. And, similarly, the new biology becomes the biologist's biology; the new chemistry becomes the chemist's chemistry; the new mathematics becomes the mathematician's mathematics; the new history becomes the historian's history; and so on. The validity of the premise that the most effective classroom consists of miniature physicists investigating physics, or miniature historians investigating history, is open to serious question.

Physics Enrollments and Career Choices

Although the PSSC course has come to be adopted widely, the percentage of high school students enrolled in physics has declined significantly over the years. Despite the national effort to improve the high school physics course and to induce more talented students to take physics, the proportion of seniors taking physics declined from 21.2 per cent in 1960–1961 to 19.6 per cent in 1964–1965.[20] This compares with 24.6 per cent in 1958–1959.[21] A study by the American Institute of Physics found that in the face of sharply rising college enrollments, the actual number of college juniors majoring in physics declined by more than 15 per cent between 1962 and 1967.[22]

During a ten-year period following Sputnik, the National Merit Scholarship Corporation (NMSC) conducted a study of the career choices of

---

[20] F. Boerker, *Enrollments in Public High School Science by Type of Course and by Sex, 1964–1965* (Washington, D.C.: National Center for Educational Statistics, November, 1966).

[21] Office of Education, *Digest of Educational Statistics* (Washington, D.C.: U.S. Government Printing Office, 1969), p. 32.

[22] Susanne D. Ellis, "Enrollment Trends," *Physics Today,* Vol. 20 (March, 1967), p. 77.

National Merit finalists. According to NMSC, these finalists represent the top 1 per cent of high school seniors who rank highest in scholastic aptitude and are regarded as "the nation's best source of brainpower." The findings reveal that where 18.8 per cent of the male finalists chose physics as their college major in 1958, only 11.1 per cent did so in 1967. Female finalists declaring physics as their college major declined from 4.1 per cent to 1.6 per cent over the same period.[23]

While the exact causes of these trends have not been established, some sources have maintained that young people have become disenchanted with the field of physics and associate it with the evils of warfare and the dehumanization of society. This problem was reported to be the most striking theme of the 1968 meeting of the American Physical Society, where one physicist described the situation as a "revulsion against science by the whole society, but especially among young people."[24] Others attribute the declining enrollments, at least partially, to excessive educational pressures and to difficulties associated with the curriculum in PSSC high school physics. An editorial in *Science,* official journal of the American Association for the Advancement of Science, puts it this way:

> Emotional shock waves following the launching of Sputnik in 1957 have been dissipated. Nevertheless, sequelae linger—notably in American education. During the late 1950's strenuous efforts were directed at improving all aspects of instruction and especially the teaching of science in the secondary schools. To achieve this a number of steps were taken. Summer institutes for science teachers were fostered. Efforts such as the Physics Secondary School Curriculum Project were launched. Campaigns to induce more students to enroll in science courses were conducted. Higher standards of performance were established. An increasing amount of homework was required. At the time, these steps generally met with enthusiastic response. However, today questions are being raised concerning the overall results of the efforts.
>
> The most recent statistics show that campaigns to increase interest in science and engineering have not been very successful. From 1960 to 1965, the number of college juniors majoring in physics dropped by about 15 per cent, while over-all college enrollment was up over 50 per cent. . . .
>
> To what extent is the current student unrest chargeable to the more stringent secondary school curricula? We do not know. However, there is a growing concern that too much is being asked of the young. . . .
>
> Responsibility for excessive pressure on secondary school students is shared by many. College admission officers, parents, new curricula, teachers, and the students themselves are involved. Results of the excessive

[23] Donivan J. Watley and Robert C. Nichols, *Career Choices of America's Most Able Youth* (Evanston, Ill.: National Merit Scholarship Corporation, 1968) (mimeographed).
[24] "A Revulsion Against the Physicist," *The New York Times,* February 4, 1968, p. 7E.

pressure seem to be especially evident in the physical sciences and engineering.

In the decade since Sputnik, scientists and others have participated in notable experiments in education. Some of the results are unexpected. Evaluation, looking toward prompt changes, is in order.[25]

Another scientist, pointing to declining enrollments and increasing student failures among the most able students in the field of chemistry, also attributes these problems to excessive pressures and contends that we have committed "a crime against a generation." [26] Ironically, critics like Bestor and Rickover, who had attracted a wide following in their attacks on the "soft pedagogy" of American education during the 1950's, fell strangely silent during the 1960's.

Growing Criticisms

Level of Difficulty. In connection with the PSSC high school physics course, leading members of the project staff have maintained from its inception that the course is intended as part of the general education of the student and "the analysis of achievement test performance by students from various levels of academic aptitude, as measured by conventional aptitude tests, clearly suggests that success in handling the ideas of the PSSC course is not limited to a narrow band of what, by traditional measures, might be called high-aptitude students." [27] However, such a conclusion is unwarranted since the correlation between scores on any standardized aptitude test with scores obtained on a given achievement test, such as the PSSC test, can be expected to be low. A low correlation should not be interpreted to mean that a given course is suitable for a wide range of students. The score on a single standardized aptitude test is simply a poor predictor of achievement. Such a test is not only an incomplete measure of aptitude, but achievement is a highly complex behavioral function. The most valid method of determining the suitability of the PSSC course for students of varied ability levels is to compare their achievement in PSSC physics with their records of prior academic achievement—particularly in academic mathematics, chemistry, and biology.

Moreover, the claim that the PSSC course is suited to a wide spectrum of students has been questioned by college professors and high school teachers who criticize the course for encompassing too much material at a level too difficult for most students. A professor of physics at Amherst

---

[25] Philip H. Abelson, "Excessive Educational Pressures," *Science,* Vol. 156 (May 12, 1967), p. 741.

[26] L. Carroll King in "High Student Failure Rate Serious Problem," *Chemical and Engineering News,* Vol. 45 (February 20, 1967), p. 44.

[27] Finlay, *op. cit.,* p. 76.

discusses this problem in terms of his own experiences in teaching a college physics course to students who completed the PSSC course in high school:

> Dealing with these students in class for several years, talking with many of them about their high school experiences, and taking several surveys of the coverage they were exposed to in the PSSC text, have convinced me that secondary school teachers are laboring under excessive pressure with respect to coverage of the text material. . . .
>
> Consequently I am convinced that it is desirable—perhaps even essential—to reduce the extent and pace of coverage in the majority of secondary school PSSC courses. . . .
>
> This will mean cutting and eliminating material that seems as dear and essential as part of one's own body, but if this is not done—with some degree of ruthlessness—the secondary school physics program is likely to show *increasing* rather than decreasing stresses and strains.[28]

Another physics professor expresses his concern over the trend toward stiffening the introductory college course in view of the improvement in the level of preparation in high school, and warns that we may be eliminating many potentially promising physics students through textbooks prepared by eminent research physicists:

> All textbooks nowadays are being stiffened to allow for an improvement in high school preparation. . . . Can we be sure that the highest intellectual achievements of the twentieth century should be stressed in the *first* college course? . . . Why the hurry?
>
> . . . If you devise a sophisticated, difficult introductory course, and screen the applicants so that only the highest ranking students are admitted, how can you be sure you are reaching the ones you want? How many of our really great physicists were wunderkinder in their youth? . . .
>
> I'm afraid that courses of the type we have been discussing might scare good B students away from physics. Physics is big enough to offer something to many grades and types of students. Why risk exposing some of them to two years of frustration? As you can see, I am not happy about this trend in physics education. Maybe I remember my own shortcomings as an elementary student. . . . Maybe I'm upset about the drop in high school and college enrollments in physics. How about calling a halt for a while until the situation becomes a bit clearer? [29]

Ironically, the decline in enrollment and the criticisms leveled at the new physics courses have come in the wake of what has been an unprecedented effort on the part of our federal government to promote course content revision and teacher education in physics and to make physics more attractive to able students. The involvement of research physicists

---

[28] Arnold Arons, "Time and Coverage," *PSSC Newsletter,* 1966, pp. 1–2.

[29] Mark W. Zemansky, "Too Far, Too Fast?," *Physics Today,* Vol. 20 (March, 1967), p. 73.

in preparing the materials for these new courses is criticized for the difficulty and remoteness of the subject matter. The major criteria for the selection of material have been based upon the concerns of the research physicist in the forefront of knowledge, and not upon the concerns, motivations, and capabilities of the representative body of college-bound students. Furthermore, the proportion of our most able students taking physics in high school and college declined steadily during the past decade. Yet the PSSC course also was intended to serve a general education function on the premise that "physics is the most basic of the natural sciences. For this reason, the study of physics is essential to the education of all of the population." [30]

"Pure" Vs. "Applied."   In developing the PSSC course in high school physics, the assumption was made that "to draw a wider group of students in the secondary schools into physics we must reduce the number of engineering applications taught in the course." [31] But some scientists have argued that "purifying" the physics course by eliminating many of the topics concerned with technology in society has made the study of physics more abstract and remote from the lives of students and the problems of society. Paradoxically, a major criticism leveled at traditional physics courses by the Physical Science Study Committee was that such courses were concerned more with the technology of society (the man-made world) than with the concerns of eminent physicists in the quest of new knowledge. The puristic approach of PSSC and its consequences have led to a reaction, not only on the part of high school students and teachers, but by scientists themselves. For example, Alvin M. Weinberg, director of Oak Ridge National Laboratory, has criticized the new curriculum reforms in the sciences as "puristic monsters." Weinberg sees a counterrevolution sprouting that will lead to courses that are more interdisciplinary and concerned not merely with the search for knowledge, but with the applications of knowledge to solve the pervading problems of mankind.[32] In recent years, several new projects have sprouted as a reaction to the PSSC high school physics course, giving tangible indication of a recognized need for pluralistic approaches in the study of physics.

Trend Toward Pluralistic Approaches

The growing concern over the abstract remoteness of the PSSC course in the face of declining enrollments caused the National Science Founda-

---

[30] Walter C. Michels, "The Teaching of Elementary Physics," *Scientific American*, Vol. 198 (April, 1958), p. 57.

[31] *Ibid.*, p. 62.

[32] Alvin M. Weinberg, *Reflections on Big Science* (Cambridge, Mass.: The M.I.T. Press, 1967), pp. 154–155.

tion to support the Engineering Concepts Curriculum Project (ECCP), which was organized in 1963 to develop a high school physics course based upon the world as man has shaped it. Intended for general education purposes in high school, the course, entitled "The Man-made World," is described as "a substantive approach to the technical bases of our society for the general student." [33] Accordingly, it is "not a course in engineering or 'preengineering.' Neither is it intended to proselytize students into engineering, the sciences or mathematics." [34] Major topics include logic and computers, models and measurements, and energy control." The Man-made World" is based on the viewpoint that engineering is synthesis-oriented and, therefore, the course is intended to represent an interdisciplinary rationale. ECCP is aimed at giving students "a start toward understanding the man-made world and how it came to be as it is. They will be aware of the influences from science and technology that will shape the future. This background will enable them to confront with enlightenment the moral issues and value judgments demanded of today's citizens." [35]

Another high school physics project, initiated in 1964 as a reaction to the excessively theoretical emphasis of the PSSC physics course and in response to the alleged "national emergency" created by the decline in physics enrollments in high school and college, is Harvard Project Physics. This course seeks to relate physics to the broader scope of human affairs.

> By avoiding overspecialized topics and making use of history of science as a pedagogic aid where appropriate, we are seeking to make the student aware of the humanistic aspects of physics. In this way we hope to respond positively to the major new developing interest in educational philosophy today: the preservation and exploitation of individual differences both in teachers and in students. The end result, one may begin to hope . . . will be a modern course that helps to bring more physics to more students.[36]

Of course, the concern for individual differences is well rooted in the progressive educational philosophy of the first half of the twentieth century. But it is significant to find a renewed concern for these differences resulting from the failure of the PSSC course to attract more high school students. Harvard Project Physics has been headed up by a three-man group composed of a physicist who is also a science historian, a professor of education, and a former high school physics teacher.

Yet another project that has grown out of the difficulties with the PSSC

---

[33] Edward E. David, Jr. and John G. Truxal, "Engineering Concepts," *Physics Today,* Vol. 20 (March, 1967), p. 39.

[34] *Ibid.*

[35] *Ibid.,* p. 40.

[36] Gerald Holton, "Harvard Project Physics," *Physics Today,* Vol. 20 (March, 1967), p. 34.

course is the Introductory Physical Science course (IPS). Designed to provide a foundation for the study of physical science in the senior high school, as well as to serve as an exposure for those youngsters who will not take physics or chemistry in senior high school, IPS is intended for the junior high school or middle school. Like PSSC, IPS is sponsored by the Education Development Center. The work on IPS began in 1963 and has led to the production of a second-year course, Physical Science II. Thus, the Education Development Center has produced three one-year courses in physical science at the secondary school level (IPS, Physical Science II, and PSSC physics). Under the auspices of the center, a textbook for the first course in college physics also has been developed. Another outgrowth of the PSSC course is the Elementary Science Study (ESS), started in 1960 through the Education Development Center with NSF funds. ESS consists of a variety of self-contained units for use in grades K through 8 which are organized around concrete rather than abstract phenomena. The National Science Foundation also has supported other projects in elementary school science, including the Science Curriculum Improvement Study established in 1959, at the University of California, Berkeley.

The growing multiplicity of course development projects in the physical sciences reflects not only the concern of the National Science Foundation and other agencies for promoting the study of such subjects from kindergarten through college, but also the growing awareness that courses in this field must be pluralistic. The contention that there is a singular, omnipresent "structure of a discipline" appears to be open to serious question. Different scholars, working from different vantage points and with different values, attitudes, and goals, will come up with different approaches in developing the content and methodological approaches for new courses.

THE NEW HIGH SCHOOL BIOLOGY

Unlike the subjects of physics and chemistry, which are taken by a minority of senior high school students, most of whom are college bound, biology is studied by the majority of students. Consequently, biology is the one field of science which serves a truly general education function in the senior high school. Among the sciences, however, physics was given first priority by the National Science Foundation for course improvement at the high school level. The cold war and the increasing development of nuclear energy had created a new urgency for course improvement in physics.

Although curriculum reform in biology has made some significant departures from the strategies of the Physical Science Study Committee, many cues have been taken from PSSC in biology, as well as in other curriculum projects. The fact that the physical sciences (along with mathematics) were first in the new wave of course improvement, the generous and prestigious support given PSSC by the National Science Foundation, the strong leadership provided by MIT faculty and administration, and the urgency of the cold war all served to make PSSC an imposing archetype for curriculum reform.

Biological Science—Variations on a Theme

The Biological Sciences Curriculum Study (BSCS) was organized in 1959 under the sponsorship of the American Institute of Biological Sciences (AIBS) through funds from the National Science Foundation. Bentley Glass, first chairman of BSCS, acknowledges that the original ideas for BSCS developed when members of AIBS took notice of "the excellent steps taken by the Physical Science Study Committee." [37] As in the case of PSSC, it was decided that BSCS would focus first on course improvement in the senior high school. The study adopted the task-force approach of PSSC, in which a group of university scientists were brought together to head up the program with the assistance of science educators (from schools of education), high school teachers, and curriculum supervisors.

Glass estimated that significant knowledge in the field was doubling every ten to fifteen years and that "the biology actually being taught in the schools today is twenty years behind the advancing front of science, and in important respects is a full century in arrears." [38] Although acknowledging great inadequacies in college level courses as well, the committee felt that their efforts should be directed first at the high school level, where most students make a choice of occupation. And, while recognizing that modern biology requires a considerable background in physics and chemistry, the BSCS committee nevertheless decided that to postpone the study of biology to the senior year of high school would decimate the number of students electing to take the course. Traditionally, biology has been placed in the tenth grade and most students take the subject as part of the general education requirement. Thus, the committee decided that the new biology would be designed to meet the general education needs for most students at the tenth-grade level.

Rationale and Objectives.   The PSSC theme of "science as inquiry" also pervades the BSCS rationale. In the study of biology Glass maintains that "real participation in scientific inquiry, and as full a participation as

---

[37] Bentley Glass, "Renascent Biology: A Report on the AIBS Biological Sciences Curriculum Study," *School Review,* Vol. 70 (Spring, 1962), p. 16.

[38] Glass, *op. cit.,* p. 17.

possible, should be provided."[39] Through BSCS, according to Glass, "for the first time . . . education in the natural sciences, at least at the secondary level, has assigned the acquisition of scientific information and concepts a place of lesser importance than the understanding of the very nature of scientific enquiry and of the scientific enterprise in which modern man is embarked." [40] Glass quotes the science historian, George Sarton, on the necessity for the average man to "understand as clearly as possible the purposes and methods of science. This is the business of our schools, not simply of the colleges but of all the schools from the kindergarten up." [41] Although BSCS has not yet ventured into the kindergarten, the romantic notion that the young child can and should be made to deal with knowledge in styles not unlike those of the mature scholar, is ever-present in the literature bearing on new curriculum projects in the sciences and even in the social studies. Here the influence of Bruner has been clearly felt. According to Bruner, "there is a continuity between what a scholar does on the forefront of his discipline and what a child does in approaching it for the first time." [42]

Stress on Inquiry

The importance of inquiry as method for teaching and learning is stressed in various descriptions concerning the features and objectives of BSCS in its program for high school biology. Thus, the BSCS program is characterized as "an *investigative* approach to modern biology in contrast to a *descriptive* approach in former biology programs. Inquiry is the method by which knowledge about biology is acquired. Biology is an open-ended field of study, not a set of encyclopedic facts." [43] Some of the earliest official statements from BSCS stress the importance of inquiry through laboratory work where "students must be given a first-hand understanding of how scientists observe and investigate, what their modes of procedures are, and the significance of the scientific approach." [44]

Although recognizing that most students studying biology in high school do not go on to college, the BSCS group maintains that hypothesis-testing in the development of new scientific knowledge should be a major theme of the biology course. "For such students, the high school biology course is the school's last opportunity, through its science cur-

---

39 *Ibid.*, p. 20.

40 *Ibid.*, p. 41.

41 *Ibid.*, p. 19.

42 Bruner, *op. cit.*, p. 28.

43 Burton E. Voss, "The Impact of BSCS Biology," *School Science and Mathematics,* Vol. 67 (February, 1967), p. 145.

44 *BSCS Newsletter No. 1* (Boulder, Colorado: Biological Sciences Curriculum Study, September, 1959), p. 2.

riculum, to teach what science and the scientific processes are and how scientists test hypotheses and develop new concepts." [45] Another member of the BSCS group stresses that "we need to imbue our courses and our exposition with the color of science *as inquiry*." [46]

Needs of the Scholar Vs. Needs of the Student. Is everyone capable of dealing with science as *inquiry*, and should this be expected of all high school youngsters? Schwab argues that scientific inquiry must be integral to the education of all, just as literacy itself has become universal.

> How many of our high school students . . . should be involved in an inquiring approach to science? The first impulse is to view inquiry as something for very few, for the top five or ten per cent of students. . . . I do not believe this to be the case. . . .
>
> . . . For most students entering high school in the next year or two, it will be a shocking change of pace. For most high school students entering college in the next few years, it will come as a similar shock. But this very sequence suggests what the future can hold. As a few teachers introduce an inquiring curriculum, more and more students will enter college who have been well conditioned to the process. They will move at a faster and more effective pace through teacher training and go out to accelerate the rate at which inquiry permeates the schools and returns its dividends to the colleges.
>
> Before we turn a skeptical ear to a forecast of such extensiveness, let us remember what happened in the case of literacy. The same apparently obvious facts about educability and the same "common sense" which may now tell us that inquiry is beyond the competence of average men and women once led to the same pronouncement about teaching the ordinary man to read and write. . . .
>
> It is not too much to hope for a similar outcome to efforts to teach science as inquiry.[47]

Although Schwab sees a temporary shock effect on students during the transition from traditional expository courses in science to inquiry-centered courses, Zacharias and White hold that "the student who is exposed to a new curriculum will have little trouble with it. If a course is presented to him as biology, he will accept it as representing biology as unquestioningly as he would have accepted the course it replaced." [48] It is the teacher and not the student, according to Zacharias and White,

---

[45] Bentley Glass, "Some Reflections on Science Education," *BSCS Newsletter No. 6, Annual Report* (Boulder, Colorado: Biological Sciences Curriculum Study, December, 1960), p. 6.

[46] Joseph J. Schwab, "Some Reflections on Science Education," *BSCS Newsletter No. 9* (Boulder, Colorado: Biological Sciences Curriculum Study, September, 1961), p. 8.

[47] *Ibid.*, p. 9.

[48] Zacharias and White, *op. cit.*, p. 75.

who will have difficulty with the transition. In this connection, teacher education has been built into BSCS through NSF institutes similar to those provided for PSSC.

Turning again to Schwab's pronouncements concerning the inquiry-centered courses in science, it is one thing to have students learn to inquire into the applications of knowledge in solving pervading problems, both personal and social, and quite another thing to have students learn like a scientist who is in the forefront of his discipline. Dewey and other experimentalists viewed inquiry in the curriculum as the chief method of education through which the learner becomes capable of dealing with personal and social problems intelligently. In this way democracy is strengthened—to the extent that its citizens are enlightened and capable of meeting new problems. But the new course-improvement projects, which have been described as "renascent" [49] and "revolutionary," [50] are concerned largely with the scholar's approach to new knowledge. Some scientists warn that university research scholars, with their narrowly puristic approach to their disciplines, have taken hold of curriculum reform at the elementary and secondary school levels, and in so doing have fragmented and abstracted the curriculum at the expense of learnings that are relevant to the urgent problems of man.[51] Applied and interdisciplinary studies are deprecated in favor of abstract and theoretical pursuits, which are the methods of the discipline-oriented university scholar. However, this problem is probably more characteristic of curriculum projects in mathematics, such as the School Mathematics Study Group (SMSG), and physics (PSSC) than of BSCS. Nevertheless, the BSCS program clearly is intended to represent the thinking of those biologists in the forefront of knowledge.

Pluralistic Approach to Course Development

Perhaps the most significant aspect of BSCS in determining course content was the decision made early in the project to develop three versions of the high school biology course. Where PSSC, SMSG, and other programs initially sought to develop the subject matter according to a singular structural scheme, following Bruner's notion of "structure of a discipline," BSCS decided on a pluralistic approach. According to Bruner, the organization of subject matter around key principles would reveal the fundamental character of the discipline and would help narrow the gap between advanced and elementary knowledge.[52] Nevertheless, the BSCS group felt that the great diversity of the life sciences precluded any

49 Glass, "Renascent Biology," *op. cit.*

50 Arnold Grobman, "The Threshold of a Revolution in Biological Education," *The Journal of Medical Education,* Vol. 36 (October, 1961), pp. 1253–1265.

51 Weinberg, *op. cit.*

52 Bruner, *op. cit.*, p. 26.

possibility of finding any one best approach in developing a high school course in biology. Glass observed that the biological sciences are more complex, diversified, and less well formulated in terms of scientific law than the physical sciences and, consequently, the notion of "structure of a discipline" would be of limited value in the practical work of selecting content and methods for new biology courses.[53] Consequently, three versions of high school biology were produced and, in subsequent years, were revised extensively: (1) the Blue version, with its molecular emphasis and biochemical treatment, (2) the Yellow version, with its orientation toward the reproductive, developmental, and evolutionary, and (3) the Green version, with its emphasis on the ecological and behavioral aspects of biology. Nevertheless, more than half the material is common for all three versions. Nine unifying threads are identified for all three versions:

1. Change of living things through time—evolution.
2. Diversity of the type and unity of pattern of living things.
3. Genetic continuity of life.
4. Complementarity of organisms and environment.
5. Biological roots of behavior.
6. Complementarity of structure and function.
7. Regulation and homeostasis: the maintenance of life in the face of change.
8. Science as inquiry.
9. Intellectual history of biological concepts.[54]

The pluralistic approach of BSCS is shown in Figure 3-1. Here we see the profiles of the biological content levels for each of the three versions. Although each version is designed for the tenth grade, the differences in emphases are apparent. Yet it can be seen that there is a common core content among all three versions. Moreover, where traditional high school biology courses have emphasized the tissue and organ level, the BSCS versions give greater treatment to the molecular, cellular, and community levels in which modern biological research is being concentrated. Differences among the three versions exemplify the various areas of interest among biologists and demonstrate that there is no single body of subject matter that must be "covered" in the tenth-grade biology course (or in the introductory college course, for that matter). The three versions represent only three of the many possible ways of organizing material for study.

Special Course for Low Achievers. Although the three BSCS versions were originally intended for all students who take biology in the tenth grade, it became apparent that these courses were far too difficult for stu-

---

[53] Bentley Glass, "Theory into Action—A Critique," *Science Teacher,* Vol. 32 (May, 1965), pp. 29–30, 82–83.
[54] *About BSCS Biology* (Boulder, Colorado: Biological Sciences Curriculum Study, August, 1967), p. 2.

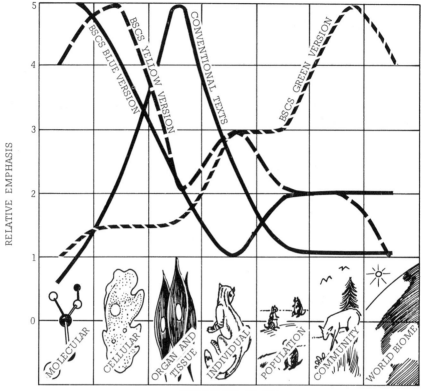

Figure 3-1. Relative Emphasis in Original BSCS Versions and Contemporary Conventional Texts

> *Source: Arnold Grobman,* The Changing Classroom: The Role of the Biological Sciences Curriculum Study *(New York: Doubleday & Company, Inc., 1969), p. 79.*

dents who are below the fortieth percentile in aptitude and achievement. Consequently, a special course was prepared for such students and made available commercially in 1966. The special course, known as *Biological Science: Patterns and Processes,* is designed to provide detailed examples and techniques for the teacher in structuring the learning situation. Although the course contains many themes and concepts from the previous versions, the vocabulary level is simpler and the amount of reading material is considerably reduced in favor of laboratory and field activities. However, even a cursory examination of the text material reveals a lack of richness in design and the absence of the attractive color plates that are characteristic of the Blue, Green, and Yellow versions. The text and other materials for the special course are undergoing considerable revision with a view toward making the course more appropriate for the intended student population. A series of paperbacks on biological topics also has been developed to enrich the text material.

Other Courses.   A second course has been prepared by BSCS for students who have completed the Blue, Green, or Yellow version. The second-year course, *Biological Science: Interaction of Experiments and Ideas,* was first made available commercially in 1965 and is designed to provide considerable experience in research-centered laboratory work. Emphasis is given to teaching science as a process of inquiry.

In addition to the second-year course, BSCS is preparing material for life sciences courses for the junior high and middle school levels. BSCS also has joined the Commission on Undergraduate Education in the Biological Sciences (CUEBS) to develop materials for a biology methods course for preservice teachers.

Systems Approach

In addition to the three BSCS versions, the special course for low achievers, the second-level course, and the special materials for teachers, BSCS has developed a variety of materials including supplementary problems for intensive laboratory work, films, paperback volumes, and special tests.

The Laboratory Blocks.   The emphasis on inquiry-discovery is enhanced further through Laboratory Blocks, which are provided in addition to the regular laboratory exercises for the three versions. Through the Laboratory Block Program, students taking one of the three BSCS versions are given the opportunity to explore intensively problems in a single area of biology, in order "to learn biology as a biologist learns it." [55] Each Laboratory Block requires six weeks of intensive investigation and is designed to be the focus of all class activities during this time period. Although BSCS has produced many Laboratory Blocks, it is recommended that only one block be used per school year. The Laboratory Blocks cover such subjects as "animal growth and development," "life in the soil," "the molecular basis of metabolism," "evolution," and "the biological effects of radiation."

Presumably, despite the fact that the teacher may have had no actual experience in conducting research, the teacher and his students, through the Laboratory Blocks, are expected "to learn biology as a biologist learns it."

---

55 Addison E. Lee, "The Use of BSCS Laboratory Blocks in a Modern Biology Program," *BSCS Newsletter No. 23* (Boulder, Colorado: Biological Sciences Curriculum Study, December, 1964), p. 5.

The Laboratory Blocks are designed to guide the student to make discoveries for himself. Some questions or problems will be posed, but no answers will be given in advance. Thus, the student is really working with the unknown. In making discoveries for himself, the student will generally follow in the footsteps of scientists who have preceded him. On some occasions, however, he may follow an entirely new approach. . . . He should be on the lookout for new problems, design new experiments to investigate these problems and, to the extent possible, carry on these investigations.

At least to some extent, the procedure outlined here should bring the student to the frontier of science for a particular subject.[56]

These are indeed lofty expectations, especially for students who are not set on research careers in science. And if, in the Laboratory Block, the student is conducting research for which no answers are provided, what about the teacher? Is the teacher also really working with an unknown?

To avoid pedagogical embarrassment, the teacher is provided with supplements to the Laboratory Blocks which contain guidelines for conducting the investigations and data to be obtained, along with the correct answers to the problems. Although the Laboratory Block Program is designed to have the student inquire and discover in much the same way that a research biologist handles a problem, the fact that the teacher has the cues and answers in advance, the time limit of six weeks (during which the student is studying other subjects, while the research scientist usually is devoting full time to the problem), and the teacher's decisions regarding organization and techniques—all serve to make the research experience somewhat less genuine. But these are perhaps necessary compromises and although the Laboratory Block Program does not justify some of the sweeping claims made for it, it must nonetheless be regarded as a significant and valuable departure from conventional laboratory exercises.

Other Materials. Batteries of tests have been developed by BSCS to assess student achievement in the various courses. These include quarterly and comprehensive examinations for which norms have been established. A problem in test development has been that of measuring inquiry objectives and applications.

Unique among the BSCS materials are the Single Topic Inquiry Films, which are designed to stimulate students to raise questions, formulate hypotheses, interpret data, and discuss various concepts and phenomena. The films are brief and are intended to be stopped on certain frames for critical discussion. As the title of the series implies, the films are to arouse student inquiry and teachers are instructed not to give answers to the problems presented.

---

56 *Ibid.,* p. 6.

A series of paperback volumes on research problems has been produced for use with gifted students. The problems are derived from areas of investigation in which active researchers are engaged. Although originally developed by BSCS for gifted high school students, these paperbacks are being used in a number of college-level courses.

ASSESSMENT: RESEARCH, OPINIONS, AND PROBLEMS

Evaluation of Achievement

During the early stages in which the three BSCS versions were being used, BSCS set out to compare differences in achievement not only among the three versions, but between BSCS students and control groups of youngsters in conventional courses of high school biology at the tenth-grade level.[57] Accordingly, BSCS would "compare performance of students in each version with a control group of students in conventional biology, in terms of measuring attainment of BSCS objectives as well as on a conventional biology test (an old College Board exam)." [58] Thus the major measurement criteria for assessing achievement in the BSCS and control groups were designated by BSCS as (1) an old College Board biology achievement examination, and (2) a BSCS Comprehensive Final Examination along with a BSCS Impact Test. The old College Board examination selected was the Cooperative Biology Test of 1948, which, though outdated, was considered to represent "conventional biology." Other tests to be administered to the BSCS and control groups were the BSCS-developed Test of Understanding of Science, later renamed the Processes of Science Test, and the Purdue Opinion Poll. The Scholastic Aptitude Test (SAT) was administered initially to both groups and statistical corrections were made between groups for differences in aptitude.

Research Criteria and Inequities. Because the BSCS Comprehensive Final Examination is specifically designed by BSCS to measure achievement in BSCS biology, whereas the Cooperative Biology Test of the College Entrance Examination Board is not designed for any specific course or textbook, this disparity must be regarded at the outset as a bias favoring the BSCS population. The use of a 1948 edition of the Cooperative Biology Test raises a serious question as to whether a thirteen-year-old test could be said to represent the "conventional" biology courses of 1961–1962.

Moreover, there appear to have been other disparate variables in favor of the BSCS population. The BSCS teachers were paid an additional 10

57 *BSCS Newsletter No. 10* (Boulder, Colorado: Biological Sciences Curriculum Study, November, 1961), pp. 2, 5.

58 *BSCS Newsletter No. 12,* Annual Report (Boulder, Colorado: Biological Sciences Curriculum Study, February, 1962), p. 10.

per cent of their annual salary for participating in the evaluation program, whereas the control-group teachers received no additional compensation. BSCS teachers also received specific training and participated in a one-week briefing session prior to the experiment. No such training programs and briefing sessions were provided for the teachers of the control groups. BSCS students received free textbooks and laboratory books, which became the property of the students (not the schools), while the BSCS teachers were given special supplementary guides. No comparable provisions were made for the control population. It was also recommended that school systems give additional support to the experimental classes, and BSCS provided for the services of university research biologists who served as resource persons for the schools using the BSCS course. Finally, the BSCS students were given a practice sample version test early in the school year to familiarize them with the type of BSCS version tests to be taken later. The BSCS classes also were given quarterly BSCS achievement tests during the year. Although both the control and BSCS populations received the BSCS Comprehensive Final Examination at the end of the year, only the BSCS population received the BSCS practice sample version test and the BSCS quarterly achievement tests.[59] Obviously, such practice could be expected to improve the scores of the BSCS students over the control students on the BSCS Comprehensive Final. Neither population received practice versions of the Cooperative Biology Test. Efforts were made to match the control and BSCS populations according to school and community characteristics.

Findings.   The findings revealed that although the BSCS population outscored the control group on the BSCS Comprehensive Final, the control group outperformed the BSCS population on the Cooperative Biology Test prepared by the College Entrance Examination Board. While these results were not entirely unexpected, the control group also showed a slight but significant superiority over the BSCS population on the BSCS Impact Test, which was designed to measure understanding of scientific principles and scientific reasoning capability.[60]

The results on the BSCS Impact Test were indeed an unanticipated outcome. Comparisons on the Test of Understanding of Science showed no significant differences between the BSCS and control groups. Nor were there significant differences on the Purdue scales designed to measure attitudes and opinions toward science and scientists. In view of the stated objectives of BSCS, one would have anticipated that the BSCS students

59 Hulda Grobman, "The Rationale and Framework of the BSCS Evaluation Program," *BSCS Newsletter No. 19* (Boulder, Colorado: Biological Sciences Curriculum Study, September, 1963), pp. 6–11.

60 Wimburn Wallace, "The BSCS 1961–62 Evaluation Program—A Statistical Report," *BSCS Newsletter No. 19, ibid.,* p. 23.

would score significantly higher than the students in conventional classes on both the BSCS Impact Test and the Purdue scales.

Turning to other findings, comparisons on achievement scores for the three BSCS versions yielded negligible and inconsistent differences. However, a subsequent study revealed that students in the Blue version obtained significantly greater gains in achievement, while those in the Green version made the lowest gains.[61] Classes participating in the BSCS Laboratory Block Program made slightly lower scores than other BSCS classes on the BSCS Comprehensive Final. This finding was not surprising in view of the fact that time spent on Laboratory Block activities is taken from time that otherwise would be devoted to the textbook materials that are covered on the achievement test.

The BSCS Evaluation Program for 1961–1962 involved more than twenty-four thousand students in tenth-grade biology. Undoubtedly the results were disappointing to proponents of BSCS. A review of other research studies, sponsored independently of BSCS, was conducted by the BSCS Research and Development Laboratory at the University of Texas. Here again, the results of these studies failed to reveal consistently significant differences between BSCS students and others on various non-BSCS achievement and critical-thinking measures.[62]

Implications. Obviously, the findings of these investigations are disappointing to proponents of BSCS. Perhaps the kinds of objectives and methods implicit in the BSCS program are not measured adequately by paper-and-pencil tests. It is conceivable that a sample study of student behavior in handling various biological problems might have been more apropos. (Surely one would not expect to measure the worth of a scientist through paper-and-pencil tests.) Or perhaps conventional courses are not nearly so inadequate as BSCS proponents would have us believe. On the other hand, teachers may tend to compensate for inadequacies inherent in the textbook and other course materials that represent "conventional" biology. Thus it is not enough in curriculum evaluation to compare learning outcomes from different course materials without taking into account the actual styles and strategies of the teacher in the classroom.

It is unlikely that a large-scale replication of this study will be undertaken by BSCS because most of the conventional textbooks have been revised extensively to include modern biological materials. Thus BSCS, which originally set out to prepare and evaluate sample course materials that could serve as models for other courses in high school biology, has

---

[61] *BSCS Newsletter No. 30* (Boulder, Colorado: Biological Sciences Curriculum Study, January, 1967), p. 5.
[62] *Ibid.,* pp. 21–25.

been successful in exerting such an influence. Moreover, many teachers of non-BSCS courses are now being reached by the NSF institutes.

Despite the disappointing outcomes in this research, it has also shown that radically new courses can be developed without danger of suffering any really great *loss* of conventional learning material. Frequently, conservative educators resist curriculum innovation on the ground that the "tried and tested" will be sacrificed.

Curriculum research is a highly complex matter, and university research scholars in the disciplines have tended to draw sweeping conclusions about the advantages and panaceas for such-and-such a discipline-oriented course in the absence of systematic research and evaluation. Too often they have reached conclusions concerning curriculum questions which should have been hypotheses for research. Moreover, they have tended to overestimate students' interests in and capacities for theoretical studies. This has been true not only of the Biological Sciences Curriculum Study, which originally set out to develop its course versions to meet the general education needs of virtually all high school youth, but also of the Physical Science Study Committee, which attempted to develop its high school physics course for the small proportion of students who study the subject. As mentioned earlier, where the PSSC course was found to lack appeal for those students who are interested in the technological aspects of physics, the three BSCS versions were found to be too difficult for 40 per cent of the students who normally take the subject in the tenth grade. One lesson to be learned is that a much more open stance toward course-content improvement is needed and this can be accomplished through multiple versions of new courses and continuous evaluation.

Research on Teaching Styles

Content Vs. Methods.   For many years, traditionalists have been critical of the attention that progressive educators have given to teaching styles or methods. Traditionalists took the position that knowledge of content should be a sufficient qualification for teaching. However, although the curriculum reform programs of the 1960's sought to give the scholar the chief role in establishing the subject matter through structural elements characteristic of the particular discipline, the question of teaching methodology and styles of learning could not be ignored. For example, it was found that merely providing high school teachers with intensive work in their subject specialties through NSF-sponsored Academic Year Institutes at universities failed to change their teaching styles. Such teachers, exposed to passive-receptive experiences emphasizing lecture classes, textbook and other readings, written assignments, periodic paper-and-pencil tests, and even independent study, continued to teach science as merely a body of established knowledge. In contrast, those teachers involved in active-participation experiences, which included discussion classes and out-of-class work with students and teachers, evidenced significant changes in their own teaching styles by treating science as thought rather than as a body of established knowledge.[63]

A study sponsored by BSCS concerning the classroom style of teachers using a specific version of BSCS material revealed great disparities among the teachers. Despite the fact that each teacher was working with identical lessons on photosynthesis in the BSCS Blue version, and although each of the classes was characterized as high in ability and achievement, an analysis of the treatment of topics, content skills, conceptual levels, cognitive styles, and teacher-student talk led the researcher to conclude that "there is no such thing as a BSCS curriculum presentation in the schools. . . . The substantial differences found in topics in terms of *goals* and *levels of abstraction* suggest that the teachers have different approaches and instructional strategies that result in different ideas and concepts being presented to the students." [64] Among the teachers studied, the range of teacher talk was from 66 per cent to 95 per cent. The investigator found that those students participating in the greatest amount of class discussion also made significantly higher scores on the BSCS tests. The findings led the researcher to conclude that "to say that a student has been through the BSCS curriculum probably does not give as much specific information as the curriculum innovators might have hoped." [65] The investigator also noted that emphasis in teacher preparation in the new programs of course-content improvement has focused on the need to improve and update the subject-matter background of teachers, while giving secondary attention to instructional methodology. He advocated that just as much explicit emphasis be given to developing instructional skills, such as how to lead a class discussion, as is given to upgrading the teacher's subject-matter preparation.

The Teacher Variable.   In curriculum innovation the teacher variable may be at least as powerful as the instructional-material variable. Regardless of what is professed, one cannot automatically assume that the "new" biology entails an inquiry approach while the "conventional" biology course is merely didactic or passive-receptive in its treatment of the subject matter in relation to the learner. Obviously, for new curricula to be implemented effectively, considerable emphasis must be given to teaching strategies.

---

[63] Howard E. Gruber, "The Process of Science Education," *Teachers College Record,* Vol. 63 (February, 1962), pp. 367–376.

[64] James J. Gallagher, "Teacher Variation in Concept Presentation in BSCS Curriculum Programs," *BSCS Newsletter No. 30, op. cit.,* p. 17.

[65] *Ibid.*

Other Evaluations

A study of the assignment of students to tracks in biology revealed an alarming degree of improper student grouping. Grobman found that although the schools in the study reported using ability tests for determining the grouping levels, between 30 and 40 per cent of the students assigned to the BSCS course for lower-ability youngsters were fully capable of handling the regular BSCS versions.[66] This may indeed be indicative of the degree of malpractice which exists in assigning students to tracks or ability levels in various other subjects in our schools, and it may also provide a clue as to why various systems of tracking and grouping youngsters fail to produce anticipated gains in achievement over nongrouping.

In addition to the many research studies of the BSCS course versions, a number of reviews of the new courses have appeared in various journals. While complimenting the Biological Sciences Curriculum Study for its fresh and challenging approaches to course-content improvement, a British educator, reviewing the BSCS versions for *Science,* found many aspects of the texts to be far too difficult for fifteen-year-olds. For example, regarding the treatment of the DNA code and RNA, he offers this criticism:

> It is good to read such lucid descriptions of the architect and builder of life, but, interesting as it is, it would appear to be outside the understanding of the 15-year-old. To take but one example from the Yellow version:
>
> "You will remember that RNA has much in common with DNA: both are made up of nucleotides. The primary differences are that the sugar of RNA is *ribose* instead of *deoxyribose,* and thymine is not present in RNA. Instead of thymine, we find *uracil* . . . a pyrimidine very similar to thymine. The two purines and two pyrimidines present in RNA, therefore, are adenine, guanine, cytosine, and uracil."
>
> I doubt whether a fraction of boys and girls would be able to do more than memorize these facts to answer the guide questions and problems that go with each chapter.[67]

The reviewer criticized the complex biochemical and theoretical notions in the BSCS material and observed that while many tenth-graders would be able to memorize the theories, it is doubtful that they would be able to really understand or judge the significance of such material. In concluding, he reiterated his position that the treatment of biology

---

[66] Hulda Grobman, "Assignment of Students to Tracks in Biology," *The American Biology Teacher,* Vol. 27 (December, 1965), pp. 762–764.

[67] J. K. Brierley, "The Biological Sciences Curriculum Study Publications," *Science,* Vol. 143 (February 14, 1964), p. 669.

in the three BSCS texts is too difficult and expressed surprise that school teachers allowed the scientists to include such material.

> To generalize greatly, the level of the texts seems to be pitched too high for the 15-year-old. It is a little surprising that the school teachers on the various committees let some of the text through, but so often a schoolmaster is humbled into silence by a scientist, intellectually quick on the draw, yet the schoolmaster's experience with boys and girls is the touchstone of the ideas being debated.[68]

Ausubel characterized the Yellow and Blue BSCS versions as "admirably thorough, accurate, and up-to-date, but so ineffectively presented and organized, and so impossibly sophisticated for their intended audience, as to be intrinsically unlearnable on a long-term basis." [69] He also criticized these versions for virtually ignoring many important applications of biological science while introducing "an absurd and unrealistic level of biochemical and biophysical sophistication for which the intended users lack any semblance of adequate background." [70] According to Ausubel, "except for the Green Version, the BSCS textbooks do not . . . constitute much of an improvement over the better conventional texts, in terms of either conceptual content or congruence with contemporary thinking in and approach to biology; and, in some substantive and most pedagogic respects, they fall below the standard of the typical conventional text." [71] He maintained that the high school biology course should concentrate on broad biological ideas for general education instead of on the physical and chemical basis of biological phenomena. Accordingly, the naturalistic approach would have greater transfer value for problem solving in the real life of the student than the laboratory centered experimental-analytical approach.

Ausubel also challenged the validity of the currently fashionable trend in course-content improvement projects to neglect applications to practical problems on the premise that only "basic science" knowledge is relevant to general principles or structure of the discipline. He contended that the applied biological sciences not only have their own general principles but are related to basic principles in biology. With this in mind, coupled with the general education needs and interests of students, there is a legitimate place in the course for dealing with biological principles through the many practical problems in health, disease, agriculture, the interaction of heredity and environment, the biological aspects of

---

68 *Ibid.*, p. 670.

69 David P. Ausubel, "An Evaluation of the BSCS Approach to High School Biology," *American Biology Teacher*, Vol. 28 (March, 1966), p. 176.

70 *Ibid.*, p. 177.

71 *Ibid.*

behavior, and so on. Ausubel criticized the Blue and Yellow versions for determining the order of learning material according to level of biological organization rather than according to what is most appropriate to the learner. According to Ausubel, the material should be organized so that the learner proceeds from the familiar to the unfamiliar instead of having to contend first with the most difficult material in the field (i.e., molecular and cellular biology). He held that the Blue version appears more appropriate as an introductory college course than as a high school course.

General Education

As discussed earlier, the subject of biology is the one science that traditionally has been studied in high school by many terminal students as well as by those who are college bound. But where the BSCS group originally set out to develop a high school course that would meet the general education needs of youngsters of average as well as superior intelligence, it soon became apparent that the three BSCS versions are too difficult for fully 40 per cent of the students. This meant that the course materials are geared mainly for those students who are indeed college bound.

But level of difficulty is only one factor in course development for purposes of general education. Another important factor raised by some critics of the new course programs in the sciences is the tendency for research scientists to deprecate the applied aspects of their discipline. They are chiefly concerned with theoretical aspects and the research frontiers of their field. Yet for general education purposes, the applied dimensions are of considerable importance in the life of the learner and to society in general. Moreover, the notion that only through the theoretical and research dimensions of a given discipline can students learn the basic principles and structure of the discipline remains a matter of debate. There is also considerable disagreement among scientists in given disciplines as to what should properly be included in an introductory college course, as well as an introductory high school course, not to mention the infinitely complex matter of agreeing on what constitutes the structure of the discipline and how this structure should permeate all levels of learning.

Course Improvement at the College Level

The American Institute of Biological Sciences (AIBS), which originally sponsored BSCS, also recognized the need to modernize the biology curriculum in higher education. Through its Commission on Undergraduate Education, it established a special panel in 1965 to develop a core curriculum that would encompass the body of knowledge essential for all biology students in college. Much of the work of the panel was supported by NSF. It will be recalled that the fear of Soviet scientific rivalry during the 1950's prompted many university scientists to blame the schools rather than the institutions of higher education for curriculum inadequacies. But after assuming leadership in various programs for course-content improvement at the precollege level, it soon became apparent to these scientists that undergraduate courses were also in need of similar reforms.

The Problem of Structure.   It will be recalled that one of the main contentions of many scholars who exercised leadership in these new curriculum programs was that new high school courses must be developed to represent the structure of each discipline and the mode of the mature research scholar in each discipline. With this in mind, the Commission on Undergraduate Education of AIBS initially identified the need to develop an ideal core curriculum in biology. However, efforts in this direction at the college level came to be rejected because of a total lack of agreement among biologists as to what should properly constitute the core of knowledge. According to the panel, it became clear that "the product of such an effort might well vary with the composition of the group and hence would carry little weight with the biological community." [72]

Thus it was far easier for scientists to join together in developing new courses and to effect the adoption of these courses in the schools than to bring about similar reforms among their own colleagues in the universities. Where the schools yielded quite readily to the weight of scientific authority and the pressures of the times, it was quite another matter for college professors to agree on the proper authority for course-content improvement.

Consequently, the panel decided to devote its efforts to compiling and analyzing existing core programs at a variety of institutions that were noted for their efforts in developing the content and organization of their biology curricula and that would be likely to receive favorable consideration by the university community. The panel proceeded to make an in-depth analysis of the content of the curricula at the selected universities. This was done by attempting to identify every item, concept, or body of information which was given at least five minutes of treatment by professors in their college classes. Interviews were conducted and various instructional materials, including the lecture notes of professors and students, reading assignments, laboratory exercises, and various other descriptive data were collected.

---

[72] Commission on Undergraduate Education in the Biological Sciences, *Content of Core Curricula in Biology* (Washington, D.C.: The Commission, 1967), p. 1.

Lack of Agreement. The findings revealed that only 7 per cent of the information items were shared in common among the institutions studied. The panel considered this to be surprisingly small and the question was raised as to whether "the multiplicity of judgments reflect uncertainty and difference of opinion concerning the central concepts and factual foundation of biology." [73] The panel concluded that "there is no short-cut to curriculum revision, nor is there a single ideal curriculum." [74]

These findings once again would seem to seriously challenge those who maintain that there exists a singular and unified structure upon which basic studies in a discipline are to be organized. The problem is further compounded for the high school where student interests, capabilities, and achievement levels are infinitely more diverse than at the college level.

THE NEW HIGH SCHOOL CHEMISTRY

The development of new courses in high school chemistry has closely paralleled the work of PSSC and BSCS, both in general rationale and in the use of a task force for creating and disseminating new materials. The two leading projects are the Chemical Education Material Study (CHEM Study) and the Chemical Bond Approach Project (CBA). CHEM Study grew out of a committee of the American Chemical Society, and in 1960, Glenn Seaborg, then Chancellor of the University of California at Berkeley, used his influence in securing an NSF grant for the purpose of organizing a group to develop a new high school chemistry course. The project has been located on the Berkeley campus since 1963. The Chemical Bond Approach Project, also supported by NSF, was initiated in 1957 at a meeting of chemistry professors and high school teachers at Reed College and subsequently was headquartered at Earlham College. Both CBA and CHEM Study are regarded as products of the "dissatisfaction with out-of-date curricula . . . which reached a crescendo of self-criticism after the launching of Sputnik I." [75]

Rationale and Objectives

As in the case of PSSC and BSCS, the leaders of CHEM Study and CBA expressed dissatisfaction with conventional courses as (1) not being in tune with modern developments on the frontiers of research, (2) presenting the subject matter in a didactic manner through which knowledge is treated as a compendium of information, (3) failing to convey to the learner the style of the scholar in discovering new knowledge through

---

[73] *Ibid.,* p. 26.

[74] *Ibid.,* p. 28.

[75] J. S. F. Pode, "CBA and CHEM Study: An Appreciation," *Journal of Chemical Education,* Vol. 43 (February, 1966), p. 98.

scientific inquiry, (4) placing excessive emphasis on rote learning instead of understanding, (5) dealing with too many practical applications of chemistry that are not of real concern to research scholars, and (6) lacking the unifying themes and principles that are the basis of organizing knowledge and discovering new knowledge in a discipline.

The major claims for the CHEM Study course are presented in the foreword of the first edition of the student's textbook:

> A clear and valid picture of the steps by which scientists proceed is carefully presented and repeatedly used. Observations and measurements lead to the development of unifying principles and then these principles are used to interrelated diverse phenomena. Heavy reliance is placed upon laboratory work so that chemical principles can be drawn directly from student experience. Not only does this give a correct and nonauthoritarian view of the origin of chemical principles, but it gives maximum opportunity for discovery, the most exciting part of scientific activity. . . .
>
> There are a number of differences from more traditional courses. The most obvious are, of course, the shift of emphasis from descriptive chemistry toward chemical principles to represent properly the change of chemistry over the last two decades. . . . Less obvious but perhaps more important is the systematic development of the relationship between experiment and theory.[76]

Some of the members of the CHEM Study project have produced material that they describe as "first-generation descendants" of CHEM Study.[77] This material is taken directly from the original CHEM Study textbook and laboratory manual and follows virtually the same principles, objectives, and pattern of organization.

Although the Chemical Bond Approach Project claims to follow the theme of the chemical bond that holds atoms together, and although CBA differs in other points of emphasis of treatment from the CHEM Study course, the two programs are very closely related in their rationales and objectives, as illustrated in this early description of the CBA course:

> The laboratory program stresses investigation as opposed to mere demonstration of facts already known. Instead of concentrating on the body of chemical knowledge built up through the ages, the course stresses the ways in which chemists arrive at such knowledge through scientific inquiry. To put it another way, the project emphasizes inquiry as well as the results of inquiry, methodology as well as recorded discovery.
>
> An outstanding feature of the new course is its emphasis on observa-

---

[76] George C. Pimentel (ed.), *Chemistry: An Experimental Science* (San Francisco: W. H. Freeman and Company, 1963), pp. vii–viii.

[77] Paul R. O'Connor and others, *Chemistry: Experiments and Principles* (Indianapolis: Raytheon Education Company, 1968).

tion and experimentation, on having the student see and do things for himself. . . .

All in all, the new curriculum attempts to present to students a bold and imaginative approach to the study of chemistry, one which brings them to the very frontiers of chemical knowledge.[78]

While both courses share the same rationale and objectives in stressing inquiry, in seeking to develop the relations between theory and experiment, and in attempting to base the material on the principles underlying modern chemistry, the CBA course is considered more advanced and sophisticated, giving greater emphasis to conceptual models and quantitative treatments. These differences illustrate how scholars in a discipline, although sharing the same rationale and objectives, will produce significantly different course materials even for the same group of students.

Systems Approach

Like their PSSC and BSCS counterparts, the two chemistry projects have organized a task force of chemistry professors, science educators, curriculum supervisors, and teachers in developing the new courses. However, the "descendant" textbooks are produced by small groups of collaborators, as is often the case in the preparation of conventional texts.

Both CHEM Study and CBA have developed teachers' manuals and series of tests in addition to the textbooks. CHEM Study also has produced a number of motion pictures to provide demonstrations that are too difficult to conduct under ordinary classroom conditions. Although these films are not as open-ended and inquiry-oriented as the PSSC and BSCS motion pictures, they are integral to the course and, together with the textbook and tests, can be said to represent a systems approach to course development.

ASSESSMENT: RESEARCH, OPINIONS, AND PROBLEMS

Evaluation of Achievement

Need for Controlled Research and Longitudinal Studies. Thus far the marked advantages claimed for the new chemistry courses have not been substantiated in controlled research. The new projects have avoided such evaluation on the grounds that "no external criterion exists with which the new course can be usefully compared." [79] This position must

---

[78] Arthur H. Livermore and Frederick L. Ferris, Jr., "The Chemical Bond Approach Course in the Classroom," *Science*, Vol. 138 (December 7, 1962), p. 1078.

[79] *Ibid.,* p. 1079.

be regarded as untenable in view of the claims made for the new courses and in view of the opportunities to conduct longitudinal studies on college achievement and career choices. Does a higher proportion of these students elect to take chemistry courses in college than of students of comparable ability who have completed a conventional high school chemistry course? Do more of the "new chemistry" students elect to major in chemistry when they get to college? Although one of the objectives of the new chemistry projects is to produce more chemistry students, as well as to improve chemical education generally, the proportions of students taking high school chemistry and majoring in chemistry in college have failed to increase. The proportion of male National Merit finalists choosing chemistry as their major field amounted to only 6.6 per cent in 1967 as compared with a peak of 8.4 per cent in 1959. Among the female finalists, only 4.6 per cent chose chemistry in 1967 as compared with 9.7 per cent in 1958.[80] While these data probably reflect factors unrelated to the new courses, the proportion of students from these courses who go on to major in chemistry in college has not been significantly greater than that of others of comparable ability who had taken conventional high school chemistry courses.[81]

On the College Entrance Examination Board's Chemistry Achievement Test, which is composed of items representing the new chemistry as well as the conventional subject matter, CBA students obtain somewhat lower scores than those in conventional chemistry courses. Only on the CBA-devised achievement tests do the CBA students produce higher scores than those in conventional classes.[82] These findings closely parallel those of PSSC and BSCS discussed earlier in this chapter.

Pointing to the failure of many able students as chemistry majors in college, a professor of chemistry has contended that our curriculum reform programs in high school have concentrated on improving the courses, equipment, and teachers while the handling of students has been a "violation of the student's right to individual attention and consideration . . . we have asked him to do too much, too fast, too soon, and we have asked him to keep at it too long." [83] This criticism has been discussed widely in scientific circles and illustrates the need for carefully conducted longitudinal studies in evaluating new curricula. Moreover, studies of teaching styles and attitude changes of students should shed

---

[80] Donivan J. Watley and Robert C. Nichols, *op. cit.*

[81] Frank X. Sutman, "What Should We Expect from High School Chemistry?" *Science Education*, Vol. 49 (April, 1965), pp. 292–293.

[82] John I. Goodlad, *The Changing School Curriculum* (New York: The Fund for the Advancement of Education, August, 1966), p. 45.

[83] L. Carroll King in "High Student Failure Rate Serious Problem," *Chemical and Engineering News, op. cit.*

considerable light on the problems of effectively implementing the new courses.

Unfortunately, the CHEM Study project has taken a position toward evaluation similar to that of PSSC and CBA.

> Inevitably the question arises, "Is this course better than (or, as good as) the traditional one?" An answer is not readily found in comparative tests. A CHEM Study student might be handicapped in a test that has little emphasis upon principles, that is heavily laden with descriptive "recall questions," or that uses obsolete terminology. Conversely, a test designed specifically for the modern CHEM Study course content would surely prejudice against a student with a traditional preparation. The issue cannot be completely resolved "objectively" because value judgments are ultimately involved. Whether CHEM Study goals are valid and the approach is reasonable must be decided with due consideration to the reported experience of teachers and to the credentials of those who developed the materials.[84]

However convincing the above argument may appear to be, the line of reasoning followed precludes any controlled experimentation for purposes of evaluating the sweeping claims made for this course over conventional courses. We are simply asked to accept these purported advantages by word of testimonials and authority—a process more characteristic of theology than of science. Such acts of faith are likely to produce an accepted dogma instead of scientific curriculum development.

Without controlled research it is not possible to evaluate the sweeping claims made by the proponents of a new course, such as "it sharply stimulates the development of more powerful styles of inquiry." [85] Moreover, if it should not be possible to produce adequate criterion measures of achievement in the new courses (although a number of educators and groups, including the College Entrance Examination Board, believe that such tests are possible), many opportunities exist for studies in problem solving, critical thinking, attitude changes, college achievement, and career choices. Moreover, since the CHEM Study and CBA projects share the same rationale and objectives, comparative studies between the two would appear to be of some value. Of course, controlled experimentation can yield embarrassing results and, moreover, unfavorable results can lead to abandonment of the project by the funding agency (NSF) and to a fatal decline in adoptions. Such political considerations may account, to some extent at least, for the propensity of the proponents of such projects to prefer testimonials and authority to controlled comparative research.

---

84 Pimentel and others, *op. cit.*, p. viii.
85 Finlay, *The School Review, op. cit.*, p. 76.

Suitability for Students of Varied Abilities.   In attempting to ascertain the suitability of the CBA course for high school students who take chemistry, CBA has administered the School and College Ability Test (SCAT) of the College Entrance Examination Board to various groups of CBA students and has compared the scores with those obtained by these students on the CBA achievement tests. The very low correlations obtained between the two sets of tests have led the CBA staff to conclude that the data "reflect primarily the unusually high performance of a fair proportion of the students who have low ability." [86] This conclusion has been emphasized repeatedly by CBA.

> Data from the evaluation studies indicate that this course is appropriate for high school and appropriate for a student group with a broad spectrum of abilities. . . . The evidence is clear that, even though modern theories of chemistry are used throughout to explain observed chemical phenomena, the course *can* be effectively communicated to students of a wide range of scholastic abilities.[87]

From similar data, CHEM Study has reached the same conclusion that "a surprising number of supposedly less able students seem to do well in the course . . . comparisons between standard aptitude measurements and performance in the course do seem to show a rather low correlation coefficient. . . ." [88]

It will be recalled that similar claims from similar data are made for the PSSC physics course, as discussed earlier in this chapter. Again, the failure of ability tests to predict achievement in a given course with any high degree of precision is no evidence that the course is suitable for students of lower aptitude. The test may simply lack validity for predicting such achievement. A more valid approach would be that of comparing students of varied achievement levels in high school science and academic mathematics taken in previous years with their achievement as measured on the CBA and CHEM Study tests. In other words, if we are interested in determining the suitability of a given course for a wide spectrum of students, the students' records of previously demonstrated achievement in related subjects may prove a more suitable basis for comparison than a single standardized aptitude test.

The relationship between scores on single aptitude tests and subsequent achievement can be expected to be low. Goslin has observed that "if test scores alone are used to predict college grades, about the highest

[86] Lawrence E. Strong, "Chemistry as a Science in High School," *The School Review*, Vol. 70 (Spring, 1962), p. 50.

[87] Livermore and Ferris, *op. cit.*, p. 1080.

[88] J. A. Campbell, "CHEM Study—An Approach to Chemistry Based on Experiments," Chapter 6 in *New Curricula*, Robert W. Heath (ed.), *op. cit.*, p. 91.

correlation on the average that can be hoped for is .50, which makes possible prediction only about 25 per cent better than chance." [89] Moreover, achievement is not merely a product of aptitude alone, although aptitude surely is an essential ingredient. Attitudes and interests, or motivation, are key factors in academic performance.

Other Evaluations

Both CHEM Study and CBA have received highly favorable reviews in the journals. A professor of chemistry at a college of science and technology in England has observed that the texts for these courses reveal chemistry "as a fascinating exploration . . . rather than the offering of a corpus of unchangeable facts and rigid interpretation for assimilation by passive students." [90] However, the reviewer observed that CBA represents a far more advanced and sophisticated course, giving the impression that it is a revision course for experienced teachers, while CHEM Study appears to be more of a beginner's course.

Another British professor opined that both courses fulfill the spirit of their aims and represent "a breakthrough in science education." [91] Nevertheless, he criticized both courses for introducing ideas without adequate discussion, and observed that because chemistry is not a logical subject, the logical emphasis of CBA can lead to difficulties. He also criticized the classroom demonstrations in the teachers' guides of both courses, and the CHEM Study films for presenting data in violation of the spirit of inquiry. One of the most serious criticisms offered, however, was directed at the neglect of the applied and utilitarian aspects of the subject.

> By concentrating exclusively on the activities and mental processes of the academic chemist, the applications of chemistry in everyday affairs necessarily occupy a small proportion of both courses. . . .
> . . . The inevitable implication that chemistry is an exclusively academic pursuit must be avoided at all costs. . . . I should be extremely unhappy to see the applied industrial aspects of the subject drop out of the school curriculum altogether.[92]

An American high school teacher of the subject also laments the inadequate emphasis given to the applied and "everyday life" treatment of the subject in CBA and contends that the course is too difficult for high school students.

---

[89] David A. Goslin, *The Search for Ability: Standardized Testing in Social Perspective* (New York: John Wiley & Sons, Inc., 1966), p. 158.

[90] P. G. Ashmore, "On Teaching High School Chemistry," *Science,* Vol. 148 (June 4, 1965), p. 1312.

[91] Pode, *op. cit.,* p. 98.

[92] *Ibid.,* p. 102.

Principles (i.e., theoretical concepts) are stressed in class. Little, if any, attention is paid to the fact that chemicals and their applications are all around us. . . . That is all *condemned* as "descriptive." The student is exposed mainly to what a previous generation learned in physical chemistry in the junior or senior year of college.

. . . The problems at the end of each chapter are of fantastic difficulty, sufficiently so as to baffle almost all students. The teacher gets a manual so that he can do the problems.[93]

Social Applications of a Discipline

It will be recalled that similar criticisms have been voiced concerning the PSSC course and, as a result, alternative courses emphasizing the utilitarian aspects of the subject are being developed. On the other hand, many of the academic purists have argued that the applied material gets in the way of the theory and principles upon which the discipline is based. Whether there is truly an antithesis between the theoretical and applied aspects of a discipline may be more of a philosophic position than a function of learning outcomes related to general education and career choices of high school students. Adolescents are interested in the applied aspects and social implications of the subjects they study. Those who would regard such treatment as irrelevant to the structure of a discipline per se are ignoring certain affective considerations that can be of inestimable consequence in the education of adolescents as citizens as well as in their choice of scientific careers. The way must be kept open for alternative approaches to course development in the high school.

SCIENCE AT THE ELEMENTARY LEVEL

Although a number of the elementary science projects have been formulated on the assumption that the child can learn to engage in scientific inquiry in a manner not unlike that of the mature scientists, there are some significant differences in the approaches taken by these projects in organizing subject matter as compared with the secondary school projects. Where the latter have produced highly structured and complete courses that are discipline-centered, some of the leading elementary projects allow for considerably greater flexibility in the teacher's selection and utilization of materials.

Project Developments

The Elementary Science Study, a project of the Education Development ment Center, has developed a wide variety of self-contained units which

---

[93] Frederick Cornell, "CBA Is Not the Answer," *High Points,* Vol. 48 (March, 1966), pp. 60–62.

can be used in different sequences and combinations for grades K through 8 at the discretion of the individual teacher and school. Each unit is designed to have children learn about a given phenomenon or series of phenomena through direct observation and manipulation of materials. Some of the titles of the units are "Animal Activity," "Bones," "Changes," "Colored Solutions," "Gases and Airs," "Growing Seeds," "Pond Water," "Light and Shadows," and "Pendulums." The Elementary Science Study has avoided the development of a prescribed curriculum in science. As implied in the wide variety of topics treated in the different units, the Elementary Science Study has engaged specialists from the several scientific disciplines and engineering to design the materials. Initiated in 1960 through grants from NSF and the Sloan Foundation, the study has made its units commercially available since 1967. As in other elementary science projects, a chief problem has been in preparing teachers to make effective use of the materials.

In contrast to the Elementary Science Study, the Science Curriculum Improvement Study is a systematic sequence of instructional units for grades K through 6 which is based upon a hierarchy of conceptual learnings. The subject matter of the units is organized sequentially so as to lead toward higher levels of abstract thinking. The focus is on the life sciences in the primary grades and physical science in the upper grades. Emphasis is given to scientific attitudes and procedures in the various pupil activities. This project was organized at the University of California (Berkeley) in 1959 through an NSF grant. Instructional materials developed by the project have been available commercially for several years.

Yet another project which is designed as a systematic course of study in science for grades K through 6 is Science—A Process Approach. This project, organized in 1963 through the American Association for the Advancement of Science, also has received funds from NSF. Science—A Process Approach is designed to develop the ability of children to employ scientific processes—observing, classifying, measuring, interpreting data, controlling variables, formulating hypotheses, and experimenting. In this sense, the objectives are no different from those of the high school science projects. However, the subject matter and activities in this project are drawn from various scientific disciplines and an attempt is made to develop some degree of relationship among these disciplines.

Research and Evaluation Needed

Although most of the elementary science projects claim to be built on the premise that children can and should learn to appreciate and make use of scientific processes, those responsible for developing these projects have tended to avoid any systematic evaluation through controlled research concerning the validity of their assumptions and the effectiveness of their approaches. Instead, they have been content to use trial and demonstration approaches in testing and promoting the acceptance of the materials. As discussed earlier, there is a critical need to assess the degree to which the new approaches actually enable children to develop higher cognitive styles, such as hypothetical thinking, as claimed by the designers of these curriculum packages.

SUMMARY

The impact of the nuclear age, the cold war, and Sputnik catalyzed an unprecedented number of federally supported projects for curriculum reform in the sciences. The key agents in redesigning the science curriculum at both the elementary and secondary levels are university scholars representing the various scientific disciplines.

Curriculum reform in the sciences has followed Bruner's premise that "intellectual activity anywhere is the same." Thus the mature scholar at the frontier of his discipline and the schoolboy investigating a particular problem are engaged in the process of inquiry-discovery. Because this principle is presumed valid at every age and grade level, the major curriculum projects have attempted to accelerate teaching and learning by introducing more advanced subject matter at earlier levels of schooling. Moreover, at the secondary level, each discipline is to be regarded as a structure through which problems are formulated, investigated, and solved, and through which concepts, generalizations, and principles are discovered, utilized, and modified in a never-ending process.

As discussed in Chapter 1, the validity of inquiry-discovery as a pervading theme of the new curriculum projects remains in question despite the sweeping claims made for this approach. Just as one can learn to appreciate and understand good music or literature without being able to create good music or literature, one can learn to appreciate and understand science without being a discoverer of scientific principles or phenomena. This does not imply that inquiry-discovery is not a sound pedagogical process in certain learning situations. But to use inquiry-discovery as a pervading theme in curriculum reconstruction on the assumption that the schoolboy is to be regarded as a miniature model of the mature scholar may prove faulty and disappointing for all concerned. Another problem is that the implications of Piaget's views on intellectual development have not been treated adequately in connection with the new science projects, particularly those designed for children in the elementary grades and young adolescents in grades 7 and 8.

Turning to yet another issue, most of the major high school science projects have been centered on the discrete subject fields. Where the Physical Science Study Committee (PSSC), for example, originally sought to develop a two-year high school course integrating physics and chemistry, what finally emerged was a one-year course in PSSC physics. Separate chemistry courses were produced under the auspices of other curriculum projects. The Biological Sciences Curriculum Study (BSCS) chose the route of developing three versions of high school biology. Although modern biology relies heavily on certain fundamental concepts in chemistry and physics, the traditional placement and function of biology as a tenth-grade subject for general education precluded the possibility of building the biology course in close articulation with the chemistry and physics courses offered in high school.

A growing number of educators and scientists have expressed concern over the tendency for certain curriculum projects, particularly PSSC and the various new mathematics courses, to sacrifice interdisciplinarity and application for the sake of purity. Despite the fact that the major curriculum projects grew out of the cold war era and were intended to attract more of our able students to scientific careers, during the past decade the enrollments in high school and college physics have declined appreciably while the enrollment in chemistry has failed to increase. Engineering enrollments in the universities have also declined. Some scientists have described the situation as a revulsion against science by young people, who see the physical sciences as contributing to the problems of man. Other observers have contended that the new high school courses in physical science reflect the esoteric and puristic research interests of university scientists who are not concerned with immediate applications of knowledge, whereas adolescents are interested in applied and interrelated knowledge. As a result, new physical science courses recently developed, such as the Engineering Concepts Curriculum Project and Harvard Project Physics, are based upon the world as man has shaped it. It is hoped that these courses will have greater relevance for the adolescent who is concerned with the influences of science and technology and the resultant moral issues and value judgments that confront modern society. The trend toward pluralism in developing new courses in science also reflects doubt that there exists a singular, omnipresent "structure of a discipline." Different scholars in the same discipline working independently on curriculum development have been producing courses that are significantly different in content and process.

Most of the claims made for the new science courses have been in the form of testimonials rather than evidence from controlled research. Although those responsible for developing the new courses initially set out to prove the superiority of the new material over conventional course work, most of the research has failed to reveal a significant improvement in learning outcomes where conventional achievement measures are employed. Moreover, the performance in college courses in science is not markedly superior for those students who are products of the new science courses in high school. Only on special achievement tests designed specifically for the new courses does one find significantly higher scores for students in these courses over youngsters in conventional courses. However, the reverse advantage would probably accrue to students in a conventional course taking an examination specifically designed for that course.

While it can be argued that controlled experimentation comparing the learning outcomes in the new courses with those from traditional courses is improper because the two approaches are so completely different, many of the difficulties appear to stem from inadequacies in experimental design and the use of improper criterion measures. Under existing circumstances, the developers of the new courses have been charged with evaluating the effects of their own efforts. As defenders and proponents of their own works, they have tended to turn away from controlled experimentation whenever their claims have not been substantiated. Such conditions make it less likely that significant improvements will be stimulated in existing projects and, consequently, new projects with different rationales and approaches must continually be created. Unfortunately, only in rare instances has the spirit of science pervaded the evaluation efforts in the science curriculum reform movement.

PROBLEMS FOR STUDY AND DISCUSSION

1. Most of the major curriculum reform projects in science are supported by NSF and are funded to provide for their own evaluation. What are some pitfalls of such an arrangement as compared with evaluation through independent agencies?

2. It has been observed that "scientists do not use the scientific method outside of science." [Robert M. Hutchins, "Science, Scientists, and Politics," *The Journal of General Education,* Vol. 16 (October, 1964), p. 201.] Do you believe that this statement is a valid criticism of the ways in which the curriculum reform projects in science have been researched, particularly in view of the claims made for these projects? Why?

3. A scientist maintains that "the professional purists, representing the spirit of the fragmented, research-oriented university, took over the curriculum reforms, and by their diligence and aggressiveness, created puristic monsters." [Alvin M. Weinberg, *Reflections on Big Science* (Cambridge, Mass.: The M.I.T. Press, 1967), p. 154.] From what you know about the major curriculum reform projects, would you be inclined to agree or disagree with this allegation? Why?

4. The quotation in problem 3 above relates to the classical dilemmas in curriculum making between *theory* and *application,* and between

specialism and *interdisciplinarity*. Do you believe that the resolution of these dilemmas is more urgent in the secondary school curriculum than in the college curriculum? Why or why not?

5. During the cold war period of the 1950's, the schools were blamed for our nation's failure to maintain scientific and technological superiority over the Soviets. Yet, despite the various federally funded programs enlisting university scientists in reforming the high school curriculum, the proportion of students taking high school physics and college physics and engineering declined during the 1960's. At the 1968 meeting of the American Physical Society, the situation was attributed to a "revulsion against science by the whole society, but especially among young people." Some scientists and educators attributed the problem to excessive educational pressures. Others pointed to the emphasis in the PSSC course on topics that are primarily of interest to research physicists, while neglecting the interests of adolescents who are more concerned with the applications and uses of knowledge.

   Do you believe that these enrollment "problems" of the 1960's could have been anticipated by the curriculum reformers? Why or why not? To what extent, if any, should adolescent interests serve as a determining factor in curriculum construction? Why?

6. The increasing number of national curriculum projects in science has created new problems for school administrators, curriculum coordinators, supervisors, and teachers in selecting the best courses for their schools. What criteria and procedures would you recommend for determining which courses to adopt? What criteria and procedures would you use for ascertaining the success of a newly adopted course?

7. Low correlations between student scores on standardized aptitude tests and their scores on achievement tests in new science courses have led some educators to the conclusion that these findings give evidence that the new courses are appropriate for students of a wide range of scholastic abilities. Why is this conclusion of doubtful validity?

8. Bruner maintains that "the curriculum of a subject should be determined by the most fundamental understanding that can be achieved of the underlying principles that give structure to that subject." [Jerome S. Bruner, *The Process of Education* (Cambridge, Mass.: Harvard University Press, 1960), p. 31.] Despite the general acceptance of this premise in the curriculum reform movement at the secondary level, a study by a commission of the American Institute of Biological Sciences revealed that college professors of biology do not agree on the content and organization of an "ideal" core course

in college biology representing the central concepts and foundations of the field.

In view of this disagreement, how do you account for the wide acceptance of Bruner's premise with regard to curriculum reform in our secondary schools?

9. It has been observed that it is far easier for scientists to join together in developing new courses and to effect the adoption of these courses in the schools than to bring about similar reforms among their own colleagues in the universities. How do you account for this?

SELECTED REFERENCES

American Association for the Advancement of Science. *The New School Science.* Washington, D.C.: The Association, 1965.

Ausubel, David P. *Educational Psychology: A Cognitive View.* New York: Holt, Rinehart and Winston, Inc., 1968. Ch. 14.

Bruner, Jerome S. *The Process of Education.* Cambridge, Mass.: Harvard University Press, 1960.

———. *Toward a Theory of Instruction.* Cambridge, Mass.: Harvard University Press, 1966.

Commission on Undergraduate Education in the Biological Sciences. *Content of Core Curricula in Biology.* Washington, D.C.: The Commission, 1967.

Dewey, John. *How We Think.* Boston: D. C. Heath & Company, 1910, 1933.

Elam, Stanley (ed.). *Education and the Structure of Knowledge.* Chicago: Rand McNally & Company, 1964. Chs. 1, 5.

Flavell, John H. *The Developmental Psychology of Jean Piaget.* Princeton, N.J.: D. Van Nostrand Company, 1963.

Ford, G. W., and Lawrence Pugno (eds.). *The Structure of Knowledge and the Curriculum.* Chicago: Rand McNally & Company, 1964.

Goodlad, John I. *The Changing School Curriculum.* New York: The Fund for the Advancement of Education, 1966.

Grobman, Arnold. *The Changing Classroom: The Role of the Biological Sciences Curriculum Study.* New York: Doubleday & Company, Inc., 1969.

Grobman, Hulda. *Evaluation Activities of Curriculum Project.* Chicago: Rand McNally & Company, 1968.

Heath, Robert W. (ed.). *New Curricula.* New York: Harper & Row, Publishers, 1964. Chs. 5, 6, 7, 8, 12, 13.

Johnson, Lloyd K., Ellsworth S. Osbourn, and Paul E. Blackwood. *Research in the Teaching of Science.* Washington, D.C.: Office of Education, U.S. Department of Health, Education, and Welfare, 1965.

Lockard, J. David. *Sixth Report of the International Clearinghouse on Science and Mathematics Curricular Developments.* College Park, Md.: University of Maryland, 1968.

Martin, W. T., and Dan C. Pinck (eds.). *Curriculum Improvement and Innovation: A Partnership of Students, School Teachers, and Research Scholars.* Cambridge, Mass.: Robert Bentley, Inc., 1966.

National Society for the Study of Education. *Rethinking Science Education,* Part I, Fifty-ninth Yearbook. Chicago: The University of Chicago Press, 1960.

Piaget, Jean, and B. Inhelder. *The Growth of Logical Thinking from Childhood to Adolescence.* New York: Basic Books, 1958.

Rickover, H. G. *American Education—A National Failure.* New York: E. P. Dutton & Co., Inc., 1963.

Rosenbloom, Paul C., and Paul C. Hillestad. *Modern Viewpoints in the Curriculum.* New York: McGraw-Hill Book Company, Inc., 1964. Chs. 4, 5, 11, 12.

Schwab, Joseph J., and Paul F. Brandwein. *The Teaching of Science.* Cambridge, Mass.: Harvard University Press, 1966.

Tyler, Ralph W., Robert M. Gagné, and Michael Scriven. *Perspectives of Curriculum Evaluation.* Chicago: Rand McNally & Company, 1967.

Watson, Fletcher G. "Research on Teaching Science," Chapter 20 in *Handbook of Research on Teaching,* N. L. Gage (ed.). Chicago: Rand McNally & Company, 1963.

Weinberg, Alvin M. *Reflections on Big Science.* Cambridge, Mass.: The M.I.T. Press, 1967.

Chapter 4

Curriculum Change in Mathematics

Regarded as essential to scientific and technological progress, mathematics was given highest priority along with science in the curriculum reform movement of the cold war era. These demands, coupled with the continued development of mathematical theory and the emphasis on mathematics as a discipline unto itself, have created a difficult issue in curriculum reform. A schism has developed between those scholars who regard mathematics as a discipline unto itself and those who find its greatest meaning in its applications to the physical world.

No other field has been subjected to greater change and controversy. The resolution of the issue concerning the "pure" and "applied" aspects of mathematics in the curriculum reform movement will necessitate considerable compromise in the coming years. In this chapter this issue is explored in the light of developments in some of the leading projects in secondary school mathematics.

RATIONALE AND OBJECTIVES OF LEADING PROGRAMS

University of Illinois Committee on School Mathematics (UICSM)

One of the first projects in the "new wave" of curriculum reform in mathematics began with the establishment of the University of Illinois Committee on School Mathematics (UICSM) in 1952. The group was composed of faculty from the colleges of education, engineering, and arts and sciences with the aim of exploring the content and teaching of mathematics in grades 9 through 12. Initially supported by the University of Illinois and the Carnegie Corporation, UICSM has received substantial funds from the U.S. Office of Education and NSF.

The UICSM program is described by its director as "an attempt to determine what the teacher must do to bring to the mind of the adolescent some of the ideas and modes of thinking which are basic in the work of the contemporary mathematician." [1] The rationale of formulating the curriculum for the child and adolescent according to the interests and styles of thinking of the mature scholar pervaded the curriculum reform movement of the 1960's—with science and mathematics leading the way.

In its efforts to bring secondary school mathematics in tune with modern concepts and processes in the discipline, the UICSM program embraced two major premises or themes: discovery and precision in language. The premise behind the discovery principle is that "the student will come to understand mathematics if he plays an active part in developing mathematical ideas and procedures . . . we must design both exposition and exercises in such a way that the student will discover principles and rules." [2] Through the development of precision in language when dealing with mathematical entities and their relationships, it is anticipated that the student will sharpen his awareness and understanding of the discipline and will be able to give clear expression to his discoveries. Thus the student should be able to discover and state generalizations from the use of precise language in dealing with various modern concepts and operations.

CEEB Commission on Mathematics

Established in 1955 by the College Entrance Examination Board (CEEB) through a grant from the Carnegie Corporation, the Commission on Mathematics studied the mathematics curriculum in grades 9 through 12 and formulated a series of recommendations. [3] While the commission was not designed to function along the lines of a typical project in course-content improvement, it nevertheless did produce some new materials —most notably a book on probability and statistics for the twelfth grade.

Although the CEEB was originally established with the primary objective of operating as an independent agency for college admissions testing, the function of constructing examinations not only serves to reflect curriculum content and practices, but also operates as a force for curriculum change. Among the major recommendations in the commission's proposals, which appeared in 1959, was the elimination of trigonometry as a separate course and of solid geometry as a full semester of work. The aim was to remove the traditional emphasis on useless calculations and

---

[1] Max Beberman, "An Emerging Program of Secondary School Mathematics" in *New Curricula,* Robert W. Heath (ed.) (New York: Harper & Row, Publishers, 1964), p. 34.

[2] *Ibid.,* p. 23.

[3] Commission on Mathematics, *Program for College Preparatory Mathematics* (Princeton, N.J.: College Entrance Examination Board, 1959).

manipulations in algebra, solid geometry, and trigonometry and to relate these areas instead to modern developments in the discipline of mathematics.

School Mathematics Study Group (SMSG)

The School Mathematics Study Group was organized as a national project in 1958 with the purpose of involving research mathematicians, mathematics educators, supervisors, and teachers in curriculum improvement for all levels of schooling (K–12). From its inception SMSG has been supported by the National Science Foundation, which has contributed several million dollars to the project. No other curriculum project in mathematics has enjoyed comparable financial support. It is significant that the establishment of SMSG grew out of a conference in 1958 in which a group of mathematicians were briefed on the operations of the Physical Sciences Study Committee under the direction of Jerrold Zacharias of MIT. Originally located at Yale, SMSG was moved to the School of Education at Stanford in 1960. Although the shortage of skilled mathematicians, which became increasingly apparent during the cold war and Sputnik era, was an important factor in the funding of SMSG by NSF, the work of SMSG has not been confined to gifted students.

SMSG has been engaged in developing courses, teaching materials, and instructional methods that are intended to provide students with understandings and competencies consonant with the basic concepts and structure of mathematics. Through a task-force form of organization, a considerable number of sample textbooks have been developed and tried out in a wide variety of classroom situations in grades K through 12. In addition to these textbooks, SMSG has produced texts for senior-level courses in analytic geometry, calculus, and computer mathematics. Besides the textbooks, a variety of supplementary material has been developed by SMSG: a series of expository monographs by outstanding mathematicians, special instructional units (including, for example, lessons on probability for the primary, intermediate, and junior high school grades), teachers' manuals, which contain the solutions to the problems in the students' textbooks along with additional guidelines and commentary on instructional methods, a series of booklets for teacher preparation, and programmed materials for students.

Recognizing the problem of curriculum compartmentalization when the focus is on producing a collection of new courses instead of a truly unified curriculum, and faced with mounting criticisms that its own course work may lean too heavily on what research mathematicians regard as significant while neglecting the utilitarian and general education aspects of mathematics, SMSG has become aware of the need for a fresh approach to curriculum development for the secondary schools:

a second look should be taken at the secondary school program, viewing it as a whole rather than as a collection of six separate courses. The hope was expressed that this project would not be just a revision or an integration of material already in the present series, but a bold, new approach that would attempt to further break down compartmentalization, to develop a logical sequence of topics that might lead to a more efficient curriculum, and to include some topics that have arisen as major forces in current mathematical developments. Every attempt would be made to deal realistically with meaningful applications of mathematics while still retaining the opportunity to understand and appreciate the spirit and structure of mathematics. It was agreed that the first part of any new sequence should be devoted to those mathematical ideas which any well-educated citizen should be acquainted with. . . .[4]

SMSG has been regarded as synonymous with the "new mathematics" and has generated considerable criticism and controversy. The nature of this criticism and controversy is discussed later in this chapter.

University of Maryland Mathematics Project (UMMaP)

Established in 1957 with the support of the Carnegie Corporation, the University of Maryland Mathematics Project has developed new courses in grades 7 and 8 through the joint efforts of the university's faculty in mathematics, education, psychology, and engineering, along with school supervisors and teachers. Additional support has been obtained from NSF. An important objective of UMMaP, similar to that of SMSG, is to develop a more effective use of language in communicating the concepts and structure of mathematics. The project also represents an attempt to improve junior high school mathematics in the light of promising developments at the senior high level. UMMaP has sought to relate its course development efforts to learning research.

Although the University of Maryland Mathematics Project represents the joint efforts of several university departments, a committee of the National Council of Teachers of Mathematics found its early materials to be lacking in applications to social problems or social situations.[5] However, the program is under continual revision and, in the light of recent criticisms, it appears likely that modifications will be made.

The Greater Cleveland Mathematics Program (GCMP)

Created in 1959 by the Educational Research Council of Greater Cleveland, the Greater Cleveland Mathematics Program has been engaged in

---

[4] E. G. Begle, "SMSG: The First Decade," *The Mathematics Teacher,* Vol. 61 (March, 1968), p. 242.

[5] National Council of Teachers of Mathematics, *An Analysis of New Mathematics Programs* (Washington, D.C.: The Council, 1963), p. 23.

developing a sequential curiculum in grades K through 12 which attempts to emphasize discovery approaches. The GCMP describes itself as "a concept-oriented modern mathematics program in which the primary emphasis has been placed upon thinking, reasoning, and understanding. . . . The child is continuously encouraged to investigate how and why things happen in mathematics. He is led to make generalizations, to test these generalizations, and to find new applications for them." [6] In developing its curriculum, GCMP has attempted to follow the recommendations of the major national groups in mathematics and mathematics education. The subject matter is organized so that key mathematical concepts and processes reappear in increasing complexity at various grade levels in an effort to follow a spiraling sequence.

A review of the GCMP materials by a committee of the National Council of Teachers of Mathematics found some applications to social problems and situations.[7]

The Madison Project of Syracuse University and Webster College

The Madison Project was organized in 1957 and, since 1961, has been sponsored jointly by Syracuse University and Webster College (Missouri) through funds from NSF and the U.S. Office of Education. The major objective of the project is to enrich and improve the mathematics curriculum in grades 2 through 8 by means of supplementary instructional material with emphasis on discovery methods. The project also has developed a complete ninth-grade course, as well as materials for individualized study in grades 6 through 12. A major objective of the Madison Project is to lead students to the realization that the discipline of mathematics is open-ended. The attempt is made to organize the curriculum into learning sequences, so that "experience without formal instruction" in the early grades forms the basis for formal instruction in the later grades. Thus concepts and operations in mathematics are designed to be repeated in spiraling fashion at increasing levels of complexity as the pupil advances in maturity. In addition to textbook material, a series of tapes and films have been developed for the in-service education of teachers.

In analyzing the early material developed by the Madison Project, a committee of the National Council of Teachers of Mathematics found that there were few social applications and that the material seemed to be "very abstract with little meaning in relation to children's experiences." [8]

[6] *Ibid.*, p. 10.
[7] *Ibid.*, p. 12.
[8] *Ibid.*, p. 19.

EVALUATION OF LEARNING OUTCOMES

Emphasis on Intuition and Discovery

In addition to reconstructing the curriculum to reflect the newer developments in the field of mathematics, the several major curriculum projects seek to develop instructional methods based upon inquiry and discovery. The Brunerian premise that it is easiest and best for the schoolboy to learn a subject by behaving like a research scholar pervades the leading curriculum projects in mathematics. Accordingly, intellectual activity anywhere is taken to be the same. The importance of intuitive thinking for creative work by mature researchers in the disciplines thus takes on great significance even in our elementary and secondary levels of schooling. A research mathematician puts it this way:

> as the student comes to the high school teachers, his mathematical equipment should have two main components—the intuitive component and the knowledge component. These are difficult to separate, particularly since the intuitive component is dependent for its growth on the knowledge component. . . . The old curriculum was designed chiefly for the knowledge component; the student was taught how to perform arithmetic and algebraic operations and how to prove theorems. But little conscious development of mathematical intuition took place. . . . In contrast to this, the new curricula should try to turn teaching of the knowledge component into a process whereby the student's intuition is actually used and developed further in acquiring the new knowledge.
>
> For example, while under the old system the student was *told* the formula for carrying out a process, under the new he should be invited to do a little guessing as to what form the process should take. This guessing and the accompanying experimentation, resulting in a decision as to the final result, develops and strengthens his mathematical intuition. In an embryonic way, this procedure is precisely the same as that pursued by the research mathematician, and in my opinion the teacher who cultivates it is doing creative teaching. And I believe that all concepts should be introduced in this way.[9]

The degree to which the new projects have enhanced intuitive processes is yet to be determined. Moreover, the selection of subject matter for the "knowledge component" and the role of intuition and discovery for the "intuitive component" are matters of considerable controversy. The issues connected with this controversy are not unlike those raised in the preceding chapter regarding the new science curriculum.

---

[9] R. L. Wilder, "The Role of Intuition," *Science,* Vol. 156 (May, 1967), p. 609.

Achievement

Experimentation involving control-group designs reveals that, on standardized achievement tests, students in the new programs fail to make higher scores, or make slightly lower scores, than those in conventional mathematics classes. On the other hand, students in the "new" mathematics classes have obtained somewhat higher scores on tests designed specifically for the projects concerned.[10] Where proponents of the "new" mathematics point out that the standardized tests are biased in favor of conventional mathematics, it should also be emphasized that the tests designed specifically for the projects concerned are clearly biased in favor of those students who are taking the courses created by these projects. These findings are similar to those obtained in evaluating the new science projects, as discussed in the preceding chapter.

Need for Careful, Continuous, Independent Evaluation. While the research findings on achievement tend to support the conclusion that students can study the "new" mathematics without suffering severe losses in competencies where traditional mathematical skills and concepts are concerned, there is little evidence that the new courses effect significant changes in patterns of thinking, in college performance, in attitudes, or in career selections. Yet it is in precisely these aspects that proponents of the new projects have discredited the conventional curriculum. The claims made for the new projects, which have yet to be substantiated through controlled experimentation, have been described as representing "a kind of wonder drug that has suddenly appeared on the mathematics horizon." [11] More careful evaluations are needed, and undoubtedly will be forthcoming, as the reform projects enter their revisionary phases.

One of the universal problems in the project approach to curriculum reform is the tendency to evaluate the total package after it has been produced. This places the project leadership in a position of defending their commitments and acting as proponents of their products, thereby closing off many promising avenues for improvement that might well lead to the attainment of the goals for which the projects were originally created. Undoubtedly, the problem of securing sustained support from funding agencies is a powerful factor in bringing about sweeping claims and unyielding loyalties.

---

[10] See E. G. Begle, *op. cit.;* also Kenneth E. Brown and Theodore L. Abel, *Analysis of Research in the Teaching of Mathematics* (Washington, D.C.: Office of Education, U.S. Department of Health, Education, and Welfare, 1965), pp. 5–6.

[11] Herbert Fremont, "New Mathematics and Old Dilemmas," *The Mathematics Teacher,* Vol. 60 (November, 1967), p. 715.

The National Longitudinal Study of Mathematical Abilities. The growing concern for a more comprehensive evaluation of the "new" mathematics led to the establishment in 1961 of the National Longitudinal Study of School Mathematics (NLSMA). This study was administered by SMSG through NSF funds. It was anticipated that the findings would be valuable in future curriculum development and in providing educators with needed information for better curriculum decision making.

In the fall of 1962, over 110,000 students from 1,500 schools in 40 states were identified for participation in the study, which was designed to investigate pupil achievement over a period of up to five years. Achievement comparisons were to be made between populations using textbook series adjudged to represent "modern" mathematics and "conventional" mathematics. Large student populations at each of three grade levels were to be tested at the beginning and end of each school year, beginning with grades 4, 7, and 10. Tests were devised by the project staff to assess the achievement of the groups using the "modern" and "conventional" curriculum materials according to levels of mathematical computation, comprehension, application, and analysis.

Although the researchers interpreted the findings as pointing to somewhat superior achievement in computation on the part of the groups using "conventional" curriculum materials and an indication of higher levels of comprehension, application, and analysis on the part of the groups using "modern" materials, the variability and overlapping in achievement were so extensive that the NLSMA research staff was forced to conclude that "there are not many clear generalizations that can be made." [12] Some of the groups using "modern" materials performed quite poorly on all measures—from computation to analysis—in comparison with the groups using "conventional" materials. Thus the findings must be interpreted as inconclusive.

NLSMA obtained no data concerning teaching styles and noncognitive outcomes. Proponents of the "new" mathematics cannot be overjoyed by the findings of NLSMA. On the other hand, this study can be valuable in pointing the way to more comprehensive and sophisticated approaches to curriculum evaluation. For the time being at least, the glowing claims made for the "revolution" in school mathematics must be reassessed. This does not call for a return to the "old" mathematics, but requires instead a more balanced and comprehensive approach to curriculum development and evaluation.

In developing new curricula, there is the tendency for many teachers

---

[12] Edward G. Begle and James W. Wilson, "Evaluation of Mathematics Programs," Chapter X in *Mathematics Education,* Sixty-ninth Yearbook of the National Society for the Study of Education, Part I (Chicago: The University of Chicago Press, 1970), p. 402.

to adopt the "knowledge component" of the new project while adhering to conventional instructional methods. Curriculum development is more than the revision of textbooks. More longitudinal or developmental studies are needed to assess not only achievement, but also attitudes, motivation, and other noncognitive outcomes. Whether SMSG is the most appropriate agency for directing such investigations is a matter of question because SMSG represents a particular rationale in an arena of great controversy.

EUROPEAN COMPARISONS

Crisis and Change

Although impetus for modernizing the curriculum in mathematics and science can be traced to the impact of the nuclear age and the cold war, it was Sputnik that triggered new attacks on the schools and catalyzed a rash of federally supported projects for improving instruction in these fields. Leading critics of American education such as Professor Arthur Bestor and Vice Admiral Hyman G. Rickover maintained that European and Soviet schools were far superior to American schools. Bestor attributed the failure of the United States to be first in space to the neglect of our schools in requiring sufficient mathematics and science of all students, and especially of the academically talented. He also maintained that the educational standards of the European nations were far superior to those of the United States.[13] Rickover argued that "some American high school graduates never get beyond quadratic equations, but every graduate of the European science-mathematics secondary school must be familiar with differential and integral calculus, analytical geometry, application of mathematics to physics, and spherical trigonometry." [14] In making such comparisons, however, these critics of American education ignored the fact that in most European countries the overwhelming majority of the students drop out of school by age sixteen, whereas over 86 per cent of the sixteen-year-olds remain enrolled in American high schools.[15]

Nevertheless, the attacks on American education came during a period of unprecedented international rivalry and consequently attracted con-

---

[13] Arthur Bestor, "What Went Wrong with U.S. Schools," *U.S. News & World Report* (January 24, 1958), pp. 68–77.

[14] H. G. Rickover, *Education and Freedom* (New York: E. P. Dutton & Co., Inc., 1959), p. 184.

[15] Despite efforts to universalize secondary education in certain European nations, recent data reveal that the gap has not been closed and the United States continues to remain pre-eminent in the attainment of universal secondary education. See Torsten Husén (ed.), *International Study of Achievement in Mathematics*, Vol. I (New York: John Wiley & Sons, 1967), p. 231.

siderable support among the nation's intelligentsia and political leadership. The special federal support provided for curriculum improvement in mathematics and science through the National Science Foundation and the National Defense Education Act of 1958 was clearly a response to cold war pressures.

THE INTERNATIONAL STUDY OF ACHIEVEMENT IN MATHEMATICS

During the late 1950's, testimony before various congressional hearings by Rickover and others alleged that American students were far behind their European compeers in achievement in mathematics and science. Rickover went so far as to include in his testimony examples of examinations administered in the schools of various European nations.[16]

In the absence of cross-national research on achievement, critics and defenders of American education had to rely on descriptive data in comparative education. The cold war period following World War II was an important factor not only in heightening the interest in comparative education, but in producing national programs for curriculum reform in the United States through federally supported programs. These developments were accompanied by growing demands for the national assessment of educational achievement in the United States, along with cross-national studies of pupil achievement.

Background and Development of the International Study

In 1958 proposals for cross-national studies of educational achievement were submitted to the UNESCO Institute of Education in Hamburg, Germany, by Professor Arthur W. Foshay of Teachers College, Columbia University, and Professor Benjamin S. Bloom of the Graduate Department of Education of the University of Chicago. Between 1959 and 1961 a pilot study was conducted to determine the feasibility of such an undertaking, and in 1960 the Council for the International Evaluation of Educational Achievement (IEA) was formed at the UNESCO Institute for Education to make plans for a full-scale study.

Mathematics was chosen as the first subject area to be studied by IEA for reasons of feasibility and because "most countries represented are at present concerned with improving their scientific and technical education, at the basis of which lies the learning of mathematics." [17] Although

---

16 H. G. Rickover, *American Education—A National Failure* (New York: E. P. Dutton & Co., Inc., 1963), pp. 343–476.

17 Husén, *op. cit.*, p. 33.

the chairman of IEA, Torsten Husén of the University of Stockholm, maintained that the rapidly growing interest in comparative education could only be superficially ascribed to post-Sputnik reactions, he acknowledged the criticisms leveled at American education by Admiral Rickover.[18]

Our federal government was vitally interested in the project, as evidenced by the fact that while each of the twelve participating nations contributed its share of the expenses for data collection within its own boundaries, the U.S. Office of Education not only assumed the costs for the United States but provided the funds for the international financing of the project. The participating nations were Australia, Belgium, England, Finland, France, Israel, Japan, the Netherlands, Scotland, Sweden, the United States, and West Germany.

National Differences. Recognizing that school holding power differs markedly among nations, it was decided that one target population would be all thirteen-year-olds since virtually all of this age group could be expected to be in school regardless of the nation. It is at age fifteen and beyond when serious attrition occurs in the schools of European nations. This point was stressed at the outset by the chairman of the study who observed that where in the United States some 70 per cent of the age group is enrolled in the senior year of secondary schooling, the figure for England is only 12 per cent, in Germany 11 per cent, and in Sweden 23 per cent.[19] The second target group was the population enrolled in full-time schooling in the senior year of secondary school. Between January and June of 1964, tests were administered to 132,775 students in 5,348 schools in the 12 countries. Questionnaires were also completed by the teachers in these schools.

Objectives of Study. Husén stressed repeatedly that the IEA study was not designed to compare countries through a type of "international contest." Instead, it was intended to analyze achievement in relation to school organization, student selection practices, student differentiation or grouping practices, curriculum design, and socioeconomic factors. For example, in the United States a number of critics, notably Admiral Rickover, were advocating that we abandon the comprehensive high school in favor of the dual system of Europe in which the "elite" students would attend separate academic schools. Paradoxically, some European nations, notably England and Sweden, were embarking on school reforms aimed at democratizing their systems by converting to the American type of

---

[18] *Ibid.,* p. 19.
[19] *Ibid.,* p. 28.

comprehensive secondary school. Thus, questions relating to school organization and student selection and differentiation practices were fundamental to the IEA study.

Findings and Controversy

Despite the warnings against interpreting the study's results as a contest among nations, the trail of Sputnik I was still dimming the American skies ten years after its launching. And so, when the IEA findings were released in 1967, the American press promptly made an "international contest" out of the study. A front-page article by Fred M. Hechinger, education editor of *The New York Times,* was captioned "U.S. Ranked Low in Math Teaching." [20] Hechinger, who was born in Germany and attended schools in that country until he came to the United States in 1937 at the age of sixteen, followed this up in the Sunday edition of *The New York Times* with a feature article entitled, "U.S. Gets Low Marks in Math." [21] In the latter article Hechinger declared that "the United States carried off no Olympic medals" and that "the American record is not inspiring." Of the twelve nations in the study, the thirteen-year-olds from Japan obtained the highest mean score and those from Sweden the lowest. Hechinger proceeded to compare the scores of American and Japanese thirteen-year-olds, pointing out that 76 per cent of the Japanese students scored above the 50th percentile as against 43 per cent of the American youngsters. Turning to the scores obtained by students in the senior year of secondary school, Hechinger maintained that "the American record was even worse." Here he observed that where only 2 per cent of the American students obtained scores in the upper tenth, more than 20 per cent of the students of England, Belgium, Japan, and Israel reached this "crucial category." Hechinger went on to label as a "mixture of apology and self-congratulation" the statement by a spokesman for the U.S. Office of Education which maintained that the study showed that the American high school system does not eliminate lower-achieving students and those of lower socioeconomic backgrounds.

However, a careful examination of the actual IEA report reveals that Hechinger chose to ignore much of the data, conclusions, and precautions that appear throughout the two-volume study. For example, Husén cautioned against comparing the achievement of thirteen-year-olds of different nations where the grade placement of mathematics topics varies considerably: "In a dual system with early transfer of the more adept students to the academic secondary school there is a tendency to introduce advanced mathematics topics earlier whereas in countries with a comprehensive system one seeks to introduce them later." [22] Thus, while

---

20 *The New York Times* (March 7, 1967), p. 1.
21 *The New York Times* (March 12, 1967), p. 11E.
22 Husén, *op. cit.,* p. 288.

the test included problems in algebra and geometry, such topics were not ordinarily treated in the eighth-grade curriculum of the American schools.

The Bias of Selectivity and Socioeconomic Status

What about the achievement levels of the secondary school seniors? In discussing the score differences between the Japanese and American students enrolled in academic programs in comprehensive high schools, Torsten Husén, chairman of IEA and editor of the official report, emphasized that "it must be remembered that the Japanese group is highly selected, comprising somewhat less than 1 per cent of the population at this level, as contrasted with 16 per cent in the United States." [23] Moreover, as mentioned earlier, the proportion of students continuing through the senior year of high school (the preuniversity year) is by far highest in the United States and lowest in the European nations where the dual educational system prevails. Thus, while 70 per cent of the age group is enrolled as seniors in American high schools, the proportion surviving at this level is only 8 per cent in Holland, 11 per cent in France, 12 per cent in England and West Germany, and 13 per cent in Belgium.[24]

Socioeconomic Bias. As a result of the remarkably high retentivity of the American educational system, contrasted with the exceedingly low retentivity of the other nations in the study, a strong socioeconomic bias is produced. Consequently, the population of American students in the preuniversity year represents by far the highest proportion of working class families among the nations in the study. And, conversely, the proportion of students whose fathers are engaged in professional or executive occupations is lowest for the American population. These data are presented in Tables 4-1 and 4-2.

Table 4-1 shows these trends for all students in the senior year of secondary school other than those who are studying mathematics as an integral part of their course toward their future university training for careers as mathematicians, physicists, engineers, and related occupations. The data for the latter population are presented in Table 4-2. The trends for both populations are very similar. In Table 4-1 we find that for this group of seniors the representation of students from working class families ranges from 47 per cent in the United States to only 5 per cent in West Germany. In this same population the proportion of students whose fathers are engaged in professional and executive occupations ranges from 56 per cent in West Germany to only 17 per cent in the United States.

---

[23] Husén, Vol. II, *op. cit.*, p. 94.
[24] *Ibid.*, Vol. I, p. 237.

Table 4-1. Relationship of Retentivity and Socioeconomic Background of Secondary School Seniors
(Students Who Are Not Studying Mathematics for Future Specialization As Mathematicians, Physicists, Engineers, etc.)

Nation	Per Cent of Age Group in Preuniversity Year	Father's Occupational Status (Per Cent)	
		Professional-Executive	Working Class
United States	70	17	47
Japan	57	21	14
Sweden	23	28	23
Scotland	18	33	41
Finland	14	23	31
Belgium	13	25	20
England	12	36	18
France	11	20	28
West Germany	11	56	5
Netherlands	8	50	14

Source: *Table constructed from data in Torsten Husén (ed.),* International Study of Achievement in Mathematics, *Vol. I (New York: John Wiley & Sons, 1967), pp. 237, 273.*

Table 4-2. Relationship of Retentivity and Socioeconomic Background of Secondary School Seniors
(Students Who Are Studying Mathematics for Future Specialization As Mathematicians, Physicists, Engineers, etc.)

Nation	Per Cent of Age Group in Preuniversity Year	Father's Occupational Status (Per Cent)	
		Professional-Executive	Working Class
United States	70	20	36
Japan	57	34	11
Sweden	23	29	24
Australia	23	34	27
Scotland	18	29	28
Finland	14	29	21
Belgium	13	17	28
England	12	27	21
France	11	25	20
West Germany	11	53	6
Netherlands	8	36	14

Source: *Table constructed from data in Torsten Husén (ed.),* International Study of Achievement in Mathematics, *Vol. I (New York: John Wiley & Sons, 1967), pp. 237, 272.*

Critical Differences in School Populations. Thus it is revealed that in the comprehensive school system of the United States the student population is representative of that nation's general population, whereas in the dualistic school systems of Europe the enrollment in the senior year of secondary school consists of a high proportion of students from the upper socioeconomic levels. According to Husén, "graduates from the academic secondary school, that is, students eligible for the university, are in most European countries, and especially in those with competitive selection to the secondary academic school, to a large extent a social elite." [25] Obviously, there is a critical difference between the composition of the high school population in the United States and that of European nations.

In observing that the United States far outdistances other nations in the proportion of the age group in school, Husén acknowledged that no other nation comes close to the ethnic heterogeneity of American students. In this connection, he made reference to studies that reveal that within the United States the highest average level of achievement is to be found in certain states of the Midwest where the population is relatively homogeneous both occupationally and ethnically.[26] Nevertheless, IEA did not separate, for purposes of analysis, the sizable number of disadvantaged nonwhite students in the American school population. An additional source of bias serving to lower the achievement levels of the American students in comparison to the other nations in the study is the high rate of population mobility in America, particularly among disadvantaged whites and nonwhites. Again, the IEA study did not provide corrections for the stability of the indigenous populations of the various countries.

Educational Yield

Yet another important finding largely ignored by the American press was that the total yield of relatively high-achieving students is highest for those nations which retain the largest proportion of the age group in school. According to Husén, "If the 'mathematical yield' of this population (preuniversity) can be described as 'how many got how far,' Sweden, the United States, Australia, and Japan have the highest yields." [27]

The Educational Elite. To determine whether the lowering of selection barriers results in a decline in achievement among the very best students, comparisons were made of groups representing the upper 4 per cent of the student populations. The findings reveal that the expansion of educa-

25 *Ibid.*, Vol. II, p. 302.
26 *Ibid.*, p. 230.
27 *Ibid.*, p. 131.

tional opportunity is not accompanied by a lowering of achievement among the most talented students. Moreover, when comparing the nations on this basis, rather than on the mean scores produced by the total school enrollments, significant changes in rankings occur.

> In general, those countries with the least restrictive policies as to who will continue in school show the greatest upward shifts, while those countries with stricter selection policies and practices show the greatest downward shifts in relative position. . . .
>
> The results indicate that the most talented students continue to achieve at a high level, even when as much as 70 per cent of the age group is enrolled in full-time schooling.
>
> The performances of preuniversity students in the Japanese and Swedish systems are two excellent examples . . . and the performance of the students in the United States, while decidedly low for the total sample, compares quite favorably with most other countries when equal proportions of the age groups are compared. Thus, it would seem that a nation need not fear for its most talented students when it contemplates the expansion of educational opportunity at the secondary school level.[28]

Dropouts and Educational Yield.   Because the IEA study was limited to the mathematical achievement of the in-school population of various nations, the failure to include school dropouts raises further the mean scores for those nations having highly selective secondary schools, and thereby gives a misleading picture of the true educational "yield" of these countries. Moreover, those who believe that the United States can improve its educational talent by adopting an elitist system after the dualistic structure of European schools receive no support from the findings of the IEA study.

> The first finding is that 13-year-old students following academic courses in specialized schools attain a higher level and show slightly less variability than do students following similar courses in comprehensive schools. At the preuniversity stage their superiority has vanished, and there is no significant difference between the scores of the two groups. On the other hand, 13-year-old students following general [nonacademic] courses do better in comprehensive schools than do students following similar courses in schools not containing academic pupils.[29]
>
> The opening up of opportunities for preuniversity education for more students and retaining students at school thus produced an elite group comparable and in some cases superior in size and quality to the one accomplished by a selective system. . . . A selective system with the dual-track school structure succeeds in bringing the few who survive

---

28 *Ibid.,* p. 123.
29 *Ibid.,* pp. 140–141.

to graduation up to outstanding accomplishments, whereas those who were not selected are left far behind. A system with a high degree of retentivity can bring a larger proportion of the students of average ability up to a higher level of performance than the selective system. An assessment of the "yield" in mathematics would have required a much more extensive testing program than was possible in the present project. Apart from testing representative samples of students at all the terminal points in the primary and secondary school, we would have had to test students who for various reasons dropped out of the secondary level.[30]

Pupil Grouping

The IEA study also found that students of average and below-average achievement "tend to be better motivated in undifferentiated classes or schools than if they are allocated to separate classes or schools." [31] Despite the fact that the selective academic schools were found to have better educational provisions and more highly qualified teachers, the achievement levels of senior students in these schools were not superior to those in comprehensive secondary schools. These findings are of particular significance in view of the criticisms leveled at the American comprehensive high school and the trend toward ability grouping in the United States during the past two decades.

Sex Differences

In Belgium, the Netherlands, France, and England, from five to seven times as many male as female students were found to be taking mathematics. On the other hand, the ratio was close to two to one in the United States, Finland, Japan, and Scotland. These data reflect the disparities in educational opportunities, with discrimination most prevalent in the schools of European nations. Although in all populations boys tended to outscore girls in achievement in mathematics, the differences were reduced significantly in coeducational schools.[32]

Teacher Education

Regarding teacher training, the study revealed that the amount of teacher preparation was positively associated with pupil achievement. However, in the preuniversity mathematics group achievement was significantly lower under university-trained teachers than under teachers

---

30 *Ibid.*, pp. 294–295.
31 *Ibid.*, p. 295.
32 *Ibid.*, pp. 304–306.

from teacher's colleges.[33] The latter finding runs counter to the generally accepted view in the United States that university-trained teachers are superior to those from teachers' colleges. Yet, ironically, the universities tend to attract and select students of higher academic caliber than the specialized teacher-training institutions.

The "New" Mathematics

The findings concerning the achievement of students who had been involved in the "new" mathematics were inconclusive. Seniors having taken the "new" mathematics did not produce higher scores than those in conventional courses, while "new" mathematics students at the lower levels tended to obtain better results than their counterparts; however, the mean for all countries in the "new" mathematics was not significantly higher than that for the populations which had not taken "new" mathematics courses.

Although a positive relationship was found between "discovery" approaches and interest in mathematics at the thirteen-year-old level, this was not the case for the preuniversity students. It was felt that the latter finding may have reflected the more conservative methods of instruction and the conforming pressures of the examination system at the preuniversity level.[34]

Future Research

According to Husén, the International Study of Achievement in Mathematics raised more problems than it solved. Most of the problems stem from the need to develop a conceptual model for identifying the key independent variables that account for the important cross-national differences. For example, it was found that "the socioeconomic background of the students has a much more powerful impact than most of the 'pure' school variables." [35] Consequently, in such research, the educational system must be analyzed in its social and political context.

Although IEA repeatedly cautioned against drawing conclusions from raw data on noncomparable populations, the American press did just that. To avoid such misinterpretations and distortions, the data would have to be developed in terms of "educational yield" or "how many are brought how far at the various levels in the school system," along with other factors relating educational achievement of in-school and out-of-

---

[33] *Ibid.*, p. 196.
[34] *Ibid.*, p. 299.
[35] *Ibid.*, p. 307.

school age groups to educational investment.[36] Those who have been swayed by Rickover's repeated allegations that one school year in the United States is worth only two thirds of a school year in Europe should be aware that the IEA study reported that "no evidence supports or refutes such a statement." [37]

THE MATH WARS

In the curriculum reform movement, no other discipline has been rocked by such controversy as mathematics. Although the leadership for the "new" mathematics programs has been primarily in the hands of university mathematicians assisted by mathematics educators, a number of distinguished mathematicians and scientists have been severely critical of the spirit and directions assumed by these programs. The chief criticism leveled against the major reform programs is that they are concerned primarily with abstract notions and operations in the more remote branches of mathematics, while neglecting the traditional elements of the discipline from which the major advances in science and technology have come about.

Abstraction and Application

The discipline of mathematics has emerged in the twentieth century as the fundamental language of thought in a widening spectrum of scientific and technological domains. Nevertheless, mathematics is also regarded as a discipline unto itself. According to the mathematician, Marshall Stone, an important change in the conception of mathematics in the twentieth century "which truly involves a revolution in ideas is the discovery that mathematics is entirely independent of the physical world . . . mathematics is now seen to have no necessary connections with the physical world beyond the vague and mystifying one implicit in the statement that thinking takes place in the brain." [38] Stone cites Bertrand Russell's famous epigram referring to the abstract nature of mathematics: "Mathematics is the subject in which we do not know what we are talking about or whether what we say is true." [39] In this connection mathematics is seen as the study of general abstract systems composed of specific abstract elements. Theoretical mathematicians are concerned not only with the intrinsic properties of various systems, but with the rela-

---

[36] *Ibid.*, pp. 307–309.

[37] *Ibid.*, Vol. I, p. 20.

[38] Marshall H. Stone, "The Revolution in Mathematics," *Liberal Education,* Vol. 47 (May, 1961), p. 305.

[39] *Ibid.*, p. 307.

tionships of the structures of different systems. While all this may seem utterly ambiguous to anyone but the theoretical mathematician, the point is that the discipline can be studied apart from any apparent connection with the physical world. And although the abstract study of mathematics can lead eventually to concrete applications, this is not the goal of the theoretical mathematician.

The Discipline and Curriculum Construction.   The legitimacy of such theoretical concerns is not seriously challenged in the mathematics community except when the problem of curriculum construction arises. Here it is maintained that the concerns of mathematicians who are on the frontiers of their discipline should be of little relevance to the schoolboy. Thus the new curriculum programs, with their emphasis on the structure of the discipline, have come under sharp attack for their relative neglect of the applied aspects of the subject.

One of the leading critics of the "new" mathematics programs is Morris Kline, professor and chairman of the mathematics department at the Washington Square College of New York University, and a research director at the university's Institute of Mathematical Sciences. He criticizes the leading reform groups (the Commission on Mathematics of the College Entrance Examination Board, the University of Illinois Committee on School Mathematics, and the School Mathematics Study Group) for their radical approaches to reconstructing the curriculum without first having made a careful study of curriculum, instruction, and learning connected with traditional programs. According to Kline, much of the material in the new programs "serves only the purposes of professional mathematicians or logicians, rather than the student who is beginning to get his first real grounding in mathematics." [40] He maintains that the new curriculum projects are formulated largely in the interests of a few researchers who are concerned with the pure and abstract side of mathematics, whereas the central line of work of most mathematicians actually lies in the real world of the expanding sciences.

Relationship to Other Disciplines.   Kline views the emphasis in the new programs on such topics as set theory, symbolic logic, abstract algebra, matrices, and Boolean algebra, along with the attention given to the derivation of the properties of the various types of numbers through strict logic, as resulting in the further isolation of mathematics from the physical and social sciences. The key approach to mathematics in the high school curriculum, argues Kline, should stem from its use as the language and essential instrument of science. He condemns the pressures

---

[40] Morris Kline, "Math Teaching Assailed As Peril to U.S. Scientific Progress," *New York University Alumni News*, Vol. 7 (October, 1961), p. 3.

being exerted on teachers and school administrators to adopt the "new" mathematics simply because the college entrance examinations would include this material, as well as the need to be innovative and current. And he criticizes the pedagogues for abdicating their roles in supporting programs that are entirely unsuitable for young people.

While acknowledging that educators traditionally have done a poor job with mathematics, Kline argues that the problem in traditional mathematics lies in the failure of teachers to deal with the actual uses made of the techniques and theorems which students are asked to learn. Thus mathematics is approached as though one were beginning to learn Chinese, instead of learning the meaning of the discipline as it relates to our civilization and culture. He estimates that only about 5 per cent of our present high school teachers have any conception of how mathematics is used in science and argues that the new programs, if adopted widely, will leave us outclassed as a nation in scientific progress. Kline sees mathematics in the high school curriculum not as a pure body of knowledge but as a means for understanding the real world:

> Mathematics exists primarily to help man understand and master the physical world and, to a slight extent, the economic and social worlds. . . . We must constantly show what mathematics accomplishes in domains outside of mathematics. If our subject did not have this value, it would not get any place at all in the curriculum.[41]

According to Kline, the so-called modern programs have been fashioned by men whose work is confined only to mathematics or to special branches of mathematics. Consequently, the new programs neglect the significant uses of the discipline in other disciplines and areas of our culture. To Kline, the heavy emphasis given in the new programs to such topics as set theory, structure of the real number system, and axiomatic geometry is more of a fetish than a need. Kline also criticizes the new programs for attempting to propel adolescents to the curriculum-makers' level of sophistication.[42]

Student Needs and the Professional Mathematician

Kline has not been alone in his attack on the new programs. In 1962 a memorandum signed by sixty-five mathematicians declared that the

> mathematics curriculum of the high school should provide for the needs of all students: it should contribute to the cultural background of the general student and offer professional preparation to the future users

---

[41] Morris Kline, "A Proposal for the High School Mathematics Curriculum," *The Mathematics Teacher*, Vol. 59 (April, 1966), p. 324.

[42] *Ibid.*, p. 323.

of mathematics . . . taking into account both the physical sciences which are the basis of our technological civilization, and the social sciences. . . .[43]

The memorandum contends that more attention should be given in the new programs to the connection between mathematics and science, and that concepts should be derived from and applied to concrete situations. The statement also criticizes the traditional high school curriculum for isolating the subject matter components within the discipline, as well as isolating the discipline from other domains of knowledge and inquiry; in the traditional curriculum, the student merely learns the manipulations and facts by rote without understanding their origins, purposes, and applications.

Some educators have expressed concern that the curriculum reform movement in mathematics has been overly concerned with certain esoteric principles and functions to the detriment of essential learning of computational skills and other very basic mathematical ideas and operations. No less distinguished a pioneer in the curriculum reform movement than Max Beberman, director of the University of Illinois Committee on School Mathematics, voices criticism of these excesses:

> We're not doing a good enough job of teaching masses of children the very, very basic ideas and skills in mathematics—the ability to compute and do arithmetic. A student with insight into computation is the kind of kid we should be turning out. Instead they are mouthing words like "commutative principles." [44]

Beberman sees the reform movement as being overly concerned with curriculum changes that are not fundamentally important. He argues for substantive reform rather than the "crazy turns" that many new projects have taken.[45]

Radical Curriculum Change Vs. Acceleration of Learning. Others argue that we need to make a more radical break with tradition by building the curriculum to fit the frontiers of mathematical thought. For example, Stone criticizes the Report of the Cambridge Conference on School Mathematics [46] for being concerned primarily with compressing the mathematics curriculum "so that what is now taught over twelve years of school plus three of college can be completed by the end of high

---

43 "On the Mathematics Curriculum of the High School," *The Mathematics Teacher,* Vol. 55 (March, 1962), p. 191.

44 Quoted in *A Decade of Comment on Education,* Mortimer Smith (ed.) (Washington, D.C.: Council for Basic Education, 1966), p. 66.

45 *Ibid.*

46 The Report of the Cambridge Conference on School Mathematics, *Goals for School Mathematics* (Boston: Houghton Mifflin Company, 1963).

school," [47] instead of endorsing the bolder changes that are being advanced in certain European quarters, both west and east. The Cambridge Report is the product of a conference of noted mathematicians, scientists, and leaders in the curriculum reform movement who sought to review the needs for shaping the precollege mathematics curriculum for the coming decades. The Cambridge Conference was held in 1963 through the support of NSF and Educational Services Incorporated (now Education Development Center, Inc.). In reviewing the Cambridge Report, Stone sees signs of a lessening of the momentum for developing a radically new mathematics curriculum—a momentum that had come about during the early efforts of SMSG and UICSM.

> Now there are signs that both SMSG and UICSM, the two most influential agents of reform in the United States, are losing momentum in the sense that neither is giving a place of importance to bold experiments with mathematical subject matter or its efficient organization into a curriculum radically different from the traditional one. This is most unfortunate, because we need to make a real break with tradition at this time, and we have already amassed enough evidence through imaginative experiments undertaken here and abroad to show that the reform demanded by current trends in mathematics . . . is pedagogically feasible.[48]

Need for Controlled Research. Much of what Stone regards as "evidence" amassed through "imaginative experiments" here and abroad actually is derived from little more than feasibility demonstrations. Carefully controlled experiments comparing students in the best of the new programs with those in the best of the traditional programs simply have not been undertaken. Because most of the evaluation studies for the new programs are administered by the specific programs concerned, it is doubtful that, under such circumstances, control groups can be constituted with the care bestowed upon the experimental groups. As mentioned at the beginning of this chapter, the fact that the National Longitudinal Study of Mathematical Abilities, financed by NSF, was administered through SMSG raises the legitimate question of why the study was not administered by an agency independent of any reform program.

Nevertheless, Stone argues that it has been demonstrated that (1) curriculum groups are capable of developing new programs that represent the frontiers of mathematical thought; (2) in the present climate of opinion, schools are ready for radical curriculum change; and (3) students can

[47] Marshall H. Stone, "Reviews and Evaluations," *The Mathematics Teacher*, Vol. 58 (April, 1965), p. 354.

[48] *Ibid.*, p. 353.

learn the material as presented in the new programs. However, as discussed earlier, many mathematicians do not agree with the premise that the secondary curriculum in mathematics should be reformulated to represent the abstract and self-sufficient side of the discipline. Noting the absence of connections with the real world in many of the postulates of current mathematics, a mathematician observed that "one can only conclude that much of modern mathematics is not related to science but rather appears to be more closely related to the famous scholastic arguing of the Middle Ages." [49]

The University Influence.   The concern for purity and abstraction on the part of research mathematicians has resulted in a tendency for various divisions at some universities to offer their own mathematics courses independent of the mathematics departments. Such fields as engineering and physics require mathematical operations that all too often are regarded as "lowbrow" by research mathematicians in the departments of mathematics. At the secondary school level, the growing need for and emphasis on vocational education make it increasingly evident that a serious gap appears between the kind of mathematics emphasized in the new programs and the kind needed for the preparation of skilled technicians.

Alvin M. Weinberg, director of the Oak Ridge National Laboratory, views the great curriculum reforms in the high schools, particularly in mathematics, as puristic monsters created by the university and reflecting the university's tendency toward purity and fragmentation of knowledge, as opposed to application and interdisciplinarity.

> These reforms started in the high schools but have now been extended, particularly in mathematics, downward to the grade schools, and in many instances upward to the colleges. . . . But, insofar as many of the new curricula have been captured by university scientists and mathematicians of narrowly puristic outlook, insofar as some of the curricula reflect deplorable fragmentation and abstraction, especially of mathematics . . . I consider them to be dangerous.
> . . . The professional purists, representing the spirit of the fragmented, research-oriented university, took over the curriculum reforms, and by their diligence and aggressiveness, created puristic monsters.[50]

The reaction on the part of certain members of the academic community against these trends toward purification, specialization, and fragmentation of the disciplines, coupled with the growing social consciousness of students and faculty on many of our college campuses, may well

---

49 R. W. Hamming, "Numerical Analysis Vs. Mathematics," *Science,* Vol. 148 (April, 1965), p. 474.

50 Alvin M. Weinberg, *Reflections on Big Science* (Cambridge, Mass.: The M.I.T. Press, 1967), pp. 153–154.

lead to a shift toward curriculum integration and interdisciplinarity in school and college, particularly for general education purposes. So far, however, the protest movement has been centered primarily in our institutions of higher education and although the established trend during the past two decades has been for the secondary schools to take their curricular cues from the universities, the development of a curricular counterrevolution is unlikely at the secondary level in the absence of significant changes in the undergraduate curriculum.

CURRICULUM COMPRESSION AND ACCELERATION

A characteristic feature of the "new" mathematics programs is the introduction of certain topics at earlier levels of schooling. In other words, more mathematics and more advanced topics are being compressed into the elementary and secondary curriculum. For example, where the theory of sets previously had not been introduced until college, it is now treated in the elementary school. And where the concept of group theory was not approached until perhaps the junior year of college, it is now introduced in the high school. Another example is the introduction of probability and statistics as a course in high school.

Advanced Placement Program

Since 1969 the Advanced Placement Program of the College Entrance Examination Board has offered two advanced-placement examinations in mathematics. These examinations are geared to two levels of calculus in high school. The high school student takes one of these examinations, according to the level of calculus completed in high school, and is placed in the college sequence of calculus according to his preparation as evidenced by his examination results. The college may offer advanced placement, credit, or both to the student who has completed the appropriate college-level course in calculus in high school and who has passed the examination. The second-level examination in calculus is designed to place the student one semester beyond the placement granted for the first-level examination.

In Table 4-3 we find examples of four high school mathematics sequences, including two sequences that provide for advanced placement. These sequences illustrate the trend toward introducing certain college-level topics and courses in the high school years.

Goals for School Mathematics: The Cambridge Conference

As mentioned earlier, the Cambridge Conference on School Mathematics sought to establish goals in mathematics education for grades K through 12. The basic premise guiding the work of the twenty-nine

Table 4-3.　Four High School Mathematics Programs

Grade	Regular Program	Regular Program (Algebra in Grade 8)	Advanced Placement Program	Advanced Placement Program—Algebra in Grade 8
9	Algebra	Plane and solid geometry	Algebra and some intermediate algebra	Plane and solid geometry
10	Plane and solid geometry	Intermediate mathematics (algebra ⅔, trigonometry ⅓)	Plane and solid geometry	Intermediate mathematics
11	Intermediate mathematics (algebra ⅔, trigonometry ⅓)	Advanced topics in algebra, elementary functions *	Intermediate mathematics (very strong course)	Elementary functions (semester), analytic geometry (semester)
12	Statistics and probability (semester), elementary functions (semester)	Statistics and probability (semester), analytic geometry (semester)	Analytic geometry and calculus	Calculus
	Begin analytic geometry and calculus in college	Begin calculus in college	Seek advanced placement in college	Seek advanced placement in college

* *We suggest that this be a one-year course containing such units as polynomial functions, circular functions, exponential and logarithmic functions, theory of equations, mathematical induction, postulational systems, matrix algebra.*

Source: *National Council of Teachers of Mathematics,* The Revolution in School Mathematics, A Challenge for Administrators and Teachers *(Washington, D.C.: The Council, 1961), p. 73.*

mathematicians, scientists, and curriculum reform leaders who participated in the Cambridge Conference was that the curriculum must be formulated according to the inherent nature of the subject matter and its organization as determined by leading scholars in the discipline, whereas small value is to be derived from what little is known about the nature of the learner. Thus the work of Piaget, for example, is promptly pushed aside as inconclusive, if not irrelevant, while the interests and needs of the non-college-bound student are virtually ignored.

> The question of what is or what is not worth teaching must be approached, initially at least, in terms of all the possibilities that are inherent in the subject matter; the question of what is not depends largely upon the organization of the subject matter. Only the very top-level of expertise is likely to be sufficient to make the necessary determinations. . . .
>
> We made no attempt to take account of recent researches in cognitive psychology. It has been argued by Piaget and others that certain ideas and degrees of abstraction cannot be learned until certain ages. We regard this question as open, partly because there are cognitive psychologists on both sides of it, and partly because the investigations of Piaget, taken at face value, do not justify any conclusion relevant to our task.[51]

The cavalier dismissal of Piaget and the refusal to give any consideration whatsoever to the nature of the learner as a basis for curriculum reform may well reflect the tenor of the times. Although the curriculum reform movement of the 1950's and 1960's embraced Bruner's conviction that "intellectual activity anywhere is the same, whether at the frontier of knowledge or in a third-grade classroom" [52]—a premise that seemingly is psychologically based—this premise actually provides the curriculum-maker with virtually complete license to formulate the curriculum according to the interests of the mature scholar. If the nature of the schoolboy as learner is not at all incompatible with that of the mature scholar, the task of curriculum determination is simplified and this task, therefore, can best be accomplished through the efforts of mature scholars who are at the frontiers of their discipline. Little or no consideration need be given to the nature of the learner if one knows the nature of the mature scholar. And who knows the nature of the mature scholar better than the mature scholar himself? It is in this sense that the Cambridge Report declares that "it would be a mistake to read this report solely in terms of the mathematics curriculum. The step which has been taken here by mathematicians is one that scholars in all the disciplines must sooner or later attempt to take." [53] Thus the Cambridge Report is held by its authors as universally valid for curriculum reform, regardless of the discipline. Interestingly, Bruner was not only one of the twenty-nine participants of the Cambridge Conference, but also served as a member of its Steering Committee.

---

[51] The Report of the Cambridge Conference, *op. cit.*, pp. 2–3.

[52] Jerome S. Bruner, *The Process of Education* (Cambridge, Mass.: Harvard University Press, 1960), p. 14.

[53] The Report of the Cambridge Conference, *op. cit.*, p. ix.

Proposals for Change: Grades K–6. The most sweeping proposal in the Cambridge Report is concerned with curriculum compression and acceleration, as discussed earlier in this chapter. Accordingly, the report advocates "that a student who has worked through the full thirteen years of mathematics in grades K to 12 should have a level of training comparable to three years of top-level college training today." [54] This would provide the student with the equivalent of two years of calculus, one semester of modern algebra, and one semester of probability theory. The speed-up would be accomplished by reorganizing and eliminating some of the traditional material, particularly the drill work and repetitious "real-life" problems in arithmetic, as well as including the kindergarten year as a formal year of schooling. The program in grades K through 6 would bring youngsters to a level of mathematical competence considerably beyond that of today's general population. In grades K through 2, treatment would be given to such topics as the real number system, geometry, logic and set theory, function, and applications of measurement. This work would not be highly formalized, but would establish a "spiral" of increasingly expanding and evolving experiences as the student deals with these and connected topics in the later grades.

In addition to dealing with these topics and concepts in "spiral" fashion as the student moves to the upper elementary grades, additional topics such as logic and foundations, theory of real functions, and applications of measurement and probability and statistics would be treated in grades 3 through 6. At the end of the sixth grade, according to the proposal, the child would have mastered what ordinarily is not reached until the completion of grade 9 at best. Whether the average child is capable of such accomplishment is subject to serious doubt. But even if such achievement were possible, it is questionable that it should be mandated for all children.

Proposals for Change: Grades 7–12. In formulating recommendations for grades 7 through 12, the Cambridge Conference encountered considerable disagreement and finally settled on two proposals prepared by two separate committees. The first proposal gives greater emphasis to abstract algebra and general mathematical concepts, while the second curriculum provides more stress on topics that ordinarily are treated in advanced calculus at the college level. Both curricula include probability in grades 7 and 8, with additional emphasis provided in this subject in grades 11 and 12. Although the two proposals include such college-level subjects as analytic geometry, calculus, probability, linear algebra, and differential equations, the second curriculum begins the calculus in grade 9 and proceeds through various topics to advanced calculus in grade 12.

---

[54] *Ibid.,* p. 7.

The Cambridge Report has been severely criticized by a number of mathematicians and educators. The mathematician Marshall Stone observes that the two curricula proposed for grades 7 through 12 are indicative of an irreconcilable conflict in philosophy that "sows the seeds for eventual confusion in a much wider circle." [55] He also noted that much of the advanced material "could have been lifted with little change from almost any good college announcement,"[56] and that the goal of compressing more advanced topics produces curriculum congestion. And although the Cambridge Report incorporates some three years of college-level material in the senior high school, it fails to give any consideration as to how this would change the college curriculum. Moreover, the proposals at the secondary level ignore the question of what should be provided for students who are not bound for college.

As discussed earlier in this chapter, the Cambridge Report rejects the view held by Stone and others that the school curriculum be organized to provide for the earliest possible treatment of material representing pure mathematics from contemporary mathematical research. The report deplores the dichotomy between "pure" and "applied" mathematics, and advocates that applications of mathematics to spheres of life be given a legitimate place in the school curriculum. Nevertheless, the primary concern of the Cambridge Report is the compression of the mathematics curriculum for pupil acceleration. In this regard, the twenty-nine scholars who produced the Cambridge Report appear to be naive and unrealistic.

THE ISSUE OF CHANGE

Revolution or Revision?

Some mathematicians have held that the revolution in mathematical thinking must be the basis for bold new approaches in developing a curriculum radically different from the traditional one. As discussed earlier, for example, Marshall Stone has expressed concern that the new mathematics programs may lose their momentum and fail to make a sufficient break with tradition. Others have pointed to the semantic difficulties in regarding the various major curriculum programs as purveyors of a truly new subject matter. Instead, they see these projects as bringing about the following revisionary trends: (1) elimination of less important topics, particularly in trigonometry and solid geometry, which are of little interest to professional mathematicians, (2) integration of certain material, such as plane and solid geometry, (3) introduction of material reflecting the more recent developments in mathematics, such as proba-

---

55 Stone, "Reviews and Evaluations," *op. cit.,* p. 357.
56 *Ibid.*

bility and statistics, (4) emphasis on the structure of the discipline, rather than treating mathematics as isolated topics and disjointed subject matters, and (5) introduction of material at earlier grade levels and the compression of more material into the elementary and secondary schools.[57]

Despite the recent tendency for certain mathematicians and mathematics educators to hold that the new programs do not really constitute a revolutionary change in the curriculum, the early literature describing these programs gave promise that a curriculum revolution was in the offing. For example, an official publication of the National Council of Teachers of Mathematics, published in 1961, was titled *The Revolution in School Mathematics, A Challenge for Administrators and Teachers*.[58] This publication was produced as a result of a series of eight regional conferences, conducted by the National Council of Teachers of Mathematics with the financial support of NSF, to provide school administrators and mathematics supervisors with information on implementing the new programs in their schools. The opening statement of this publication flatly describes the changes in mathematics as a revolution: "The changes in mathematics at the present time are so extensive, so far-reaching in their implications, and so profound that they can be described only as a revolution." [59]

The various new programs, supported and promoted by NSF during the era of the cold war and the space race, attracted unprecedented fanfare. Magazine and newspaper articles attempted to describe the "new" mathematics, while cartoons satirized the inability of parents to help their youngsters with their new homework. A new market was created for books designed to explain the "new" math to parents with the forewarning that "the current revolution in school mathematics has just begun." [60] By 1970 more than two dozen different curriculum projects in mathematics were being sponsored and promoted throughout the United States. The profusion of curriculum projects in mathematics and science in this country and abroad led to the establishment of the International Clearinghouse on Science and Mathematics Curricular Developments in 1962 through funds from NSF.[61]

The most influential of the mathematics projects are university based

[57] Allen F. Strehler, "What's New About the New Math?" *Saturday Review* (March 21, 1964), pp. 68–69.

[58] National Council of Teachers of Mathematics, *The Revolution in School Mathematics, A Challenge for Administrators and Teachers* (Washington, D.C.: The Council 1961).

[59] G. Baley Price, "Progress in Mathematics and Its Implications for the Schools" in *The Revolution in School Mathematics, ibid.,* p. 1.

[60] Ralph T. Heimer and Miriam S. Newman, *The New Mathematics for Parents* (New York: Holt, Rinehart and Winston, Inc., 1965), p. 109.

[61] J. David Lockhard, *Sixth Report of the International Clearinghouse on Science and Mathematics Curricular Developments* (College Park, Md.: Science Teaching Center, University of Maryland, 1968).

and NSF sponsored. Considerable confusion has been created among school administrators under the pressure of keeping their schools in tune with the leading proposals. Not infrequently does one find the arbitrary and abstract manipulations characteristic of the traditional mathematics curriculum being substituted by a "modern" program that replaces the old manipulations with new abstractions that are equally meaningless.

In describing the reform movement as a revolution, the National Council of Teachers of Mathematics has maintained that "the content of any subject matter field must be based on an appeal to authority—the authority of leading scholars in that field." [62] Thus the chief criterion for curriculum reform is the authority of the research mathematician and not the nature of the learner or the nature of man in dealing with the physical world. Moreover, as we have stressed throughout this chapter, the reform movement has been marked by serious and often irreconcilable controversy among the scholars as to what should properly constitute the mathematics curriculum of the future. The only real agreement is that the traditional mathematics curriculum must be changed substantially.

The premise that the schoolboy and the research scholar share the same kind of intellectual activity—a premise that has served as a basis for the curriculum reform movement during the past two decades—has come to be challenged not only in the sciences, as discussed in Chapter 3, but also in mathematics and other curriculum fields. Serious questions are being raised about the validity of fashioning the school curriculum in accordance with the interests of research mathematicians who are on the frontiers of their discipline in studying mathematics for its own sake. The abstractions in investigating mathematical structures may be elegantly appealing to many scholars, but whether the schoolboy can and should share the concerns of such scholars remains an unsettled and growing controversy.

SUMMARY

Although mathematics, along with science, enjoyed highest priority in the curriculum reform movement of the 1950's and 1960's, mathematicians became sharply divided on the shape and directions of the new programs. The major reform programs were criticized for being concerned primarily with the study of mathematics for its own sake, while neglecting the traditional elements of the discipline through which the major advances in science and technology have been made possible.

In essence the community of mathematicians was divided between those who regard mathematics as a discipline unto itself and those who regard

---

[62] *The Revolution in School Mathematics, op. cit.*, p. 69.

the discipline as the fundamental language of thought in a widening spectrum of scientific and technological domains. Thus the major curriculum programs, with their emphasis on the structure of the discipline, have come under attack for neglecting the applied aspects of mathematics. The new programs are accused of emphasizing purism at the expense of application and interdisciplinarity. The resolution of this issue most likely will take the form of compromise in the coming years, rather than victory of one group over another.

As in the curriculum reform movement in science, the leading mathematics projects embrace the Brunerian premise that it is easiest for the schoolboy to learn the structure of a discipline by employing modes a thought characteristic of the mature scholar on the frontiers of knowledge. In this connection, a great deal of emphasis is given to discovery methods and the importance of intuitive thinking. However, the degree to which this rationale has been successful remains a matter of debate. Many of the claims made for the new projects have yet to be verified through controlled experimentation. Although it has been shown that students can engage in the new programs without suffering any significant impairment in traditional mathematical skills and concepts, there is little evidence that these programs have effected significant improvement in cognitive processes, college performance, and career motivation.

In addition to the fundamental changes in restructuring the subject matter and incorporating modern topics in the mathematics curriculum while de-emphasizing outmoded content, an important trend in the reform movement has been the compression of more advanced material in the elementary and secondary schools. Certain proposals, such as the Report of the Cambridge Conference on School Mathematics, have been criticized for their unrealistic concern for compressing too much into the elementary and secondary phases of schooling, for ignoring the non-college-bound student, and for dismissing the implications of Piaget's research on intellectual development.

The rationale for pushing more advanced material down into the lower levels of schooling appears to stem from Bruner's notion that "intellectual activity anywhere is the same, whether at the frontier of knowledge or in a third-grade classroom." While such a declaration appears at first thought to be psychologically based, it actually has served to give the mature scholar complete license to impose his own interests, convictions, and biases in formulating the curriculum for the child and the adolescent. When Bruner's notion is regarded as a principle to be followed rather than as a hypothesis to be tested, the interests of the mature scholar take precedence over the interests, needs, and capabilities of the schoolboy.

No other discipline has been rocked by so much controversy. But no other discipline has been subjected to greater revision and reform.

PROBLEMS FOR STUDY AND DISCUSSION

1. Bruner states that "if you wish to teach the calculus in the eighth grade, then begin it in the first grade by teaching the kinds of ideas and skills necessary for its mastery later." [Jerome S. Bruner, *Toward a Theory of Instruction* (Cambridge, Mass.: Harvard University Press, 1966), p. 29.] Does this statement conflict with Piaget's theory concerning the stages of human development? Why or why not?

2. The following statement is taken from a memorandum signed by sixty-five mathematicians alleging certain undesirable features in the various curriculum improvement projects in mathematics at the secondary level. Do you agree with this statement? Why or why not? Do you find this statement to be applicable to many of the curriculum projects in disciplines other than mathematics? Why or why not?

    Mathematicians reacting to the dominance of education by professional educators who may have stressed pedagogy at the expense of content, may now stress content at the expense of pedagogy and be equally ineffective. Mathematicians may unconsciously assume that all young people should like what present-day mathematicians like or that the only students worth cultivating are those who might become professional mathematicians. ["On the Mathematics Curriculum of the High School," *The Mathematics Teacher*, Vol. 55 (March, 1962), p. 191.]

3. In the same memorandum, cited in the preceding problem, the mathematicians contended that "what is bad in the present high school curriculum is not so much the subject matter presented as the isolation of mathematics from other domains of knowledge and inquiry, especially from the physical sciences. . . ." [*Ibid.*, p. 193.] How do you account for this isolation? Do you believe that a similar problem has emerged in the curriculum projects in English and social studies? Why?

4. The curriculum reform projects in mathematics at the secondary level have been criticized for being concerned almost exclusively with developing programs for the college-bound student while virtually ignoring the mathematical needs of the terminal and vocational student. How do you account for this in view of the fact that most secondary school pupils are not college bound?

5. Bruner offers this criticism and recommendation for curriculum-makers:

    Research on the instructional process—in mathematics as in all disciplines—has not been carried out in connection with the building of curricula . . . psychologists have come upon the scene, armed with evaluative devices, only after a curriculum has already been put into operation. Surely it would be more efficient and useful if embryonic instructional materials could be tried out under experimental conditions so that revision and correction could be based upon immediate knowledge of results. [Jerome S. Bruner, *Toward a Theory of Instruction* (Cambridge, Mass.: Harvard University Press, 1966), p. 54.]

Why have the major curriculum projects tended to regard research and evaluation primarily as operations which follow curriculum development and promotion? Is there a fallacy in regarding research and evaluation as entities separate from the processes of curriculum development? Why or why not?

6. A review of articles on the "new" math appearing in popular magazines over the ten-year period from 1956 through 1965 revealed that during most of this period the articles "defer almost blindly to the new curricular innovators in mathematics" and that "not until the final year of the decade, 1965, do authors appear in these magazines to question the validity and appropriateness of the innovators' handiwork." [Francis J. Mueller, "The Public Image of 'New Mathematics,'" *The Mathematics Teacher,* Vol. 59 (November, 1966), pp. 619–620.] How do you account for the long absence of criticism in the popular press?

7. The Cambridge Report maintains that "the question of what is or what is not worth teaching must be approached, initially at least, in terms of all the possibilities that are inherent in the subject matter; the question of what is teachable and what is not depends largely upon the organization of the subject matter." [The Report of the Cambridge Conference on School Mathematics, *Goals for School Mathematics* (Boston: Houghton Mifflin Company, 1963), pp. 2–3.] How important are (a) sociopolitical forces and (b) the nature of the learner in determining what is worth teaching and what is teachable?

8. What problems other than language differences must be considered in conducting and interpreting research comparing educational achievement among nations?

9. In the International Study of Achievement in Mathematics, the concept of "educational yield" was developed as a result of the emergent problems in determining the "productivity" of the school systems of different nations. What is meant by the concept of "educational yield"? Why is this concept particularly applicable to education in the United States?

10. The researchers in charge of the International Study of Achievement in Mathematics cautioned repeatedly in reporting their findings that the study was not designed to compare countries against one

another and that it was not to be conceived as an "international contest." Nevertheless, the education editor of *The New York Times* opened his news story with the statement that "in the first international comparison of educational achievement, the United States carried off on Olympic medals." [Fred M. Hechinger, "The U.S. Gets Low Marks in Math," *The New York Times* (March 12, 1967), p. 11E.] How do you account for this interpretation or misinterpretation of the nature and intent of the research?

11. More than thirty years ago, a mathematics educator interviewed each of twenty-five high school students who had just enrolled in a geometry class. He asked the students why they were studying geometry and found that at least nineteen of the twenty-five members of the class were taking the work only because it was required. The interviews also revealed that twenty-two of the twenty-five students had a negative attitude toward further work in mathematics. [Harold P. Fawcett, *The Nature of Proof*, Thirteenth Yearbook of the National Council of Teachers of Mathematics (New York: Teachers College, Columbia University, 1938), p. 29.] If you were to interview the members of a high school class in geometry today, do you think you would come up with the same findings? Why or why not?

SELECTED REFERENCES

American Educational Research Association. "Science and Mathematics Education." *Review of Educational Research,* Vol. 39 (October, 1969).

Bereday, G. Z. F. *Comparative Method in Education.* New York: Holt, Rinehart and Winston, Inc., 1964.

Brown, Kenneth E., and Theodore L. Abell. *Analysis of Research in the Teaching of Mathematics.* Washington, D.C.: Office of Education, U.S. Department of Health, Education, and Welfare, 1965.

Bruner, Jerome S. *The Process of Education.* Cambridge, Mass.: Harvard University Press, 1960.

————. *Toward a Theory of Instruction.* Cambridge, Mass.: Harvard University Press, 1966. Chs. 1, 2, 3, 8.

Butler, Charles H., and F. Lynwood Wren. *The Teaching of Secondary Mathematics,* 4th ed. New York: McGraw-Hill Book Company, Inc., 1965. Chs. 1, 2, 3, 4, 5, 6.

Cambridge Conference on School Mathematics. *Goals for School Mathematics.* Boston: Houghton Mifflin Company, 1963.

Commission on Mathematics. *Program for College Preparatory Mathematics.* Princeton, N.J.: College Entrance Examination Board, 1959.

Dewey, John. *How We Think.* Boston: D. C. Heath & Company, 1910, 1933.

Fawcett, Harold P. *The Nature of Proof,* Thirteenth Yearbook, National Council of Teachers of Mathematics. New York: Teachers College, Columbia University, 1938.

Flavell, John H. *The Developmental Psychology of Jean Piaget.* Princeton, N.J.: D. Van Nostrand Company, 1963.

Ford, G. W., and Lawrence Pugno (eds.). *The Structure of Knowledge and the Curriculum.* Chicago: Rand McNally & Company, 1964.

Goodlad, John I. *The Changing School Curriculum.* New York: The Fund for the Advancement of Education, 1966.

Heath, Robert W. (ed.). *New Curricula.* New York: Harper & Row, Publishers, 1964. Chs. 1, 2, 3, 4, 12.

Henderson, Kenneth B. "Research on Teaching Secondary School Mathematics," Chapter 19 in *Handbook of Research on Teaching,* N. L. Gage (ed.). Chicago: Rand McNally & Company, 1963.

Husén, Torsten (ed.). *International Study of Achievement in Mathematics,* Vols. I and II. New York: John Wiley & Sons, 1967.

Johnson, Donovan A., and Robert Rahtz. *The New Mathematics in Our Schools.* New York: The Macmillan Company, 1966.

Lockard, J. David. *Sixth Report of the International Clearinghouse on Science and Mathematics Curricular Developments.* College Park, Md.: University of Maryland, 1968.

National Council of Teachers of Mathematics. *The Revolution in School Mathematics, A Challenge for Administrators and Teachers.* Washington, D.C.: The Council, 1961.

———. *Evolution in Mathematics,* 26th Yearbook, Washington, D.C.: The Council, 1961.

———. *An Analysis of New Mathematics Programs.* Washington, D.C.: The Council, 1963.

———. *Research in Mathematics Education.* Washington, D.C.: The Council, 1967.

National Society for the Study of Education. *Mathematics Education,* Sixty-ninth Yearbook, Part I. Chicago: The University of Chicago Press, 1970.

Piaget, Jean, and B. Inhelder. *The Growth of Logical Thinking from Childhood to Adolescence.* New York: Basic Books, 1958.

Rickover, Hyman G. *Education and Freedom.* New York: E. P. Dutton & Co., Inc., 1959.

———. *American Education—A National Failure.* New York: E. P. Dutton & Co., Inc., 1963.

Tyler, Ralph W., Robert M. Gagne, and Michael Scriven. *Perspectives of Curriculum Evaluation.* Chicago: Rand McNally & Company, 1967.

Weinberg, Alvin M. *Reflections on Big Science.* Cambridge, Mass.: The M.I.T. Press, 1967.

Williams, S. Irene. A Survey of the Teaching of Mathematics in Secondary Schools. Princeton, N.J.: Educational Testing Service, 1969.

Willoughby, Stephen S. *Contemporary Teaching of Secondary School Mathematics.* New York: John Wiley & Sons, Inc., 1967. Chs. 1, 2, 15.

Wooten, William. *SMSG—The Making of a Curriculum.* New Haven: Yale University Press, 1965.

Chapter 5

Curriculum Change in the Social Studies

In George Orwell's *Animal Farm,* the tenet is advanced that "all animals are created equal . . . except some are more equal than others." The same tenet can be said to characterize the status of subjects in the secondary school curriculum as a result of nationalizing influences on the curriculum during the 1950's and 1960's. As discussed in the preceding chapters, the cold war and Sputnik gave priority to curriculum reform in the sciences, mathematics, and modern foreign languages. It was not until 1962 that the federal government, through the Office of Education, initiated the Social Studies Program by establishing curriculum development centers at various universities. These efforts, along with the establishment of a considerable number of other projects in the social studies during the 1960's, have generated a proliferation of new curriculum proposals at the elementary and secondary levels. Nevertheless, the level of support in the social studies has not been comparable to that given the sciences and mathematics. Furthermore, where the curriculum reform movement in the sciences and mathematics has produced a number of dominant programs that have exerted a marked influence on the secondary school curriculum, no comparable programs have emerged in the social studies.

In view of the great proliferation of specialized projects in the social studies at the secondary level, no attempt is made in this chapter to describe systematically the various projects that are seeking recognition and influence. Instead, the main focus of this chapter is on the great flux and ferment that presently characterize the curriculum in the social studies, as influenced by the forces and trends of recent history.

BACKGROUND TRENDS AND FORCES

With relatively few exceptions, the trend in the social studies during the 1960's was mainly in the direction of developing programs through the specialized disciplines that comprise this broad field. In comparison, the 1930's, 1940's, and early 1950's were characterized by notable efforts to dissolve the subject boundaries in the social studies in the hope that the problems of youth and society could be analyzed and attacked on a molar level. Although the student protest movement at some of our colleges and universities during the 1960's generated a number of significant efforts toward improving the articulation and integration of the social sciences through multidisciplinary and interdisciplinary courses for general education in these institutions, no comparable efforts were manifested in the secondary schools.

The Traditional Dominance of History

At the turn of the century, the four-year sequence followed by many high schools consisted of ancient history, medieval and modern European history, English history, and American history and government. The advent of World War I gave rise to demands for reorganizing the curriculum to include modern history and contemporary social studies.

A report of the Committee on Social Studies of the NEA's Commission on the Reorganization of Secondary Education, published in 1916, advocated the modernizing of the curriculum in the social studies so as to develop the learner's potentials for more effective membership in society. As shown in Table 5-1, the sequence of courses recommended by the committee was divided into two cycles, one for grades 7 through 9, and the other for grades 10 through 12.

Table 5-1. Social Studies Curriculum Proposed by the NEA Commission on the Reorganization of Secondary Education, 1916

	Grade	Subject
Cycle I	7	European history (one semester geography optional)
	8	One semester American history
		One semester civics
	9	One year civics, or civics and economic history
Cycle II	10	European history (through 17th century)
	11	American history and/or modern European history
	12	Problems of democracy

Source: Commission on the Reorganization of Secondary Education, The Social Studies in Secondary Education *(Washington, D.C.: Bureau of Education, Bulletin No. 28, 1916), p. 35.*

The Problems Approach. The curriculum proposed by the 1916 commission became widely adopted and persisted as the dominant pattern, with minor variations, until the curriculum reform movement of the 1960's. The proposal for the "problems of democracy" course is significant because it represented, first, the recognition of the importance of giving greater emphasis to the modern social sciences in the high school curriculum and, second, the need to integrate these disciplines (i.e., political science, sociology, and economics) through problems that are of vital importance to society and that meet the needs and interests of students. However, many schools adopting this recommendation failed to integrate the material and simply organized the course as separate blocks of subject matter. Furthermore, the committee's proposal did not de-emphasize history, but called for the treatment of modern history in the curriculum and provided options allowing for the traditional three years of history in grades 10 through 12.

In 1920 a committee of the American Historical Association recommended that the association adopt the proposal for eliminating ancient history as a required course and that a course in social problems be provided in grade 12. But these recommendations were rejected by the American Historical Association. This rejection was attacked in an editorial in the *School Review,* which accused the American Historical Association of attempting to "blockade a movement which is in fact going forward in the schools." [1] At the same time, committees of the National Association of Secondary School Principals, the American Political Science Association, and the American Sociological Association went on record in favor of increased emphasis on the social studies in the secondary schools, while the American Sociological Association specifically endorsed the "problems of democracy" course for grade 12. Although Krug views the stance taken on this issue by the National Association of Secondary School Principals and the *School Review* as possible beginnings of conflict between historians and educationists,[2] the sanctity of history in the secondary school curriculum came to be challenged as the result of a host of changing forces.

Emergence of the Contemporary Social Sciences. The emergence of the United States from World War I as an international power, the growing recognition of the social sciences in the colleges and universities, and the increasing enrollments and diversity of the high school population, gave sufficient cause for a reassessment of the secondary school curriculum. Even some historians recognized the need for relating the study of his-

---

1 "Conservatism in History," *School Review,* Vol. 28 (March, 1920), p. 167.

2 Edward A. Krug, *The Shaping of the American High School* (New York: Harper & Row, Publishers, 1964), p. 360.

tory to the modern social sciences. The historian Carl Becker had advocated during World War I that the high schools provide "a carefully coordinated course in which history, economics, civics, and sociology should all find their properly related place." [3] Although notable attempts were made to articulate and integrate history and the social studies during the 1930's, 1940's, and early 1950's, the issues raised between those favoring the traditional emphasis on history, as opposed to those advocating a significant place for the contemporary social sciences in the curriculum (particularly that which is labeled the "social studies"), reached new crescendos following World War II and throughout the 1950's.

Growing Concern for Curriculum Articulation and Integration

The period from the 1930's to the mid-1950's was marked by proposals and attempts to integrate the social studies and to articulate the subject matter of this field with other subjects, notably English, through block-time and core classes. While these developments are discussed in greater detail in Chapter 2, it is significant that the overwhelming majority of schools offering block-time and core classes were focusing these classes on the social studies as a broad field in correlation with English. As recently as the 1956–1957 school year, almost a third of the separately organized junior high schools in the nation were offering block-time or core classes. Of these schools, 20 per cent reported that the subjects were unified around a central theme, units of work, or problems, while 12 per cent indicated a core curriculum based upon the personal-social needs of adolescents.[4]

Although most of the secondary schools continued to adhere to the traditional practice of offering separate courses with no planned efforts toward correlating the different subject matter fields, the fact remains that a significant proportion of the schools were attempting to improve the articulation of the general education curriculum, particularly with regard to the social studies and English. Much of the curriculum literature of the 1930's, 1940's, and early 1950's recommended the integration of the general education phase of the secondary school curriculum through block-time and core classes. Many colleges and universities during this period were making radical changes in their general education programs, particularly in the direction of developing integrated courses in the social sciences. Without doubt, such efforts in higher education

---

[3] Carl Becker, "History in the High School Curriculum," *Educational Administration and Supervision*, Vol. 2 (June, 1916), p. 378.

[4] Grace S. Wright, *Block-Time Classes and the Core Program in the Junior High School* (Washington, D.C.: Office of Education, U.S. Department of Health, Education, and Welfare, 1958), p. 20.

exercised significant influences on curriculum workers in the secondary schools.

THE BATTLE FOR CURRICULUM INTEGRATION

Report of the Educational Policies Commission

Recognizing the need for concerted planning in developing the secondary school curriculum for all youth during the post-World War II period, the NEA's Educational Policies Commission issued a volume in 1944, *Education for ALL American Youth,* which was intended as an example of how school systems and communities might meet the educational needs of all youth. The commission gave considerable attention to the social studies in general education through its proposed program in "common learnings." The purposes of the "common learnings" were designated "to help youth grow in six areas: (1) civic responsibility and competence, (2) understanding of the operation of the economic system and of the human relations involved therein, (3) family relationships, (4) intelligent action as consumers, (5) appreciation of beauty, and (6) proficiency in the use of language." [5]

Emphasis on Integrated Studies for General Education.   Through block-time classes, large problems could be studied from a number of subject fields with the "common learnings" teacher being assisted by other teachers whenever desirable. Although the "common learnings" would focus strongly on the social studies, literature and the use of language would be an important and integral function of the course. To summarize the "common learnings" sequence, grades 7, 8, and 9 would include the study of the community and state, and the principles of American democracy. Grade 10 would concentrate on the city at work or community studies and civic projects, consumer economics, and family life. A separate but closely correlated course in science ("The Scientific View of the World and of Man") would be offered in grade 10 as part of the "common learnings." The theme of civic competence would continue in grade 11 along with the study of American history ("Man's Efforts to Achieve Freedom and Security"). National and international problems would receive major attention in grade 12, along with the study of literature and the arts of various nations. Additional work in the social studies would be available through elective courses.[6]

The proposals of the commission in connection with the "common

---

[5] Educational Policies Commission, *Education for ALL American Youth—A Further Look* (Washington, D.C.: National Education Association, 1952), p. 238.

[6] *Ibid.,* pp. 239–251.

learnings" course obviously gave the social studies a dominant role. The social studies were to be integrated through molar problems geared to contemporary life and closely correlated with literature, while the development of skills in oral and written communication was to be a functional outgrowth of "common learnings."

Although relatively few schools actually adopted the commission's curriculum model for general education, at mid-century a significant proportion of junior high schools throughout the nation were offering block-time and core classes giving major emphasis to the social studies in correlation with English. Nevertheless, despite these notable efforts the predominant pattern of the social studies curriculum in our secondary schools continued to be based largely upon the program recommended in 1916 by the Committee on Social Studies of the NEA's Commission on the Reorganization of Secondary Education.

The Label of Progressivism.   While the commission's proposals were labeled by Cremin as "the progressive dream" and "patently the logical outcome of the progressive education movement," [7] the membership of the Educational Policies Commission included James B. Conant, then President of Harvard University. Furthermore, Conant, who was generally regarded as a moderate conservative on educational matters, served as chairman of the commission at the time that the revised edition, *Education for ALL American Youth—A Further Look,* was approved for publication in 1951.

In retrospect it appears odd that Conant would endorse a document representing such a patently progressive educational philosophy. But Sputnik was years away. Conant had still to serve as U.S. High Commissioner and ambassador to West Germany, not to mention his later position as the leading educational statesman and spokesman for the nation's interest during the cold-war era under appointment of John Gardner of the Carnegie Corporation.

Report of the Harvard Committee

Another document concerned with curriculum policy and practice in the post-World War II years is *General Education in a Free Society,* published in 1945 as the Report of the Harvard Committee. The Harvard Committee, appointed in 1943 by President Conant of Harvard University, was composed of professors of arts and sciences and education. Where *Education for ALL American Youth* represented a progressive educational philosophy, the Harvard Report assumed an eclectic stance.

---

[7] Lawrence A. Cremin, *The Transformation of the School* (New York: Alfred A. Knopf, Inc., 1961), p. 332.

The brief review of the Harvard Report in this chapter is limited to those recommendations concerned with the social studies phase of the curriculum in general education.[8] Here the report emphasized the need to provide a course on community life and civics and a course in American history in grades 7 and 8 in schools where a large proportion of students drop out before grade 11. For those students who are likely to graduate from high school, the report stressed the need to avoid curricular repetition and duplication by leaving the formal study of American history and civics until the last years of high school. No specific recommendations were made concerning the social studies courses to be offered such students in grades 7 and 8.

While acknowledging that students should not necessarily be required to take work in the social studies throughout the four years of high school, the report recognized the need for developing curriculum continuity and viewed with favor the adoption of two two-year sequences in the social studies in the high schools. This would provide for the study of European history, or general history and geography, in grades 9 and 10, followed by a two-year sequence of American history and problems of American life in grades 11 and 12. A considerable amount of work should be provided in the history of modern civilization for all students going on to graduate from high school, because America owes much of its heritage to European antecedents. The study of geography should be linked closely with general history.

The Place of History. The report deplored the practice of exposing students to American history year after year through repetitive courses. Yet the course in American history should be part of a sequence of courses in history and the social studies. Uniform coverage, chronological completeness, and rote learning should be avoided so as not to dull the student's interest in history. Students should develop historical skills instead of forming judgments without evidence.

Study of Contemporary Society. The fitting culmination of all work in the social studies, according to the Harvard Report, is a course on the nature of contemporary society. Such a course would be concerned with the goals, values, organization, processes, problems, and conflicts in the political structure, economic life, and social relationships of our nation. Although this course should deal with some of the unsolved problems of modern political and economic life, the historic roots of such problems should be given considerable emphasis.

Throughout the social studies, greater emphasis should be given to

---

[8] Report of the Harvard Committee, *General Education in a Free Society* (Cambridge, Mass.: Harvard University Press, 1945), pp. 137–150.

interpretation, but theorizing should be well rooted in the knowledge of the field. The attempt to cover too much material has resulted in students learning too little about too much. Finally, the report emphasized that the social studies should not be expected to imitate the rigorous exactitude of other disciplines, such as mathematics, because social and political life is shaped by emotions and manifold variables and unknowns, which allow for societal change and improvement.

An Eclectic Approach.   The Harvard Report represented an attempt to preserve the traditional elements of the social studies curriculum while providing some opportunity for experimentation and change through the inclusion of the study of contemporary society. Although the Harvard Report sought to reconcile the differences between those committed to the traditional dominance of history through the subject-centered curriculum and those calling for an integrated curriculum based upon the problems and needs of youth and society, the report tended to favor a social studies curriculum rooted in the cultural heritage.

Integration in the Social Sciences:
The Dilemma of Diversity and Specialism

Efforts to integrate the social sciences for purposes of general education have stemmed from the recognition that "man can be only partially studied in the segmented contexts of the separate disciplines, that social, economic, political, psychological, geographic, and ideational influences do not exist in isolation, and that what is needed is . . . a systematic interrelating of the verified hypotheses concerning human behavior.[9]

Emphasis on Specialization.   Scholars in each of the social science disciplines tend to regard their own specialties as the basis for curriculum development. Thus, historians, sociologists, economists, political scientists, geographers, and anthropologists would tend to favor their own specialties in determining course content, sequence, and methodology. Many historians, for example, have resented the inroads made in the high school curriculum by the contemporary social sciences. One historian puts it this way: "Fortunately most of the courses labeled 'social studies' in the public schools are still basically courses in history. Before it is too late, the label 'history' should be restored to them. Unless this is done, the processes of erosion will continue. More and more of these courses will surrender to the fad of contemporaneity."[10]

---

[9] Arthur Naftalin, "Social Science in General Education," Chapter VI in *General Education*, Fifty-first Yearbook of the National Society for the Study of Education, Part I (Chicago: The University of Chicago Press, 1952), p. 122.

[10] Arthur Bestor, *The Restoration of Learning* (New York: Alfred A. Knopf, Inc., 1955), p. 128.

The bias that university scholars have for their own disciplines is illustrated in the 1960 curriculum survey of the San Francisco public schools. The survey committee, appointed by the San Francisco Board of Education during the height of the post-Sputnik I furor against the public schools, was composed of liberal-arts professors from the University of California (Berkeley) and Stanford University. Representing the social sciences were a Stanford professor of history and a University of California professor of economics. In citing the difficulties associated with the term *social studies,* the survey report concluded that "the only way to remedy this situation is to return to the teaching of the more clearly defined subjects of history and geography." [11] With the exception of one semester of civics in grade 12, the committee recommended that the required social studies sequence in grades 7 through 12 be limited to geography and history. In recommending that current affairs be eliminated, the committee held that the aims of such studies would be "best achieved by the study of history, whose subjects, more remote in space or time, render easier an objective analysis of conflicting opinions and interests." [12]

Diversity and Conflict. Thus, scholars in each of the social science disciplines tend to regard their own specialties as the focal point for curriculum development. Add to this the differences in philosophical orientation, and one can begin to comprehend the great conflict and diversity of opinion as to what should properly constitute the social science or social studies component of the general education curriculum in high school and college.

> The bewilderment that besets planners of general education programs in social science is reflected in an immense diversity of courses described as "social science," "social studies," or "social problems." . . . For example, some planners develop their courses around the notion of preparation for citizenship in the specific sense of acquainting the student with the institutions and processes of government. Others seek to transmit an understanding of the cultural heritage through courses in contemporary civilization; still others offer a diagnosis of contemporary social, economic, and political problems, or they deal directly with the application of the scientific method to the problems of society, or they emphasize a study of the patterns of cultural organization. Some courses are "student-centered" in the instrumentalist sense, while others, place primary, if not exclusive, emphasis upon "subject-matter" without paying any particular attention to how the course content will ultimately

---

[11] *Report of the San Francisco Curriculum Survey Committee* (San Francisco: San Francisco Unified School District, April 1, 1960), p. 52.
[12] *Ibid.,* p. 53.

affect the behavior of the individual student. Teaching methods likewise reveal a wide range of techniques.[13]

The tendency on the part of specialists—historians, political scientists, geographers, economists, sociologists, and so on—to argue that their own disciplines should serve as the focal point, even in the case of "integrated" approaches in the social studies, raises the danger of compartmentalization characteristic of the traditional subject curriculum. Because the experts are at odds, the schools are caught in a bind as to which formula should be adopted. And because no unified approach has emerged from the national curriculum projects characteristic of the curriculum reform efforts in the sciences and mathematics, the schools have tended to adhere to the traditional sequence while making minor additions and subtractions of subjects and topics.

Opposition to Integrated Approaches in the Social Studies

"Back to the Fundamentals."   Leading essentialists have held that the secondary schools must be concerned primarily with the "fundamental disciplines" of history, mathematics, science, English, and foreign languages. They have opposed the efforts over the years toward the integration of the social studies curriculum in the secondary school and the revision of the curriculum to include the contemporary social sciences in place of history.

Historian Arthur Bestor, one of the most influential spokesmen for the essentialist position during the 1950's, recommended that the social studies program in the secondary school consist of ancient history, medieval and early modern European history, world history of the nineteenth and twentieth centuries, American history, and American constitutional history and governmental structure (though not necessarily in the order given).

Opposition to Contemporaneity.   Bestor conceded that courses such as geography and economics might be offered outside the regular sequence.[14] According to Bestor, the uniqueness of history as a discipline requires that it not be submerged in the contemporary social sciences under the label of "social studies." He argued that "the shortsighted worship of contemporaneity is producing its most devastating effects within the area which educationists call 'social studies.' This label has itself contributed so greatly to educational confusion and stultification that it ought to be abandoned forthwith." [15]

---

13 Naftalin, *op. cit.,* p. 121.

14 Bestor, *op. cit.,* p. 326.

15 *Ibid.,* p. 126.

Dominance of History. In connection with the need for interdisciplinary approaches, Bestor contended that this could be provided for in the history courses, where "the teacher of history can draw data and concepts from economics and political science without having to be re-baptized to do so." [16] On the other hand, according to Bestor, one cannot expect the integration of history in the contemporary social sciences because the latter are taught by teachers who "have merely picked up a capricious assortment of credits in miscellaneous courses classified among the social sciences." [17] Bestor's logic as to why the social studies curriculum should be limited primarily to history, and why history teachers are more competent in their discipline than those who have specialized in one or more of the contemporary social sciences, is predicated on the belief that "history bears approximately the same relationship to the social sciences that mathematics does to the natural sciences." [18] Such reasoning, carried to its logical conclusion, would virtually eliminate the natural sciences as a fundamental discipline in the secondary school curriculum. Yet Bestor manages to include the sciences in the secondary school curriculum along with mathematics, history, English, and foreign languages "because contemporary intellectual life has been built upon a foundation of these particular disciplines." [19]

Opposition to Integrated Frameworks. In attacking various approaches toward the integration of knowledge through broad fields, core, and the common learnings, Bestor held that one cannot deal effectively with life problems until he has marshaled the array of separate intellectual powers. Thus the "attempt to coordinate the distinctive disciplines in an orderly attack upon complex, intertwined problems should come as the culmination of long-continued study, so that the intellectual powers applied may be as fully developed as possible." [20] Bestor sees this fruition of the powers of mental discipline as occurring in the college years, although here too he is critical of the omnibus introductory courses at the college level. "We must remember, however, that the various disciplines can only be coordinated; they cannot be fused." [21] However, Bestor acknowledges that some integrated work might be appropriate during the senior year of high school for those youngsters who are not going on to college.

The belief that one cannot deal with molar problems or phenomena as they occur in life until one has developed his mental abilities through a fund of elemental knowledge derived from the basic disciplines, under-

---

16 *Ibid.,* p. 129.
17 *Ibid.,* p. 128.
18 *Ibid.,* p. 127.
19 *Ibid.,* p. 40.
20 *Ibid.,* p. 63.
21 *Ibid.,* p. 65.

lies Bestor's position against integrated studies. Bestor also holds that "one cannot take the unresolved chaos that comes to us in experience and deal with it directly, if one expects the mind to play any role in the process. Practically all 'integrated' courses in the high school, and many of those in college, have overlooked this simple fact." [22]

However, studies on the psychology of learning have failed to support the doctrine of mental discipline. Cronbach, for example, concludes that "the studies supposed to improve the mind had no more effect on mental test performance or on ability to master other subjects than did the studies believed to lack disciplinary value." [23] This does not mean that no curriculum priorities need be established so far as areas of knowledge are concerned. It simply means that the discipline of mathematics, or of Latin, for example, holds no unique attributes over other studies in the "cultivation of the intellect." Furthermore, the mastery of Latin or mathematics is not requisite for disciplined thinking in unrelated fields, such as history or political science. Where areas of knowledge are closely related, as in the case of the physical sciences and mathematics, or in the case of the social sciences, the isolation of these areas of knowledge in the curriculum through separate and independent subjects inhibits learning transfer.

Bestor's premise that the context of life experience is far too complex for effective learning to take place, as far as the child and adolescent are concerned, must be regarded as untenable. Whitehead, for example, observed that perhaps the most complex form of learning, oral communication, is learned by the child before he even enters school. The child learns basic oral communication because it is essential to social life and because it is developed through the natural context of social life. Thus the criterion of difficulty, or the assumption that the simplest elements of learning must precede the complex, would appear to be invalid where intellectual tasks are derived from life experience. According to Whitehead, "the uncritical application of the principle of the necessary antecedence of some subjects to others has, in the hands of dull people with a turn for organization, produced in education the dryness of the Sahara." [24]

Turning again to the matter of integrated studies, the limited body of research comparing the learning outcomes from integrated curricula in comparison to traditional separate-subject curricula fails to support Bestor's notions against integrated approaches. In assessing the research related to integrated courses, Lindgren concludes that "theoretically, at

---

[22] *Ibid.*, p. 60.

[23] Lee J. Cronbach, *Educational Psychology*, 2nd ed. (New York: Harcourt, Brace & World, Inc., 1963), p. 315.

[24] Alfred North Whitehead, *The Aims of Education and Other Essays* (New York: The Macmillan Company, 1929), p. 26.

least, such courses should succeed not only because they make better sense but also because students would be more highly motivated to participate in the learning process." [25] But although the general literature in curriculum tends to regard integrated approaches most favorably, the problem of developing the scope and sequence of content often has been left to the decisions of groups of classroom teachers who have neither the time nor the resources for such tasks. The result often has been the failure to develop adequate criteria and priorities in the selection of content and, consequently, the emerging program of studies has become vulnerable to criticism for appearing to be arbitrary and frivolous.

As discussed later in this chapter, efforts to focus on the separate disciplines of knowledge in curriculum building reached unprecedented proportions through the curriculum reform movement in the social sciences during the 1960's. The attempt of mature scholars to organize knowledge systematically and logically according to its structural elements raises serious questions, however, as to whether such formulations will serve to fragment the curriculum into separate disciplines or domains which, in turn, will create new problems of synthesis for the immature learner. In 1916 Dewey warned that "the segregation which kills the vitality of history is divorce from present modes and concerns of social life." [26] And in 1917 Whitehead called for the eradication of "the disconnection of subjects which kills the vitality of our modern curriculum." [27]

The opposition to integrated approaches in the social sciences is accompanied by even greater opposition to efforts that are directed at correlating and integrating this field with other fields, such as the language arts (literature). The concern for the study of human problems is not the exclusive province of the social studies. Indeed, it is manifested in literature and the arts. But to build a larger and more comprehensive framework for curriculum integration in general education, through a common-learnings or core approach, presents obstacles that are far too difficult for most schools to surmount by themselves. For not only are national curriculum groups tending to focus their efforts on the separate disciplines, but the university scholars appear to be engaged in a kind of power struggle in which they seek to promote their own specialties.

Ironically, the mounting social conflicts and crises in our cities during the 1960's have resulted in the creation of certain interdisciplinary programs, such as urban studies, in a number of colleges and universities. However, in view of the trend toward specialization, there is the likelihood that many such programs will become highly specialized, depart-

---

[25] Henry Clay Lindgren, *Educational Psychology in the Classroom*, 3rd ed. (New York: John Wiley & Sons, Inc., 1967), p. 387.

[26] John Dewey, *Democracy and Education* (New York: The Macmillan Company, 1916), p. 250.

[27] Whitehead, *op. cit.*, p. 10.

mentalized, and separated from the various social science departments of the university.

Conant's Report on the High School

In 1959, under the auspices of the Carnegie Corporation, James B. Conant presented his "first report to interested citizens" on the American high school in a small volume titled *The American High School Today*.[28] Conant's study was conducted during a period of mounting criticisms leveled at American education as the result of cold war tensions and Sputnik I. Conant's recommendations for the social studies curriculum were not radically different from what was being practiced in many traditional high schools of the day. According to Conant, the graduation requirements for all students in the comprehensive high school should include from three to four years of social studies. This would consist of two years of history (one of which would be American history) and a senior course in American problems or American government.

A Course in American Problems. Although Conant's proposal for a senior course in American problems or American government was virtually identical to the proposal of the 1916 NEA Commission on the Reorganization of Secondary Education, he discussed this course in some detail while offering no specific recommendations concerning the nature and scope of the other required courses in his proposed social studies curriculum. And while Conant recommended that students be grouped according to ability, subject by subject, in the required courses, he proposed that the senior course in American problems or American government be heterogeneously grouped. Accordingly, each class in this course would represent a cross section of the total student population of the school. That this course would exemplify a living embodiment of our democratic society is reflected in Conant's description of the twelfth-grade social studies (American problems or American government).

> This course should develop not only an understanding of the American form of government and of the economic basis of our free society, but also mutual respect and understanding between different types of students. Current topics should be included; free discussion of controversial issues should be encouraged. This approach is one significant way in which our schools distinguish themselves from those in totalitarian nations. This course, as well as well-organized homerooms and certain student activities, can contribute a great deal to the development of future citizens of our democracy who will be intelligent voters, stand

---

[28] James Bryant Conant, *The American High School Today* (New York: McGraw-Hill Book Company, Inc., 1959).

firm under trying national conditions, and not be beguiled by the oratory of those who appeal to special interests.[29]

These are indeed noble and far-reaching objectives for an entire curriculum, let alone a single course. Conant did not explain how such objectives could be realized through a single problem-centered and heterogeneously grouped course in the senior year, especially in view of his recommendation that all other required work, taken earlier in the social studies, consist of subject-centered and homogeneously grouped courses in history. If so much can be expected from a problem-centered approach and heterogeneous grouping, then why not carry this rationale throughout the entire required or general education sequence in the social studies? Academically talented pupils would still be able to pursue advanced courses in the social studies beyond those courses which constitute the general education sequence required of all students. Yet Conant offered no explanation for the apparent inconsistency in his proposed social studies curriculum. While his professed faith in the comprehensive high school as the great democratizing institution of our society was reflected in his proposal for the heterogeneously grouped senior course in American problems, this rationale was strangely absent from his social studies curriculum for grades 9 through 11.

Subject-Centered Curriculum. The emphasis given to the integration of the general education curriculum through a problem-centered common-learnings course, as proposed by the Educational Policies Commission under Conant's chairmanship in 1952, was abandoned completely in *The American High School Today.* Conant simply reverted to the departmentalized school and the separate-subject framework, while ignoring the question of curriculum integration so prominently featured in the 1952 report, *Education for ALL American Youth—A Further Look.* Apparently, the crisis of Sputnik I called for a return to the traditional separate-subject framework of curriculum organization as advocated by leading essentialists of the day.

Conant's Report on the Junior High School

Conant's report for the Carnegie Corporation on the senior high school was followed in 1960 with a similar document on the junior high school. In recommending that all students in grades 7 and 8 be required to take social studies (with emphasis on history and geography), Conant advocated that a block of time be set aside in grade 9 in which one teacher would work with the same group of students, generally in English and the social studies.

---

29 *Ibid.,* pp. 75–76.

However, Conant's advocacy of block-time teaching was not intended for purposes of curriculum articulation and integration, but rather to have the block-time teacher working with fewer students over a longer time period so that the teacher would be able to serve also in a counseling capacity. Presumably, this would provide for a smoother transition for the student from the self-contained classroom of the elementary school to the departmentalized structure of the junior high school. Except for this block-time arrangement in grade 7, Conant recommended a strictly departmentalized curriculum framework in the junior high school. In connection with the block-time teaching in grade 7, subject matter boundaries (i.e., between English and social studies) would be retained. Consequently, Conant's advocacy of block-time teaching was not to be construed as an endorsement of core teaching.

> The block-time teaching I am discussing need not break down subject-matter lines. Occasionally, one finds a school in which efforts to integrate or fuse subjects are successfully made. These "core" programs are oriented to the problems of young adolescents and involve considerable teacher-pupil planning. . . . Though I am not opposed to experimentation with the core approach, I must make it plain that my advocacy of block-time teaching does not presuppose an endorsement of core teaching.[30]

As in the case of his study of the senior high school, the common-learnings core, advocated in the 1952 report of Conant's Educational Policies Commission, was noticeable by its absence in Conant's 1960 report on the junior high school. The pressures of the times appeared to warrant a return to the safety of the traditional and time-tested subject curriculum.

RECENT FORCES AND TRENDS

Proposals by Professional Societies

Recognizing the impact of the curriculum reform movement in the sciences and mathematics, the American Council of Learned Societies, a federation of national organizations concerned with the humanities, embarked on a cooperative venture with the National Council for the Social Studies in 1960 for the purpose of formulating the general and content objectives of the social studies in general education. As the result of this joint effort, a volume of position papers was published in 1962. Except for two papers on geographic areas, and a culminating paper by a committee of the National Council for the Social Studies, each of the

---

[30] James Bryant Conant, *Education in the Junior High School Years* (Princeton, N.J.: Educational Testing Service, 1960), p. 23.

position papers focused on a major social science discipline: history, geography, political science, economics, cultural anthropology, sociology, and psychology.

Efforts to View the Whole Curriculum in the Social Studies.   One of the reasons cited for this undertaking was that, in efforts to improve and update the social studies curriculum over the years, "no serious effort has been made to view the separate parts with reference to the whole, and, lacking a general framework within which to operate, the experts in the several disciplines have frequently worked at cross purposes." [31] It was also observed that despite local deviations, the social studies curriculum in the senior high school in the early 1960's was still based on the 1916 report of the NEA's Commission on the Reorganization of Secondary Education. Thus, the general pattern to be found was civics or world geography in the ninth grade, world history in the tenth, U.S. history (usually by state law) in the eleventh and, occasionally, problems of democracy in the twelfth.[32] Also criticized was the widespread practice of preparing most teachers of the social studies with a major subject emphasis in history, while neglecting the behavioral sciences.

Separate Position Papers.   Although this joint effort on the part of the American Council of Learned Societies and the National Council for the Social Studies was conceived for the purpose of relating the various component disciplines into a general framework, the end result was a series of position papers representing, for the most part, the specialist's view of his own discipline. Thus, in one of these papers a historian maintains that, first, history must be the core of the social studies curriculum because "it is hardly possible to begin the analysis of social behavior until a number of historical facts have been absorbed"; second, "the narrative tone of history sustains student interest better than the analytical approach of other social sciences"; and, finally, "the historical context is closer to the real situations that students will face later in life." [33] Not only are such claims unsupported by research, but the increased emphasis on the modern social sciences in the curriculum in recent years has been justified on the grounds that the absorption of historical facts does not enhance analytical thinking, and that the modern social sciences evoke greater interest and commitment on the part of students because such studies are indeed closer to the problems of contemporary life than is the traditional study of history. In this vein, a geographer, writing in the

---

[31] American Council of Learned Societies and the National Council for the Social Studies, *The Social Studies and the Social Sciences* (New York: Harcourt, Brace & World, Inc., 1962), p. vi.

[32] *Ibid.*, p. 4.

[33] *Ibid.*, p. 24.

same volume as the above-quoted historian, maintains that "there is a growing demand that the schools should provide a more effective treatment of world affairs, and a better understanding of the significance of the arrangement of people, resources, and political organization in the modern world. This purpose is not well served by using the behavioral concepts in a historical framework." [34] And, again in the same volume, a political scientist argues that in the social science curriculum of the high schools, "history is queen, and this tends to be a history taught with little if any critical appreciation for the social science generalizations embedded in its common-sense narrative." [35]

Emphasis on the Separate Disciplines. Although not all scholar-specialists contend that their particular disciplines must necessarily be represented in the high school curriculum as separate courses, they nevertheless advocate that their disciplines be given considerably greater emphasis. However, the proper curriculum framework for such learnings is either completely avoided or is given but cursory treatment by these scholars. As a consequence, the schools are criticized by the scholar-specialists for not properly imparting the essential areas of knowledge and competencies that comprise each of the major social science disciplines, while these very same critics skirt the questions of curriculum frameworks, priorities, diversity of the student population, time limits, and changing pressures to which the schools are subjected. Thus an economist argues that "economic understanding of a quality and on a scale required for the successful exercise of government in a world crowded with public economic issues will not just happen. It can be had only if the task of providing it is set explicitly for, and accepted wholeheartedly and carried out vigorously by, the schools." [36] And a sociologist recommends that "sociology should be made available as an avenue of study for the academically talented high school student; and that a much more thorough treatment of sociology should be incorporated in existing social studies for all students." [37]

It is easy for university scholars to point to the gaps between the secondary school curriculum and the advances in scholarly knowledge and methodology. In the eyes of many university scholars, the high schools should provide for a more thorough and effective treatment of the specialized scholarly disciplines so that the students, upon entering college, would be able to pursue more advanced work while the colleges could, in turn, eliminate the troublesome survey courses.[38] Many university scholars see the ideal high school as a microcosm of the university and,

[34] *Ibid.,* p. 45.
[35] *Ibid.,* p. 101.
[36] *Ibid.,* p. 116.
[37] *Ibid.,* p. 169.
[38] American Council of Learned Societies, *op. cit.,* p. 40.

as a result, conceive of the high school curriculum as serving primarily a college-preparatory function. In turn, the high school youngster, regarded as a miniature college student, is denied curricular experiences that are designed to meet his authentic needs and interests. Moreover, the terminal student is virtually disregarded and the problem of student diversity is treated mainly through ability grouping rather than through curriculum redesign.

As we have seen, the joint effort on the part of the American Council of Learned Societies and the National Council for the Social Studies to view the separate social science disciplines with reference to a general framework resulted, for the most part, in a series of position papers in which individual scholars seek to extoll the essential role of their own disciplines. Yet the National Council for the Social Studies sees the development of desirable sociocivic behavior as the ultimate goal of education in the social studies. If this be the case, then there must be an essential difference between the social sciences as specialized disciplines and the social studies in the schools, because the social sciences purport to be scientific and neutral and desirable sociocivic behavior is not the exclusive concern of any individual discipline.[39] Nevertheless, the growing efforts to influence the social studies curriculum in our secondary schools during the 1960's, on the part of such learned societies as the American Historical Association, American Economic Association, American Anthropological Association, Association of American Geographers, American Political Science Association, and American Sociological Association have been concerned with promoting the separate disciplines in the schools.

The Social Studies Program of the U.S. Office of Education

As mentioned at the beginning of this chapter, the unprecedented federal support of curriculum improvement projects in the sciences and mathematics during the immediate post-Sputnik period through NDEA and NSF led some educators to point to the danger of curriculum imbalance. As a result, the U.S. Office of Education established the Social Studies Program (originally called Project Social Studies) in 1962.

In comparison to the level of support given the projects in the sciences and mathematics, however, the Social Studies Program has received meager, if not token, support. Through this program, more than a dozen centers were established at colleges and universities throughout the nation for purposes of redefining the goals, scope, content, materials, and techniques of the social studies curriculum, and to evaluate and disseminate the new materials. These projects have been designed to provide for the collaboration of professors and school teachers, and many of them pur-

---

[39] *Ibid.*, p. 290.

port to follow an inductive or inquiry approach while employing a variety of audiovisual resources.

Although most of these projects have sought to shift the orientation of the social studies curriculum from the traditional historical-descriptive emphasis to an empirical-analytical emphasis characteristic of the modern social sciences, they are criticized on a number of grounds. Like other curriculum reform projects in the social studies, the projects connected with the Social Studies Program of the U.S. Office of Education have sought to model themselves after the exceedingly well-endowed curriculum projects in the sciences, particularly the physical sciences, both conceptually and operationally. From the operational standpoint the social studies projects, because of their meager financial resources, have been utterly unable to come anywhere near a resemblance to the giant organizational framework and scope of functions characteristic of the projects in the sciences. From the conceptual standpoint, the validity of using the sciences as a model for curriculum construction in the social studies is yet to be demonstrated. This issue is discussed later in this chapter.

Support by the National Science Foundation

The National Science Foundation has joined various professional societies in supporting curriculum projects in the areas of anthropology, economics, geography, and sociology. However, the level of support provided these social studies projects by NSF is minuscule compared to the funds allocated by this agency for course-content improvement in mathematics, physical science, and biological science. Where the anthropology project is designed to develop material to be used in high school history courses and possibly for introductory social studies courses during the early grades of the secondary school, the projects in economics, geography, and sociology include the development of new high school courses in these disciplines.

The relatively low level of support provided by NSF for the curriculum projects in the social studies, in comparison to the sciences and mathematics, can be traced to the historical bias against the social sciences on the part of this agency. Although NSF was established in 1950 with a division of biological sciences and a division of mathematical, physical, and engineering sciences, the social sciences were not accorded divisional status until 1961. Furthermore, this division was limited to the social science disciplines of anthropology, economics, and sociology on the grounds that these are the most scientific of the social sciences.[40] In recent years some modest grants have been made by NSF for support of research in political science.

---

[40] Laurel N. Tanner, "BIG SCIENCE and little social science," *The School Review*, Vol. 77 (March, 1969), pp. 18–31.

MAJOR CHARACTERISTICS AND CRITICISMS

The Mature Scholar As Model for the Schoolboy

As discussed in Chapter 3, the assumption that "intellectual activity anywhere is the same, whether at the frontier of knowledge or in a third-grade classroom," [41] originally was formulated as a fundamental premise for guiding the curriculum reform movement in the sciences. This premise, embraced by university scholars seeking curriculum reform in the sciences at the elementary and secondary levels, also was adopted by their counterparts in the social sciences. The university scholar who assumes that "what's good for me is good for the kids" virtually absolves himself from the complex task of ascertaining the appropriateness of the material in relation to the psychological development of children and adolescents. Thus the university scholar's model is that of himself and not of the child or youth who must learn the material. As mentioned earlier, not only is this an unproved assumption, but it eliminates the need to explore and evaluate alternative approaches to curriculum development.

Unsubstantiated Claims. The premise that the schoolboy's mode and motives for effective learning are identical to those of the mature scholar has resulted in the production of curriculum materials that are more noted for their promotional claims than for their contributions to determining the most effective patterns of curriculum and instruction in the social studies. For example, the director of a leading curriculum project in economics for grades 1 through 12 offers us the Bruner-derived claim that "children, even at the beginning of first grade, can see the great contours of the economic world." [42] He goes on to state that "it has been this writer's observation that the first grader's curiosity is sharper than that of first-year college students." [43] The author offers no experimental evidence in support of these remarkable claims even though his project is entitled "A New Experiment in Economic Education." From our review of the theories of Dewey and Piaget, discussed in Chapter 1, the premises and claims of the author are subject to serious challenge.

Need for Research. Following the mandate of Bruner and the Physical Science Study Committee, which holds that the task of the student be modeled after that of the mature scholar, Fenton argues that "students must learn the rules by which historians collect evidence and use it to interpret the past if they are to read or write history intelligently. . . .

---

[41] Jerome S. Bruner, *The Process of Education* (Cambridge, Mass.: Harvard University Press, 1960), p. 14.

[42] Lawrence Senesh, "The Organic Curriculum: A New Experiment in Economic Education," *The Councilor,* Vol. 21 (March, 1960), p. 3.

[43] *Ibid.,* p. 13.

Teaching the mode of inquiry of history and the social sciences lies at the heart of the new social studies." [44]

Ironically, while Fenton maintains in one publication that students "must be able to judge whether an author's conclusions are supported by the evidence he presents," [45] in another publication he acknowledges that his position regarding his own curriculum is not supported by research evidence. "Although we have discovered no research data to support our position," writes Fenton, "we believe that the ability to use questions associated with analytical concepts from the social sciences correlates highly with creative achievements in history and the social sciences. . . . This process is likely to produce a generation of students who are able to think creatively about society." [46] Thus Fenton expects teachers and curriculum workers to accept his premises at face value while, on the other hand, high school students are required to judge an author in history and the social sciences according to the evidence in support of the author's conclusions.

This is not to imply that all curriculum programs be thoroughly researched before they are put into practice. Surely there is need for new and promising changes in fields notorious for their didactic-memoriter methods, which are known to be deadening to the student. However, we need to question the assumption that the student learning history, or social science, or physics, must perform like a professional historian, social scientist, or physicist. Is it realistic to assume that the high school student studying four or five major disciplines can be expected to assume the role of the mature scholar in each of these disciplines? Are the student's interests, aspirations, needs, and talents so closely interwoven with those of the mature scholar? Dewey cautioned that "there are certain features of scholarship . . . which get in the way of effective teaching." [47]

Emphasis on Inquiry or Induction

The new projects characteristically seek to stress a mode of inquiry through which new concepts, skills, and generalization are developed. The traditional emphasis on rote learning of factual information as an end in itself is rejected. Some of the projects have developed a sequence of steps representing the inquiry process with the assumption that by learning to follow this mode, students should be able to investigate problems independently and in a disciplined manner. One such schema, devel-

---

[44] Edwin Fenton, *Teaching the New Social Studies in Secondary Schools* (New York: Holt, Rinehart and Winston, Inc., 1966), p. 150.

[45] *Ibid.*

[46] Edwin Fenton, *Developing a New Curriculum: A Rationale for the Holt Social Studies Curriculum* (New York: Holt, Rinehart and Winston, Inc., 1967), p. 7.

[47] John Dewey, *Democracy and Education, op. cit.,* p. 215.

oped at one of the projects in the Social Studies Program supported by the U.S. Office of Education, lists the following steps in a mode of inquiry:

1. Recognizing a problem from data
2. Formulating hypotheses
   a. Asking analytical questions
   b. Stating hypotheses
   c. Remaining aware of the tentative nature of hypotheses
3. Recognizing the logical implications of hypotheses
4. Gathering data
   a. Deciding what data will be needed
   b. Selecting or rejecting sources
5. Analyzing, evaluating and interpreting data
   a. Selecting relevant data
   b. Evaluating sources
      (1) Determining the frame of reference of an author
      (2) Determining the accuracy of statements of fact
6. Evaluating the hypotheses in light of the data
   a. Modifying the hypothesis, if necessary
      (1) Rejecting a logical implication unsupported by data
      (2) Restating the hypothesis
   b. Stating a generalization.[48]

Dewey's Reflective Steps.   Such attempts at identifying the elements of the inquiry process are not new. They are as old as Plato. And, as discussed in Chapter 1, such a schema was proposed in 1910 by Dewey in his five steps in reflection: (1) a felt difficulty; (2) its location and definition; (3) suggestion of possible solution; (4) development by reasoning of the bearings of the suggestion; (5) further observation and experiment leading to its acceptance or rejection.[49] However, Dewey cautioned that the phases "do not follow one another in a set order" and "no set rules can be laid down on such matters." [50] An assumption underlying the projects in the "new" social studies is that "the child, regardless of his age, can fruitfully engage in discovering solutions to psychological and intellectual problems." [51]

Developmental Stages.   Both Dewey and Piaget see hypothetical thinking as a process that is developed as the youngster matures, and not an ability that can be mastered at any age. According to Piaget, hypothetical thinking first becomes manifest between late childhood and early adoles-

---

[48] Fenton, *Developing a New Curriculum, op. cit.,* p. 6.
[49] John Dewey, *How We Think* (Boston: D. C. Heath & Co., 1910), p. 72.
[50] *Ibid.,* pp. 115–116.
[51] Byron G. Massialas and C. Benjamin Cox, *Inquiry in the Social Studies* (New York: McGraw-Hill Book Company, Inc., 1966), p. 137.

cence.[52] Nevertheless, many of the social studies projects have developed their curricula according to the Brunerian notion that the mode of inquiry characteristic of the mature scholar is appropriate at any level of schooling. Thus the "new" social studies projects often include lists of abilities in critical thinking for children and youth which closely resemble those designed for college students. For example, in 1954 Dressel and Mayhew identified the following critical abilities for college students in the social sciences:

1. To identify central issues
2. To recognize underlying assumptions
3. To evaluate evidence or authority
    a. To recognize stereotypes and clichés
    b. To recognize bias and emotional factors
    c. To distinguish between verifiable and unverifiable data
    d. To distinguish between relevant and nonrelevant
    e. To distinguish between essential and incidental
    f. To recognize the adequacy of data
    g. To determine whether facts support a generalization
    h. To check consistency
4. To draw warranted conclusions.[53]

Without indicating the appropriate age levels for the development of critical-thinking skills, Massialas and Cox offer the following list for the social studies curriculum:

1. The skills of understanding
    a. Summarizing
    b. Having sensitivity to new, ambiguous, or specialized words
    c. Detecting bias
    d. Assessing competence
    e. Judging the validity of data and their sources
    f. Identifying strong and weak arguments
    g. Developing analogies
    h. Distinguishing fact from opinion
2. The skills of hypothesizing or stating problems
    a. Perceiving possible solutions and stating them as tentative generalizations
    b. Detecting material or intellectual problems
    c. Developing and identifying different types of generalizations
3. The skills of exploration
    a. Identification of assumptions
    b. Developing valid inferences and tracing logical implications

---

52 Jean Piaget, *The Psychology of Intelligence* (New York: Harcourt, Brace & World, Inc., 1950), pp. 87–158.

53 Paul L. Dressel and Lewis B. Mayhew, *General Education—Explorations in Evaluation* (Washington, D.C.: American Council on Education, 1954), pp. 38–40.

      c. Recognizing dogmatism or emotion in statements

      d. Seeking and utilizing evidence

  4. The skills of concluding

      a. Accepting, modifying, or rejecting a hypothesis

      b. Developing solutions and consensus on solutions

      c. Testing a generalization.[54]

While the preceding list contains many important critical-thinking skills worthy of development, no effort is made to ascertain which are appropriate for seventh-graders, for example, and which are suitable for high school seniors. Moreover, it would appear that the preceding list, intended for the secondary school, is considerably more complex than that developed by Dressel and Mayhew for college or university students.

Inductive Teaching.   Another point of confusion has resulted in the use of the term *inductive teaching* in connection with a number of the "new" social studies projects. As we have seen, the so-called "inductive" or "inquiry" approach closely resembles Dewey's reflective teaching. Dewey's warning against laying down set rules and rigid steps in reflection should be carefully heeded in any curriculum package in the social studies that purports to be based on the "inductive approach." The misleading implication behind set methods or sequential steps is that two individuals should derive the same conclusions or solutions from the same set of data. But in the fields of history and other social sciences, scholars with differing sociopolitical philosophies frequently tend to come up with conflicting interpretations and conclusions on problems and issues, even when they have access to identical sources of evidence. While this should be expected, especially where issues are involved, the proponents of the "inductive" mode have often tended to ignore the reality of conflicting interpretations and conclusions being derived from the same data, while teachers and students seek to find the "right" answers through the proper method.

Consequently, although the "new" curriculum packages claim to employ the inquiry or inductive approach, in many cases the students must reach conclusions or solutions that are predetermined by the authors of these packages, while the teacher is expected to ensure these outcomes. In this respect the inquiry or inductive approach is in sharp conflict with Dewey's reflective experience. For Dewey, the reflective experience cannot lead to predetermined conclusions and solutions if it is to be truly reflective. Moreover, conclusions and solutions must be tentative and must be regarded as open to revision as they are tested in various connections and in view of the consequences in the real world. "There is

---

[54] Massialas and Cox, *op. cit.,* pp. 73–74.

no completion in the act of thinking. . . . Our most elaborate and rationally consistent thought has to be tried in the world and thereby tried out. And since it can never take into account all the connections, it can never cover with perfect accuracy all the consequences." [55]

Dewey also cautioned that unless a problem becomes the learner's problem, it will be just another externally imposed requirement involving steps toward "solution" which may have little to do with the development of reflective thinking.[56] Thus it is possible to follow an "inductive" or "inquiry" sequence of steps in a particular curriculum package in the social studies without becoming engaged in a truly reflective experience. The student has simply learned to meet another externally developed requirement.

The use of the term *inquiry* appears to be replacing the term *induction* as a label for the "new" curricula in the social studies. But it is not enough to use labels, however attractive they may appear. We will need to evaluate these projects carefully if any significant contribution is to be made to improving the social studies curriculum.

Absence of Experimental Research

As mentioned earlier, the "new" social studies projects often bear the label of "A New Experiment" and the claim is made that these projects constitute a curriculum revolution. It is ironic that while these projects commonly expect the child and the adolescent to follow an inquiry approach in testing hypotheses and evaluating alternatives for the solution of problems, the projects themselves have, for the most part, avoided the scrutiny of controlled experimentation as a means of evaluating their effectiveness in comparison to alternative curriculum packages.

The common practice has been to demonstrate the efficacy of the new projects through field trials. But merely showing that children are capable of learning certain concepts, skills, and generalizations does not answer the basic question as to whether such material *should* be included in the curriculum, or whether such material actually produces more effective learning outcomes than alternative materials. According to Hunt and Metcalf, "the projects, with few exceptions, are non-experimental. Rather than test hypotheses, projects have developed 'new' and 'exciting' instructional materials based upon unexamined assumptions. . . . Little effort has been made to evaluate systematically the learning that results from teaching the new materials." [57]

The task of evaluating the various curriculum packages in the social

---

[55] John Dewey, *Democracy and Education, op. cit.,* pp. 176–177.

[56] *Ibid.,* p. 182.

[57] Maurice P. Hunt and Lawrence E. Metcalf, *Teaching High School Social Studies,* 2nd ed. (New York: Harper & Row, Publishers, 1968), p. 279–280.

studies may prove to be far more complex than evaluating projects in the sciences and mathematics, because the social studies are infinitely more diverse. Moreover, whereas the sciences and mathematics tend to fit into lawful patterns, human behavior is far more complex and unpredictable. Thus the task of selecting content for the social studies tends to be far more arbitrary than that of selecting content for curricula in science or mathematics. As discussed in earlier chapters, even in the sciences and mathematics, curriculum workers have not found common agreement as to what should properly constitute a first course in high school physical science, seventh-grade mathematics, or college biology. But this does not imply that carefully controlled experimentation in evaluating learning outcomes from alternative curriculum approaches is unnecessary or without value. For unless the grandiose claims are carefully evaluated, we will not know whether we are moving forward or backward through our innovations. It is not only unfruitful but dangerously misleading to make claims for curriculum packages that are unsubstantiated and that are not subjected to the scrutiny of controlled research. For without such research, students and teachers are expected to accept the new material as dogma or theology.

Discipline Qua Discipline: The Search for Structure

The priority and prestige accorded the sciences in the curriculum reform movement during the 1960's seduced many of those responsible for curriculum reform in the social sciences into the belief that the sciences are an ideal model. Thus, for example, Fenton contends that "generalizations holding for PSSC physics also hold true for most of the materials produced at Project Social Studies centers" [58] (the Social Studies Program of the U.S. Office of Education). However, those responsible for constructing the PSSC course have encountered considerable difficulty in validating the assumptions upon which this course was built. In attempting to develop the PSSC course according to the fundamental structure of the discipline, much of the course content not only became separated from the world of practical applications, but also had limited appeal for even those adolescents of high ability. Moreover, even if an ideal structure in the physical sciences could be created as a sound basis for curriculum construction in this discipline, its applicability to other disciplines must be carefully scrutinized.

> There are very few social scientists who do not believe that the physical sciences are in some sense a paradigm for science. There are exceptions, but typically a sociologist is likely to agree that he would like to see sociology develop in the direction of becoming more like field theory in physics, with its greater precision, its greater powers of prediction,

---

[58] Fenton, *Teaching the New Social Studies, op. cit.,* p. 497.

its more complicated theories, and its more exciting theories. The same applies to the psychologist. Indeed, there has been a long history of psychologists who have attempted to produce theories of learning, for example, which are patterned upon classical physical theories. In my view, all of this is now a waste of time and a seriously misleading way of looking at the social sciences.[59]

In Chapter 3 we discussed the futile efforts of the American Institute of Biological Sciences in developing an "ideal" core course in college biology representing the central concepts and foundations of this field. After studying the biology curricula of four high quality universities that had recently given careful attention to the development of curriculum content, it was found that only 7 per cent of the information items identified in the core programs of these universities were shared in common.[60] If such a lack of agreement is characteristic of a first course in biology as found in four high quality universities, one cannot expect to find social scientists in general agreement as to the concepts, generalizations, principles, and structure of the social science disciplines. Yet most of the social studies projects have attempted to base their work on the dubious premise that there is a structure for each of the social science disciplines and that the model to be followed for discovering this structure is that of the Physical Science Study Committee.

Multidisciplinarity Vs. Interdisciplinarity.   Although Scriven acknowledges that no subject within the social studies curriculum is devoid of contamination by other subjects, he opts in favor of the multidisciplinary approach as opposed to the interdisciplinary mode of curriculum organization on the grounds that the social sciences, while linked together, do not emanate from a common core.[61] But while the multidisciplinary approach does not negate the value of focusing on broad social problems, because this can be done by treating these problems from the vantage point of each of the separate disciplines which constitute the social sciences, the breakdown occurs when the learner is left entirely to his own devices in synthesizing the various disciplines so that the problem can be solved in reality. When one dissects a frog, one can learn a great deal about the parts of the organism, but the poor creature can never be brought to life again.

59 Michael Scriven, "The Structure of the Social Studies," in G. W. Ford and Lawrence Pugno, *The Structure of Knowledge and the Curriculum* (Chicago: Rand McNally & Company, 1964), p. 97.

60 Commission on Undergraduate Education in the Biological Sciences, *Content of Core Curricula in Biology* (Washington, D.C.: The American Institute of Biological Sciences, 1967), p. 21.

61 Scriven, *op. cit.*, pp. 92, 94.

The Separate Disciplines. With few exceptions, the trend of the curriculum reform movement in the social studies has been away from problems that require integrative approaches to curriculum construction and toward the building of concepts, generalizations, skills, and theories, which are believed to comprise the structure of each of the separate disciplines. Although the current movement rejects the factual-descriptive-chronological treatment of subject matter characteristic of the traditional curriculum in which memorization is the key intellective process, the new focus is on the internal logic of the discipline qua discipline.

Even where attempts are made to include each of several major social science disciplines at a given grade level, separate units are derived for each discipline and these units appear to be insulated from other units that stem from other disciplines. For example, the so-called organic curriculum, developed by Senesh and others, attempts to deal with the fundamental concepts and ideas of each of several disciplines (economics, political science, sociology, anthropology, and geography) at every grade level. Through separate units representing each of the disciplines, the learner, beginning in the first grade, is "exposed to each of the social science disciplines in an undiluted form." [62] The approach is called organic because the different disciplines are treated in each grade level through separate units appropriate for the grade level. Yet each unit has a solo role and no systematic effort is made to integrate the various disciplines. The material is "organic" only insofar as each of the separate disciplines is given a solo role at each grade level. The fundamental ideas for two of the social science disciplines developed through this approach are presented in Figures 5-1 and 5-2.

After having formulated these fundamental ideas for each of the major disciplines in the social sciences, Senesh gives this account of his observations in first-grade classrooms: "I visited first grade classes to find out how many of these ideas could be related to the first graders' experiences. I found that the children's experience in social matters is potentially so meaningful that the fundamental knowledge can be related to their experience." [63] Unfortunately, Senesh offers no research evidence to support his conclusions. He simply contends that the material within the same structure of knowledge should grow in depth and complexity as the student advances from grade to grade. No attention is given to synthesizing the separate disciplines by relating them to broad themes, major issues, or pervading problems of man which transcends the individual disciplines. Instead, the learner is expected to develop his own mosaic from

---

[62] Lawrence Senesh, "Organizing a Curriculum Around Social Science Concepts," Chapter 3 in Irving Morrissett (ed.), *Concepts and Structure in the New Social Science Curricula* (New York: Holt, Rinehart and Winston, Inc., 1967), p. 24.

[63] *Ibid.*, p. 23.

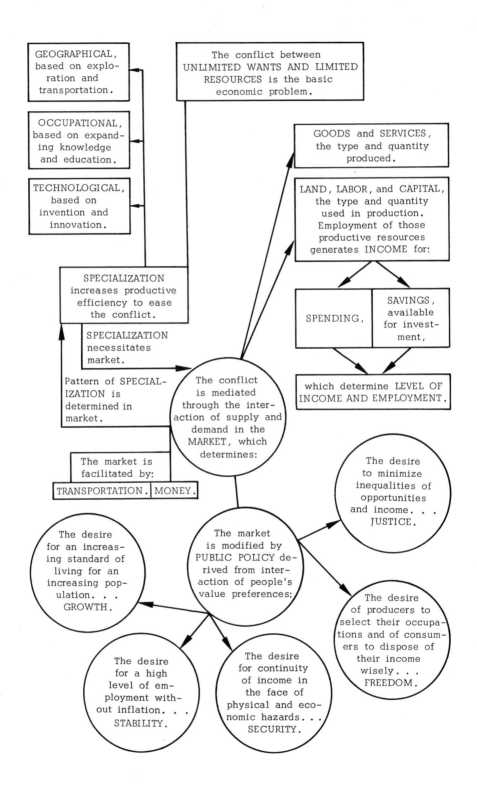

GEOGRAPHICAL, based on exploration and transportation.

OCCUPATIONAL, based on expanding knowledge and education.

TECHNOLOGICAL, based on invention and innovation.

The conflict between UNLIMITED WANTS AND LIMITED RESOURCES is the basic economic problem.

GOODS and SERVICES, the type and quantity produced.

LAND, LABOR, and CAPITAL, the type and quantity used in production. Employment of those productive resources generates INCOME for:

SPENDING, | SAVINGS, available for investment,

SPECIALIZATION increases productive efficiency to ease the conflict.

SPECIALIZATION necessitates market.

Pattern of SPECIALIZATION is determined in market.

which determine LEVEL OF INCOME AND EMPLOYMENT.

The conflict is mediated through the interaction of supply and demand in the MARKET, which determines:

The market is facilitated by:

TRANSPORTATION. | MONEY.

The desire to minimize inequalities of opportunities and income. . . JUSTICE.

The desire for an increasing standard of living for an increasing population. . . GROWTH.

The market is modified by PUBLIC POLICY derived from interaction of people's value preferences:

The desire of producers to select their occupations and of consumers to dispose of their income wisely. . . FREEDOM.

The desire for a high level of employment without inflation. . . STABILITY.

The desire for continuity of income in the face of physical and economic hazards. . . SECURITY.

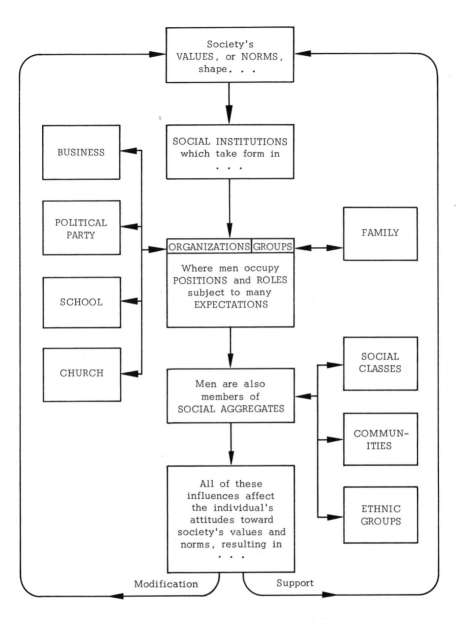

Figure 5-2 *(Above).* Fundamental Ideas of Sociology

Source: Lawrence A. Senesh, "Organizing a Curriculum Around Social Science Concepts," Chapter 3 in Irving Morrissett (ed.), Concepts and Structure in the New Social Science Curricula *(New York: Holt, Rinehart and Winston, Inc., 1967), p. 31.*

Figure 5-1 *(Left).* Fundamental Ideas of Economics

Source: Lawrence A. Senesh, "Organizing a Curriculum Around Social Science Concepts," Chapter 3 in Irving Morrissett (ed.), Concepts and Structure in the New Social Science Curricula *(New York: Holt, Rinehart and Winston, Inc., 1967), p. 25.*

the separate disciplines developed by specialists in each of the disciplines. According to Senesh,

> It is the job of the academic departments of universities to stimulate more social scientists to pay attention to the problem of structuring the knowledge of their own discipline. Such logical patterns of ideas will serve the social scientists as a map to identify new areas of research, and will serve the curriculum worker as a guide to build a curriculum which can be adjusted to incorporate new ideas as the frontier of knowledge expands.[64]

The Issue of Desirable Sociocivic Behavior as an Educational Goal

Although a 1962 report of the National Council for the Social Studies opens with the assertion that "the ultimate goal of education in the social studies is the development of desirable sociocivic behavior," [65] such a goal has come to be criticized by some academicians who hold that if their discipline is to be a science of human behavior, then it must not be committed to any ideology such as that embraced by "desirable sociocivic behavior." A sociologist offers this argument:

> the plain fact is that many college and university teachers of sociology are not primarily interested in "educating citizens." . . . For the profesfessional sociologist, his discipline is—or at least is in the process of becoming—a science of human behavior. . . . The spirit of free inquiry and objectivity is the foundation of sociology, just as it is the foundation of all other liberal arts and sciences; and it cannot help but be undermined if the study of society is curbed and channeled by the demands of an ideology, even a democratic one.[66]

An identical position is taken by Scriven who calls such objectives "sociocivically repulsive," [67] while an economist takes the opposing view that "to enlist the teaching of economics explicitly in the service of citizenship is in no sense to debase economics or to pervert economics as a science." [68] In response to this issue, one can well argue that this goal is indeed legitimate in the social studies in the secondary school as contrasted with the social sciences in the universities. But regardless of this point, it is difficult to see how it is possible even to select content, how-

---

[64] *Ibid.,* pp. 37–38.

[65] National Council for the Social Studies, "The Role of the Social Studies," *Social Education,* Vol. 26 (October, 1962), p. 315.

[66] Gresham M. Sykes, "Sociology," in *The Social Studies and the Social Sciences, op. cit.,* p. 158.

[67] Scriven, *op. cit.,* p. 101.

[68] Ben W. Lewis, "Economics," in *The Social Studies and the Social Sciences, op. cit.,* p. 107.

ever noncontroversial, without bias. Moreover, if in a democracy, one of the "desirable sociocivic objectives" is "the willingness to be open to the ideas and opinions of others," then such an objective might actually facilitate inquiry and "scientific" openmindedness. Nevertheless, the obsession with "scientific neutrality" on the part of many academicians in the behavioral sciences has raised an issue that probably suffers more from the lack of definition of what are "desirable sociocivic objectives" in a democracy, than from an ideological conflict in curriculum building.

The Persistent Question of Interdisciplinarity

The focus on fundamental concepts within each of the major disciplines that comprise the social sciences has wittingly and unwittingly resulted in the identification of concepts that are not necessarily within the exclusive domain of a singular discipline. Such developments are probably outgrowths of the discipline-centered trend of curriculum reform, rather than expressions of opposition. One project identified the following concepts, among many others, which can be related to more than one discipline:

> *Conflict*—its origin, expression, and resolution (biology, anthropology, psychology, sociology, political science, economics).
> *Industrialization-Urbanization* (ecology, anthropology, psychology, sociology, political science, economics).
> *Secularization* (anthropology, political science, sociology).
> *Compromise* and *Adjustment* (anthropology, psychology, sociology, political science, economics).
> *Power* (political science, sociology, economics, anthropology, psychology).
> *Morality* and *Choice* (anthropology, sociology, psychology, philosophy).
> *Institution* (anthropology, sociology, political science).[69]

Added to the above are many "value" concepts such as the dignity of man, loyalty, freedom, equality, and so on—each of which may be treated through more than one discipline. Moreover, there are many methodological concepts—such as objectivity, evidence, analysis, synthesis, and so on—which are common to all the social science disciplines.

If the search for the fundamental concepts that comprise the structure of each of the separate disciplines in the social studies also produces concepts that apply to several disciplines, one is led to ask whether the emphasis on the separate disciplines is the only valid procedure for curriculum construction. For such cross-disciplinary and interdisciplinary

---

[69] Adapted from Roy A. Price, Warren Hickman, and Gerald Smith, *Major Concepts for Social Studies* (Syracuse, N.Y.: Social Studies Curriculum Center, Syracuse University, 1965), pp. 8–18.

concepts continually appear, even when one is not seeking relationship and synthesis between and among the separate disciplines.

The Place of History

The emphasis on the separate social science disciplines has begun to challenge the traditional dominance of history in the secondary school curriculum. Although the secondary schools continue to emphasize history over any of the other social science disciplines, the proliferation of curriculum projects has been accompanied by efforts to find room for the newer social sciences as distinct disciplines. Krug takes the position that "history (should) remain the core of the social studies curriculum but that history teachers be encouraged and instructed to select and use often insights, concepts, and modes of inquiry from the social sciences." [70] To accommodate the social sciences within the framework of history, Krug sees the teacher employing an eclectic approach. He feels that such accommodation can be effected by history teachers who are also knowledgeable in at least one of the social sciences.

However, as discussed earlier in this chapter, many social scientists hold that history is an inadequate framework for the modern social science disciplines because these disciplines must retain their essential structural and methodological characteristics if they are to be authentic. Moreover, past experience has provided little evidence that history can be conceived as such a unifying core. Yet the battle among the university academicians seeking a place for their particular disciplines in the curriculum of the secondary school raises the specter of increasing fragmentation in an already fragmented curriculum.

THE COUNTERFORCE OF CURRICULUM INTEGRATION

Despite the unmistakable trend emphasizing the separate disciplines in the social studies curriculum during the past decade, a few notable counterefforts have appeared, as though to say: "We must stop acting as though nature were organized into disciplines in the same way that universities are." [71] If the curriculum is to have the authenticity characteristic of life, then cross-disciplinary and interdisciplinary modes of curriculum organization may yield results that go far beyond the sum total of the individual disciplines that make up the social studies. This does not imply that discipline-centered inquiry is wrong, but rather that it is not sufficient if we are to deal effectively in education with the total sys-

---

[70] Mark M. Krug, *History and the Social Sciences* (Waltham, Mass.: Blaisdell Publishing Company, 1967), p. 134.

[71] Russell L. Ackoff, "Systems, Organizations, and Interdisciplinary Research," *General Systems*, Vol. 5, 1960, p. 6.

tem of reality. Thus the passion for discipline-centered inquiry can lead to many blind spots in dealing with life problems.

The Issues Approach As an Integrative Schema

Contending that the specialized and fragmented disciplines, as constituted in the universities, are an inadequate model for the secondary school curriculum, Oliver and Shaver have developed a "jurisprudential approach" in which contemporary public issues are examined in the light of data from many sources.[72] Through the "jurisprudential approach," two or more legitimate sides of an issue bearing on an important question of public policy are studied. As discussed earlier, where a number of social scientists are opposed to sociocivic objectives as organizing elements in curriculum building, Oliver and Shaver hold that such objectives are not only legitimate but essential if the learner is to come to understand the role of the citizen in the community.

In the "jurisprudential approach" a controversial situation is presented through a dialogue which, in turn, evokes a disputative discussion requiring careful analysis of the issue or problem. When the teacher acts as one of the principals in the dialogue, he assumes a Socratic role. He is not merely concerned with opinions, but must be capable of helping students gain insights to evaluative, legal, and ethical aspects of the issue from both a contemporary and a historical perspective. Thus the teacher and students must be open to evidence pertinent to all sides of the issue, and they must engage in a process aimed at clarifying, if not resolving the issue.

Oliver and Shaver claim that the "jurisprudential approach" involves intellectual processes or strategies that are much more complex than those that have been described as "critical thinking" in the educational literature. However, this is debatable because many efforts at identifying the critical-thinking processes include the investigation of issues.[73] Nevertheless, the "jurisprudential approach" provides opportunities for investigating controversial issues through a methodology that heretofore has been neglected in the classroom. It provides for the careful analysis of political discussion through the identification of such specific areas of disagreement as the use and meaning of words, the principles governing social and political conduct, and the accuracy or plausibility of events in our society and among nations. It is assumed that through dialogues constructed in situational contexts the student is more likely to become personally involved in important issues and problems of public policy

---

[72] Donald W. Oliver and James P. Shaver, *Teaching Public Issues in High School* (Boston: Houghton Mifflin Company, 1966).

[73] Dressel and Mayhew, *op. cit.*

than if he merely is exposed to subject matter information that is primarily factual. Moreover, the systematic analysis of each issue, incorporating both contemporary and historical material, provides an integrated framework that is absent from the usual practice of treating "current events" as a supplement to the regular course in government or history.

Research Findings.   Where most of the curriculum projects in the social studies have not been subjected to controlled research, the "jurisprudential approach" has been evaluated to some extent with experimental and control groups. The findings revealed that students exposed to this approach did not suffer in their knowledge of conventional social studies content while they displayed greater retention of historical material than did the control groups. However, where the paper-and-pencil tests revealed that the students could learn effectively many of the abstract conceptual terms through the "jurisprudential approach," clear-cut results were not obtained with regard to carrying over the "jurisprudential" skills to more complex situations in student-led discussions during the second year of the program. Despite other methodological problems in conducting this research, the findings point to the conclusion that traditional subject-centered approaches are not superior to integrative approaches even in the knowledge of subject matter retained. According to Oliver and Shaver, "these results might well warrant the substitution of such an experimental curriculum for a conventional two-year United States history course in schools where receptive and capable teachers could implement the program." [74]

Rejection of "Structure of the Discipline."   Of great significance in this integrative approach is the rejection of the "structure of the discipline" as the key model for curriculum reform in the social studies, especially for purposes of general education. It openly challenges the premise that the learner and the teacher can function productively only when they adhere to the styles and norms of the university scholar.

> it seems that the social scientist's perception of public issues is, perhaps, as often blocked as facilitated by the rigor of his own conceptual schemes.
> . . . It is not at all certain that the social science scholar has made such a compelling contribution to clarifying or resolving major societal issues that his mode of thought is *the* model to be followed and taught. The somewhat parochial nature of the average academician's orientation as indicated by much scholarly work leads us to two major reservations about this basis for the social studies curriculum. First, there are models

---

[74] Oliver and Shaver, *op. cit.*, p. 284.

of reflection and action which obviously are relevant to social studies objectives but are all but ignored by the social scientists in their academic work. And, second, the social scientist seems especially prone to generalize from the fact that *his* structures make the social world meaningful and exciting to him to the proposition that the same structure will appear meaningful and exciting to all comers and especially to restless children and adolescents.[75]

Treatment of Values and Value Conflicts. The "jurisprudential approach" treats value judgments as a central concern in the study of public issues. While recognizing that it is possible and desirable to apply scientific methods toward the resolution of value conflicts that arise from errors and inconsistencies of fact, the "jurisprudential approach" also allows for the exposure of value conflicts that cannot be resolved through scientific methods, such as those stemming from fundamental differences in social philosophy. Where the traditional curriculum in the social studies either failed to treat value conflicts or reduced them to inane moralisms, the "jurisprudential approach" seeks to open these conflicts to careful analysis for the purpose of developing a realistic understanding of public issues.

Reflective Thinking As an Integrative Schema

Hunt and Metcalf also have challenged the validity of the premise that knowledge of the structure of the disciplines is essential to general education and that the "revolutionary" claims of the "new" curricula should be accepted in the absence of rigorous assessment.[76] They contend that a radical change in the aims, content, and methodology of the social studies is needed if we are to enable youth to understand and deal effectively with social problems, and that with the possible exception of the "jurisprudential approach," the current projects do not give promise of meeting this need.

Emphasis on Reflective Thinking. Borrowing from Dewey's model of reflection, Hunt and Metcalf propose that the content of learning not be restricted to formally organized bodies of knowledge but, instead, that the content of learning or subject matter "may be regarded as the data of acts of reflective thought." [77] They recommend that teaching materials focus on problematic areas involving "(1) broadly social and highly controversial issues of the culture; (2) knowledges, values, and attitudes of students; and (3) relevant data of the social sciences." [78]

---

[75] *Ibid.*, pp. 230–231.
[76] Hunt and Metcalf, *op. cit.*, p. 280.
[77] *Ibid.*, p. 281.
[78] *Ibid.*, p. 288.

Curriculum Integration Through Problematic Areas.   Because the problematic areas are related to life problems, they will invariably cut across the usual subject matter boundaries. While acknowledging that the pedagogical complications of the core curriculum or "common learnings" course has not always been well understood by teachers, Hunt and Metcalf recommend a block-time core that is problem centered and represents the pervasive cultural contradictions that are shared by most students and our society as a whole. Such a curriculum closely resembles the problem-centered core or "common learnings" course found in the mid-century literature of the progressives; [79] but where the latter conceived of the core or "common learnings" course as encompassing virtually all of general education, Hunt and Metcalf propose that the core concentrate mainly on social problems in place of the traditional subject-centered divisions in the social studies. Acknowledging that such a core would not only integrate the social studies but would embrace data from other fields as well, they see it being limited clearly to social problems and the acts of reflection that are brought to bear on these problems. The reflective process is outlined as (1) recognition and definition of a problem, (2) formulation of hypotheses, (3) elaboration of logical implications of hypotheses, (4) testing hypotheses, and (5) drawing conclusions.[80] The problems studied through the reflective process must challenge the inadequacies or incompatibilities in the beliefs, concepts, or values of the students. Otherwise, these problems will lack authenticity for the student.

Prospects for Integrative Problem-Centered Approaches

Whether the discipline-centered emphasis of recent years will be reversed in favor of interdisciplinary problem-centered approaches remains doubtful. But as the discipline-centered projects are carefully evaluated in the coming years, and as the traditional curriculum fails to meet the "relevancy" criterion demanded by many college and high school students, it is likely that integrative problem-centered curricula will emerge into new importance.

In recent years, the Social Studies Curriculum Program of the Educational Development Center has come to recognize the need for developing courses of study that are organized through the perspective of several interrelated disciplines. Acknowledging its "honest mistakes" of the past, and noting that "emphasis on specific disciplines obscures the unifying

---

79 See Educational Policies Commission, *Education for ALL American Youth—A Further Look, op. cit.,* and Harold B. and Elsie J. Alberty, *Reorganizing the High School Curriculum,* 3rd ed. (New York: The Macmillan Company, 1962).

80 Hunt and Metcalf, *op. cit.,* pp. 68–69.

questions of man's experience," [81] the Social Studies Curriculum Program has attempted to develop materials in response to our society's deepening crisis in cultural values and human relations. At the upper elementary level, "Man: A Course of Study" deals with the nature of man in contrast to other animal species, while also examining man in society. At the secondary level, several courses have been developed, such as "Inventing the Western World," "From Subject to Citizen," "The American Experiment," and "Modernization." In these courses, historical coverage is subordinated to the goal of developing an understanding of root political and social issues. Contemporary and historical documents serve as key source materials and a variety of audiovisual resources have been developed for classroom use. Although the Social Studies Curriculum Program has had only a limited impact on the schools, the fact that it has come to reject the discipline principle as the sole basis of curriculum reform is highly significant.

Many examples can be cited of attempts to develop broadly integrative problem-centered courses at the college level. One such example are the all-college courses at Livingston College of Rutgers University. Opened in the fall of 1969 as a residential, coeducational institution, many of Livington's general education courses are intended to be interdisciplinary and problem-centered. Moreover, some of these courses carry up to eight semester hours of credit to provide large blocks of time for students to investigate problems not only as treated in the literature of several disciplines, but also as found in the community. These "super courses" are taught by a team of specialists whose interests go beyond a single discipline. Such course titles as "Life in Cities" and "The Black Experience in America" attest to the interdisciplinary and problem-centered opportunities that are possible when educational institutions reject traditional discipline-centered models in course building. Some of the other courses in the general education curriculum are "Problems in Population and Environment," "Some Contemporary Moral Issues," and "The Formation and Justification of Beliefs and Attitudes." [82]

Whether such courses are truly interdisciplinary will depend not only on the nature of the problems selected for study, but the degree to which the specialized expertise of the faculty is able to relate the various disciplines to one another so that the problems can be exposed to concerted treatment. Otherwise, each expert may simply demonstrate how a particular discipline parcels out its body of knowledge in terms of only one segment or perspective of a molar problem.

---

[81] *EDC Social Studies Curriculum Program* (Cambridge, Mass.: Educational Development Center, Inc., 1968), p. 1.

[82] *Livington College Catalogue, 1970–1971* (New Brunswick, N.J.: Rutgers University, 1970), pp. 31–32.

The Demand for "Relevance" and the "Black Experience"

In recent years a number of secondary schools, particularly those in urban areas, have added new courses in history and the social studies as a means of meeting student demands for "relevancy" in the curriculum. But merely adding some courses in Afro-American or black studies does not change the essential nature of the traditional subject-centered approach in the general education curriculum. Such material may be treated as just another course or series of courses within a subject-centered curriculum. An alternative approach is to develop the material through a problems-and-issues framework in recognition of the dynamic and contemporary character of the subject matter. While many colleges are instituting new courses and programs in black history and culture, some urban high schools are making notable efforts to incorporate this material into existing courses in history and problems of democracy.

A number of the new social studies projects are giving increasing attention to black history and culture. For example, Oliver and Shaver's "jurisprudential" curriculum includes the problem area of racial and ethnic conflict, in which such topics as school desegregation, civil rights, housing, job opportunities, and black power are investigated. In this context, such values as equal protection, due process, and brotherhood of man are examined in the light of their conflict with the values of peace and order, property and contract rights, personal privacy, and right to association.[83]

A matter of critical concern is that the treatment of black history and culture will be developed in a distorted and propagandistic way to pitch black against white or to glorify the black past in an effort to compensate for the perverse neglect in our textbooks of the black man's role in our nation's history. A professor of history makes this appeal:

> I appeal to you to give a contemporary emphasis to the role that black people have played in the American past, but on the other hand to avoid the new distortions which would come from a propagandistic use of history to promote Negro cultural nationalism and separation. . . . Both the historian and the teacher have an obligation to a broad and balanced search for truth about the past which transcends ethnic or ideological loyalties. To fulfill this function, to promote a humanistic understanding of our fellow humans, we need to take account of a black past that has villains as well as heroes, sufferings as well as successes, shades of gray as well as black and white.[84]

We are warned that the promotion of black nationalism and separatism will result in a distorted education to serve the purposes of ideological

---

[83] Oliver and Shaver, *op. cit.*, p. 142.
[84] Louis R. Harlan, "Tell It Like It Was: Suggestions on Black History," *Social Education*, Vol. 33 (April, 1969), p. 395.

propaganda. Although there are those who would justify this on the basis of our neglectful past, the lessons of history have exposed time and time again the dangers of nationalistic propaganda in any form.

SUMMARY

Most of the curriculum reform projects in the social studies during the 1960's may be criticized for (1) the emphasis on the individual disciplines without giving adequate attention to the total social studies curriculum and the total school curriculum, (2) the stress on the "structure of the discipline" as the basis for developing content, while neglecting problem-centered approaches that span more than one discipline, (3) the assumption that the learning style of the mature scholar is the most appropriate model for children and adolescents, (4) the tendency to concentrate on cognitive skills while neglecting the affective dimension of learning, and (5) the failure to become engaged in experimental research as a means of evaluating their effectiveness in comparison to alternative curriculum frameworks. Moreover, as each of the discipline-centered projects competes for a place in the social studies curriculum of the secondary school, little attention is given to the need for balance and relationship in an increasingly pressurized curriculum.

A multiplicity of social studies projects has emerged but, unlike the curriculum reform movement in the sciences and mathematics, none of the social studies projects has attained a position of dominance in the curriculum of the secondary school. Yet most of the social studies projects have attempted to imitate the prestigious projects in the sciences and mathematics by enlisting university scholars and by following a discipline-centered approach. The infinitely greater diversity of the social studies, coupled with the relatively low level of the principles, generalizations, and tools that characterize this broad field, raises serious questions as to whether the separate, discipline-centered approach is valid, particularly for purposes of general education.

Although integrative and problem-centered frameworks are distinctly in the minority and run counter to the general trend toward specialization, there is evidence that such interdisciplinary approaches are gaining interest and are beginning to be of influence. For example, the growing demand for curriculum "relevance" on the part of student activists in our colleges and universities has been followed by similar demands on the part of students in our urban high schools. This has produced some limited attempts at introducing problem-centered courses built around contemporary issues. But, essentially, the traditional discipline-centered courses have remained intact—even those that are intended for general education.

Despite the trend toward specialization as opposed to interdisciplinarity, a discernible resurgence of problem-centered and interdisciplinary studies, especially for purposes of general education, may come about as a result both of the growing demand for curriculum relevance and of the failure of discipline-centered projects to provide for curriculum balance and coherence. This does not mean a return to the "common learnings" or core approach in which virtually all of general education was to be theoretically integrated through molar problems. Instead, the problem or issue-centered approaches in the social studies may seek to concentrate on interdisciplinary studies that fall more definitively within the realm of this broad field.

While the discipline-centered projects in the social studies claim to emphasize the inquiry mode or style of teaching, such a style can also be developed in problem or issue-centered curricula that are interdisciplinary in nature. But there is confusion as to whether students, through the inquiry mode, are to be led to predetermined conclusions or whether they are to be allowed to reach their own conclusions in matters of great controversy.

Of all the curriculum areas, the social studies stand out as the center of the current curriculum reform demands in our schools and colleges. And probably no curriculum area is in such a stage of flux, controversy, and confusion as are the social studies today.

PROBLEMS FOR STUDY AND DISCUSSION

1. How do you account for the paucity of controlled research in evaluating the curriculum projects in the social studies?

2. Do you agree that the development of desirable sociocivic behavior is a legitimate goal for the social studies in the secondary school? Why or why not?

3. Contrary to the marked trend toward disciplinarity and structure is the view that "while the concept of the structure of a discipline may well be an appropriate basis for determining what should be taught in a *social science course,* it is not adequate as the basis for the social studies curriculum." [James Shaver, "Values and the Social Studies" in Irving Morrissett (ed.), *Concepts and Structure in the New Social Science Curricula* (New York: Holt, Rinehart and Winston, Inc., 1967), p. 123.]

   What differences, if any, do you see between the *social studies* and the *social sciences?*

4. Are the sciences an adequate model for curriculum reform in the social studies? Why or why not?

5. What are the chief differences between *multidisciplinary* and *interdisciplinary* approaches in the social studies?

6. What are the advantages and limitations of integrated problem-centered approaches in comparison to the separate discipline-centered approaches in curriculum building?

7. Do you agree with the contention that history should serve as the core of the social studies curriculum and that the demand for treating the modern social sciences can be accommodated simply by having history teachers make use of concepts and modes of inquiry from the social sciences? Why or why not?

8. The proliferation of curriculum projects in the social studies has created confusion as to which projects should be adopted by the schools. Assuming that you are the chairman of a social studies department in a secondary school, what criteria and procedures would you apply in determining which curriculum projects to adopt? How would you ascertain the success of newly adopted projects?

9. How do you account for the fact that support for curriculum projects in the social studies on the part of the National Science Foundation has been limited primarily to the fields of anthropology, economics, geography, and sociology?

SELECTED REFERENCES

Alberty, Harold B. and Elsie J. *Reorganizing the High School Curriculum,* 3rd ed. New York: The Macmillan Company, 1962.

American Council of Learned Societies and the National Council for the Social Studies. *The Social Studies and the Social Sciences.* New York: Harcourt, Brace & World, Inc., 1962.

Bestor, Arthur. *The Restoration of Learning.* New York: Alfred A. Knopf, Inc., 1955.

Bruner, Jerome S. *The Process of Education.* Cambridge, Mass.: Harvard University Press, 1960.

Conant, James Bryant. *The American High School Today.* New York: McGraw-Hill Book Company, Inc., 1959.

———. *Education in the Junior High School Years.* Princeton, N.J.: Educational Testing Service, 1960.

Cremin, Lawrence A. *The Transformation of the School.* New York: Alfred A. Knopf, Inc., 1961.

Dewey, John. *Democracy and Education.* New York: The Macmillan Company, 1916.

———. *How We Think.* Boston: D.C. Heath & Co., 1910, 1933.

Educational Policies Commission. *Education for ALL American Youth— A Further Look.* Washington, D.C.: National Education Association, 1952.

Fenton, Edwin. *Teaching the New Social Studies in Secondary Schools.* New York: Holt, Rinehart and Winston, Inc., 1966.

———. *The New Social Studies.* New York: Holt, Rinehart and Winston, Inc., 1967.

Ford, G. W., and Lawrence Pugno. *The Structure of Knowledge and the Curriculum*. Chicago: Rand McNally & Company, 1964.

Fraser, Dorothy M. (ed.). *Social Studies Curriculum Development: Prospects and Problems*. Thirty-ninth Yearbook. Washington, D.C.: National Council for the Social Studies, 1969.

Fraser, Dorothy M., and Samuel P. McCutchen (eds.). *Social Studies in Transition: Guidelines for Change*. Washington, D.C.: National Council for the Social Studies, 1965.

Gibson, John S. *New Frontiers in the Social Studies*. New York: Citation Press, 1967.

Hunt, Maurice P., and Lawrence E. Metcalf. *Teaching High School Social Studies*, 2nd ed. New York: Harper & Row, Publishers, 1968.

Krug, Edward A. *The Shaping of the American High School*. New York: Harper & Row, Publishers, 1964.

Krug, Mark M. *History and the Social Sciences*. Waltham, Mass.: Blaisdell Publishing Company, 1967.

Krug, Mark M., John B. Poster, and William B. Gillies, III. *The New Social Studies*. Itasca, Ill.: F. E. Peacock Publishers, Inc., 1970.

Kuhn, Alfred. *The Study of Society: A Unified Approach*. Homewood, Ill.: Richard D. Irwin, Inc., and the Dorsey Press, Inc., 1963.

McLendon, Jonathon C. *Social Studies in Secondary Education*. New York: The Macmillan Company, 1965.

Massialas, Byron G., and C. Benjamin Cox. *Inquiry in the Social Studies*. New York: McGraw-Hill Book Company, 1966.

Metcalf, Lawrence E. "Research on Teaching the Social Studies," Chapter 17 in *Handbook of Research on Teaching*, N. L. Gage (ed.). Chicago: Rand McNally & Company, 1963.

Moreland, Willis D. (ed). *Social Studies in the Senior High School*. Washington, D.C.: National Council for the Social Studies, 1965.

Morrissett, Irving (ed.). *Concepts and Structure in the New Social Science Curricula*. New York: Holt, Rinehart and Winston, Inc., 1967.

National Society for the Study of Education. *General Education*. Fifty-first Yearbook, Part I. Chicago: The University of Chicago Press, 1952.

Oliver, Donald W., and James P. Shaver. *Teaching Public Issues in High School*. Boston: Houghton Mifflin Company, 1966.

Piaget, Jean. *The Psychology of Intelligence*. New York: Harcourt, Brace & World, Inc., 1950.

Report of the Harvard Committee. *General Education in a Free Society*. Cambridge, Mass.: Harvard University Press, 1945.

Smith, Frederick R., and C. Benjamin Cox. *New Strategies and Curriculum in Social Studies*. Chicago: Rand McNally & Company, 1969.

Womack, James G. *Discovering the Structure of Social Studies*. New York: Benziger Brothers, 1966.

Chapter 6

Curriculum Change in English

Scholars have marveled at the processes through which children learn spoken language. Although this must be regarded as one of the most complex intellectual tasks, it is learned readily and continuously in early childhood in the absence of formal and systematized instruction because it is so immediate to the child's environment and because it is so essential to human life.[1] Even the amazingly complex task of learning written language is begun as soon as the child commences his formal schooling. Yet relatively little is known about (1) the ways through which children learn their native language, (2) how and at what stages youngsters gain awareness of the language they have come to use, and (3) how this awareness and understanding create possibilities for the continued learning and functioning of language.[2] Moreover, as we shall see later in this chapter, many of the fundamental assumptions guiding certain traditional practices in the teaching of English have persisted despite a growing body of research that shows such practices to be ineffectual.

The modern curriculum reform movement, which began in the sciences and mathematics, reached English belatedly when the English Program of the U.S. Office of Education was initiated late in 1961. Like the social studies, English was accorded low priority in the allocation of federal funds. Despite the modest level of support, the reform movement in English has caused educators to raise fundamental questions concerning the content and processes to be developed in the teaching of English. The raising of such questions has produced considerable ferment and constructive effort in a field that has been regarded as the least clearly defined subject in the curriculum, with the possible exception of

---

[1] Alfred North Whitehead, *The Aims of Education and Other Essays* (New York: The Macmillan Company, 1929), p. 25.

[2] John Dixon, *Growth Through English* (Reading, England: National Association for the Teaching of English, 1967), p. 76.

the social studies.[3] As in the social studies, current efforts for curriculum reform in English are characterized by a large number of specialized and uncoordinated projects throughout the nation. In this chapter we shall review some of the major trends and forces leading to the current conflicts and directions in the teaching of English in our secondary schools.

THE PROBLEM OF IDENTITY

As virtually all the subjects in our schools are taught in English, it can be said that all teachers are involved, consciously or otherwise, in the teaching of English. In the science class, for example, students learn to use English in a highly precise and specialized way. English as a school subject encompasses much more than the development of communication skills to be used for servicing other disciplines and areas of knowledge. Because the study of English includes literature, and because literature represents all human experiences, the study of literature must reach into many fields of knowledge. Thus the study of English, although classified as a separate subject in the secondary school, presents opportunities for curriculum integration that cannot be ignored.

Content and Sequence

Perhaps because it is indispensable to the learning of virtually all school subjects, the teaching of English has long been marked by considerable controversy and confusion. This has been compounded by the growing trend toward specialization within the field of language and literature. To this day there is no generally agreed-upon body of content and sequence, not to mention instructional methodologies, for the English curriculum in the secondary school. As one specialist stated the matter several years ago, "the secondary school English field has survived for the last half century without discovering any commonly accepted body of knowledge about language thought clearly to be teachable and worth teaching to high school students." [4]

Structure of a Discipline. Since the 1960's, many of the curriculum reform projects in English have attempted to embrace the notion of "structure" in imitation of curriculum projects in the sciences and mathematics. Yet the subject of English encompasses a wide galaxy of experiences and competencies, which have been classified according to a number of spe-

---

[3] Herbert J. Muller, *The Uses of English* (New York: Holt, Rinehart and Winston, Inc., 1967), p. 4.

[4] Donald K. Smith, "English, Speech, and the Language Arts," in Stanley B. Kegler (ed.), *The Changing Role of English Education* (Champaign, Ill.: National Council of Teachers of English, 1965), p. 69.

cialties, ranging from literature and composition to speech and the newer mass media. Ironically, although the major impetus for promoting English as a discipline comes from the universities, the universities themselves have partitioned many of these specialties into separate departments of English, drama, journalism, speech, and so on. Nevertheless, no other subject in the curriculum has such complex and necessary interrelationship with other subjects.

Although the notion of "structure of a discipline" is embraced by many educators as the key to the development of a universally valid and acceptable body of content and sequence, given the complex nature and function of English in the curriculum and in life, it may be utterly naive to assume that universally valid and acceptable formulas are possible. Instead, the creation of a variety of alternative curriculum patterns that are teachable and worth teaching may emerge from the current curriculum reform efforts.

The Problem of Definition and Disciplinarity

English is the one subject that all students are required to study throughout their school years. Yet, ironically, the literature reveals not only considerable debate as to the proper content and sequence of English in the secondary curriculum, but wide disagreement over defining the subject. For example, the Commission on English of the College Entrance Examination Board recommends "that the scope of the English program be defined as the study of language, literature, and composition, written and oral, and that matters not clearly related to such study be excluded from it." [5] The identical position was expressed in a 1962 report sponsored by the NEA's Project on Instruction, which declared that "the major revolution is made up of the growing conviction that English as a subject consists of just three things and no more: English is literature, language, and composition. These are its subject matter." [6]

A Narrow Definition. This narrow conception of English can hardly be said to represent a revolution. It merely represents an attempt to narrow the focus of English teaching to three constituent areas and to exclude any formal consideration for relating and integrating this subject matter with other subjects in the curriculum. For example, it should be recalled that the NEA, through its agencies such as ASCD and the Educational Policies Commission, has long championed the integration of English with the social studies and other areas of the curriculum for pur-

---

[5] Commission on English, *Freedom and Discipline in English* (New York: College Entrance Examination Board, 1965), p. 13.

[6] Report of the Disciplines Seminar, *The Scholars Look at the Schools* (Washington, D.C.: National Education Association, 1962), p. 12.

poses of meeting the general education needs of youth. But the pressures of the 1960's called for a specialized and disciplinary approach to subject matter. And the NEA was ready to change its tune with the times.

Turning again to the conception of English as a subject consisting of "just three things and no more," there are few who would contend that language, literature, and composition do not belong to English. But the notion that the subject of English must be limited to this tripartite model is regarded as narrow and ill-conceived for a number of reasons:

> composition is not unique to the subject of English, and it is an art or skill rather than content. Literature belongs pre-eminently to English, but does not the content of literature embrace all aspects of human experience and deal with the content of many other school subjects? And what about speech, dramatics, journalism, the mass media of communication, remedial reading, and listening? All of these have been questioned by those who deplore the diversity of activities characteristic of modern high school English. . . .
>
> From a practical point of view, the triad theory has only limited applicability. The study of language, it is true, is fairly self-contained, although it is encountered constantly in composition and literature. . . . But composition? When we write, we need content, which we must borrow from every subject in the curriculum. Literature? It is art, language, history, economics, psychology, ethics, religion—the whole spectrum of human concerns. Thus while language, composition, and literature are obviously central to the English program, the tripartite design is not especially helpful to the curriculum planner.[7]

Other Weaknesses.   Thus the definition of English as a tripartite division into language, literature, and composition not only fails to fit the criterion of disciplinarity, and not only neglects to indicate how English must be related to other subjects in the curriculum, but omits many important areas such as drama as a performing art, journalism, and the newer mass media. Such a definition also fails to indicate the relative emphasis and articulation to be provided within the triad of language, literature, and composition. Some English educators maintain that the core of the curriculum in English should be language; others make a convincing case for literature, while many critics point to the need for major emphasis on composition under the allegation that this is one of the most neglected and essential activities in the total school curriculum. Thus the definition of English as "the understanding of language, the manipulation of language, and the appreciation of language"[8] is deemed imbalanced because it regards language as the central theme or core of

---

[7] John J. DeBoer, "The New English," *The Educational Forum,* Vol. 32 (May, 1968), pp. 398–399.

[8] H. A. Gleason, Jr., "What Is English?" *College Composition and Communication,* Vol. 13 (October, 1962), pp. 1–10.

the English curriculum, whereas equally convincing cases can be made for different organizing principles.

Disciplinarity. Similarly, the definition of English as "the study of the English language and of its use as a medium of communication" [9] is not only criticized for its arbitrary focus on language, but is regarded as far too broad to be useful in attacking the problem of scope and sequence, as well as the problem of how English is to be related to other studies. Regarding the latter problem, for example, the study of English as a medium of communication receives considerable emphasis in the social studies in connection with propaganda analysis. Nevertheless, many specialists in English education prefer to conceive of English as a discipline unto itself rather than as a broad field that is closely interwoven with other areas of the curriculum.

It is contended that English is a separate discipline because its unifying element is the study of language and that the study of language can be justified for its own sake. [10] While those holding this view believe that a "new" English is in the making, in a vein not too dissimilar to the "new" mathematics and the "new" science, the unprecedented activity in English education during recent years has resulted in wide disagreement as to the principal aims, areas of emphasis, and methods to be employed in the English curriculum. Despite the significant developments in the various areas of specialization within the field of English, the current scene is marked by considerable fragmentation of effort, leaving the classroom teacher without a coherent and unifying rationale that can be said to represent a discipline.

The emphasis on disciplinarity has led specialists to reject the conception of English as simply that subject matter which is directed at the development of effective skills in thinking through listening, speaking, reading, and writing. Such a functional definition, with its emphasis on skill development, runs counter to those who regard English as a discipline or as an amalgamation of specialized disciplines.

In the face of the recent trend toward disciplinarity, some English educators warn against conceiving of English as a discipline unto itself or as a set of specialized disciplines. They contend that curriculum development in English should not be fashioned after the discipline-centered approaches that have been in vogue in many other subject fields during the past decade. DeBoer advises teachers of English to proceed in accordance with the following three principles, and warns against treating English as a discipline sharply separated from other subjects:

---

[9] Harold B. Allen, "The 'New' English Anew," *The Bulletin of the National Association of Secondary School Principals,* Vol. 51 (April, 1967), p. 18.

[10] *Ibid.,* pp. 18–19.

> (1) That English shares in the task of the high school as a whole; (2) that a certain amount of integration of English, within its own field and with other subject fields, is necessary; and (3) that English encompasses many activities which are not necessarily connected with a certain organizing theme. . . .
>
> The sharp distinction between English and the social studies cannot possibly be defended. And if the subject fields are no longer realms unto themselves, they cannot be divided into such separate subjects as language, composition, and literature. The effort made no sense in the beginning.
>
> The question whether English should constitute a structure or a group of three substructures is less appropriate than a similar question applied to such subjects as mathematics or science.[11]

Although DeBoer goes on to acknowledge that English should have a central organizing strategy that holds its parts together, however loosely, he sees this not as a representation of the "structure of a discipline," but as the body of human anxieties and aspirations that might be said to represent an "idea curriculum." Such a curriculum would deal directly with the problems of youth and of society and, of necessity, would call for considerable correlation and integration with the social studies. DeBoer's proposals are strikingly similar to the curriculum reform efforts of the progressive era and clearly appear to be in tune with the current demands for curricular "relevance" as voiced by student activists in our high schools and colleges. However, the trend in English education during the past decade has been away from personal and societal problems and away from correlation and integration with the social studies. As mentioned earlier, the recent curriculum reform efforts in English have been directed toward specialization and disciplinarity in an attempt to be in line with the trends in certain other disciplines.

As we shall see in our discussion of some of the major current trends in English education, important contributions are being made; however, no coherent patterns have been emerging to help the classroom teacher in his quest for balance and relationship in the English curriculum. Spokesmen for the many specialties and vantage points that comprise the complex field of English education are competing for curriculum priorities, leaving the classroom teacher with the dilemma of what to do with material so much of which is fragmented and incompatible. The challenge of the 1970's is to develop some integrated and coherent sequences for experimentation and field testing in our secondary schools.

A "New" English?

Although several major movements in the teaching of English have gathered notable momentum in recent years, the current scene is marked

---

11 DeBoer, *op. cit.*, pp. 399–401.

by fragmentation of effort and conflict of viewpoint among the specialists. As we have emphasized, a coherent and unifying rationale, which can be said to represent the discipline of English, is not likely to emerge from these disparate approaches. Moreover, the conglomerate nature of the subject, with its multiplicity of scholarly specialties, raises doubt that a unifying structure can be said to exist.

Nevertheless, there are those who have maintained that a "revolution in English is taking place" [12] on a scale comparable to other areas of the curriculum. It is pointed out that a "new" method has emerged, which is geared to the characteristics of the material to be learned, rather than to the interests, needs, and abilities of the learner.[13] But such a "new" method is, by itself, merely an attempt to refocus the emphasis away from the learner and toward the subject matter. And while there are those who maintain that a "new" rhetoric and a "new" criticism have been created, it has been shown that these "new" approaches are essentially a return to earlier practices.[14]

Linguistics. The development of linguistics has begun to challenge our traditional classroom practices. Linguistics has been described as the study of language in a scientific way or as the process of inquiring and discovering knowledge about language. This has led to the rejection of traditional or prescriptive grammar, in which our language was treated so as to conform to sets of rigid and unchanging rules. Structural and transformational grammar, as outgrowths of linguistics, treat language as dynamic and evolving.

Yet there is little evidence that these new grammars will produce more effective writing and speech. And although linguistics has provided us with new understandings concerning the styles of language and the relativity of "correctness," there is much disagreement among linguists about the best approaches for investigating language. But even if these differences were to reach a general resolution, it is doubtful that high school students will best develop their language power by investigating language in the manner of the linguistic scholar.

Semantics. As an important branch of linguistics, semantics focuses on how man uses language to codify and communicate meaning. In other words, it seeks to reveal, scientifically, the relationships among language, thought, and behavior. By exposing us to linguistic conventions, semantics opens the way to new approaches and understandings. By learning

---

[12] Francis A. Ianni and Lois S. Josephs, "The Curriculum Research and Development Program," in Robert W. Heath (ed.), *New Curricula* (New York: Harper & Row, Publishers, 1964), p. 197.

[13] William H. Evans and Jerry L. Walker, *New Trends in the Teaching of English in Secondary Schools* (Chicago: Rand McNally & Company, 1966), p. 33.

[14] DeBoer, *op. cit.,* p. 393.

to make critical distinctions about different kinds of language and how man's world of reality is shaped by language, it is hoped that students will become freed from the linguistic conventions that restrict and stereotype our thinking. In this regard semantics fosters critical thought.

Although a convincing case might be made to show that linguistics will spearhead a revolution in the teaching of English, it nevertheless represents only one important and specialized aspect of a highly complex and diverse field known as English. Even among college teachers in departments of English, not to mention teachers in our secondary schools, those who are highly knowledgeable about linguistics and semantics are a small minority who have chosen to specialize in these domains of scholarship. And, as discussed earlier, the Brunerian notion that students will best attain language power by learning to emulate the methods of the linguistic scholar remains a moot question.

THE FAILURE OF TRADITIONAL APPROACHES

Before continuing with our analysis of major current forces, trends, and issues, we shall review briefly some background developments in the teaching of English. Our brief review of the failure of traditional approaches is organized in terms of the triad of language, literature, and composition.

Language

The traditional emphasis on Latinate grammar can be traced to the transplantation of the Latin-grammar type of school from England to America during the early Colonial period. The chief function of this school was to prepare boys for college where they would receive training for the ministry. As Latin was the language of religion and learning, it was the chief language of the Latin-grammar school and of the college, although some elements of Greek were also taught. The admission requirements of Yale College in 1745, similar to those of Harvard, indicated clearly what was expected of the Latin-grammar school:

> That none may be expected to be admitted into this College unless, upon Examination of the President and Tutors, They shall be found able Extempore to Read, Construe and Parce Tully, Vergil, and the Greek Testament; and to write True Latin in Prose and to understand the Rules of Prosodia and Common Arithmetic, and Shall bring Sufficient Testimony of his Blameless and inoffensive Life.[15]

---

[15] Ellwood P. Cubberley, *Public Education in the United States,* rev. ed. (Boston: Houghton Mifflin Company, 1947), p. 30.

Latinate Grammar. Despite the decline of the Latin-grammar school and the rise of schools stressing the more practical subjects, English was not introduced as a broad-field subject until the latter part of the nineteenth century. Instead it was treated atomistically under an array of such course titles as grammar, rhetoric, logic, English literature, composition, and elocution. Although these came to be consolidated under the broad field of English, the study of English grammar continued to be treated prescriptively in a manner patterned after the study of the classical languages. Thus the prescriptive treatment provided rules that dictated the correct forms of oral and written language. Because tradition had established Latin as the most logical language, the rules for English were formulated according to Latin models. Students were required to follow rules that were derived from Latin even though many of these rules were of limited applicability to modern English usage and style. Nevertheless, prescriptive grammar had become a recognized discipline with an entrenched position in the English curriculum. And it gave assurance to those searching for immutable and finite determinants of correctness.

> There was a readily discernible need for such a prescriptive attitude in the nineteenth-century American school. Some educational discipline, however arbitrary, was needed both to refine the crudities of much frontier speech and to provide clear-cut models for the waves of immigrants. . . . Millions of people were desperately eager to discover an objective standard of correctness, and the prescriptive textbook and teacher provided it. And, since people looked to the grammarian as one who must be capable of describing each linguistic infelicity in a rigorous way, ideas about grammar and usage became inextricably confused. This confusion still prevails in many quarters.[16]

During the early decades of the twentieth century an increasing number of educators held that the usage of language does not follow ironbound prescriptions and that language must evolve with the dynamic qualities of life. This viewpoint was supported by a growing body of investigations revealing that prescriptive grammar as a separate discipline had little or no effect upon written and oral language skills. Yet many English teachers continued to assume that drill in traditional grammar will automatically become transformed into written and oral skills, and that grammar skills are best attained by making language conform to various atomistic rules and constructs.[17]

---

[16] Commission on English, *Freedom and Discipline in English, op. cit.*, pp. 19–20.

[17] Henry C. Meckel, "Research on Teaching Composition and Literature," Chapter 18 in N. L. Gage (ed.), *Handbook of Research on Teaching* (Chicago: Rand McNally & Company, 1963), p. 974.

Emergence of Newer Approaches.   In recognition of the failings of pre-scriptive grammar, some efforts were made by progressive educators dur-ing the 1930's and 1940's to develop a more functional and integrative approach to the study of grammar. Through this approach, grammar is studied as problems emerge in literature, composition, and oral expres-sion. The rigid rules and drills of prescriptive grammar are thus elimi-nated, along with the study of grammar as a separate discipline in the English curriculum. Ironically, while functional grammar represented a categorical rejection of the traditional prescriptive grammar, it came to be criticized by those modernists interested in the scientific study of lan-guage, namely, the linguists. Thus the functional approach was attacked for failing to provide for a scientific and systematic analysis of language.

Literature

The notion that there should be a universally prescribed canon of liter-ary works required to be read by all secondary school students persists in some quarters to this day. The practice of listing prescribed books for the college entrance examinations in English began at Harvard in 1874 and was adopted by many New England colleges. The book list for the examinations of 1885, as announced in the Harvard catalogue of 1882–1883 contained such works as *Macbeth, The Merchant of Venice,* the first two books of *Paradise Lost,* Emerson's *Essay on Eloquence, Silas Marner,* and *A Tale of Two Cities.*[18]

Lack of uniformity among the lists prescribed by the different colleges led to the formation of the Conference on Uniform Entrance Require-ments in English, whose membership reached beyond New England to include the Middle States Association, the Southern Association, and the North Central Association. With the establishment of the College Entrance Examination Board soon after the turn of the century, the lists of prescribed "classics" came to be used as the basis for the board's exami-nations in English. The opposition to college domination over the high school curriculum in English, led by representatives of the North Central Association, helped to bring about the decline of the National Conference just before World War I. Nevertheless, the lists of "classics" continued to influence the curricula of high schools for many years, despite the fact that most students were not college bound.[19]

Rejection of Prescriptive Lists.   Although the College Entrance Exami-nation Board during its early history relied on lists of prescribed "classics" as the basis for the English examinations, a 1965 report by the board's

---

18 *Harvard University Catalogue, 1882–1883,* p. 67.

19 Edward A. Krug, *The Shaping of the American High School* (New York: Harper & Row, Publishers, 1964), p. 364.

Commission on English makes clear the folly of prescribing a definitive list of literary works for all secondary schools.

> If the Commission could claim for the study of literature a definiteness as apparent as that of other subjects in the curriculum, it might specify them; but all attempts to prepare a canon of literary works deserving a special place in the secondary school curriculum meet serious obstacles. Who can claim the authority to draw up any such master list? Or to require it, once drawn? Even granting satisfactory answers to those questions, one must face others no less troublesome. What conceivable principles can govern inclusion and exclusion? What effects would ensue from precise curricular prescription? [20]

"Great Books."   Some college professors of English who might hesitate to draw up a definitive list of prescribed literary works for all college freshmen have not hesitated to do so for high school students. One need not turn to Robert M. Hutchins and Mortimer Adler's Great Books program to find prescriptive listings of literary works that purport to exemplify the permanent content of a proper literary education. For example, the 1960 Report of the San Francisco Curriculum Survey Committee, whose membership included a professor of English from Stanford University and a professor of English from the University of California (Berkeley), suggested the following prescription of basic readings for all students in grades 9 through 12:

The 9th Grade
   Classic Mythology (Bulfinch or Edith Hamilton), the *Odyssey* . . . , a book of the Bible in the King James version . . . , *Sir Gawain and the Green Knight* . . . , some Malory, *Don Quixote,* a Shakespeare play complete (a minimum of one Shakespeare play should be read in each of the four years), *Robinson Crusoe, Great Expectations,* one of Tennyson's *Idylls,* and a modern novel like Lewis's *Arrowsmith.*

The 10th Grade
   . . . short stories from Poe to Hemingway or even Salinger, . . . perhaps another and more difficult Dickens or a novel from one of the American masters—Cooper or Howells . . . , some short biographies of Macaulay . . . , a modern play . . . Bernard Shaw or Sean O'Casey . . . , a second play by Shakespeare . . . a group of his sonnets . . . , a sampling of famous short poems written during the past three hundred years.

The 11th Grade
   . . . Franklin's *Autobiography* and Crèvecoeur's *Letters from an American Farmer;* . . . a selection of Emerson's essays, *Walden, The Scarlet Letter,* and poems by Whitman and Emily Dickinson; . . . Park-

---

[20] Commission on English, *Freedom and Discipline in English, op. cit.,* p. 42.

man's *The Oregon Trail* . . . , *The Adventures of Huckleberry Finn,* . . . some of Abraham Lincoln's Civil War papers . . . , *The Red Badge of Courage;* the poems of Robert Frost . . . , the poems of T. S. Eliot . . . , a play by Eugene O'Neill . . . (and) the third Shakespeare play.

The 12th Grade

. . . *The Canterbury Tales* (the Prologue and a tale or two) in the original . . . , Spencer's shorter poems, the fourth Shakespeare play, Milton's *Comus* and *Lycidas* . . . , the *Areopagitica.* Johnson's *Preface to Shakespeare* and his *Life of Milton* . . . , Pope's *Rape of the Lock* . . . , Johnson's *Life of Pope, Tom Jones,* . . . a very intensive study of the short poem . . . , *Middlemarch* . . . , the dramatic monologues of Browning and the lyrics of Tennyson . . . , Mill's *On Liberty* or Ruskin's *Crown of Wild Olive* . . . , a Hardy novel, Conrad's *Heart of Darkness,* the poems of Hardy and Housman.[21]

Problems of Selection, Relevance, and Relationship. Aside from the fact that such a prescribed listing fails to take into account the tremendously diverse population of students attending the public schools, not to mention the specific needs of the disadvantaged, no criteria or principles are advanced for the selection of works on the list. Teachers are expected to accept the prescribed list on authority. But other authorities would likely devise quite different lists. Moreover, lacking criteria and principles for inclusion and exclusion, how are new works to be selected and old works culled out? While it is easy to advance such prescriptions for the curriculum, the most challenging and significant task of how to make the readings relevant to the abilities, interests, and aspirations of adolescents is virtually ignored by the authorities.

In making these prescriptions, the authorities give no consideration as to how the study of these ordained literary works is to relate to the total English curriculum, not to mention relationships with other subject fields. Indeed the essentialist attitude is to conceive of the "discipline" as a self-serving entity. In the eyes of these scholar-specialists, "everything else is irrelevant to the English curriculum." [22] Knowledge is compartmentalized by subjects or "disciplines" while interdisciplinary considerations and the task of integrating knowledge are left entirely to the devices of the student.

Yet literature is not created in a vacuum. Literature is in our history just as history is in our literature. And literature can bring valid and unique insights into contemporary social problems. To isolate literature from the social studies is to isolate literature from life. This is not to mean that the study of literature should be completely absorbed by the

---

[21] Report of the San Francisco Curriculum Survey Committee (San Francisco: San Francisco Unified School District, 1960), pp. 33–34.

[22] *Ibid.,* p. 23.

social studies any more than one would advocate that the social studies be completely absorbed by the study of literature. Curriculum correlation and integration do not require the loss of identity of subject matters. By bringing certain subject matters or disciplines together into new combinations, it is possible to explore significant problems, themes, and topics that might otherwise remain untreated or unrelated. Some educators are concerned that the unique art forms that we call literature will lose their identity when they are closely related to other subjects in the curriculum and to life problems. However, it is equally erroneous to assume that the study of literature on its own terms is the only way to cultivate the adolescent's tastes for good literature.

The Chronological-Historical Approach. One of the traditional approaches to the study of literature is through a chronological-historical survey. This approach has been followed as a convenient means of sequencing the literary works to be studied and not as a strategy for correlating and integrating literature with the curriculum in the social studies. The historical pattern frequently has taken the form of a rapid survey of a large number and variety of literary works at the sacrifice of depth of treatment. Perhaps a more satisfactory approach is to limit the number of works and authors so that an effective balance of breadth and depth is developed.

Nevertheless, the historical approach can be criticized because it solves the problem of sequence through mere chronology, whereas student concerns might well require a radically different sequence and treatment. Furthermore, although the historical pattern is intended to develop an understanding and appreciation of literary history, it is often followed without any formal attempt at relating the material with the subject matter in the social studies. And there is no evidence that a chronological approach is indeed the best way of gaining historical perspectives and appreciations.

The Thematic Approach. In recognition of the inadequacies of the chronological-historical pattern, a thematic approach is developed that relates literary works to major themes and problems in human experience. Because such themes and problems in life are not necessarily confined to chronological periods and do not necessarily occur in chronological order, the historical pattern is deemed inadequate.

Through the thematic approach literary works from various time periods can be integrated into combinations that are not possible through mere chronological sequencing. The thematic approach also lends itself to relating the subject matter in some degree to the concerns of the student, because contemporary themes and problems of man are given a recurrent perspective.

Nevertheless, the thematic approach is criticized for the tendency sometimes to fit literary works arbitrarily into preconceived themes. The use of the thematic approach as a means of correlating and integrating the study of literature with other subjects, particularly the social studies, became closely associated with the progressive educational practices of the 1930's and 1940's. Many specialists in literature attacked such efforts on the grounds that the study of literature should serve literary purposes rather than social or philosophical goals. In other words, they maintained that literature as a unique art form must be studied for its own sake.

The Genre Approach. The emphasis on disciplinarity that characterized the curriculum reform movement of the 1960's stimulated a resurgence of effort to return to the traditional practice of studying literature for its own sake. The focus is on literary genres or types. Rhetorical and structural forms through which literature is manifested become the central concerns of the course of study. It is ironic that this traditional approach of the literary scholar-specialist is labeled as the "new" method of teaching literature.

> There can be little doubt that the teaching of literature, more than any other area of language study, has been revolutionized by the new method. The time when literature was taught mainly for its sociological and historical values is past. It is becoming less common to find literature still selected, organized, and taught primarily as a means of gaining insight into life and its problems. Today, literature is being taught chiefly as means of gaining insight into literature itself.[23]

As mentioned earlier, the teaching of literature by genre or type can hardly be described as a new and revolutionary development. But this approach has been embraced by many specialists during the decade of the 1960's when the rallying cry was "structure of the discipline." Emphasis on genre or type has been criticized not only because it becomes a convenience of classification and prescription, thereby limiting the possibilities for experimentation and uniqueness, but also because it often leads to "juiceless formalism and an excessive preoccupation with terminology and analysis."[24] Perhaps the most severe criticism leveled against this approach, however, is that it suits the needs of certain literary experts and not those of adolescents.

Relevance. Despite the emphasis on disciplinarity during the 1960's, many influential sources were beginning to stress the desirability of avoiding total commitment to a single approach and the need to develop a

---

[23] William H. Evans and Jerry L. Walker, *op. cit.,* p. 37.
[24] Commission on English, *Freedom and Discipline in English, op. cit.,* p. 53.

balanced treatment that will make time, form, and value significant in the critical study of literature. The cry for "relevance" by many young people today cannot go unnoticed. The rebellion against the overformalism of our curriculum in school and college has challenged the preoccupation with disciplinarity that characterized the curriculum reforms of the 1960's. Not since the Great Depression of the 1930's has there been such demand for linking the study of literature to contemporary social problems. But merely adding an elective course or two on "black literature" will not by itself effect a fundamental change in the structure and function of the curriculum.

Composition

During the early years of this century, great emphasis was given to the traditional liberal arts of grammar and rhetoric in the teaching of composition. Recognizing the failure of traditional approaches in developing effective writing ability, coupled with the trend toward universal secondary education, the appeal for more pragmatic approaches began to be heard. The old emphasis on rigid rules and inherited principles was no longer adequate to the diversified demands for written expression in a changing society. Where the traditional stress was on rules to be followed, the pragmatic conception was on the development of ability in written communication to fit a wide variety of situations in the lives of students.

Progressive Influences. The period from World War I until the mid-1950's witnessed a series of publications by the National Council of Teachers of English advocating a pragmatic conception in the teaching of English. Based upon the findings of many research studies, which revealed negligible results in developing composition skills through emphasis on traditional grammar, the council recommended that grammar and usage be taught functionally through composition. Also advocated was the use of literature as a model for pupil writing. The practice of drawing from other school subjects in assigning topics for English composition was encouraged as a demonstration of the universality of expository writing. Moreover, efforts toward correlating, fusing, and integrating English with other subjects, particularly the social studies, provided new opportunities for relating composition to a broad spectrum of topics.

Essentialist Influences. The cold war era and the immediate post-Sputnik period were accompanied by essentialist demands to return to the fundamentals. Among the deficiencies most cited in criticizing the secondary schools was the alleged inability of students to write effectively. Many college professors of English accused the secondary schools of neglecting the art of writing. Although the most avid defenders of the schools were on record as recognizing the need for improving the teaching of composition, as evidenced by a series of reports by the National Council of Teachers of English,[25] the pressures of the times forced the schools into a defensive posture. An example of the allegations appearing in the national press was an article in *Harper's Magazine* which made the bizarre claim that American college freshmen were unable to write as well as ten- and twelve-year-old British schoolboys.[26] No research evidence was offered to support this contention. A common sport for many educational critics of the day was to claim that the teaching of writing had deteriorated beyond belief since the days when they were students in high school.[27] Yet one could cite sources revealing similar deficiencies in our schools and colleges before the turn of the century. A Harvard professor, writing in a pamphlet published in 1896, recalled past years when "graduates of our best colleges could not write a letter home describing their own commencement without making blunders which would disgrace a boy twelve years old." [28]

Problem of Articulation. Where the late 1950's found critics calling for simplistic solutions through a return to the fundamentals of drill in rhetoric and formal grammar, the 1960's were marked by unprecedented efforts toward improving instruction in composition through a variety of approaches. Nevertheless, the trend of the 1960's was away from the correlation, fusion, and integration of English composition with other subjects in the curriculum. Yet the problem of articulating composition with other activities in the English curriculum continues to remain a serious one. The body of research in the teaching of composition has been largely unfruitful in pointing the way toward solving the problem of articulation. Newly conceived studies are needed. As discussed later in this chapter, the perennial problem of teacher load has limited the amount of time that English teachers are able to devote to composition assignments. With one hundred and fifty students in a daily schedule, few teachers are about to assign and evaluate carefully a theme a week, as recommended by many authorities.

CONFLICTING DEMANDS FOR CHANGE

Throughout the twentieth century many proposals have been made for improving the English curriculum of the secondary school. The

---

25 Meckel, *op. cit.,* p. 967.

26 Derek Colville, "British and American Schools," Vol. 215 (October, 1957), p. 58.

27 See Clifton Fadiman, "The Case for Basic Education," in *The Case for Basic Education,* James D. Koerner (ed.) (Boston: Little, Brown and Company, 1959), pp. 8–10.

28 A. S. Hill in *Twenty Years of School and College English* (Harvard University, 1896).

sources of these proposals include the National Council of Teachers of English, the NEA's Educational Policies Commission, the College Entrance Examination Board, the Council for Basic Education, and the reports of James B. Conant that were commissioned by the Carnegie Corporation. A brief review of some of the most influential proposals should serve to illustrate how certain trends and forces have evolved during periods of shifting expectations and demands.

The National Council of Teachers of English

The first comprehensive report sponsored by the National Council of Teachers of English appeared in 1917.[29] Calling attention to the growing recognition of the high school as an institution for all the youth of all the people, this report went on to observe that college preparation was now only a relatively minor function of the high school. Accordingly, the trend toward universal secondary education required that the curriculum be diversified to meet the social needs of a heterogeneous student population. The proposed solution would be to broaden the range of subject matter without sacrificing the common educational goals of our common culture. Instead of devising a limited set of curriculum essentials and facts, as divided into language, literature, and composition, English should be conceived as a complex of interrelated competencies of communication skills in reading, writing, speaking, and listening. The report provided sequences to illustrate how continuing strands could be developed from grades 7 through 12. The lists of suggested readings went far beyond the traditionally prescribed classics to include a broad variety of literary sources.

Although not a radical document, this report called for significant changes in the English curriculum in tune with the changing role of the secondary school. Despite the passage of over half a century since the publication of this report, it remains relevant to the current controversy as to whether English should be conceived as a distinct discipline or as a broad field having necessary interrelationships with other subjects in the curriculum for purposes of meeting social needs.

As implied in the title, *An Experience Curriculum in English,* published by the NCTE in 1935, recommended that teachers develop the English curriculum according to a series of significant experiences representing increasing scope and complexity as students progress through the grade levels.[30] Through these "experience strands," the curriculum would have continuity and would serve the life needs of children and youth. This report represented an elaboration of the 1917 NCTE document,

---

[29] James J. Hosic (compiler), *Reorganization of English in Secondary Schools* (Washington, D.C.: U.S. Bureau of Education, 1917).

[30] National Council of Teachers of English, *An Experience Curriculum in English* (New York: Appleton-Century-Crofts, 1935).

calling for a more diversified and functional approach to curriculum construction while rejecting the notion of a national curriculum for all secondary school students.

One year later, *A Correlated Curriculum* presented a variety of approaches for correlating, fusing, and integrating the study of English with other subjects in the curriculum.[31] This report was designed as a review of a variety of proposals and practices illustrative of significant approaches to curriculum correlation and integration in the secondary school. Although it was not intended as a specific guideline for curriculum reconstruction, the report reflected the growing interest of the times in curriculum reform based upon progressive educational theory and the emerging literature in the psychology of learning. The inadequacies of the traditional picture-puzzle curriculum with its bits and pieces of separate and unrelated subjects called for "a carefully integrated curriculum so taught that the connection of each subject with every other subject and with the whole of life will be unmistakable for the student." [32]

The need for curriculum correlation, fusion, and integration was considered urgent as a result of the growing chaos in urban life, the hyperspecialization of labor in society, the knowledge explosion, and the sociopolitical confusion of a nation faced with the crises of the Great Depression. Because English is the language by which knowledge is communicated and developed in our society, the study of English must be regarded as the pivotal and binding element of the total school curriculum.

In 1952 the NCTE published *The English Language Arts*.[33] This volume extended many of the ideas proposed in the earlier NCTE reports while pointing to the need to update the curriculum by incorporating activities relating to semantics and the newer mass media. The concept of English, as represented in this report, is the activities of reading, writing, speaking, and listening—not a body of separate subject matters and not a discipline to be studied for its own sake. The report identified ways of developing the curriculum in English according to student needs, experiences, and interests.

However, the forces for specialization and disciplinarity in the curriculum, catalyzed by the cold war and Sputnik, brought the term of "English language arts" into disfavor. As an integrative concept, this term was considered acceptable perhaps for the elementary level of schooling, but inappropriate for the discipline-centered high school.

---

31 National Council of Teachers of English, *A Correlated Curriculum* (New York: Appleton-Century-Crofts, 1936).

32 *Ibid.*, p. 1.

33 National Council of Teachers of English, *The English Language Arts* (New York: Appleton-Century-Crofts, 1952).

Other Proposals of the Progressive Era

The influences of the progressive era on proposals for curriculum reform in English were evidenced not only in reports by the NCTE but also in the documents of other agencies. For example, the report of the NEA's Educational Policies Commission, *Education for ALL American Youth,* which was published in 1944 and revised in 1952, contained important implications for the English curriculum in its comprehensive and utopian vision of the American secondary school during the post-World War II period.[34] A proposed program of common learnings, developed from grades 7 through 14, would provide a daily block of time for addressing the imperative personal-social needs of youth. Through broad problem areas, subject matter would be drawn from the fields of citizenship, economics, family living, literature and the arts, and use of the English language. Thus the common-learnings program would provide for the complete integration of English, the social studies, and the arts for purposes of meeting the general education needs of youth. Approximately one half of the student's schedule in grades 7 through 9, and one third of his time in grades 10 through 12, would be devoted to the common-learnings program in a continuous time-block. In addition to the integrated problem-centered approach of the common-learnings program, special courses in remedial English and electives in literature would be provided.

Although this report was widely read and discussed by professional educators, common-learnings programs along the lines proposed in *Education for ALL American Youth* were limited to only a small proportion of junior high schools and some university laboratory schools. However, a 1957 national survey of block-time and core classes in junior high schools revealed that almost 20 per cent of these schools had block-time programs and that the subjects most frequently combined were English and social studies.[35]

Proposals for Retrenchment

The era of the cold war and Sputnik elevated the essentialists to a new level of prominence. Advocating a return to basic education, as exemplified by the traditional academic disciplines, the essentialists viewed the efforts toward developing student-centered curricula through correlated, fused, and integrated studies as a vast life-adjustment con-

---

[34] Educational Policies Commission, *Education for ALL American Youth—A Further Look* (Washington, D.C.: National Education Association, 1952).

[35] Grace S. Wright, *Block-Time Classes and the Core Program in the Junior High School* (Washington, D.C.: Office of Education, U.S. Department of Health, Education, and Welfare, 1958), pp. 63–64.

spiracy to destroy the traditional academic curriculum. Writing for the Council for Basic Education, a professor of literature attacked reports of the National Council of Teachers of English for allowing literature to become the mere tool of social studies,[36] and for promulgating student-centered doctrines.[37] In an earlier treatise, Bestor viewed the core curriculum and common-learnings program as "intellectual anarchy" and argued that curriculum integration or synthesis is not possible until one has "marshaled the array of separate intellectual powers" that are the province of the traditional academic disciplines.[38] The proper place for such curriculum integration, according to Bestor, is not in the high school but in college.[39]

While the essentialist position attracted a wide audience among the nation's intelligentsia during the 1950's, the curriculum reform efforts of the 1960's were to go far beyond the simplistic solution of returning to the traditional academic subjects. Unprecedented efforts were made to reconstruct the curriculum through each separate and specialized subject field or discipline. As we shall see later in this chapter, although the reform movement in English received lower priority than that given the disciplines of mathematics and science, the efforts toward specialization and disciplinarity in English were to be influenced considerably by developments in these higher priority disciplines.

Proposals to Meet National Needs

Although Conant's 1959 report on the American high school was intended as an analysis of the entire curriculum of the comprehensive high school, the recommendations pertaining to the teaching of English attracted particular attention. In addition to recommending that all students be required to complete four years of English, Conant advocated that approximately half the total time in English be devoted to composition and that every student be required to write an average of one theme a week to be corrected by the teacher.[40]

Theme Writing and Teacher Load. Recognizing the enormous task of correcting student themes under typical teacher-student ratios, Conant recommended that each English teacher be assigned no more than one hundred pupils. An earlier study had revealed that when the teacher-

---

36 Douglas Bush, "Literature," in *The Case for Basic Education,* James D. Koerner (ed.), *op. cit.,* p. 114.

37 *Ibid.,* p. 108.

38 Arthur Bestor, *The Restoration of Learning* (New York: Alfred A. Knopf, Inc., 1956), p. 60.

39 *Ibid.,* p. 63.

40 James B. Conant, *The American High School Today* (New York: McGraw-Hill Book Company, Inc., 1959), pp. 50–51.

student load was over one hundred and fifty, the number of compositions assigned during the school year averaged only four.[41] But while Conant's ratio of one hundred students per English teacher represented a significant reduction in student load, his recommendation still meant one hundred themes to be corrected by each teacher weekly.

Only a relatively small proportion of high schools adopted Conant's recommendation on teacher load in English, partly because of cost factors and partly because of the implied preferential treatment accorded teachers of English. Teachers of the social studies, for example, who also assign student themes as an integral part of the course work, could very well make a convincing case for load reductions. And at a time when mathematics and the sciences were being given the highest priority through federally supported curriculum projects, the field of English was unable to gain any preferential treatment.

Ability Grouping.   Perhaps the most widely adopted of Conant's recommendations was one calling for ability grouping in English and other subjects. Essentially, this provided for the establishment of at least three types of classes: one for the more able student, one for the average, and one for the slow reader. The average group would be divided further into two or three ability levels, according to Conant. However, despite the assumption that ability grouping will enable English teachers to make use of differentiated methods and materials, recent research reveals that ability grouping not only is seldom accompanied by the anticipated differentiation of instructional practices, but fails to produce consistent gains in student achievement.[42]

Other Conant recommendations called for schoolwide tests in English composition, remedial and developmental reading programs, and an advanced placement course in college-level English for highly gifted pupils.

The Junior High School and Block-Time Teaching.   Conant's report on the junior high school advocated heavy emphasis on reading and composition, three levels of ability grouping in academic courses, departmentalized instruction, and a load of no more than one hundred pupils per English teacher.[43]

Although recognizing that a significant number of junior high schools

---

[41] Paul B. Diederich, "Innovations in English Teaching" in *Needed Research in the Teaching of English* (Washington, D.C.: Office of Education, U.S. Department of Health, Education, and Welfare, 1963), pp. 72–73.

[42] James R. Squire and Roger K. Applebee, *High School English Instruction Today* (New York: Appleton-Century-Crofts, 1968), pp. 239–240.

[43] James B. Conant, *Education in the Junior High School Years* (Princeton, N.J.: Educational Testing Service, 1960).

provided block-time or core programs for purposes of correlating, fusing, or integrating the curriculum, particularly in the areas of English and the social studies, Conant recommended that block-time teaching should not serve the function of breaking down subject-matter boundaries. Instead, it should be limited to grade 7 for the purpose of having a teacher spend more time with a given group of pupils so that he may get to know them better, and to serve as a mechanism for ensuring a smooth transition between the self-contained elementary classroom and the departmentalized teaching of the secondary school.

Conant's opposition to core programs for curriculum correlation and integration and his advocacy of departmentalization in the junior high school years clearly reflected the growing national trend toward disciplinarity in the curriculum. If the United States was to meet the demands of the cold war and the space age, the schools must provide for specialization of instruction.

CHANGING MODELS FOR CHANGING TIMES

Evolution of Models for the Teaching of English

Literacy. In viewing major curriculum developments in perspective, a number of epochal models can be identified.[44] One model is concerned primarily with the development of language skills for the purpose of fostering initial literacy. This model was given major stress as recently as the early decades of the twentieth century, when the schools of our major cities were attempting to assimilate the children of immigrants and when the secondary schools were beginning to embrace the ideal of universal education.

However, the functional character of this model came to suffer from the forces of formalism. For example, formal grammar was taught virtually as an end in itself and consequently bore little relationship to the development of functional language usage. Moreover, with the attainment of general literacy, the pressures mounted for a return to an earlier model.

Cultural Heritage Through Literary Works. A second model, emphasizing the cultural heritage through literary works, actually represented a return to an earlier era in which the universities designated with great authority and specificity those works on which entrance examinations were based. Secondary schools found this model attractive because it conformed perfectly to the expectations of the prestigious universities, it exemplified a notion of rising intellectuality, and it represented a simple solution to the problem of curriculum construction. One could

---

[44] See Dixon, *op. cit.*, pp. 1–13.

look to the universities for leading sources of authority in identifying the best literary works to be taught at various levels of schooling. But just as the skills model came to be treated as an end in itself through an overly formalized curriculum, the cultural heritage model was imposed in such a manner as to ignore the demanding social and personal problems of contemporary life.

Personal and Social Growth. In an attempt to make the curriculum relevant to the realistic demands of contemporary life, a third model emerged during the era of progressive education—a model emphasizing personal and social growth. In implementing this model no sharp lines of demarcation could be drawn between personal and social problems that were properly within the province of English and those that were in the domain of the social studies. As a result, efforts were made to correlate and integrate the subject matter through broadly conceived thematic studies and problem-centered core programs.

These efforts suffered from a lack of adequate curriculum materials to match the noble intent of this progressive model, not to mention the tendency to include much trivial material in the absence of sound criteria for the selection of content. The emphasis on personal and social growth also became vulnerable to the savage attacks of the essentialists during the cold war period. But even during the height of the progressive era, the proportion of schools committed to a curriculum geared to this model was limited. The inertia of tradition was dominant in most schools, which continued to adhere to curricula stressing formal drill in grammar and the study of literary works that were largely irrelevant to life and outside the main currents of a changing society.

Structure, Function, and Disciplinarity. A fourth and contemporary model places key emphasis on the analysis of the structure and function of language as interaction. This model is based on the premise that language, like life, is ever changing. Accordingly, the learner should be making new discoveries in the process of using language from experience. Thus man not only is engaged in the constant reshaping and enrichment of his language so that it portrays his environment more realistically, but he uses language to control and influence his environment.

While this fourth model may appear to be related to the previous model that emphasizes personal and social growth, the focus of the fourth model is on the analysis of the structure and function of language in interaction rather than on broadly conceived individual and social problems. Moreover, as an outgrowth of the general trend of the 1960's toward disciplinarity, the fourth model represents a swing away from the correlative and integrative approaches with the social studies that characterized the curriculum reform efforts of the progressive era. It also represents the approach and perspective of the university scholar in staking out a domain for specialized study and commitment.

Thus, despite the promising aspects of a model that conceives of language as dynamic, the utilitarian quality of this model has been overshadowed by the specialized and esoteric concerns of university scholars. The emerging scene is marked by growing confusion as differing rationales and specialties are created which compete for a place in shaping the curriculum (i.e., the "new" linguistics, the "new" rhetoric, and the "new" literary criticism). These developments are an outcome of the recent efforts to treat the subject of English as a discipline. In the face of the enormous claims made for many of the "new" developments, relatively little is known concerning the degree to which these approaches are successful in helping youngsters to use language more effectively.

MAJOR CURRENT DEVELOPMENTS AND PROPOSALS

Earlier in this chapter we reviewed some of the arguments against treating English as a discipline sharply separated from other subjects in the school curriculum. Nevertheless, the power and momentum of the reform movement in the sciences and mathematics during the 1960's gave cause for efforts to fabricate a "new" English in the image of these other disciplines. And although federal funds became available for curriculum projects in English, the magnitude of these funds was modest in comparison to the level of support provided for the "national defense" disciplines of science, mathematics, and modern foreign languages.

Yet the field of English is undergoing considerable change in the midst of growing controversy. Whether this change actually represents a "newness" in curriculum characteristic of the "new" mathematics or the "new" physics is a matter of debate. But regardless of the outcome of this debate, the decade of the 1960's witnessed unprecedented activities in training in-service teachers of English, in funding curriculum development projects in universities and school systems, and in supporting scholarship in various language specialties, such as linguistics.

The English Program of the U.S. Office of Education

The generous federal support through NDEA and NSF for curriculum projects in the sciences and mathematics led to the criticism that a dangerous imbalance was being created. With the establishment of Project English in the fall of 1961, now known as the English Program, the U.S. Office of Education moved to support curriculum development in English. Although the level of federal support in English amounted to only a very small fraction of the funds provided for the sciences and mathematics, the English Program created widespread interest and activity toward improving instruction in English at all levels.

An important feature of the English Program has been the establishment of a number of small centers at universities throughout the nation for the purpose of developing and disseminating curriculum materials. These centers are intended to bring together specialists in English and English education to develop promising curriculum innovations in cooperation with school systems and state departments of education. Also supported through the English Program are a number of research projects and in-service programs for teachers. Beginning in 1965, NDEA funds were made available for in-service institutes for teachers in English.

Imitation of Science and Mathematics Projects.   While this support has stimulated unprecedented activity in developing new curriculum packages in English, none of the projects has commanded attention and produced an impact on the schools comparable to the leading projects in the sciences and mathematics. Although the areas of focus in these projects differ widely, many of the centers have patterned their efforts after the specialized discipline-centered approaches characteristic of the first projects in the modern curriculum reform movement in the sciences and mathematics.

None of the English projects has sought to correlate or integrate the study of English with the social studies. According to Goodlad,

> There is little doubt that the "new" English will be characterized by carefully structured curricula taught inductively; by literature courses that emphasize depth and analysis, and lead the student to appreciate literary craftsmanship and its relation to meaning; and by an interest in structural linguistics, in generative grammar, and in speech as an integral part of the curriculum.[45]

Needed Evaluation.   Nevertheless, no definitive research findings have yet been produced that point to superior learning outcomes through these "new" curriculum packages in comparison to conventional approaches. The mixed findings in evaluating the effects of the major projects in the sciences and mathematics would appear to indicate that definitive results are unlikely in the more disparate and ambiguous field of English. Furthermore, as a subject involving developmental skills, the evaluation of instruction in English requires longitudinal research and experimentation—the kind of investigations that have commanded no concerted commitment on the part of English scholars.

Limited Resources.   Another serious shortcoming of the English Program stems from the initial strategy of sponsoring a relatively large number of modestly financed projects at different centers which operate concurrently

---

[45] John I. Goodlad, *The Changing School Curriculum* (New York: The Fund for the Advancement of Education, 1966), p. 76.

and with virtually no interdependent lines for the development of a coordinated and continuous approach to curriculum development. This probably was the outcome of attempting to spread limited financial resources as much as possible during a period in which the major sources of federal funds for curriculum development were being directed at the chosen fields of mathematics and the sciences.

The "Basic Issues" Report

Under a grant from the Ford Foundation, twenty-eight scholars and teachers from the field of English participated in a series of four conferences in New York City during 1958. These conferences were sponsored by the National Council of Teachers of English, the Modern Language Association, the College English Association, and the American Studies Association. Taking their cue from the burgeoning curriculum projects in the sciences, mathematics, and modern foreign languages, the conferees declared that "there is as much reason to believe that English teaching can be radically improved, given the right approaches to the problems and an effort of sufficient magnitude and strength, as there is to suppose that we can strengthen education in mathematics, science, and foreign language." [46]

Emphasis on Need for Sequential and Cumulative Curricula.   Although the purpose of the series of conferences was to formulate the basic issues in the teaching of English, and to "present these issues in no partisan, doctrinaire, or contentious spirit," [47] the "Basic Issues" report did indeed take a stance on many of these issues. For example, one identified issue was whether basic programs in English can be devised that are sequential and cumulative from the kindergarten through the graduate school. After raising this question it was concluded that unless such programs can be devised, "we must resign ourselves to an unhappy future in which the present curricular disorder persists and the whole liberal discipline of English continues to disintegrate and lose its character." [48]

English As a Discipline.   The commitment to a discipline-centered approach is revealed by the first question raised by the conferees—"What is English?"—followed by an expression of concern that the "fundamental liberal discipline of English" is being extended to include public speaking, journalism, listening, remedial reading, letter writing, and general academic orientation. The report goes on to point out that the high

---

[46] Modern Language Association, *The Basic Issues in the Teaching of English* (New York: The Association, 1959), p. 5.

[47] *Ibid.*, p. 6.

[48] *Ibid.*, p. 7.

school teacher of English is troubled by the practice of combining English with the social studies through block-time and core courses. Although it was agreed that English includes composition, language, and literature, uncertainty was expressed as to whether other activities belong within the boundaries of the "fundamental liberal discipline of English."

The view that English properly consists of composition, language, and literature certainly provides no earth-shaking revelation to teachers and curriculum theorists. Moreover, this conception of English fails to show how the subject is a "fundamental liberal discipline." The determination of the content to be included in the course of study and the sequential arrangement of this content are matters of arbitrary decision under such a loosely conceived notion of what properly constitutes the "discipline" of English. Undoubtedly, it is possible for academicians to conduct many conferences and to publish many volumes seeking a proper definition of English without shedding light on how English is to be taught and what should be the proper determinants for the selection and sequence of subject matter.

Although the "Basic Issues" report stresses the need for a sequential and cumulative curriculum in English from the kindergarten to the graduate school, it is unlikely that any fundamental agreement can be reached when the universities have dissected and apportioned English into a myriad of specialized domains. Moreover, the body of research on the teaching of English, while useful in identifying certain promising practices, fails to point the way to a systematic schema for curriculum design. Even in the sciences and mathematics there is great debate concerning the selection and sequence of subject matter. To pattern English after the fields of mathematics and science, as implied in the "Basic Issues" report, may only add to the existing confusion in view of the infinitely more complex and eclectic nature of the subject of English.

False Dichotomies. The "Basic Issues" report is distinguished by its attempts to raise the wrong questions and to fabricate false issues. For example, on the matter of composition, the question is asked, "Should students be taught to 'express themselves' or to 'communicate'?" [49] It is ridiculous to think that "self-expression" and "communication" can be separated—and even if it were possible it would be foolhardy to build a wall between the two or to assign definitive priorities. Another nonsensical question is phrased this way in the report: "Is learning to write primarily a matter of learning to think?" [50] This is like the account given in *Gulliver's Travels* concerning the endless controversy and conflict between the empires of Lilliput and Blefuscu on the question of whether a soft-

---

[49] *Ibid.*, p. 9.
[50] *Ibid.*

boiled egg should be broken at the large end or at the small end. Although leading scholars of both empires published many hundreds of large volumes on this question, they were unable to find a solution.

The Sputnik Syndrome. Having convened only three months after the launching of Sputnik I, the "Basic Issues" conference was particularly mindful of our nation's new obsession with the development of scientific talent. Thus, another "wrong" kind of question was raised by the conferees: "Should the basic program in English be modified for students who are primarily interested in science, technology, or related fields? This issue concerns those students who may have very great ability but whose interests and educational programs lead them toward technical subjects. Should they be grouped together for their study of English?" [51] To segregate scientifically talented students from other students, and to create a special English curriculum geared to their scientific leanings, may augur well for a scientific-technological nation, but raises ominous implications for a democratic society. Furthermore, if such segregation and specialization in English is afforded those who are scientifically talented, should not special classes and separate curricula in English be devised for those whose exceptional talents are evidenced in the arts, the social sciences, and other fields?

Other Issues. Yet another question of dubious value is put this way: "Should certain literary works be required at each of the various levels in a basic program?" [52] Unless one embraces the "One Hundred Great Books" philosophy, such a question leads us nowhere, because the literary experts have never been able to agree on an absolute and definitive list of works to be read by each student at the various grade levels.

Reflecting the nationalizing trends in testing, the report offers this question: "Could national standards for student writing at various levels be established, and what would be their value?" [53] In view of the great disagreement on the assessment of writing ability, it would appear that the establishment of national standards would be limited to those elements of composition which can be easily measured and standardized. But writing also has stylistic and creative dimensions that defy standardization.

And, finally, the report pointed out that "English offers a great opportunity for foundation support to exert an effective and pervasive influence upon American education." [54] Through such support, according to the

---

51 *Ibid.*, p. 8.
52 *Ibid.*, p. 3.
53 *Ibid.*, p. 9.
54 *Ibid.*, p. 15.

"Basic Issues" conferees, a sound sequential and cumulative curriculum from kindergarten through graduate school could be developed.

Looking back at the "Basic Issues" report, it is unfortunate that a distinguished group of experts on the teaching of English would devote so much thought and effort in advocating that educators seek the right answers to so many wrong questions. But the times were such that the "Basic Issues" report gained widespread credence while attracting negligible criticism. It is noteworthy that none of the "Basic Issues" was concerned with the disadvantaged in school and society.

The Commission on English of the College Entrance Examination Board

Established in 1959 for the purpose of facilitating a nationwide improvement in the English curriculum, particularly for college preparatory students, the work of the commission was culminated with a report in 1965, *Freedom and Discipline in English*. The foreword to the report, written by the president of the College Entrance Examination Board, states that "the report should be viewed as a part of the curricular reform that . . . has swept over the schools. It should take its place with comparable reports in other subjects, particularly in mathematics, the sciences, and foreign languages." [55] Despite this ambitious intent, the report was not followed as a blueprint for curriculum reform in English. Instead, it stimulated considerable discussion and debate.

Ignoring the Disadvantaged. One of the most obvious and least discussed aspects of the report was its failure to deal with curriculum problems relating to the education of the disadvantaged. Of dubious validity was the report's basic premise "that the sooner the program in English for college preparatory students can be given sound underpinnings, the sooner corollary programs for other students can be thoughtfully designed." [56] This wishful premise reflected the tenor of the times in which the curriculum reform efforts in the disciplines were being designed primarily for our academically talented and college-bound students. The assumption that it is best to begin curriculum reform with this student clientele in mind also is a reflection of the traditional role of the high school as a college preparatory institution. And, paradoxically, this narrow vision has resulted in the failure of the curriculum to meet the diversified educational needs of a cosmopolitan pupil population.

With the majority of the high school enrollment not going on to higher

---

[55] Commission on English, *Freedom and Discipline in English, op. cit.*, p. vii.
[56] *Ibid.*, p. 4.

education, serious problems can be anticipated when curriculum reform is directed narrowly at our most academically able students. This does not mean that our priorities should be reversed. For it would be equally erroneous to assume that the academically talented will be served best when highest priority in curriculum reform is directed at the terminal student population. The point is that efforts toward curriculum improvement must be balanced if all the children of all the people are to be served well by the schools.

A Narrow Definition.   Another aspect of the report that deserves critical scrutiny is the definition given for the scope of the English curriculum. As stated earlier in this chapter, the report defines the English program as a tripartite group of disciplines: language, literature, and composition. Again, this is a reflection of the specialized discipline-oriented syndrome led by the curriculum reform movement in the sciences and mathematics during the 1950's and 1960's. The inadequacies of such a narrow conception of the English curriculum were discussed earlier in this chapter. The relationship of English to other subjects in the curriculum, a matter of great concern on the part of curriculum workers in English during the 1930's and 1940's, is virtually ignored in the report.

Grammar.   The commission pointed out that existing grammatical approaches do not deal effectively with the problems of language as encountered by the secondary school student. In this connection, the need to relate the study of grammar to constant and meaningful application through literature and composition was stressed. Accordingly, attention should be given to the changing nature of language and how usage often changes despite the "proven" canons of grammar which, in turn, must change with usage. Students should become aware of how language characterizes social and economic levels, variety of occasion, and cultural attitudes.

Literature.   Categorically rejected by the commission is the idea of a national curriculum in English, along with the specification of a canon of literary works for the secondary school. The tendency for teachers to allow textbooks to do their curricular thinking for them also was deplored. Instead, the school's English department should be selecting literary materials through a continually evolving consensus on the part of competent faculty.

Despite such pronouncements, for several years the College Entrance Examination Board has issued a suggested list of authors and works for reading in "Advanced Placement English." While this list is not intended as a prescriptive syllabus, it is preceded by this bit of advice: "Probably the most useful syllabus designed from these suggestions will include a few works from each of the genres." [57] Although there is great disparity and lack of agreement among college departments of English as to what readings should be required in the first college course in literature, many college teachers applaud any effort in the direction of building uniformity or standardization in the secondary school curriculum through approved book lists.

> Revision of the English curriculum is not exclusively a matter of what is being done in composition. Quite as exciting are the developments in literature. . . . In literature one begins to see, unexpectedly perhaps, a move in the direction of uniformity or a standardized curriculum—an approved list of books. The evidence to support this notion is admittedly slight. . . . But it is notable that the Committee on English of the Advanced Placement Program has recently issued a revision of its course and examination description in which it indicates very specifically the areas in literature in which students taking the Advanced Placement Examinations in English in the future can expect to be tested. The committee does not mean that the list should be rigidly prescriptive—of course not. But the results of issuing such a list are not difficult for anyone to imagine, if he has had any connections with high school English teachers. Make no mistake about it. Next May quite a number of able high school youngsters will go to the Advanced Placement Examination in English meticulously prepared in every selection even hinted at by the list.[58]

Ironically, while the practice of prescribing literary canons for college entrance examinations is almost a century old, this tradition is applauded in the above quotation, which is taken from a chapter entitled "New Approaches to College Preparatory English." Apparently, despite the battle of the first quarter of the twentieth century to free the high schools from rigidly prescriptive curricula in literature, there are those who view such standardization as a "new" and needed development. There is a double irony in this inasmuch as the advent of the paperback heralded a long-promised freedom for the teacher to discard the traditional anthology, as well as the rigidity of outdated prescriptive lists.

An important aspect of *Freedom and Discipline in English* is the emphasis given to the use of critical questions to enhance the critical process. According to the report, this not only is important while a literary work is being read by the student but also after the reading is completed, so that the student becomes more personally engaged with the total impact of the work. Here it is important for students to ask

---

[57] College Entrance Examination Board, *1968–70 Advanced Placement Course Descriptions* (Princeton, N.J.: The Board, 1968), p. 74.

[58] Edwin H. Sauer, "New Approaches to College Preparatory English," Chapter 11 in Robert W. Heath (ed.), *New Curricula* (New York: Harper & Row, Publishers, 1964), p. 223.

questions of their own and to evaluate these questions. In this critical process, teachers and students will analyze material through questions of form, rhetoric (the relationship of the work to the writer or speaker, its setting, and its audience), meaning, and value (personal response and the relative excellence of the work). According to the commission, "critical questions" should constitute the dominant approach to the study of literature if a spirit of inquiry is to be developed. The use of objective-type tests in the English class should be limited because such items fail to deal with some of the most searching, interesting, and significant aspects of the subject matter.

Composition. Turning to composition, the Commission on English advocated that each assignment require the student to discover something new and should evoke the best from him. A good assignment might take the form of a proposition that challenges the learner to react with commitment. It might furnish data to start from and stipulate the audience to be addressed. Although the commission acknowledged the need to vary the kind of composition assignments, it recommended that the expository essay be the staple of the course in grades 11 and 12 at least. Such writing, according to the commission, not only best prepares the student for college writing but constitutes the most common form of human discourse.

Recognizing the problem of time in reading and correcting compositions carefully, and acknowledging that individual conferences with students take more time than any teacher can provide, the commission pointed to the value of certain substitute mechanisms. These include the employment of lay readers, the use of a laboratory hour in which the teacher may tour the room while the class is engaged in writing and correction, the exchange of student papers for the correction of mechanical errors, and the use of selected student themes (anonymous) for class demonstration and criticism. The use of lay readers continues to be a controversial matter, although the College Entrance Examination Board and Educational Testing Service have supported such measures. This procedure is discussed later in this chapter.

Another procedure recommended by the commission is the use of topical commentary in which a grade (number, letter, or single word) substitutes for discursive commentary for each of the principal topics of ordinary correction (writing skills, organization, reasoning, and content). This method, employed in national CEEB examinations, is recommended on the dubious assumption that students will be able to translate such codes into their equivalent meaning in discursive commentary.

Yet another controversial method proposed by the commission is the sampling of student compositions for correction by the teacher. Here the teacher might correct carefully only a sampling of one third of the compositions at any one time. Student objections to such a method should not be too surprising; for when a student is asked to do an assignment, he rightly expects the teacher to give it a careful reading. Moreover, not to provide a careful reading and evaluation of each assignment may simply allow the student to repeat his errors and compound his problems during a time in which he should be making continuous progress in invention, style, and organization.

Disciplinarity. Although the commission recommended that the English teacher be assigned no more than four classes daily with an average class size not to exceed twenty-five students, the commission's position favoring a discipline-centered approach precludes the use of block-time classes for curriculum correlation and integration and for reducing the number of different students assigned to each teacher daily. And while some educators continue to maintain that a sharp division between English and the social studies leads to inexcusable curriculum fragmentation, the decade of the 1960's was a period in which many leading curriculum specialists in English sought to emulate the discipline-centered fervor of their colleagues in the sciences and mathematics. It is no small wonder, then, that the Commission on English of the College Entrance Examination Board embraced the concept of English as a discipline to be treated separately from other subjects in the curriculum of the secondary school.

The Anglo-American Conference

In the late summer of 1966 a group of about fifty educators met at Dartmouth College for the Anglo-American Conference on the Teaching of English—or the Dartmouth Seminar, as it came to be called. Twenty of the participants were from the United Kingdom, one was from Canada, and the rest were from the United States. Hailed as the first large-scale international meeting devoted to English, the Dartmouth Seminar was sponsored by the Modern Language Association of America, the National Council of Teachers of English, and the National Association for the Teaching of English (United Kingdom). The seminar was supported by a grant from the Carnegie Corporation. The purpose of the Dartmouth Seminar was to provide for an international exchange of ideas concerning curriculum problems in English as a school subject.

It will be recalled that a similar meeting of thirty-four scientists, mathematicians, psychologists, and other educators met at Woods Hole on Cape Cod in the fall of 1959 to determine how education in science might be improved in our elementary and secondary schools. The report of the Woods Hole Conference, *The Process of Education* by Jerome S. Bruner, proved to have unprecedented impact as a rationale for shaping the school curriculum not only in the sciences and mathematics, but in virtually every subject that is considered a discipline. Although the Dartmouth Seminar made no mention of the Woods Hole Conference, the parallel between the two is clear. Moreover, it should also be noted that the Carnegie Corporation, which provided the financial support for the Dartmouth Seminar, had also joined other agencies in planning the Woods Hole Conference. Nevertheless, where two fifths of the membership of the Dartmouth Seminar was composed of British educators, all but one of the thirty-four participants in the Woods Hole Conference were Americans.

Conflicting Values.   The participation of a large representation of British educators in the Dartmouth Seminar proved significant not only in view of the international intent of the conference, but because the British educators tended to assume a more progressive stance toward curriculum reform than their American counterparts. Ironically, it was the Americans who supported the traditional ideal of intellectual discipline, while the British argued for greater individual freedom in a vein remarkably similar to the progressive ideal that had characterized American educational theory in an earlier era.

In essence, where the Americans were caught up in the nationalizing trends toward curricular specialization and efficiency, the British educators were concerned with individual development. Thus, while most of the Americans sought to emulate the discipline-centered approach, as developed at Woods Hole for the fields of science and mathematics, the British favored a student-centered curriculum.

Discipline-Centered Emphasis.   In the United States, the Brunerian influence had already established itself in many of the centers connected with the federally financed English Program (formerly known as Project English) and consequently the American participants in the Dartmouth Seminar were prepared to follow a discipline-centered model in their deliberations. In short, their preconceived perception of an appropriate strategy for curriculum development was "to redefine the particular subject in the light of the best knowledge available, to identify its central and organizing principles, to select and arrange applications and illustrations of those principles in an orderly sequence appropriate to the capacity of children of various ages, and finally to write radically new textbooks embodying these concepts." [59] Such a strategy involves a process of definition in which "the scholar looks at the 'subject' in abstraction from the pupils who will be using and operating in it. Necessarily the

---

[59] John Dixon, "Conference Report: The Dartmouth Seminar," *Harvard Educational Review,* Vol. 39 (Spring, 1969), p. 368.

work of the scholar comes first; only when his 'definition' is complete can schoolteachers begin to 'select and arrange applications.' " [60]

Learner-Centered Emphasis.   The British opposition to the discipline-centered model resulted in some redirection of the seminar's attention toward a more learner-centered approach. According to the British author of one of the seminar reports, the latter approach, based upon concrete classroom experience, offers these advantages over the subject-definition model:

> (1) it does not separate what is learned from the way it is learned and the use to which it is put . . . , (2) by not assuming an exclusive interest in the subject, one realizes that continuities of learning are of two kinds: within subject boundaries and across them . . . , (3) it leads us to discuss . . . how in his everyday living a student comes to use what he has learned.[61]

The Elusive Structure.   Nevertheless, the polarities between the two models, as represented by the American and British educators at the Dartmouth Seminar, remained unresolved. For example, at the beginning of the seminar, the participants sought to define "What is English?" Although it was never acknowledged that such a question is unanswerable, the seminar soon abandoned its attempts at deriving a definition, because the "logical structure of the discipline" could not be determined. Instead, the seminar attempted to describe "What is English?" in terms of the multifarious processes and activities that the learner experiences through the use of language.

Closely related to the problem of definition is the applicability of Bruner's "structure of a discipline" to the subject of English. Although the linguists agreed that this concept of "structure" can indeed be applied to the study of language, most of the participants were of the opinion that the concept of "structure" fails to indicate clearly the means for teaching students to read, write, speak, and listen effectively. Yet it was noted that in the teaching of English "there is no generally accepted philosophy to guide decisions about what the study should be centered on, what should be its primary aims—not to mention how best to achieve those aims." [62]

Problem of Priorities.   While pointing out that many teachers regard literature as the heart of the subject, and that the main focus of the English departments in the colleges and universities is on literature, it was also observed that there is much confusion as to the kinds of litera-

---

60 *Ibid.*
61 *Ibid.*, pp. 369–370.
62 Muller, *op. cit.*, p. 4.

ture to be taught and the purposes to be served by doing so. For example, should the development of proficiency in reading be the primary objective? And what about the problem of values and critical thinking?

Then there are those who contend that English should focus mainly on language. This, in turn, raises the question of priority in composition. What emphasis should be given to expository, functional, and creative writing? And while the development of fluency in oral expression is recognized in the professional literature, in most high schools this is left to an elective course in speech, rather than being treated as integral to the subject of English. Also, the place of rhetoric, logical thinking, and critical analysis has not been given adequate attention in developing the curriculum in English.

Also present in all this debate is the need to assess the impact of the new science of linguistics on the ability to read and write more effectively. For although linguistics bears an aura of respectability in our scientific age, we are still unclear as to whether this specialty, with its production of new grammars, will emerge as a discipline unto itself, or whether it will lead to learning outcomes that are functionally applicable to language usage by all citizens.

Pupil Grouping or Streaming.   Turning to the issue of pupil grouping or streaming, both the American and British participants in the Dartmouth Seminar condemned such practice and recommended that other approaches be explored for meeting different abilities and interests.

One suggested approach is the British "workshop" method where heterogeneous classes are divided into a number of groups, some self-chosen, which work together on different assignments related to a larger class project. Many seminar members observed that the practice of grouping has served not only to stigmatize the disadvantaged student and reinforce his self-concept of inadequacy, but also has deprived this student of stimulation by peers who are higher achievers. Moreover, it isolates students so that they are denied opportunities to learn from others of different cultural backgrounds.

> When language is used for interaction in talk and drama, it is essential for a class to have a wide range of experience and background. Of course, if a social group becomes segregated, whether in predominantly Negro schools in the U.S., or in the predominantly working class streams of the U.K., it will inevitably retreat into its own subculture and dialect, and the difficulties of encouraging a broader cultural awareness will become highly intractable.[63]

It was noted that grouping does not produce sufficient incremental achievement for the abler student; on the other hand, it often causes

---

[63] Dixon, *Growth Through English, op. cit.,* p. 101.

detrimental effects for the disadvantaged youngster. Nevertheless, there was considerable disagreement on this issue. The practice of grouping continues to persist in many elementary schools and in most of our larger secondary schools. Although streaming has long been the official policy in the schools of England and Wales, this policy is meeting growing opposition.

Correctness and Style.   Another matter given considerable attention in the seminar concerns the tendency of teachers of English to impose a single, fixed, and "correct" form of standard English on their students. Although this notion has been discredited by language experts, many teachers continue to follow a dogmatic path of "righteousness" in treating language as a set of absolute and unchanging rules.

Teachers need to understand how language, like life, is ever changing in style and that correctness is determined through usage, which, in turn, evolves according to man's expanding experiences. Moreover, the concept of usage as relative to the situation and the purpose to be served, including dimensions of time and place, needs to be better understood by teachers. The treatment of spoken English as an inferior form of written English, rather than as a different form, along with the tendency to regard colloquial language as a corruption, was deplored by the seminar members. This does not imply that sloppy usage is to be applauded or tolerated. The point is that too many teachers have treated English as a dead language through prescriptive rules that are unchanging. While all students need to learn standard English, they should not be made ashamed of their own familiar dialect forms which have been developed from their home, family, and neighborhood environment. Nevertheless, many disadvantaged youngsters encounter great difficulty in learning to make "language switches" which are necessary not only for purposes of accommodating to the standard English found in much of our printed materials, but also in oral communication where new situations call for new social roles in the mainstream of society. Obviously, this has special meaning for the role of the English teacher in a fluid society where the school is a key agent of cultural change.[64] Yet it must be acknowledged that relatively little is known about how such learning might be effected through the English curriculum. Seminar participants agreed that a great deal of experimental work is needed on this problem.

The Linguistics Debate.   The seminar participants criticized the tendency of teachers to devote considerable time to drill and memorization in formal grammar. It was pointed out that many teachers were operating under the discredited notion that such exercises will produce more

---

[64] *Ibid.,* p. 22.

effective writing and speaking. It was observed that the teaching of conventional grammar has been chiefly a waste of time. Although prescriptive grammar has been discredited, many seminar participants expressed skepticism concerning the work of linguists in producing the new "generative" or "transformational" grammar. Here doubts were raised concerning the extent to which such new grammars can actually improve written and spoken English. For it has yet to be demonstrated that a theoretical understanding of such grammars will carry over to usage.

Furthermore, the new grammars appear to impose their own formalisms on the learner. In the words of the author of one of the seminar reports, "Looking over a book on it [transformational grammar], I found it rather forbidding, with diagrams and formulas that at first glance looked like esoteric versions of diagraming I once had to do." [65] Most of the British members of the Dartmouth Seminar opposed such systematic approaches to the teaching of language and held that occasional "implicit" teaching as the need arises should be sufficient. On the other hand, the linguists argued that while there is no research evidence regarding the utility of linguistic study, it can be justified for its humanistic value, good for its own sake. Nevertheless, even the linguists could not reach agreement as to what specific elements should be included in the curriculum in English. One of the hopeful conclusions of the seminar was that linguists, particularly those grounded in psychology and sociology, could shed needed light on the ways in which young people learn language.

Literature.   Although the seminar members avoided listing the specific literary works or authors to be studied, they recommended that, in addition to major representative works in English and American literature, the curriculum should include some foreign literature in translation, "reservoir" literature in the background of our culture (classical mythology, European folk and fairy tales, and the Bible), and some attention to the newer media (motion picture, radio, and television). The traditional teaching of knowledge about literature, particularly through literary history, should be eliminated. Opposition was expressed to the growing trend toward imitating college courses in literary history in the high school and emphasizing literary forms, genres, and techniques. The curriculum in literature should be concerned primarily with the expansion of the learner's experience, rather than with the promulgation of a formal knowledge of literature. Nevertheless, it was recommended that reading materials be selected for their literary value, with the goal of improving adolescent tastes.

The use of basic themes as an organizing principle for the study of literature was debated. The thematic approach, whereby literature is

---

[65] Muller, *op. cit.*, p. 69.

related closely to life, was contrasted with the method of approaching literature for its aesthetic qualities and uniqueness as an art form. Although this issue was not resolved, it was clear that the seminar participants had failed to give high priority to the study of literature for the purpose of developing a better understanding of broad social problems, issues, and values.

Concerning literary criticism, the British educators warned against teaching students to analyze works according to the "right things" as established by the teacher, the textbooks, or the English professors—at the expense of enjoying literature and exercising independent judgment. One British participant put it this way: "The dryness of schematic analysis of imagery, symbols, myth, structural relations, et al. should be avoided passionately at school and often at college. *It is literature, not literary criticism, which is the subject.*" [66]

Although some mention was made of the need to relate literature to the diverse and conflicting values that the individual faces in a pluralistic society, the relationship of literature to the social studies was totally ignored.

Writing and Talking. It was observed that, except for the writing of term papers in college, few students will ever have the need to produce the kind of writing required in the typical composition assignment. Even the college composition course was severely criticized for assignments that are dull and artificial. The need to stimulate student interest through lively class discussions was stressed. Students should be given the opportunity to write for audiences other than the teacher if they are to be stimulated to write with their hearts as well as their minds. Interest and confidence should not be stifled by stressing error and correctness.

It was also pointed out that there are no clear criteria for "effective" writing. The failure of research to point the way to newer and more efficient methods of teaching composition was cited. But it was agreed that emphasis on traditional grammar not only had a negligible effect on the improvement of writing, but served to squander time that might better have been spent on writing. Although a number of American participants advocated that the curriculum be centered on rhetoric (the principles underlying the effective use of language), the British favored greater attention to personal and creative writing. While mention was made of the need to work with teachers of other subjects concerning the use of language across the whole curriculum, no explicit recommendations were offered as to how such cooperation might be implemented.

Seminar participants agreed that the teaching of speech or "talking" was being neglected in the English curriculum in both British and Ameri-

---

[66] *Ibid.*, p. 88.

can schools. In American secondary schools, as in the colleges and universities, the practice has been to provide separate courses in speech, which are distinguished from English and which are not required of all students. Furthermore, the speech course tends to focus primarily on the more formal or public kinds of speech, while informal speech as a means toward personal development is being virtually ignored. Here, too, the need for research on the role of speech in the acquisition of personal identity has been given little attention.

The need to provide for group discussion in the English class through student study groups, so that students may learn to talk to one another more effectively, was stressed. In too many classrooms the teacher dominates the discussion and pupil talk is invariably a response to teacher talk. Also recommended was the practice of using panel discussions, rather than speeches or formal debate, to promote an open market of ideas consistent with democracy. Through heterogeneous classes, such panel discussions would be enriched by a greater variety of dialect, vocabulary, and viewpoints. The importance of learning to listen critically is vital to all citizens of a democracy. Yet little attention has been given to the development of listening skills in the English class.

Concerning the recent passion for imitating other disciplines in centering the curriculum on the "innate" structure of the subject, it was observed that "the structure of the subject must be meshed with the structure of the student. A major failure of education has been to consider the logic of one almost to the exclusion of the psychologic of the other." [67]

Creativity and Drama. It was observed that the teaching of creative writing in American schools usually stops at about the fifth grade, after which writing assignments tend to be concentrated on exposition and drills in mechanics. In recent years, many British schools have given increased emphasis to creative writing as a means of individual development. The seminar participants noted that creative writing should enable the student to appreciate language more fully by freeing him from stultifying mechanization, standardization, and regimentation so characteristic of the traditional lesson with its obsession for unbending rules. Teachers must realize that creative expression is not limited to the subject of English but should pervade the entire curriculum. Despite the imprecision of the term *creativity,* it was felt that it can be recognized not only in the greater works in the arts and sciences, but in certain efforts of children and youth. Thus it is a useful concept for anyone interested in vitalizing the curriculum.

Turning to drama, the seminar members recommended that this be made an integral part of the English curriculum. Although British educa-

---

[67] *Ibid.,* p. 110.

tors have stressed the importance of continuing to emphasize drama as a performing art throughout the school years, in American secondary schools it has been studied as literature while the performance aspect has been relegated to separate drama classes and to extracurricular activity. Moreover, it is ironic that drama, an art form directly intended to promote interaction among people, has emerged in the English class chiefly as literature to be read. In conceiving of drama as a performing art it is important to develop dramatic activity for the sake of the student's own education and not as a "show" for parents and others. Obviously, we will need to free students from the restrictions of the boxlike classroom and the fixed rows of desks if such activity is to be conducted effectively.

The Mass Media. Recognizing the profound influences of the motion picture, radio, and television in shaping our interests, attitudes, and behaviors, it was agreed that some study of the mass media be included in the English curriculum. With regard to television, the situation in Britain was acknowledged as significantly different from the United States in that the British television industry, through the BBC, is not dominated by a Madison Avenue syndrome, evidences greater public responsibility than do the American networks, and offers more valuable programs for use in English classes.

Despite the expressed concern on the part of the seminar group for the study of the mass media in the English curriculum, few concrete suggestions were offered as to how such material might be incorporated. Moreover, little attention was given to the place in the curriculum of an older, pre-electronic medium—the press. Here the seminar group made no recommendations concerning the treatment of propaganda and how our news may be slanted, distorted, or even suppressed. Obviously, such matters should be of vital concern to the teacher of the social studies as well as to the teacher of English. Yet the seminar report made no suggestions as to how such learning activities in the two subject fields might be complemented.

The potential of the newer media for improving instruction was discussed, and although it was agreed that we have hardly begun to utilize technological aids effectively, skepticism was evident concerning the benefits of programmed instruction and "canned" or videotaped lectures. In this connection, critical questions were raised concerning the use of programmed materials as a testing process: "What was tested? Was it attitudes, personal development, sensitivity to values, stimulus to creativity? Or was it not merely knowledge and proficiency? The answer was that it was chiefly the latter." [68]

---

[68] *Ibid.*, p. 150.

Examinations. British seminar members soundly criticized the traditional British practice of administering "external" examinations which set national standards for admission to the university. It was felt that these examinations not only serve to prevent many students of high potential from entering the university but exert an undesirable influence on the curriculum generally. For example, teachers tend to drill students for these examinations. Furthermore, separate examinations are given in language and literature at the General Certificate level, thereby dividing subject matter that should be treated as a whole. Moreover, at the advanced level, the examination is on literature alone. This results in the tendency for traditional schools to de-emphasize language teaching for this age group.

Many British members of the Dartmouth Seminar expressed shock over the growing influence of the College Entrance Examination Boards as an important criterion for determining admission to colleges in the United States. It was also felt that such "external" tests have caused teachers to cram students so that they might have a better chance of obtaining needed scores. Both the British and American educators also criticized the National Assessment examinations in the United States and warned that such tests, along with the College Boards, will only serve to exert an undesirable influence on the curriculum and will further aggravate the deleterious effects of grouping or streaming students in our schools. A systematic review of these examinations was recommended. The British educators, in particular, expressed concern over the tendency for our schools to bow to the pressures of technocracy, with individual development being sacrificed in the interests of economy and efficiency.

A Unitary Approach. An important outcome of the Dartmouth Seminar was the decision to advocate a unitary approach to English. This runs counter to the prevailing practice in many schools of dissecting the study of English into periods and courses in which composition, language, literature, speech, and drama are treated as separate entities and as abstract processes divorced from the real purposes of using language. In curriculum development there has been a tendency to focus on specialized content, with the end result that a system of abstract schemas becomes the course of study.

One way to unify classroom activity is to center the work around important themes of human experience. Although the seminar recommended this as a viable strategy, it failed to give credit to the earlier efforts of progressive educators in utilizing the thematic approach for purposes of curriculum integration. A proposed solution to the problem of utilizing the competencies of specialists when a unitary approach is being implemented may be found in team teaching. Thus colleagues with different specialities can learn by working together toward common goals. However, as mentioned earlier, the Dartmouth Seminar made no effort to explore the many possibilities for relating the curriculum in English to other subjects and vice versa. Yet one of the seminar reports quoted from a fifty-year-old British study, which had declared that "it is impossible to teach any subject without teaching English." [69] In this connection, the Dartmouth Seminar merely acknowledged that, unfortunately, little effort has been made to examine the precise ways in which such teaching is being conducted.

Structure of the Discipline. Criticism was directed at the traditional practice of developing the subject matter so that the studies are "force fed" at each grade level for the specific purpose of preparing students for the next grade level. This not only stuffs children with concepts before they are ready, but stifles interest and curiosity. "We should never, in other words, impose the future upon the pupil unless we can find some way to translate it into the present." [70]

Regarding the question of knowledge and the "structure of a discipline," it was concluded that decisions in life are reached by affective as well as cognitive processes and that attitudes, feelings, and desires have their own forms of organization. The danger of organizing the subject matter according to its "inherent" logical framework is that it deflects the learner from translating such knowledge into self-directed action. Moreover, efforts to construct a sequential curriculum according to the principles of structure have been arbitrary, deflective, and restrictive, and have yet to be supported by research on learning.

> In the first place, there is no body of agreement as to the nature of this structure, nor does any such agreement seem attainable; it is not even clear whether it should be looked for within the discipline of literary criticism or that of linguistics. Secondly, the search for this kind of 'structure' as a guiding principle leads to a retrogressive emphasis on 'knowledge' (knowledge *about* the language, or *about* literature) as opposed to 'ability to use.' And, thirdly, the desire for a step-by-step articulation leads to a demand that the English teacher's field of activity be restricted to that which can be made incremental.
>
> . . . the hopes for a definition in terms of 'the great and simple structuring ideas' are fed by the illusion that all subjects are akin to Mathematics. Not much consideration is needed to show that Mathematics and English are worlds apart. . . . English is the meeting point of experience, language and society. It implies a developmental pattern whose origin and momentum comes from outside the school situation.[71]

---

69 Dixon, *op. cit.,* p. 67.
70 *Ibid.,* p. 78.
71 *Ibid.,* pp. 84–85.

Other Criticisms and Recommendations.   It was suggested that teachers at the secondary level would do well to make some use of the "workshop" approach, pioneered in a number of the primary schools here and in England, where learners are stimulated to exercise responsibility in pursuing independent and group work. The departmental organization and teacher specialization in the secondary school leave teachers in relative isolation and create a situation where the teacher is regarded as the only means through which students can learn. Through team teaching and workshop approaches, teachers as well as pupils should find new opportunities to learn from one another. Furthermore, the workshop approach should enable students of "mixed abilities" to work together more successfully through cooperative enterprises.

The pressures exerted upon the schools by the colleges and universities have caused secondary school teachers to conceive of educational objectives as ground to be covered and examinations to be passed. Under such pressures the schools are not free agents and tend to limit their curriculum innovations to prepackaged programs handed down by the universities. An urgent recommendation of the seminar was the sponsorship of an international experiment, conducted over several years in selected school districts, to explore new approaches to English in concert with analogous approaches in other subjects. The study would be longitudinal, along the lines of the Eight-Year Study. However, it would be distinguished from the Eight-Year Study in that the focus would be on new subject approaches. Streaming or tracking would be eliminated, along with external examinations, and the universities would agree to admit students on the basis of joint school-university consultation. Unfortunately, however, neither the sponsors nor the participants of the seminar followed through on this recommendation.

RECENT MAJOR STUDIES

The National Study of High School English Programs

One of the most comprehensive studies ever made of English teaching in our high schools was conducted during the 1960's under the sponsorship of the National Council of Teachers of English through a grant from the U.S. Office of Education.[72] The major purpose of this study was to identify the characteristics of English programs that were producing students of superior achievement. Schools consistently producing award winners in the NCTE Achievement Award Program were matched with a sample of schools of good reputation in English education, but which were not producing award winners. The NCTE Achievement Award

---

[72] James R. Squire and Roger K. Applebee, *High School English Instruction Today*, *op. cit.*

Program is a national attempt to identify high school students of outstanding achievement in English through various tests and measures.

Focus on the Superior Student.   With the national curriculum reform movement of the 1960's focused on the talented student, it is not surprising that the NCTE should concentrate its study on a nucleus population of schools producing NCTE Achievement Award winners. No attempt was made to identify those schools which were attaining significant results with students representing the entire spectrum of abilities and socioeconomic backgrounds.

Comparisons of Characteristics of the School Samples.   The investigators were unable to find any significant differences in the characteristics between the schools that were noted for their high production of NCTE award winners, and those schools not producing award winners but otherwise having been identified as possessing strong programs in English. No attempt was made to identify the number of schools in the latter population that chose not to participate in the NCTE testing program. In view of this methodological lapse, and because of the newness of the NCTE Awards Program, it was decided to treat the two populations of schools as a single population of 158 high schools in 45 states. A total of more than 1,600 classes were observed directly in the 158 schools.

Major Findings.   The following are some of the major findings of the study: (1) teachers in the schools studied were better prepared, were more active professionally, and had more opportunities for in-service education than teachers nationally; (2) the English curriculum was characterized by a strong emphasis on literature and, although there was some evidence of a decline in reliance on the literary anthology, the anthology was being used in a significant number of schools; (3) more than half of the class time was being devoted to the study of literature; (4) few schools gave evidence of having developed carefully integrated and sequential programs of study; (5) widespread confusion was reported on the part of many teachers with regard to content and method in language instruction; (6) although frequent and varied composition experiences were provided, insufficient time was being allocated to rhetoric and the processes of writing; (7) instructional methods were less varied than anticipated by the investigators, with insufficient use being made of discussion techniques and audiovisual resources; (8) although two thirds of the teachers appeared to have wide latitude in the selection of instructional materials, in many cases these teachers gave evidence of self-censorship by citing real or imagined community pressures; (9) comparatively little instructional experimentation or innovation was found; (10) instructional programs in the skills of reading were found lacking in purpose, organization, and impact; (11) most efforts to individualize instruction were directed at the academically able student, while the non-college-bound student and slow learner were receiving insufficient attention; (12) students appeared to be more concerned with academic success than other students nationally, but efforts to assess the intellectual climate in the selected schools yielded only tenuous evidence; (13) while there was a close relationship between the size of the school library and the quality of the book collection, students showed preference for the public libraries with their larger and more accessible resources; school libraries not only were far below the standards formulated by the American Library Association, but were lacking in relevant contemporary material; and (14) teacher-made tests, including end-of-term examinations, gave excessive emphasis to rote learning and to encyclopedic knowledge of literary history.

Conclusions and Implications.   With our national emphasis on the academically talented student during the late 1950's and through the decade of the 1960's, it is not surprising that virtually every school in the study was found to be neglecting the needs of the terminal, non-college-bound student. Characteristically, the most experienced and effective teachers were being assigned to the advanced and honors classes, while the terminal students were tracked into classes characterized by dull and mechanical instructional routines.

Although the teachers in the study claimed that they were devoting over 70 per cent of class time to discussion and Socratic questioning, actual classroom observation revealed that barely 20 per cent of class time was used in this way. The need for greater emphasis on appropriate teaching methods in both in-service and preservice programs was cited as imperative.

Even in the stronger schools, there was a notable lack of coherence in the curriculum. The elements of the language arts were lacking in coordination, and important relationships among language, literature, composition, speech, and reading were being ignored. The curriculum, in short, was highly fragmented. The only well-developed courses of study that were found were those designed for the advanced college-bound students.

Although considerable emphasis was being given to literature, student preferences were largely ignored and major controversial works in twentieth-century literature tended to be neglected so as to avoid threatened censorship. And while 16 per cent of class time was being given to composition, little instruction was directed at the writing process. In this connection the teaching was largely error-oriented. Teacher-pupil conferences and the use of cumulative folders were rarely in evidence.

In the area of language, the teachers revealed a growing confusion as a result of the recent scholarly developments in our universities. Even if the confusion concerning new developments in grammar and usage were to be resolved, the problem of integrating such materials with other areas of the language arts would require special attention.

Perhaps one of the most important and least emphasized finding in the study was the almost nonexistent place of a reading program integral to the English curriculum. Although almost half of the schools employed a reading specialist, most teachers tended to regard remedial and developmental reading as unrelated to their own classroom work.

Similarly neglected were speech and oral language skills. Typically, a semester of speech is provided in the tenth grade, but little effort is made in developing oral language skills at other levels and relating such work to other elements of the English curriculum.

Among the schools claiming experimental and individualized programs, the "individualized" approaches were almost always accompanied by large group lectures, which appeared to be an ineffective method for instruction in English. Although humanities courses were found in 20 per cent of the schools, such studies were designed for advanced studen's only. On the whole, experimental programs were found to be lacking in effective coordination and evaluation.

In conclusion, if the preceding deficiencies and needs are characteristic of the schools that nationally have the best English programs, it is clear that English remains one of the most neglected and disjointed subjects in the high school curriculum, particularly for the terminal student.

A National Survey of the Teaching of Reading

With a grant from the U.S. Office of Education, the Curriculum Study Center at the University of Illinois conducted a national survey in late 1968 and early 1969 to determine the status of reading instruction in our public high schools.[73] More than 2,000 questionnaires were mailed to a random sample of the membership in the secondary school section of the National Council of Teachers of English. After eliminating those returns from teachers in nonpublic schools and those returns judged to be unusable, an analysis was made of 912 questionnaires. It was estimated that, of the active public high school teachers of English included in the sample, between 55 and 60 per cent completed the questionnaire. No attempt was made to sample the population of English teachers who were not members of NCTE.

Major Findings. Although more than 80 per cent of the respondents agreed that the teaching of reading should be a major responsibility of the high school, a majority considered themselves poorly prepared for such work. More than 80 per cent of the teachers had never taken a

---

[73] George K. McGuire, *The Teaching of Reading by English Teachers in Public High Schools* (Urbana, Ill.: Illinois State-Wide Curriculum Study Center, 1969).

course on the teaching of reading at the undergraduate level. Of those who *had* taken a course in English methods, more than 70 per cent reported that the teaching of reading was treated to little or no extent. More than 80 per cent of all the teachers reported that the English departments in their schools do not give the teaching of reading sufficient attention for reading to be considered a major departmental concern.

Although a significant number of English teachers reported that they were engaged in recommended practices in reading instruction, they considered themselves to be most effective in meeting the needs of the superior student and least effective with the below-average student.

Conclusions and Implications.   The findings of this survey do not contradict those of the National Study of High School English Programs. Where the questionnaire study was based on the respondents' perceptions of their own practices, the National Study of High School English Programs provided for direct observation of classroom practices. Although the questionnaire study found that the overwhelming proportion of teachers regarded reading as a major responsibility of the high school, both studies revealed that this responsibility is not being met.

From both of these studies it is apparent that English departments in our high schools need to give concerted attention to the teaching of reading, both remedial and developmental. Although a distinction must be made between reading instruction and the teaching of literature, reading should be integral to all elements of the English curriculum. It should not be separated from the English curriculum and regarded as being under the sole jurisdiction of the reading specialist in the high school. Preservice and in-service programs of teacher preparation in English should include systematic work in the teaching of reading, and such work should be coordinated and integrated with preparation in all other areas of the English curriculum.

Because the survey was limited to a sample of members of the National Council of Teachers of English, one could reasonably conclude that a survey of all teachers would reveal findings that are even less favorable. An encouraging note in the national questionnaire study is that so many of the teachers expressed their recognition of the importance of the teaching of reading in the high school English curriculum.

Survey by Educational Testing Service

A national survey, involving over more than 2,300 eleventh- and twelfth-grade students in public, independent, and parochial schools, was conducted by Educational Testing Service in 1969 for the purpose of determining the various student activities and assignments in the English curriculum.[74] Questionnaires were distributed to those juniors and seniors in high school who had taken the English Composition Test of the College Entrance Examination Board. Thus, the survey was limited to a selected college-bound population. The questionnaire divided English into the areas of composition, language, and literature—a tripartite organization of the subject as proposed earlier by the College Board's Commission on English.

Major Findings. In estimating the frequency of various composition activities, only 21 per cent of the eleventh-graders reported that they had "frequently" engaged in the writing of essays, while 41 per cent indicated that they "rarely" or "never" were required to write essays. Only 12 per cent of these students reported that they "frequently" wrote papers based upon personal experience. Virtually identical responses were found for the twelfth-graders. In reporting on how their papers were corrected by teachers, less than 20 per cent of the eleventh- and twelfth-graders revealed that their teachers commented on the style of writing or on the students' ideas on the topic.

Concerning activities in literature, only approximately one out of every four students reported that they had engaged "frequently" in outside reading for their classes. And only 9 per cent of the students indicated that they "frequently" gave oral reports. This compares with 54 per cent reporting that they "rarely" or "never" gave oral reports. Over 70 per cent of the eleventh- and twelfth-graders indicated that they "rarely" or "never" participated in panel discussions. Emphasis on listening skills consisted mainly of taking notes on teacher lectures.

The majority of students reported that they "frequently" read literary selections from an anthology. More than half of all students indicated that they "rarely" or "never" read a biography. And almost three out of every four students stated that they "rarely" or "never" gave an oral book report.

Implications. As the survey was limited to juniors and seniors who had taken the College Board's English Composition Test, the population in this study comprises a highly selected group of college-bound students. In fact, compared with a national sample of college entrants, these students ranked close to the 75th percentile on the Scholastic Aptitude Test in both verbal and mathematical scores.

Thus, this is an extremely able group of students and consequently the findings of the study are of special significance. When extremely able

---

[74] Fred I. Godshalk, *A Survey of the Teaching of English in Secondary Schools* (Princeton, N.J.: Educational Testing Service, 1969).

students do not engage frequently in the writing of essays, when their teachers seldom comment on these students' ideas and style of writing, when relatively few of these students are engaged in outside reading assignments for their classes, and when these youngsters rarely give oral reports and participate in panel discussions, one wonders what the picture is with regard to less able students. Listening and speaking skills are just as important for the less able and the disadvantaged youngster as for the most talented student. When such activities receive little emphasis in the curriculum with our most able students, we cannot conclude that the picture is better for others. If anything, it is likely to be even less encouraging, because our most qualified teachers and our best resources have been specifically directed toward serving the needs of our most able student population during the decade of the 1960's.

The fact that such research is directed at and limited to an extremely able population of college-bound students bespeaks our continued concern for the most academically talented segment of our population. Obviously, such research can and should be designed to encompass a more representative profile of our high school population if we are to make significant steps toward improving the English curriculum at all levels. This does not mean that we need not concern ourselves with our most talented students. While the College Entrance Examination Board is legitimately concerned with the college-bound population only, educators cannot be so selective if the individual and society are to be served by our schools.

Other Research

A comprehensive review of the research in the language arts is made periodically through the American Educational Research Association. A review in 1967 revealed that (1) better coordination of research on reading in the secondary school is needed; (2) such research should be conducted through interdisciplinary approaches; (3) listening ability can be improved by instruction; (4) more studies of critical listening are needed; (5) the basic problem of judging the worth of student compositions has not been solved; (6) English teachers devote much less than one third of class time to composition; (7) although experimental studies on the teaching of literature are on the increase, the findings tend to be inconclusive; and (8) few of the English curriculum centers supported by the U.S. Office of Education are engaged in research studies to test hypotheses connected with the new materials and methods which they were promulgating.[75]

---

[75] "Language Arts and the Fine Arts," *Review of Educational Research,* Vol. 37 (April, 1967).

An earlier survey of research on teaching included a comprehensive review of the studies on reading, composition, literature, and grammar, but failed to include research on speaking and listening.[76]

Since 1956, Educational Testing Service has studied the use of lay readers as a means of relieving English teachers of the enormous time required for the correction of student compositions. Although the use of "outside" readers enables teachers to assign a greater number of compositions, such approaches have not been accompanied by significant levels of improvement in writing skills.[77] Unfortunately, the major motive for supporting this program has been on the managerial aspect of reducing student load per teacher rather than on improving writing skills.

SUMMARY

The past decade has witnessed unprecedented efforts toward reformulating the curriculum in English at the secondary school level. Nevertheless, the reform movement in English is characterized by numerous specialized and uncoordinated projects, resulting in considerable controversy and confusion. It has been said that English is the least clearly defined subject in the curriculum with the possible exception of the social studies.

The pursuit of the notion of "structure," in imitation of the curriculum projects in the disciplines of science and mathematics, has not produced the promised solutions for building a unified and coherent curriculum in English. The wide galaxy of content and skills that comprises the subject of English suggests that other strategies may be far more fruitful in curriculum development.

Despite the unprecedented activity in the many specialized areas that make up the conglomerate subject of English, a "new" English has not emerged. While the new linguistics is gaining significant attention and is beginning to influence classroom practices, this is only one specialized field. Moreover, linguists are themselves divided by specialists, and the curriculum implications of their work have yet to be demonstrated in terms of learning outcomes for the ordinary pupil.

Studies of classroom practices in the teaching of English in our secondary schools reveal that insufficient time is being allocated to activities that are generally regarded as desirable by curriculum workers in English. For, despite the numerous areas of specialization and vantage points that encompass the subject of English, recent comprehensive surveys on the teaching of English in our nation's high schools reveal that groups of

---

[76] N. L. Gage (ed.), *Handbook of Research on Teaching* (Chicago: Rand McNally & Company, 1963).

[77] William W. West, "Written Composition," Chapter V in *Review of Educational Research, op. cit.*, pp. 159–161.

English educators can and do agree on certain approved practices. A fundamental step toward improving the English curriculum would be to develop in representative schools model programs that are characterized by a constellation of well-articulated approved practices. Through careful longitudinal research and evaluation, significant contributions can be made toward the continual improvement of the curriculum.

Emphasis on disciplinarity during the past decade has created a wider breach than ever between English and the social studies. Efforts to correlate and integrate English and the social studies during the 1930's and 1940's for purposes of common learnings or general education, particularly in the junior high school, were not accompanied by concomitant investments in curriculum resource materials and programs of teacher education. In the face of the growing areas of specialism in the field of English, the problem of developing a unified and coherent program of studies in English presents enormous difficulties, not to mention the complexities in attempting to create bridges between English and the social studies. Yet the growing demand for curriculum relevance through problem-centered approaches may present new opportunities for overcoming past obstacles. Ironically, efforts to develop cross-disciplinary and interdisciplinary studies are being undertaken anew in some of our colleges and universities, while our secondary schools continue to live with a highly fragmented curriculum.

PROBLEMS FOR STUDY AND DISCUSSION

1. What are the implications of the following statement for curriculum construction? Do you believe that this statement is valid for disciplines or subjects other than English? Why or why not?

    subject specialists in, say, history or geography are concerned among other things with developing cognitive frames of reference which will help account for certain areas of experience. But in ordinary living we judge, choose and make decisions in terms of feelings, desires and attitudes which have their own forms of organization. The structuring of experience that we aim for in English certainly involves the affective as well as the cognitive. This raises a difficult choice when we try to define the English syllabus or curriculum, whether in terms of experience to be organized or in terms of frames of reference to be developed. [John Dixon, *Growth Through English* (Reading, England: National Association for the Teaching of English, 1967), p. 80.]

2. Do you agree with the following statement? Support your position.

    The sharp distinction between English and the social studies cannot possibly be defended. [John J. DeBoer, "The 'New' English," *Educational Forum*, Vol. 32 (May, 1968), p. 401.]

3. At the Dartmouth Seminar, the following criticism was leveled at attempts to derive a rational sequence for the teaching of English from the "internal structure" of the subject. What is your opinion on this issue?

In the first place, there is no body of agreement as to the nature of this structure, nor does any such agreement seem attainable. . . . Secondly, the search for this kind of "structure" as a guiding principle leads to a retrogressive emphasis on "knowledge" as opposed to "ability to use." [John Dixon, *Growth Through English, op. cit.*, p. 84.]

4. What arguments can you offer in critizing the following definition of the scope of the English program in our secondary schools?

Recommendation: That the scope of the English program be defined as the study of language, literature, and composition, written and oral, and that matters not closely related to such study be excluded from it. [Commission on English, *Freedom and Discipline in English*, New York: College Entrance Examination Board, 1965), p. 13.]

5. A series of conferences in 1958, involving representatives from various leading national organizations concerned with the teaching of English, led to the statement below expressing uncertainty as to whether anything other than English composition, language, and literature should be included in the curricula of our schools. How do you account for such a narrow conception of English? Should such media as television and the motion picture have a legitimate place in the English curriculum? Why or why not? What about drama as a performing art, rather than as a segment of literature?

What is "English"? We agree generally that English composition, language, and literature are within our province, but we are uncertain whether our boundaries should include world literature in translation, public speaking, journalism, listening, remedial reading, and general academic orientation. [Modern Language Association, *The Basic Issues in the Teaching of English* (New York: The Association, 1959), p. 8.]

6. As discussed in this chapter, a national survey of college-bound eleventh- and twelfth-graders ranking in the top quartile of the Scholastic Aptitude Test revealed, among other findings, that (a) more than 70 per cent of these students "rarely" or "never" participated in panel discussions in class; (b) almost 75 per cent "rarely" or "never" gave an oral book report in class; (c) a majority "rarely" or "never" read a biography; and (d) almost half of the students "rarely" or "never" wrote a paper based upon personal experience.

Do these findings surprise you? Why or why not? As a teacher, what proportion of your students participate "frequently" or even "occasionally" in panel discussions?

7. What arguments can you offer to challenge the following statement by the College Board's Commission on English?

> The Commission believes that the sooner the program in English for college preparatory students can be given sound underpinnings, the sooner corollary programs for other students can be thoughtfully designed. [Commission on English, *Freedom and Discipline in English, op. cit.,* p. 4.]

SELECTED REFERENCES

American Educational Research Association. "Language Arts and the Fine Arts," *Review of Educational Research,* Vol. 37 (April, 1967).

Basic Issues in the Teaching of English, The Supplement to *College English,* Vol. 31 (October, 1959).

Bruner, Jerome S. *The Process of Education.* Cambridge, Mass.: Harvard University Press, 1960.

Commission on English. *Freedom and Discipline in English.* New York: College Entrance Examination Board, 1965.

Conant, James B. *The American High School Today.* New York: McGraw-Hill Book Company, Inc., 1959.

————. *Education in the Junior High School Years.* Princeton, N.J.: Educational Testing Service, 1960.

————. *The Comprehensive High School.* New York: McGraw-Hill Book Company, Inc., 1967.

Corbin, Richard. *The Teaching of Writing in Our Schools.* New York: The Macmillan Company, 1966.

Dixon, John. *Growth Through English.* Reading, England: National Association for the Teaching of English, 1967.

Evans, William H., and Jerry L. Walker. *New Trends in the Teaching of English in Secondary Schools.* Chicago: Rand McNally & Company, 1966.

Godshalk, Fred I. *A Survey of the Teaching of English in Secondary Schools.* Princeton, N.J.: Educational Testing Service, 1969.

Goldstein, Miriam B. *The Teaching of Language in Our Schools.* New York: The Macmillan Company, 1966.

Heath, Robert W. (ed.). *New Curricula.* New York: Harper & Row, Publishers, 1964. Chs. 10 and 11.

Hogan, Robert F. (ed.). *The English Language in the School Program.* Champaign, Ill.: National Council of Teachers of English, 1966.

Kegler, Stanley B. (ed.). *The Changing Role of English Education.* Champaign, Ill.: National Council of Teachers of English, 1965.

Marckwardt, Albert H. *Linguistics and the Teaching of English.* Bloomington, Ind.: Indiana University Press, 1966.

McGuire, George K. *The Teaching of Reading by English Teachers in Public High Schools.* Urbana, Ill.: Illinois State-Wide Curriculum Study Center, 1969.

Meckel, Henry C. "Research on Teaching Composition and Literature,"

Chapter 18 in N. L. Gage (ed.), *Handbook of Research on Teaching.* Chicago: Rand McNally & Company, 1963.

Moffett, James. *Teaching the Universe of Discourse.* Boston: Houghton Mifflin Company, 1968.

Muller, Herbert J. *The Uses of English.* New York: Holt, Rinehart and Winston, Inc., 1967.

National Society for the Study of Education. *Innovation and Change in Reading Instruction,* Sixty-seventh Yearbook, Part II. Chicago: The University of Chicago Press, 1968.

————. *Linguistics in School Programs,* Sixty-ninth Yearbook, Part II. Chicago: The University of Chicago Press, 1970.

Postman, Neil, and Charles Weingartner. *Linguistics, A Revolution in Teaching.* New York: Dell Publishing Co., 1966.

Shugrue, Michael F. *English in a Decade of Change.* New York: Pegasus, 1968.

Squire, James R., and Roger K. Applebee. *High School English Instruction Today.* New York: Appleton-Century-Crofts, 1968.

Thomas, Owen. *Transformational Grammar and the Teaching of English.* New York: Holt, Rinehart and Winston, Inc., 1965.

Reeves, Ruth. *The Teaching of Reading in Our Schools.* New York: The Macmillan Company, 1966.

Wilson, Graham. "The Structure of English," in G. W. Ford and Lawrence Pugno (eds.), *The Structure of Knowledge and the Curriculum.* Chicago: Rand McNally & Company, 1964.

Chapter 7

Curriculum Change in the Modern Foreign Languages

The curriculum reform movement not only has changed radically the methods and materials of instruction in the modern foreign languages, but it has been accompanied by a marked surge in the number and proportion of students studying languages at the elementary and secondary levels. Nevertheless, while these developments often are described as "revolutionary," our high school courses, by and large, are not producing bilingual students. Moreover, as discussed in this chapter, many problems in the teaching of languages in our schools remain unresolved.

CHANGING GOALS AND FUNCTIONS

Decline of the Classical Tradition

Our early leaders, themselves products of the classical curriculum provided by the grammar schools and universities of England, established similar schools in the New World. Because the main task of education was training for the ministry and salvation, the classical languages, particularly Latin, occupied an exalted position in the curriculum of the Colonial schools and colleges.

The eighteenth and nineteenth centuries witnessed new educational demands as a result of economic and scientific developments. Benjamin Franklin's proposal in 1749 called for the replacement of the Latin-grammar school by a new kind of school, the academy, which would offer practical studies, including modern foreign languages. However, the forces of tradition remained strong and, although the academies used English as the basic language instead of Latin, the subject of Latin remained dominant over the modern foreign languages. The academies reached their peak during the first half of the nineteenth century and declined rapidly with the rise of the public high schools during the latter part of the nineteenth century and early years of the twentieth century.

Even as late as 1900 more than half of the public high school students studied Latin, while less than a quarter were studying a modern foreign language, mainly German or French. By 1915 the proportion of students studying Latin had declined to 37.3 per cent while those taking modern foreign languages had risen to 35.9 per cent (of which 2.7 per cent were enrolled in Spanish).[1]

The influences of World War I on our social and industrial life were accompanied by demands for a more modern curriculum. While the study of German became a casualty of the anti-German sentiments of the war, Latin was attacked for its lack of relevance and utility in a dynamic, technological world. In a paper published in 1916, Abraham Flexner, a former teacher of classics who had gained a reputation for his monumental Carnegie study of American medical education, criticized the claims made for the study of ancient languages and attacked the doctrine of mental discipline.[2] Later he wrote in the *Atlantic Monthly* that "Latin has no purpose." [3] He was joined by former Harvard President Charles W. Eliot, who argued that Latin should not be compulsory and that the subject was not even necessary for the study of ancient civilization, literature, or religion.[4] At that time most of the colleges and universities were no longer requiring Latin for either admission or for their A.B. degree programs.

While the classicists fought hard to defend Latin, the trend was clear. The call of the twentieth century was for the modern and practical studies. Where a majority of public high school students studied Latin in 1900, less than 4 per cent of the students in public secondary schools were studying Latin in 1970.

Nevertheless, in the face of the dramatic decline in the proportion of high school students enrolled in Latin classes, some educators continued to argue that Latin deserves an important place in the curriculum. Although, in the second half of the twentieth century, very few educators were defending Latin on the basis of the generally discredited doctrine of mental discipline, it was being defended for its literary and cultural values. For example, writing for the Council for Basic Education, a Harvard professor of English literature contended, "It may seem utopian, though it should not, to ask that the upper section of high school students

---

[1] William R. Parker, *The National Interest and Foreign Languages*, 3rd ed. (Washington, D.C.: U.S. Department of State, 1961), p. 86.

[2] Abraham Flexner, *A Modern School*, Occasional Papers, No. 3 (General Education Board, 1916).

[3] Abraham Flexner, "Parents and Schools," *Atlantic Monthly* (July, 1916), p. 30.

[4] Charles W. Eliot, "The Case Against Compulsory Latin," *Atlantic Monthly* (March, 1917), pp. 356–359.

should have a working knowledge of two foreign languages, of which I would say that one should be Latin. . . . Latin is a door to literature and civilization. . . ." [5]

However, as discussed later in this chapter, education during the 1960's was to be reshaped to meet national goals. And because the United States was the acknowledged leader of the "free world," our federal government came to recognize the modern foreign languages as worthy of special support in view of their importance to our national defense and world leadership role.

The Decline and Rise of Modern Foreign Languages

The sharp decline in the study of German during World War I, the recognition of the importance of practical and vocational studies as a result of the war, the dropping of foreign language admission requirements on the part of many colleges, and the demand for more diversified curricula to meet the needs of an increasingly heterogeneous high school population, all served to reduce the proportion of students enrolled in foreign language classes during the years from World War I to midcentury.

Prior to World War II, foreign language instruction in our secondary schools was concentrated mainly on formal grammar, with the general objective of developing the ability of students to read and write the language. However, the development of real proficiency in reading and writing, not to mention listening and speaking, rarely was attained in the typical sequence of studies. The curriculum not only was saturated with grammatical rules and constructs to be analyzed incessantly in English, but often the teacher was lacking in bilingual fluency and consequently was unable to employ a functional approach. While such teachers were incapable of serving as models of language fluency, they were able to drill the class in textbook exercises with heavy reliance on English. Moreover, the typical sequence in many high schools was a two-year course of study in a given language.

During World War II, the U.S. Army established intensive foreign language programs that emphasized primarily the development of the ability to comprehend the spoken language and to speak with reasonable fluency. The goal was functional fluency rather than literary and cultural heritage appreciation. The instructors themselves were models of functional fluency and the language was used incessantly as the means of communication throughout the training period of nine months. The men worked in small groups and employed a variety of audiovisual methods.

---

[5] Douglas Bush, "Literature," in James D. Koerner (ed.), *The Case for Basic Education* (Boston: Little, Brown, and Company, 1959), p. 112.

The intensive nine-month training period probably was at least equivalent in time to four years of college in addition to two years of high school. Following the war, efforts to adapt the Army methods to nonintensive high school and college courses were unsuccessful. Moreover, relatively few high school teachers possessed sufficient language fluency to employ highly functional methods, and many college instructors persisted in following a literary emphasis in their courses.

During the early 1950's the proportion of the high school enrollment in modern foreign languages had declined to some 14 per cent as against almost 40 per cent in 1916.[6] One educational historian describes the situation as a "catastrophic decline . . . amounting to a state of collapse."[7] However, if we take into account that only a small minority of our youth was enrolled in high school in 1915, whereas universal high school education was a virtual reality at midcentury, a very different picture emerges. While it is true that, by 1950, the foreign languages no longer played a dominant role in the high school curriculum, the actual number of students enrolled in modern foreign language classes at midcentury was almost double that of the year 1915. Nevertheless, no renaissance in the modern foreign languages was to emerge until the late 1950's when the pressures of the cold war placed the teaching of such languages at a level of national priority commensurate with that of the sciences and mathematics.

Cold War Criticisms and Reactions

The Essentialists. During the cold war of the 1950's, leading essentialists cited the decline in the proportion of high school students in foreign language classes as evidence of our educational decadence. Rickover blamed our schools for the fact that few American ambassadors had a working knowledge of the language of their host countries.[8] However, Rickover chose not to mention that ambassadorships generally are assigned as political awards rather than according to criteria of linguistic and diplomatic capability. And although it would be most desirable for ambassadors to have bilingual and even multilingual capabilities, the emergence of English as an international language has made it possible for ambassadorial posts to be assigned without serious concern for foreign language fluency. Of course, a convincing case can be made for the need to have functional fluency in the target language if one is to understand the culture and serve effectively as a United States ambassador. But

---

[6] Parker, *op. cit.*

[7] Edward A. Krug, *The Secondary School Curriculum* (New York: Harper & Brothers, Publishers, 1960), p. 258.

[8] Hyman G. Rickover, *Education and Freedom* (New York: E. P. Dutton & Co., Inc., 1959), p. 109.

the realities of our political system have given low priority to this very important qualification.

Although foreign languages traditionally have been regarded as within the province of college preparatory studies in the American high school, Bestor advocated that the foreign languages be included in the "five great areas" that must constitute the fundamental secondary school program: mathematics, science, history, English, and foreign languages. He recommended that students be required to take at least five years of work in each of these fields, with two foreign languages being offered.[9] In response to Sputnik I, Bestor argued that the study of language is just as important to us as a world power as the study of mathematics. "Also, I believe in it as an intellectual discipline," [10] he declared.

The Conant Reports. The influential Conant report on the American high school recommended that students with language ability complete a four-year sequence in one foreign language for the purpose of developing "the ability to read the literature published in the language and . . . to converse with considerable fluency and accuracy with an inhabitant of the country in question." [11] Conant contended that such fluency is not attainable by taking two years in each of two different foreign languages. He proceeded to offer several arguments for developing a mastery of a foreign language: (1) without something approaching a mastery of a foreign language, one has missed an educational experience of the first importance; (2) such mastery makes available a new approach to human problems, because certain ideas are not always translatable; (3) mastery of one foreign language facilitates the learning of a second language, even where the second language is unrelated to the first; (4) such study will provide the opportunity for youth with special language abilities to develop their talents; and (5) "grim competition with the Soviet Union in newly developing countries turns quite as much on an adequate supply of competent linguists as on our ability to send competent engineers and businessmen to these nations." [12] Conant also pointed to the trend of starting foreign language instruction in the elementary grades as a movement worth watching.

In his report on the junior high school, Conant recommended, "Some, if not all, pupils should start the study of a modern foreign language on

---

9 Arthur Bestor, *The Restoration of Learning* (New York: Alfred A. Knopf, Inc., 1956), p. 326.

10 Arthur Bestor, "What Went Wrong with U.S. Schools," interview in *U.S. News & World Report,* Vol. 44 (January 24, 1958), p. 74.

11 James B. Conant, *The American High School Today* (New York: McGraw-Hill Book Company, Inc., 1959), p. 69.

12 *Ibid.,* p. 72.

a conversational basis with a bilingual teacher in grade 7." [13] Here he called for an articulated and sequential program from grades 7 through 12 in the same language so that something approaching mastery could be attained. He also warned that in view of the fact that only a small fraction of high school graduates actually attended elementary school in the same system, the practice of starting foreign language instruction in the lower elementary grades carries the danger that such study may very likely be interrupted, thereby resulting in a loss of time and effort.

Although the foreword of the Conant report on the American high school, written by John W. Gardner (then president of the Carnegie Corporation which sponsored the Conant studies), maintained that Conant found little relevance in comparing Soviet education with ours, the one subject field in which Conant made specific mention of Soviet competition was that of foreign language. However hard he tried, the pressures of the cold war could not be ignored in Conant's evaluation of our secondary schools.

Education for National Defense.   During the early 1950's, the Modern Language Association (MLA), with foundation support and encouragement from the U.S. Commissioner of Education, investigated the status of modern foreign language instruction and proposed a number of reform measures. It was clear that the cold war had created a new urgency for foreign language learning. As a result of its study, the MLA proposed longer sequences, the establishment of foreign languages in the elementary schools (FLES), and the utilization of language laboratories and technological aids. Where the MLA in an earlier era had taken the position that secondary schools should concentrate on reading skills,[14] the Association now endorsed an audiolingual or aural-oral approach.

The passage of the National Defense Education Act of 1958 gave recognition to the modern foreign languages as essential to our national interest, along with the sciences and mathematics. Suddenly tens of millions of dollars became available through the federal government for improving instruction in the modern foreign languages in our elementary and secondary schools. Funds were available for equipment and language laboratories in the schools and for teacher institutes in colleges and universities.

The pressures of the times were such that California enacted a law in 1961 requiring instruction in foreign languages in grades 6, 7, and 8—despite the opposition of school administrators, who pointed out that the law provided no financial allocations to support the program. Moreover,

---

13 James B. Conant, *Education in the Junior High School Years* (Princeton, N.J.: Educational Testing Service, 1960), p. 17.

14 Algernon Coleman, *The Teaching of Modern Foreign Languages in the United States* (New York: The Macmillan Company, 1929).

in enacting the law, the legislature had given no consideration as to how an army of qualified teachers could be recruited for the mandatory instruction. The result was the institution by many California schools of television lessons without adequate follow-up by qualified classroom teachers.

Nevertheless, throughout the nation, foreign language instruction in the elementary school (FLES) developed rapidly during the 1960's. By beginning such instruction at earlier levels of schooling, when children purportedly are most readily open to such learning, it was hoped that our schools would be able to develop a new bilingual generation to meet our nation's expanding economic, political, scientific, technological, and military commitments throughout the world.[15]

Educational organizations which, in an earlier era, had championed progressive education now saw the schools as instruments for serving national goals in meeting the crisis of the cold war. For example, a publication of the NEA's Association for Supervision and Curriculum Development, an organization noted for its long commitment to maintaining balance in the curriculum and orienting the curriculum to student needs, opened with the declaration that "it has become a matter of national interest to increase the number of Americans who can understand and speak a foreign language." [16] An earlier report of a seminar sponsored by the NEA's Project on Instruction was so carried away with the "pursuit of excellence" and the role of our schools in meeting national goals for world leadership that it managed to reach this ridiculous conclusion: "By 1980 anyone who speaks only two languages will be ill-equipped to cope with situations that will confront him daily. We no longer will live a monolingually isolated life. Our world role will make increasing demands, which we are now only beginning to meet." [17]

Cultural Appreciation

Although the midcentury drive to produce a large population of bilingual students has been supported mainly as a reaction to the pressures of the cold war and our nation's growing world-leadership role, foreign language educators also contend that learning should lead to a better understanding and appreciation of other cultures. A humanistic rationale behind such learning is that one cannot fully understand and

---

15 Philip H. Coombs, *The World Educational Crisis—A Systems Analysis* (New York: Oxford University Press, Inc., 1968), p. 103.

16 Edward D. Allen, Leona M. Glenn, and Frank Otto, *The Changing Curriculum: Modern Foreign Languages* (Washington, D.C.: Association for Supervision and Curriculum Development, NEA, 1968), p. 1.

17 Project on Instruction, *The Scholars Look at the Schools* (Washington, D.C.: National Education Association, 1962), p. 15.

appreciate one's own culture unless he is able to perceive how other peoples, through other languages, perceive reality. Furthermore, by understanding and appreciating the languages of other cultures, one is better able to understand and appreciate his own language and culture. Thus it is held that "study of a people through the foreign language can give students an intimacy that they cannot get through other disciplines. . . . The students get to know a people in greater detail in foreign language study than through the social studies." [18]

Unfortunately, however, the research literature on this question is inadequate to support the generalization that the study of a foreign language actually produces such outcomes. In all likelihood, the degree to which a given course, whether in the social studies or in a modern foreign language, is successful in developing certain kinds of cultural understandings and appreciations is dependent on the teacher's goals and competencies. While it cannot be denied that language learning has unique properties that are not treated in other areas of the curriculum, unless the teacher has the commitment and capability of providing learning experiences relevant to such goals the outcomes are likely to be disappointing.

CONTEMPORARY DEVELOPMENTS AND PRACTICES

Within a few years following the passage of NDEA, the high school enrollment in foreign language classes more than doubled—far outstripping the increase in the high school population during the same period. By mid-1960, more than one out of every four high school students was studying a modern foreign language and the percentage was increasing.[19] However, as we entered the 1970's, the proportion of elementary and secondary students enrolled in foreign language classes entered a decline. And an increasing number of colleges and universities were abolishing the undergraduate language requirement. The growing demand for relevance, coupled with the failure to develop students with a speaking knowledge of the target languages, contributed to the decline. A reassessment of the goals and functions of foreign languages in the curriculum appeared to be in order.

Turning to other developments, many of our larger high schools, in response to the cold war syndrome of the 1950's, instituted classes in Russian, while some schools introduced the study of Chinese (Mandarin). However, in too many cases such programs were more successful in attracting attention than in developing students with functional fluency.

---

[18] Peter F. Oliva, *The Teaching of Foreign Languages* (Englewood Cliffs, N.J.: Prentice-Hall, Inc., 1969), p. 163.

[19] Allen, Glenn, and Otto, *op. cit.,* p. 1.

During the late 1960's and early 1970's, some efforts have been made in response to demands by militant student groups to institute the study of African languages in our colleges and in a small number of high schools. But such programs at the high school level are still so limited in their application and impact that they have remained outside the main-stream of the curriculum reform movement in foreign language educa-tion.

The Objectives of Functional Fluency

The new national need called for the development of functional fluency in modern foreign languages. Traditional methods and materials, with emphasis on drill work in the rules of formal grammar and analysis in English, were inadequate to the task. The old approaches had failed and, at mid-twentieth century, the time had come for radical change.

> Present-day teaching of modern foreign languages aims toward mas-tery of all four skills—understanding, speaking, reading, and writing. Mastery of skills requires a longer sequence of study. The change in instructional objectives therefore necessitates extending the sequence of study to four or more years. The aim is not merely to expose students to the language by "covering" a great deal of material, but, by intensive and continuous drill, to lead them to a high degree of mastery or near-native proficiency in the language.[20]

Is the development of near-native proficiency a realistic goal of foreign language education in a society where few citizens are required to use a second language in daily life? In other words, is it realistic to expect our students to develop such fluency from experiences that are limited almost entirely to the academic setting? At midcentury, most of the proponents of the "new" audiolingual approach were of the opinion that such an objective was indeed attainable if only the "new" approach were adopted by our schools and if the study sequence were extended down to the ele-mentary grades.

The Grammar-Translation Method

Before discussing the audiolingual rationale in detail, it will be helpful to review some of the inadequacies of the traditional grammar-transla-tion method. This approach derives from the study of Latin and Greek through logical analysis and memorization of grammatical rules. When the study of Latin could no longer be justified on utilitarian grounds, it was heralded as being valuable as an intellectual discipline. Consider-able emphasis was given to the rigorous study of grammatical rules and

---

[20] *Ibid.,* p. 11.

their application to the reading and translation of texts. Through such methods it was contended that the intellectual powers would be strengthened while, at the same time, students would gain an appreciation of the classical heritage. Modern languages, on the other hand, were regarded as less valuable for mental discipline and for developing an understanding of our classical heritage.

With the discreditation of the doctrine of formal discipline and the growing utilitarian needs for communicating in the modern languages during the early part of the twentieth century, Latin and Greek began to be replaced by modern languages. Ironically, however, the study of modern languages was commonly modeled after the traditional grammar-translation methods developed in the teaching of the ancient languages. Textbooks and classroom methods in the teaching of modern languages tended to copy the traditional approaches, which were preoccupied with memorizing grammatical rules and vocabulary, and applying such material to tedious translation exercises, usually of a literary character.

Yet where Latin was not taught for its use in communication, the modern languages were supposed to be learned for the utilitarian purpose of communication. Although the grammar-translation method presented some utilitarian value for those whose sole goal was to become translators of printed materials, it failed to develop students capable of functional oral communication in the target language.

The Direct Method

Around the turn of the century, as a reaction to the inadequacies of the traditional grammar-translation method, a number of language theorists were advocating the direct method. This method, which gained a considerable following in Scandinavia and certain other European countries, also attracted some adherents in the United States.

The direct method is based upon the premise that classroom activities should represent a re-creation of the conditions under which children learn their native tongue. Thus the target language is used exclusively in the classroom. Students learn the second language by direct and incessant exposure, and no reference is made to translation into native-language equivalents. Objects and actions are used to convey meanings. After some degree of oral fluency is attained, the student progresses to reading. In learning to read in the target language, the direct method seeks to avoid the intermediate steps of translating the material into the native language. Instead, as the student encounters the printed material, he is expected to learn to think directly in terms of the target language. Obviously, in order to make the direct connections between the oral and written modes of communication in the target language, considerable emphasis is given to phonetics.

Through the direct method, patterns of language usage are learned by inference and induction, and not through the formal and explicit analysis of grammar as in the grammar-translation approach. Grammar is not ignored in the direct method, but is learned in a functional context. As the student advances in his mastery of the target language, the systematic study of grammar may be undertaken directly in the target language itself rather than through the native language.

Although the direct method gained great success in countries where the target language is widely used, offering the student the opportunity to communicate in the target language outside the classroom, it has not been successful in the United States, where coordinate bilingualism is not characteristic of our population. Thus in Scandinavia and the Netherlands, where English is a second language for large segments of the general population, students are afforded the opportunity to use English in their daily lives. In contrast, the target language in the United States tends to remain a foreign language rather than becoming a second language, because students do not commonly have the opportunity of using the new language outside the classroom. Under such circumstances, the basic premise of the direct method, which holds that one learns a second language in essentially the same manner in which he learned his native language, becomes open to serious question simply because the conditions are not the same. Moreover, the adolescent student encountering a foreign language for the first time is significantly different in his psychological framework from the infant who is learning his native tongue as it is directly used in life situations.

Yet another problem in the direct method is that it requires teachers who are fluent in the target language and who are enormously skillful in their teaching methods. Relatively few American teachers have such mastery. Consequently, the traditional grammar-translation method remained dominant until midcentury, when new demands and expectations called for radical changes.

The Audiolingual Approach

Through NDEA funds, the Modern Language Association was able to develop a variety of materials for six-year sequences (grades 7–12) in several modern foreign languages, including Russian. The A-LM approach ("Audio-Lingual Materials"), as it came to be designated, represented a "new" rationale. In the audiolingual approach, the chief emphasis is on the learning of language through the development of listening and speaking skills. The audiolingual approach also has been called the "aural-oral" approach. Some foreign language educators have referred to this approach as the "American" method.

Intended to follow the natural way in which language is first learned— by observing, listening, and speaking—the audiolingual approach is augmented through a variety of visual as well as auditory materials. These include motion pictures, film strips, videotapes, and charts—along with language laboratories, audiotapes, records, and totally new textbooks. Since the "new" rationale places great emphasis on seeing or observing, as well as on listening and speaking, a more adequate designation might be the "audiovisual-lingual" approach. However, the term *audiolingual* has gained the most widespread use.

Some educators have the misconception that the audiolingual approach ignores the teaching of grammar or structure. Actually, the rationale of the approach calls for considerable work on grammar or structure; but instead of treating this as an end in itself, it is learned through the functional and authentic use of the target language.

Pattern Practice. In place of the traditional grammar-translation method requiring the memorization and application of formal rules, A-LM employs pattern practices in which the learner is taught through analogy and imitation of controlled models. Pattern practice is designed to develop language dexterity and control without the burden of grammatical analysis and explanation. Pattern practice provides for rapid oral drill on pattern problems so that the problems are treated in the context of communication rather than translation. By learning through analogy rather than by analysis, the student's responses become habitual and automatic.

Each drill is concerned with a specific structural pattern and the pattern is gradually varied as the students gain mastery. It is important that the structural patterns be developed in authentic contexts of foreign language discourse, so that the student will learn to relate the material to other structural elements in the target language.

Pattern practice is based upon some of the significant developments in linguistics. As the linguists have pointed out, language is not logical and is not learned through rules of correctness. Neither is language based upon writing.

Some efforts have been made to fashion pattern practice to fit the theory of operant conditioning. However, there is evidence of widespread dissatisfaction among students and teachers who complain of the boredom and tedium from repetitive drilling and "conditioning." [21] Criticisms of operant conditioning are discussed later in this chapter.

Dialogues. The teacher serves as a model for expected behaviors and eventually, after the teacher develops a speaker-listener relationship with individual students and the total class, students begin to communicate with one another while the teacher listens. This leads to situational dia-

---

[21] Leon A. Jakobovits, "Research Findings and Foreign Language Requirements in Colleges and Universities," *Foreign Language Annals,* Vol. 2 (May, 1969), p. 437.

logues in which the students develop language skills in a more realistic and dramatic context. Where pattern practice is designed to develop automatic and habitual response skills, it is not communication in the real sense. But the skills developed through pattern practice are essential for the communication required in dialogue.

Language is learned most effectively in meaningful situational contexts. Models of pronunciation, word-order sequence, and language structures are designed to represent the conversation of native speakers. As the student comprehends the varying elements of dialogues in meaningful settings, he also imitates and learns a great deal through inference so that, eventually, he is capable of using the new language with reasonable effectiveness in new situations. Errors are corrected promptly and the student, through the newer media, is given opportunities to devote considerable time to modeling his skills so that they eventually become automatic. As students learn to communicate with one another in meaningful dialogues, their motivation is enhanced when they experience the rewards of using their audiolingual skills more naturally. Following the initial stages of audiolingual learning, reading and writing skills are developed.

Application of Linguistics

An important aspect of the "new key" is the application of structural (or scientific) linguistics to the study of languages. Actually, linguistic science was used during World War II in analyzing the lesser known languages for the military. Because structural linguists regard each language as having its own structure of sounds, forms, and meanings—rather than being based upon some other language, such as Latin—it is necessary to view a language "structurally" or "descriptively" and not "prescriptively."

Structural linguists maintain that because written language is a system of symbolizing the symbols of oral language, the study of oral language should precede the study of written language. To study writing first only creates unnecessary obstacles to the learning of spoken language, according to the structural linguists. The audiolingual method is based upon this important premise.

Linguistic science seeks to improve foreign language teaching through scientific study of the language, including analysis of:

(1) The system of mutually contrasting basic sounds ("phonemes") and the conditions under which they appear.

(2) The grammar, stated not in traditional terms of Western philosophy but in terms of form classes, inflections, constructions, sentence types, and actually functioning "rules" as determined by analysis of utterances.

(3) The study of *contrasts* between the learner's mother tongue and the language being learned.

(4) Considerations of the nature of *language itself,* which characteristically exists as a system of *spoken* communication and only derivatively as a system of written communication.[22]

In summation, language is speech, not writing; "rules" are summaries of language usage or behavior; grammatical constructs are not derived from the mother tongue, but are integral and authentic to the target language and must be used in a functional context; and, languages are different. Thus, in the audiolingual approach, grammar is learned inductively through pattern drills and not through prescriptive rules. Authentic models of oral communication in the target language are intended to enable the student to encounter and learn to use the language in its most "natural" forms. Although structural linguistics has made important contributions to modern approaches to the teaching of foreign languages, many aspects of linguistic science remain controversial and unexplored, while many teachers do not fully comprehend the major tenets of linguistic science.

Recommended Procedures

Some of the recommended classroom procedures for developing bilingualism are identified by one authority:

The modeling of all learnings by the teacher.

The subordination of the mother tongue to the second language by rendering English inactive while the new language is being learned.

The early and continued training of the ear and tongue without recourse to graphic (reading-writing) symbols.

The learning of structure through the *practice* of patterns of sound, order, and form, rather than by explanation.

The gradual substitution of graphic (reading-writing) symbols for sounds after sounds are thoroughly known.

The summarizing of the main principles of structure for the student's use when the structures are already familiar, especially when they differ from those of the mother tongue. (But he is never formally asked to regurgitate these rules.)

The shortening of the time span between a performance and the pronouncement of its rightness or wrongness, without interrupting the response.

The minimizing of vocabulary until all common structures have been learned.

The study of vocabulary only in context.

---

[22] Parker, *op. cit.,* pp. 74–75.

> Sustained practice in the use of the language only in the molecular form of speaker-hearer-situation.
>
> Practice in translation only as a literary exercise at an advanced level.[23]

Although the procedures listed above make no specific mention of visual techniques, considerable inferential and direct learning occurs through gestural-visual actions. The teacher as a model and the use of visuals for developing situational contexts are important in language learning. However, care must be taken to ensure that gestural techniques are natural and visual materials are pertinent, if distraction and interference with audiolingual skills are to be avoided.

It should be stressed again that the audiolingual approach emphasizes hearing-speaking during the early stages of language learning and separates these skills from reading-writing. Because hearing-speaking and reading-writing are different kinds of skills, it is felt that the early mixing of the two sets can lead to interference. Furthermore, it is essential that the language be used in communication rather than translation.

The Language Laboratory

One of the most important and useful instruments for implementing the audiolingual method is the language laboratory. Unfortunately, many schools, in their haste to provide language laboratories for their classes, obtained inferior and often unnecessarily expensive equipment from manufacturers. Of equal importance is the teacher's ability to make effective use of the facilities.

Through the electronic equipment in the language laboratory, the student listens to models recorded on tape and is able to respond to the program material while hearing his own voice in comparison to the models. The teacher can tune in on the students without being detected, and he is also able to talk to individual students or to the entire class. The teacher controls the programming through a console or control desk. Students are stationed in individual booths. In some installations students are able to select from among several broadcast channels by means of a switch or dial.

In addition to the broadcast system, which is suited to simultaneous use by the entire class under the teacher's direct supervision, the library system is used where it is desirable to have students make use of the equipment on a flexible individual schedule. In the library system, students are able to select from a large number of programs or lessons.

Some schools have a combination laboratory where most of the booths are of the broadcast type, containing headsets and volume controls, while

---

[23] Nelson Brooks, *Language and Language Learning, Theory and Practice,* 2nd ed. (New York: Harcourt, Brace & World, 1964), p. 142.

being connected to the teacher console as the source of the lessons. In addition, several library-type booths, containing tape decks, are available for individual programming. The library units also are connected to the teacher console.

Finally, the effectiveness of the language laboratory not only is dependent upon the teacher's skill in preparing students to use it properly, but is limited to the quality of the recorded materials and the efficiency and dependability of the electronic equipment. Properly conceived and utilized, the language laboratory can provide excellent models of communication and opportunities for the development of audiolingual skills outside of class.

PROBLEMS AND PROSPECTS

While the decade of the 1960's witnessed an unparalleled rate of growth in enrollments in foreign language classes at all levels of schooling, and although new instructional methods and media were instituted during this period, the national goal of producing a large population of native-born bilingual and multilingual students has not been realized. Despite the financial support of NDEA, the adoption of "revolutionary" methods and materials, the introduction of second language study at the elementary level, the lengthening of the study sequence, and the development of new and intensive programs of teacher preparation, the results, as measured against our initial goals, must be regarded as disappointing. Why is it that we have been unable to produce a bilingual student population in the face of a major national effort toward this end?

National Differences

Although, as mentioned earlier, the audiolingual approach is called new and even revolutionary, and is termed by some the "American" method, a type of direct approach has been used in Danish schools since the turn of the century. And while it is assumed in the United States that one should be academically talented and college-bound if he is to study a foreign language in high school, the writer has observed non-college-bound thirteen-year-olds in Danish schools engaged in lessons conducted entirely in English. These students, who were only in the beginning of the second year of English, had attained an adequate level of conversational ability. Such mastery is regarded as rather typical in the schools of Denmark.[24]

However, as mentioned earlier in this chapter, it should be recognized that, unlike the United States, Denmark is a bilingual nation. Because of

---

[24] Edmund J. King, *Other Schools and Ours,* 3rd ed. (New York: Holt, Rinehart and Winston, Inc., 1967), p. 22.

the small size of the country and because of the exceedingly limited use of the Danish language elsewhere, coordinate bilingualism is common in the daily lives of many residents of the larger cities. Thus the Danish youngster is not limited to the academic setting in learning and using a second language. Similar conditions are to be found in Sweden, Norway, and the Netherlands, where large segments of the populations use two or more languages in everyday communication. Under such conditions, bilingual fluency is developed not by learning a "foreign" language, but by learning a second language.

Society and Culture

Unlike the Scandinavian nations and the Netherlands, where two or more languages are found to be used commonly in daily life, most Americans spend their formative years in a culture where English is the only language to be learned and used. Thus the first encounter of most native Americans with the learning of a foreign language is not in everyday life in the community, but in the academic setting of the school.

Directly related to the limits set by one's culture is the opportunity to practice a second language. Despite the case that is made for America's necessary leadership role in world affairs, the typical American student does not have the opportunity to practice and develop second-language skills through natural communication.

Full coordinate bilingualism is most readily developed by living in a bilingual culture. As American students undertake the study of a second language long after they have learned only to understand, speak, read, and write English, their monolingual habit system interferes with second-language learning. That is, they have a predisposition to think in their native language as they learn and use a second language. Thus the second language remains a truly foreign language and fails to be mastered. And it appears unlikely that the study of a foreign language beginning in the early elementary grades can overcome the language limitations of our society and culture. Unless the classroom is supported by a societal environment in which the target language is used in natural settings, coordinate bilingualism appears to remain an unrealistic objective, in whatever grade study of the language is begun.

The promotion of FLES (Foreign Language in the Elementary School) programs on the grounds that the child's capacity for learning a foreign language is superior to that of the adult must be subject to question, as such superiority is evident in natural settings rather than in classroom situations.[25] In the natural setting children are able to converse incessantly

---

[25] Robert L. Politzer and Louis Weiss, "Developmental Aspects of Auditory Discrimination, Echo Response, and Recall," *The Modern Language Journal*, Vol. 53 (February, 1969), p. 75.

with peers and adult models in the target language and consequently language learning seems to occur easily and rapidly. It would appear that FLES programs could be improved markedly to the extent that the classroom environment can be made to approximate the natural setting. Nevertheless, the physical nature of classroom conditions, and the time factor which provides for an exposure of less than an hour per day, five days per week, jointly place severe limitations on the amount and quality of learning that can be expected—not to mention the constant variable of the teacher's proficiency. Moreover, when FLES programs are introduced, something has to give way in the curriculum of the elementary school.

Humanistic Objectives

The goal of developing functional fluency in a second language has obvious utilitarian values. However, in the face of our general failure to develop second-language fluency with the large majority of our pupil population, many educators seek to justify the study of modern foreign languages on humanistic grounds. In the words of one educator, "Ultimately the teaching of foreign languages (or for that matter, any academic subject beyond the sixth-grade level) must justify itself on the basis of a humanistic rather than a utilitarian rationale, as an end in itself rather than as a means to some end, however practical or however noble." [26]

But modern languages are used for communication and are not ends in themselves. If a modern language is not learned for purposes of communication, it is doubtful that it will have great humanistic value for the student. One might just as well study *about* the language and *about* the culture with the hope of gaining some humanistic and ornamental residue. On the other hand, by learning the language for communication, one should also learn to appreciate how a different culture views the universe. Utilitarian and humanistic goals should be inseparable.

Habit-Skill Emphasis in the Audiolingual Approach

The habit-skill emphasis in the audiolingual approach has been criticized not only for its boring and tedious attributes, but because it is based upon too many unproven tenets of operant conditioning and because it has not produced the level of language proficiency that is claimed for it by its proponents. In view of the disappointing results with the habit-skills emphasis, in some quarters a "generative" approach is advocated in which the learner would utilize structural patterns and rules in developing language proficiency.[27]

---

[26] Frank M. Grittner, "A Critical Re-examination of Methods and Materials," *The Modern Language Journal*, Vol. 53 (November, 1969), p. 468.

[27] Jakobovits, *op. cit.*, pp. 436–437.

Unlike the traditional grammar-translation method, the "generative" approach is intended to develop the structure and rules of the target language inductively and without translation exercises. In this sense the "generative" approach is similar to the audiolingual method. However, where repetitive pattern drills for the formation of habit-skills are commonly included in the audiolingual method, the "generative" approach rejects such drill work.

But while there is no definitive empirical research to support the habit-skill emphasis in pattern practice, the superiority of the "generative" approach is yet to be demonstrated. The habit-skill emphasis is intended to develop the learner's capacity to use the target language without translating each thought or expression into its English equivalent. In the absence of the natural home and out-of-school conditions in which coordinate bilingualism begins to take root, the habit-skill emphasis in the classroom is designed to fill an environmental void. But under conditions where a second language is commonly used in the home and society, the roots of coordinate bilingualism take hold in natural communication contexts and in the absence of tedious drill. If the habit-skill emphasis is to be successful, it would appear that it must take place in conjunction with activities in settings that approximate the natural situations in which two or more people communicate with each other.

In contrast to the audiolingual habit theory, in which language skills are developed in the target language without conscious references to English equivalents, some psychologists favor the cognitive code-learning theory, in which the differences between the target and the native languages are learned by the student.[28] Obviously, there is a sharp conflict between these two theories. In the absence of definitive research on the issue, it appears likely that the habit-skill rationale will continue to be emphasized.

Our failure to develop bilingualism in our students appears to be a result of the absence of out-of-school situations in which a second language is used incessantly under natural conditions. As we have already mentioned, unless that habit-skill emphasis is accompanied by classroom conditions that somehow approximate the natural settings in which coordinate bilingualism is developed, we are likely to have limited success in second-language learning, regardless of the theories to which we subscribe. And unless the teachers themselves can serve as fluent models of bilingualism, it is unrealistic to assume that pupils will reach levels of competence that their mentors have found unattainable for themselves.

---

[28] John B. Carroll, "The Contributions of Psychological Theory and Educational Research to the Teaching of Foreign Languages," Chapter 6 in Albert Valdman (ed.), *Trends in Language Teaching* (New York: McGraw-Hill Book Company, Inc., 1966), pp. 101–103.

Intensive Practice

While some efforts have been made to depart from the traditional class schedule of some fifty minutes per day, five days a week, so as to provide for longer time-blocks, the typical secondary school course fails to provide sufficient time in the schedule for intensive practice. Because the student does not have the opportunity to use a second language in daily life outside the classroom, the intensity of practice throughout the course itself becomes an important factor in skill development.

Even with modular scheduling, however, the allocation of a larger time-block on one day requires a correspondingly smaller time-block on another day since other subjects have earned their own priorities in the curriculum and school schedule. While modular scheduling also is intended to provide for flexibility in class size, so as to relate the size of the group to the particular learning task, economic feasibility requires that small instructional groups be counterbalanced by large classes. Consequently, while the course sequence can be extended to four, five, or more years in a second language, it is not possible under present curriculum and scheduling pressures to increase appreciably the intensity of such courses.

Teacher Competency and Instructional Practices

Through language institutes for teachers, conducted at many colleges and universities with NDEA funds, teacher competency has been improved markedly. These institutes are concerned not only with developing proficiency in utilizing the newer methods and media of instruction, but with providing teachers with opportunities for intensive practice in language usage.

Nevertheless, many teachers of foreign languages are not truly bilingual. Deficiencies in audiolingual skills are found to be common not only among older teachers but among the "new wave" of college students who were preparing to enter the profession during the late 1960's. A national study involving almost 2,500 seniors, including prospective teachers, majoring in modern foreign languages at 203 institutions revealed that the median graduate was able to speak and comprehend the language at a level somewhere between a "limited working proficiency" and a "minimum professional proficiency." [29]

When one considers that the major goal of language study in the secondary school is to develop bilingualism, failure of many teachers to have attained such a level of proficiency creates a serious predicament. The

---

[29] John B. Carroll, "Foreign Language Proficiency Levels Attained by Language Majors Near Graduation from College," *Foreign Language Annals*, Vol. 1 (December, 1967), pp. 131–151.

use of the target language incessantly in the classroom, while minimizing the student's native language, is of crucial importance in the audiolingual approach. But because many teachers do not have sufficient command of the target language, they tend to carry on much of the instruction in English.

A study of classroom practices in secondary school courses, enrolling over 5,300 students who had taken the College Board modern language achievement tests, found a surprisingly high incidence of the use of English by teachers and students at all grade levels.[30] Yet the student population in the study ranked close to the 75th percentile in both verbal and mathematical scores on the Scholastic Aptitude Test. If such classroom practices are found in courses serving an extremely able population, it would appear unlikely that better practices are to be found in classes serving more typical students. Another investigation, involving schools claiming to follow the audiolingual approach, revealed that teachers were doing the talking in the classroom 80 per cent of the time and that most of the teacher talk was in English.[31]

How can we expect secondary school students to develop bilingual fluency when the teachers themselves lack such proficiency? Some educators actually maintain that it is not necessary for teachers to be fluent in the target language, even though the goal is to develop bilingual fluency in the learner.[32] It is argued that teacher deficiencies can be overcome through the use of proper learning materials. Aside from the question of whether it is fair to expect students to attain a level of proficiency that the teacher himself has been unable to reach, the existing research evidence fails to support this notion.

Some school administrators have employed foreign-born persons under the assumption that all that is really necessary for teaching a foreign language is native fluency. However, the research does not indicate that foreign-born teachers are preferable to American-born teachers.[33] On the other hand, there is evidence that a year of study abroad is most valuable in upgrading the competencies of teachers and prospective teachers. In effect, "those who do not go abroad do *not* seem to be able to get very far in their foreign language study, on the average, despite the ministra-

---

[30] Neale W. Austin and John L. D. Clark, *A Survey of the Teaching of French, Spanish, and German in Secondary Schools* (Princeton, N.J.: Educational Testing Service, 1969), p. 19.

[31] Frank M. Grittner, *Teaching Foreign Languages* (New York: Harper & Row, Publishers, 1969), p. 327.

[32] Wilga M. Rivers, *Teaching Foreign Language Skills* (Chicago: The University of Chicago Press, 1968), pp. 210–211.

[33] John B. Carroll, "Research on Teaching Foreign Languages," Chapter 21 in N. L. Gage (ed.), *Handbook of Research on Teaching* (Chicago: Rand McNally & Company, 1963), p. 1093.

tions of foreign language teachers, language laboratories, audiolingual methods, and the rest." [34] Apparently, fluency in the target language and teaching skill must be intricately connected for effective teaching and learning.

Yet another point of difficulty is that many teachers are themselves products of the traditional grammar-translation approach. Although the language institutes are designed to retrain such teachers in the "new key" or audiolingual approach, teachers who have managed to get by with the grammar-translation method without themselves being fluent in the language encounter severe difficulties with the audiolingual rationale. Language institutes have attempted to solve this problem by combining the work in methods and materials with intensive instruction in language usage.

Undoubtedly, the widespread adoption of modern audiolingual methods and materials constitutes a revolutionary change in the teaching of foreign languages in our schools. But in many schools teachers are lacking in bilingual fluency, and the audiolingual approach may be more of a slogan than an actual day-to-day practice.

Length of Study

The rationale behind FLES (Foreign Language in the Elementary School) programs is predicated on the assumption that (1) language is most easily learned at early stages of human development, and (2) high proficiency in language learning requires a protracted period of study. Studies reveal that children learn pronunciation more easily than older people, although in other respects the rate of classroom learning is slower for children.[35]

The value of protracted study should be obvious. Research shows that there are distinct advantages when the study of a foreign language is begun in elementary school and continued to the point of majoring in a language in college. However, this does not necessarily mean that such advantages will accrue to the greater majority of students who have taken FLES programs. Much depends upon the quality of the FLES programs and whether there is continued study and use of the language.

In reviewing the research on FLES programs, it is concluded that "many FLES programs have failed because of lack of well-defined objectives, poor teacher preparation, uncertainty of methods, lack of materials, failure to secure continuity, lack of administrative understanding of lan-

---

[34] John B. Carroll, "Foriegn Language Proficiency Levels Attained by Language Majors," *op. cit.*, p. 137.

[35] *Ibid.*, p. 871.

guage learning, and false expectations. . . . [But] however good the materials, the outcomes of FLES depend upon the teachers." [36]

OTHER RESEARCH FINDINGS AND PROBLEMS

The great urgency in instituting modern foreign language classes in our elementary and secondary schools during the past two decades has resulted in the implementation of many policies and practices based upon intuitive notions and practical judgments in the absence of definitive research. Although researchers completed numerous empirical studies on the teaching and learning of languages during this period, many of the findings have been inconclusive, contradictory, inapplicable to practical conditions, or lacking in rigorous methodology. In reviewing the status of the research on teaching foreign languages, Carroll reached this conclusion:

> Educational research has contributed very little to foreign language teaching methodology aside from general knowledge concerning the construction of achievement tests, the role of foreign language aptitude in the learning process, and the psychology of bilingualism. Psychologists who have tried to investigate elements in the foreign language teaching process have frequently failed to produce useful results because their experimental settings and materials have not been sufficiently similar to those of the actual teaching situation as it occurs in the classroom or in the language laboratory. At the same time, research undertaken by foreign language teachers has only rarely been adequate with respect to research methodology.[37]

Despite this discouraging assessment, Carroll concluded that "there remain many questions which could be profitably investigated by rigorous psychological and educational research, and it is clearly within the realm of possibility that the results of such research could make language teaching more effective and efficient." [38]

Audiolingual Vs. Grammar-Translation Methods

Research Findings and Problems.   Many studies have been undertaken to assess the effectiveness of different methods of foreign language teaching. As mentioned earlier, however, research difficulties still leave us without definitive conclusions. A widely cited study attempting to compare audiolingual methods with traditional grammar-translation approaches at the college level found that students following the audiolingual course were

---

36 Emma Birkmaier and Dale Lang, "Foreign Language Instruction," Chapter VIII in *Review of Educational Research,* Vol. 37 (April, 1967), pp. 190–191.

37 Carroll, "Research on Teaching Foreign Languages," *op. cit.,* p. 1094.

38 *Ibid.*

far superior in listening and speaking skills, while the traditionally trained students were significantly better in reading and writing. It was also found that the audiolingual group developed more desirable attitudes toward language learning.[39]

Studies at other levels of schooling are in general agreement with the above findings, leading Carroll to the conclusion that "differences between the audiolingual and traditional methods are primarily differences in objectives; not surprisingly, students learn whatever skills are emphasized in the instruction." [40] Nevertheless, the Modern Language Association and a large body of professional literature have endorsed the audiolingual approach while holding the traditional grammar-translation method in disrepute.

The Pennsylvania Project. A large-scale experiment conducted in 104 Pennsylvania secondary schools of all types in diverse geographic and socioeconomic areas was conducted between 1965 and 1967 in order to assess the effectiveness of various teaching strategies and types of language laboratories. Known as the Pennsylvania Project, and financed by the U.S. Office of Education, the investigation involved 1,090 students in French and German classes.

The two major objectives of the Pennsylvania Project were (1) to determine whether the traditional (grammar-translation), audiolingual, or modified audiolingual approach is most effective in accomplishing the four objectives of the foreign language program in the secondary school (listening comprehension, speaking fluency, reading, and writing), and (2) to determine which type of language-laboratory system is most effective for language learning. The modified audiolingual approach combined the functional skills method with emphasis on formal grammar. Three types of language-laboratory systems were included in the research: (1) the use of tape recorders as program sources for the practice of listening skills and, in a limited way, the practice of oral drills; (2) the listen-respond, audioactive system in which the student is able to hear his own voice through the headset as he emulates the model speaker's recorded performance; and (3) the listen-respond-compare, audioactive-record system, in which the student records and compares his responses directly with the model speaker.

The Pennsylvania Project attracted considerable attention because of its large-scale design and because it sought answers to key issues and questions concerning the effectiveness of methods and facilities. At the time the study was undertaken, it was felt that "no sufficiently realistic and

[39] George A. C. Scherer and Michael Wertheimer, *A Psycholinguistic Experiment in Foreign Language Teaching* (New York: McGraw-Hill Book Company, Inc., 1964).

[40] John B. Carroll, "Modern Languages" in Robert L. Ebel (ed.), *Encyclopedia of Educational Research,* 4th ed. (New York: The Macmillan Company, 1969), pp. 869–870.

generalizable research had been undertaken to shed light on specific questions on modern foreign language instruction facing the American school." [41] Yet the audiolingual approach had received the endorsement of the Modern Language Association and most professional educators.

Schools selected for participation in the Pennsylvania Project were required to meet certain characteristics: commitment to following the research requirements, availability of the necessary equipment and facilities, the offering of a three- and/or four-year sequence of French and German, availability of teachers trained in audiolingual techniques and laboratory procedures, and availability of teachers having a reasonable command of the target languages. Teacher participants were required to demonstrate their proficiency through a standardized test. Workshops were conducted prior to the implementation of the research to acquaint teachers with the necessary guidelines for the study. All participating classes were required to adopt specific texts in order to control this important variable. Teachers were provided with printed guidelines to further ensure adherence to the research treatments. Project classes were observed regularly by field consultants whose duty was to evaluate the classroom activities in terms of the assigned research strategies. Student achievement was assessed through pretest and posttest procedures using the *MLA Cooperative Classroom Tests,* so that statistical adjustments could be made for differences in student aptitude and prior achievement.

The findings revealed no statistically significant differences among the three approaches after two years, except that the "traditional" classes had achieved significantly higher measures of reading, grammar, and writing at the end of the first year. It was also concluded that none of the three types of language laboratories, used twice weekly, had a discernible effect on achievement. Regarding student attitudes, it was found that their opinions of foreign language study declined over the two-year period regardless of the teaching strategy employed. Finally, it was found that there was no relationship between teacher experience nor scores on the *MLA Teacher Proficiency Tests* and class achievement.

Storm of Controversy. With the findings of the Pennsylvania Project failing to support the commonly accepted and recommended practices as advanced in much of the professional literature, an entire issue of *The Modern Language Journal* was devoted to a "Critique of the Pennsylvania Project." [42]

Among the major criticisms leveled at the Pennsylvania Project were those questioning the (1) adequacy of classroom observation procedures

---

[41] Philip D. Smith, Jr., and Helmut A. Baranyi, *A Comparison Study of the Effectiveness of the Traditional and Audiolingual Approaches to Foreign Language Instruction Utilizing Laboratory Equipment,* Final Report (Washington, D.C.: U.S. Office of Education, October, 1968), p. 11.

[42] *The Modern Language Journal,* Vol. 53 (October, 1969), pp. 386–428.

to ensure strict adherence to the specific teaching strategies; (2) appropriateness of the tests that measured teacher proficiency and student achievement; (3) failure to provide for the assessment of teacher competence in the classroom as contrasted with teacher proficiency measured by the standardized test battery; (4) failure to make a detailed accounting of what was actually done in the classroom and laboratory—including analyses of classroom interaction; and (5) inadequacies in the actual research design to ensure proper treatment of the necessary variables.

While many of these criticisms are well grounded, the major findings of the Pennsylvania Project are not at odds with the general body of research literature.[43] Absolutely strict adherence to all of the restrictions and controls necessary for a classically flawless experimental design may well have obviated the practical setting in which this large-scale project was undertaken. This does not mean that sloppy research methods are to be excused, but rather than the rigor of the experimental design and procedures is invariably affected by the practical conditions and limitations of large-scale field research.

Consequently, it is essential that the research results be carefully interpreted and replicated under a variety of conditions. In this connection, it would be misleading to conclude from the Pennsylvania Project that one method is as good as another, or that the type of language laboratory is of no importance in language learning. Some possible lessons of value from such studies as the Pennsylvania Project are that, regardless of the general acceptance of a certain methodological rationale in the professional literature, the widespread application of that specific methodology may produce results less perfect than what may be anticipated. Surely we are a long way from implementing the audiolingual approach under near-optimum conditions in a large proportion of our schools. Thus the successful use of a specific methodology is directly dependent upon the teacher's classroom competence.

As new rationales and methods are developed and gain acceptance in principle, there remains a gap between such commitment and actual practice in the field. Often the result is more of an eclectic set of field practices which may or may not have transitional value toward the actual adoption of the approved rationale and method. This is particularly the case in the teaching of foreign languages in our schools, where so many of our teachers, lacking in functional fluency and methodological competence, are imperfect exemplars of the new approach.

Antipathy Toward Research

In other chapters we discuss the tendency for the developers of new curricula to become wedded to their own work. Instead of using inde-

---

[43] Carroll, "Modern Languages," *op. cit.*, pp. 869–870.

pendent research to find clues for improving their new curricula, they often attack the viability of any research studies that yield findings that fail to support their most cherished beliefs. Thus the managing editor of *The Modern Language Journal,* in his preface of the "Critique of the Pennsylvania Project," writes, "Where common sense formerly was a reliable guide in all human activity and the base upon which man reached the frontiers, now study, reseach, and experimentation destroy its last vestiges." [44]

A weakness evident in this argument is that it precludes any use of common sense in designing, conducting, and interpreting research. And what one person regards as his own common-sense notions may be regarded by others as mere dogma. One can well imagine what the reactions of blind proponents of their own works will be if research clearly supports their notions. More than likely they will cite such research as valid.

Curriculum development is not theology. The successful development of curricula depends upon careful and continuous evaluation and modification. Until careful assessments are made, the claims made for new rationales, methodologies, or total curriculum packages should be regarded as hypotheses for eventual testing.

OTHER MEDIA AND METHODS

Programmed Instruction and Operant Conditioning

Promises and Potentials.   Some of the professional literature in foreign language education regards programmed instruction as having great potential. A 1961 publication of the U.S. Department of State, after discussing certain advantages of teaching machines and programmed instruction, declared that "an even more encouraging thing about the development of a mechanical tutor for beginning language instruction is that it comes at a time when there are not enough 'live teachers' to meet the growing demands for such instruction, and at a time when the real *effectiveness* of this instruction is everywhere under scrutiny." [45]

At a 1963 colloquium sponsored by the College Entrance Examination Board, it was predicted that the revolution in American foreign language teaching and learning would be followed by yet another revolution through the use of programmed instruction: "The principles of programmed instruction have been developed through a careful study of the learning processes, and their detailed application is already preparing

---

[44] Robert F. Roeming, "Critique of the Pennsylvania Project: Preface," *The Modern Language Journal, op. cit.,* p. 387.

[45] Parker, *op. cit.,* p. 69.

the way for yet another revolution in teaching and learning." [46] An ASCD report in 1965 noted that "programmed learning courses are very much on the horizon in the learning of languages," and concluded that programmed instruction "can take care of individual differences, one of the most neglected areas in modern language teaching." [47]

Caution and Controversy. In contrast to the glowing optimism during the early 1960's concerning the potential of programmed instruction, the more recent literature is cautious. One educator holds that sound and recording facilities must accompany programmed instruction and that visual elements be included to facilitate learning.[48] The writer warns, however, of "the danger that a purely self-instructional foreign language course will teach very thoroughly the elements of the language in certain contexts without giving the student facility and confidence in using these at a level of active communication." [49] Because functional language fluency is normally developed in situations of face-to-face communication, the use of programmed materials has obvious limitations.

Despite the early optimism, the research literature remains inconclusive on the effects of programmed instruction in language learning.[50,51] Although Skinner's theory of operant conditioning, is not accepted by all proponents of programmed instruction, it has come to influence the thinking of many language educators. Thus we find a considerable portion of the literature in foreign language education emphasizing "habit formation," "repetition," "reinforcement," and other terms in the lexicon of the behaviorist. In studying the behavior of lower organisms, Skinner contends that "the results hold surprisingly well for human organisms" and "if our current knowledge of the acquisition and maintenance of verbal behavior is applied to education, some sort of teaching machine is needed." [52] Through such devices, Skinner maintains, contingencies of reinforcement are provided to alter the behavior of humans systematically and efficiently.

In criticizing Skinner's work, Chomsky has argued that inducing a rat to press a lever in order to obtain a food pellet is very different from human verbal behavior and that Skinner's claims are arbitrary, dogmatic,

---

[46] Joseph C. Hutchinson, "The Technology of Modern Language Learning," in *Curricular Change in the Foreign Languages* (Princeton, N.J.: College Entrance Examination Board, 1963), p. 54.

[47] Emma Birkmaier, "Foreign Languages," Chapter 4 in *New Curriculum Developments* (Washington, D.C.: Association for Supervision and Curriculum Development, NEA, 1965), p. 32.

[48] Rivers, *op. cit.,* pp. 93–94.

[49] *Ibid.,* p. 94.

[50] Birkmaier and Lange, *op. cit.,* p. 192.

[51] Carroll, "Modern Languages," *op. cit.,* pp. 872–873.

[52] B. F. Skinner, *The Technology of Teaching* (New York: Appleton-Century-Crofts, 1968), pp. 32–33.

and in conflict with a considerable portion of the research literature on verbal behavior.[53] Challenging the validity of Skinnerian principles and programmed instruction in foreign language learning, another psycholinguist argues that significant language learning does not occur through the isolation of language into small units, but through the development of patterns and relationships.[54]

Although some educators have predicted a revolution in foreign language teaching through programmed instruction, the current picture is tempered with caution and controversy, and no prospect for a revolution appears on the immediate horizon.

The Motion Picture and Television

The enormous potential of the motion picture and television in language teaching has not been realized. As media of instruction, their value is dependent upon the programming itself and upon the skill of the classroom teacher in utilizing that programming. Unfortunately, where television has been heralded as a "window to the world," much programming in instructional television is limited to series of lessons not unlike the kinds of lessons provided by a good "live" teacher in the classroom. Neither the motion picture nor television has been used extensively for providing experiences, such as dialogues in natural situational contexts, which would not otherwise be possible in the ordinary classroom. The result of using television as an imitation of conventional classroom instruction is the failure of experimental studies to reveal any advantages of television instruction over conventional teaching.

It is also unfortunate that, as a means of justifying the uses of television, the medium has often been promoted as an automation device to solve the shortage of foreign language teachers and to provide instruction for more pupils without raising educational expenditures. Many of the uses of television in FLES programs have been centered on this rationale. Such a rationale conceives a television as a substitute for conventional teaching, while neglecting the potential uses of the medium in doing what the ordinary teacher is unable to do in the classroom. Moreover, the combined use of television and the motion picture with the language laboratory has never been adequately explored.

In this review of the status of modern language instruction, Carroll makes no references to television and only a single reference to the motion picture.[55] Such omission is likely to convey the impression either that no significant research has been undertaken in evaluating the uses

---

[53] Noam Chomsky, "Review of *Verbal Behavior* by B. F. Skinner," *Language*, Vol. 35 (1959), pp. 26–58.

[54] Jakobovits, *op. cit.*, p. 438.

[55] Carroll, "Modern Languages," *op. cit.*, p. 872.

of these media, or that these media are not being used to any considerable extent in foreign language teaching. As mentioned earlier, some use *has* been made of television and the motion picture in FLES programs. To a considerably lesser extent, these media have been used at other levels of foreign language instruction, including teacher education. And while a notable number of research studies have been undertaken on the effects of these media on conventional learning, there is a dearth of studies designed to ascertain the values of using these media to provide learning experiences that are not possible in the conventional classroom setting. This would include the use of television and the motion picture to develop a better understanding and appreciation of foreign cultures, as well as to develop second-language proficiency. For example, a major criticism of the conventional drills, exercises, and dialogues used in the audiolingual approach is that they are "so devoid of logical, consistent, situational reality that they do not provide the student with significant life experience in the foreign language" and *do not give him anything meaningful to talk about.*" [56] The effective use of television and the motion picture could provide situational reality and vicarious lifelike experience to exploit the student's inductive and analogical capabilities in a manner not otherwise possible in the conventional classroom setting.

Linguistics and Psychology

Chomsky has expressed skepticism concerning the contributions of linguistics and psychology in the teaching of languages and finds it "difficult to believe that either linguistics or psychology has achieved a level of theoretical understanding that might enable it to support a 'technology' of language teaching." [57] In supporting Chomsky's position, Brooks notes that linguists and psychologists have tended to concentrate on language as individual behavior and have assumed that communication in language is through codings in the form of words. On the other hand, Brooks emphasizes that when language is used to communicate with others, at least two individuals are involved in a situational context. Thus the operation is not one of coding interferences or switches, but the absence of interference or switching in the effective situation.[58] As the linguists and psychologists come to focus on language in terms of the context of communication, rather than on isolated word codings, it is hoped that more significant contributions will be made in the teaching of languages.

---

[56] A. Bruce Gaarder, "Beyond Grammar and Beyond Drills," *Foreign Language Annals,* Vol. 1 (December, 1967), p. 110.

[57] Noam Chomsky in *Northeastern Conference Reports* (New York: Modern Language Association, 1966), p. 43.

[58] Nelson Brooks, "The Meaning of Bilingualism Today," *Foreign Language Annals,* Vol. 2 (March, 1969), p. 308.

Achievement and Proficiency

Through the efforts of the Modern Language Association (MLA) in cooperation with Educational Testing Service (ETS), a series of standardized tests has been developed to measure achievements in listening, speaking, reading, and writing. The MLA-Cooperative Tests are regarded as a significant improvement over earlier tests in their usefulness in measuring speaking proficiency.

However, since standardized tests measure achievement in terms of norms, they do not indicate the absolute level of proficiency in performing in the language. Thus a score in the 99th percentile after a year of study does not guarantee that a student is able to read a newspaper with ease in the target language.[59] Similarly, the number of credit hours amassed in the study of a language may not accurately represent one's ability to read, converse, or write in the language.

In Table 7-1 we find an example of an absolute proficiency scale for assessing the ability to speak and write the target language. This scale was developed by the Foreign Service Institute of the Department of State and presents some interesting possibilities for assessing student achievement in school and college. Earlier in this chapter, we discussed the results of a national study designed to assess the proficiency of college seniors, including prospective teachers, who were majoring in modern foreign languages. The study included a sample of 2,500 seniors, out of a total population of 12,000, enrolled in 203 colleges and universities. When the results on the MLA skill tests were compared with the "absolute proficiency ratings" shown in Table 7-1, it was found that "the median graduate with a foreign language major can speak and comprehend the language only at about an FSI (Foreign Service Institute) Speaking rating of '2+,' that is, somewhat between a 'limited working proficiency' and a 'minimum professional proficiency.'"[60] These results are strikingly poor. Furthermore, it was found that those who refused to take the tests had significantly lower grade-point averages than the tested population, indicating that the proficiency levels of our language graduates probably are somewhat lower than reported in the study.

The use of absolute proficiency ratings is exceedingly valuable in providing information that is not available through college grades and scores on standardized tests. If our new generation of language teachers has such a low proficiency level, it would appear ridiculous to expect their pupils to reach standards that the teachers themselves have not attained.

It should be pointed out that the FSI scale shown in Table 7-1 does not include writing ability and knowledge of the culture(s) in which the language is used. A similar proficiency scale has been developed by the

---

59 Carroll, "Research on Teaching Foreign Languages," *op. cit.*, p. 1092.
60 Carroll, "Foreign Language Proficiency Levels," *op. cit.*, p. 134.

Table 7-1. Absolute Language Proficiency Ratings, Foreign Service Institute

Level	Speaking Skill (S)	Reading Skill (R)
Elementary proficiency	(S-1) Able to satisfy routine travel needs and minimum courtesy requirements.	(R-1) Able to read elementary lesson material or common public signs.
Limited working proficiency	(S-2) Able to satisfy routine social demands and limited office requirements.	(R-2) Able to read intermediate lesson material or simple colloquial texts.
Minimum professional proficiency	(S-3) Able to speak with sufficient structural accuracy and vocabulary to satisfy representation requirements and handle professional discussions within a special field.	(R-3) Able to read nontechnical news items or technical writing in a special field.
Full professional proficiency	(S-4) Able to use the language fluently and accurately on all levels normally pertinent to professional fields.	(R-4) Able to read all styles and forms of the language pertinent to professional needs.
Native or bilingual fluency	(S-5) Speaking proficiency equivalent to that of an educated native speaker.	(R-5) Reading proficiency equivalent to that of an educated native speaker.

Source: *"Absolute Language Proficiency Ratings," Circular, Foreign Service Institute, U.S. Department of State, May, 1963.*

Modern Language Association for teachers of modern foreign languages; it includes descriptions of proficiency levels in aural comprehension, speaking, reading, writing, language analysis, culture, and professional preparation.[61] Such measurements should be most useful in improving the quality of our foreign language programs in school and college.

Survey of Classroom Practices

Earlier in this chapter we discussed some of the results of a national survey of classroom practices involving over 5,300 high school seniors who had taken the College Board achievement tests in modern foreign languages.[62] Conducted by Educational Testing Service, the questionnaire survey was undertaken after an earlier feasibility study had shown that high school students are able to give valid accounts of their classroom

---

[61] Parker, *op. cit.*, pp. 156–158.

[62] Austin and Clark, *A Survey of the Teaching of French, Spanish, and German, op. cit.*

experiences. The study was designed to ascertain the kinds of classroom practices being followed, in view of the great curriculum reform movement of the 1960's.

Although this national study was directed at an atypical population of extremely able students who ranked close to the 75th percentile on the Scholastic Aptitude Test and who were enrolled in better-than-average schools, some of the findings indicate that there is a serious discrepancy between the approved practices found in the literature and the practices as reported in the classroom. For example, as discussed earlier in this chapter, it was found that one of the most frequent classroom activities was the use of English by the teacher to explain grammar and vocabulary, with the student responding in English. Although there is little theoretical justification for juxtaposing foreign and English tests and making word-for-word comparisons of two languages, a considerable amount of classroom time was devoted to such activity.

Student self-ratings indicated that the audiolingual revolution had not had the far-reaching results commonly claimed in the literature, because the students rated their reading skills as significantly higher than their listening and speaking skills. Virtually none of the students had used the language laboratory in elementary school. The use of the language laboratory by students, however, increased from 15 to 20 per cent in grade 7 to a majority in grades 10, 11, and 12. Nevertheless, the use of the language laboratory was restricted to two periods or fewer per week for the vast majority of students.

During their first year of language study, almost all of the students were given homework based almost entirely on reading materials instead of on listening and speaking exercises. However, the majority of students reported that they had started with listening and speaking skills before being introduced to reading and writing in the target language.

In summary, the survey revealed a serious discrepancy between the revolution in methods and materials claimed in the literature and the practices as reported in the classroom. Undoubtedly, had a similar survey been undertaken a decade earlier, the results would have shown even less use of the language laboratory and greater emphasis on reading and writing skills and grammatical results as opposed to listening and speaking. But the predicted revolution still remains a long way off.

Bilingualism and the Disadvantaged

In recent years special attention has been directed at problems of language learning for our large Puerto Rican populations in New York and other major cities, and for our populations of Mexican-Americans in the Southwest. Almost one fourth of the students in New York City's public schools are from Puerto Rican families.

Some educators have maintained that such children should receive bilingual schooling. It is contended that under present circumstances, where these youngsters receive instruction solely in English, their school achievement is retarded because their home language is Spanish. Through bilingual schooling, it is argued, these students will develop a better appreciation of their cultural heritage.

Many advocates of bilingual schooling recommend that instruction in all subjects be conducted both in the home language and in English as a second language. Since 1968 bilingual school programs have been undertaken on a limited scale in New York City, San Diego, and elsewhere, in selected schools that have a high concentration of Spanish-speaking children.

Whether bilingual schooling will prove successful in overcoming the achievement deficits of these children remains to be seen. Some educators are highly optimistic in their belief that achievement deficits can be overcome through bilingual schooling.[63] However, they often choose to ignore the influences of socioeconomic deprivation and cultural isolation on achievement. In other words, providing for bilingual schooling may prove of limited value in overcoming achievement deficits as long as the conditions of socioeconomic deprivation and cultural isolation prevail.

Other educators point out that too much may be expected from bilingual schooling where the home language of disadvantaged youngsters is not an adequate cultural exemplar. On the other hand, this can serve as a convincing argument in support of school instruction in the native language as a means of overcoming the limitations and defects of the language as used in the home.

Historically, many minorities have seen the schools as opening the doors to Americanization rather than as reinforcing the bonds of cultural isolation. Proponents of bilingual schooling contend that by helping youngsters toward higher achievement, such education will enable more children and youth to enter the mainstream of American life while strengthening their cultural heritage. Then there are others who warn of the danger of breeding too much cultural isolation through such specialized programs. The success of bilingual schooling in meeting the expectations of its advocates, in the face of socioeconomic disadvantagement and cultural isolation, is yet to be determined.

SUMMARY

The resurgence of modern foreign language teaching in our secondary schools during the past two decades has been accompanied by radical

---

[63] Donald D. Walsh, "Bilingualism and Bilingual Education," *Foreign Language Annals,* Vol. 2 (March, 1969), pp. 298–303.

changes in objectives, rationale, methods, and materials. Where the traditional emphasis was on reading as prerequisite to other forms of language learning, the audiolingual approach holds that language begins with listening and speaking. Where foreign languages in the past were approached through the analysis of rules and constructs of formal grammar, the modern approach provides for the learning of grammar inductively and through analogy as the language is used in functional contexts. Where lengthy vocabulary word lists used to be committed to memory in terms of their native-language (English) equivalents, vocabulary is now treated in the context of the actual communication process. Where the study of a target language formerly was approached through English as the intervening medium, the aim now is to develop a classroom environment in which the target language is the means of communication and English is used only where absolutely necessary for enhancing meaning. Where students once were limited primarily to printed materials, the language laboratory has become a kind of audiolingual "book." Where the abstract study of language was justified in the past for its alleged mental disciplinary values, language is now included in the curriculum because it is necessary for effective communication with other peoples and because it enables us to gain intercultural insights not otherwise thought possible.

Nevertheless, these radical changes have not been fully implemented in our classrooms. Many of our language teachers are themselves lacking in native or near-native fluency in the target language and, consequently, are imperfect exemplars or models. Excessive reliance on English is the result, and many teachers continue to adhere to traditional practices.

A further limitation on our success in second-language learning is that most of our students do not have the opportunity to use the target language in everyday life outside the classroom. Yet the incessant use of language in action is necessary for the development of bilingualism. Consequently, although our stated goals call for the development of functional fluency, relatively few schools have made notable progress toward this end.

As an outgrowth of the cold war, the 1950's witnessed an unparalleled emphasis on the study of modern foreign languages in our elementary and secondary schools. The goal was to develop a large bilingual population that would serve our nation's world leadership role. In recent years, such objectives have yielded to the more humanizing goals of developing competence in communication in order to further sociocultural awareness and understanding. Fresh attention also is being given to bilingual programs for disadvantaged children and youth who must encounter English as a second language.

Despite the notable influences of the great curriculum reform movement in foreign language education during the past two decades, our goals for developing bilingualism and cultural appreciation are far from becoming accomplished facts. Without the opportunity to use the target language in daily life outside the classroom, our students and their teachers will continue to labor under severe handicaps.

PROBLEMS FOR STUDY AND DISCUSSION

1. The novelist Arthur Koestler states: "I would only have to press a single mental button to continue writing this page in French—or Hungarian; but that does not necessarily mean that I am to be regarded as a jukebox." [Arthur Koestler, *The Ghost in the Machine* (New York: The Macmillan Company, 1967), p. 44.]

    What implications does Koestler's statement have for foreign language teaching?

2. Do you agree with the following statement? Why or why not?

    By 1980 anyone who speaks only two languages will be ill equipped to cope with situations that will confront him daily. We no longer will live a monolingually isolated life. Our world role will make increasing demands, which we are now only beginning to meet. [Project on Instruction, *The Scholars Look at the Schools* (Washington, D.C.: National Education Association, 1963), p. 15.]

3. Observe a beginning secondary school class that is purportedly following the audiolingual approach. What proportion of the class time involves the use of English? In what context is English used (i.e., translation of the target language, classroom communication, enhancement of meaning only where absolutely necessary)? Would you conclude that the class was actually following the generally accepted practices associated with the audiolingual approach? Why or why not?

4. Examine a variety of college catalogues to ascertain what foreign language admission requirements, if any, are indicated. Do you believe that such requirements where indicated are justified? Why or why not?

5. Do you agree that "it is possible for a teacher who is not a fluent speaker of the language to teach the speaking skill by an audiolingual approach" [Wilga M. Rivers, *Teaching Foreign Language Skills* (Chicago: The University of Chicago Press, 1968), pp. 210–211.] What justification can you offer in supporting or opposing this opinion?

6. What is your opinion of the position taken by the author of the following quotation?

    How about foreign languages in elementary schools? Frankly, I cannot see any excuse for them at all. . . . The elementary years may seem valuable to the teacher of languages. They seem equally valuable to the teachers of any other subject, for they are the years of greatest plasticity in the person. If cultural relativism is a valuable thing to learn, why should it not be sought through cultural anthropology, which would surely be a much more effective means?

None of the values claimed for the study of languages can be achieved, I think, short of mastery of the tongue. [James E. Russell, *Change and Challenge in American Education* (Boston: Houghton Mifflin Company, 1965), p. 57.]

SELECTED REFERENCES

Allen, Edward D., Leona M. Glenn, and Frank Otto. *The Changing Curriculum: Modern Foreign Languages.* Washington, D.C.: Association for Supervision and Curriculum Development, NEA, 1968.

Austin, Neale W., and John L. D. Clark. *A Survey of the Teaching of French, Spanish, and German in Secondary Schools.* Princeton, N.J.: Educational Testing Service, 1969.

Brooks, Nelson. *Language and Language Learning,* 2nd ed. New York: Harcourt, Brace & World, 1964.

Carroll, John. "Research on Teaching Foreign Languages," Chapter 21 in N. L. Gage (ed.), *Handbook of Research on Teaching.* Chicago: Rand McNally & Company, 1963, pp. 1060–1100.

―――. "Modern Languages," in Robert L. Ebel (ed.), *Encyclopedia of Educational Research.* New York: The Macmillan Company, 1969, pp. 866–878.

Chomsky, Noam. *Aspects of the Theory of Language.* Cambridge, Mass.: The M.I.T. Press, 1965.

Conant, James B. *The American High School Today.* New York: McGraw-Hill Book Company, Inc., 1959.

Grittner, Frank M. *Teaching Foreign Languages.* New York: Harper & Row, Publishers, 1969.

Lado, Robert. *Language Teaching: A Scientific Approach.* New York: McGraw-Hill Book Company, Inc., 1964.

Moulton, William G. *A Linguistic Guide to Language Learning.* New York: Modern Language Association of America, 1966.

Oliva, Peter F. *The Teaching of Foreign Languages.* Englewood Cliffs, N.J.: Prentice-Hall, Inc., 1969.

Parker, William Riley. *The National Interest and Foreign Languages,* 3rd ed. Washington, D.C.: U.S. Government Printing Office, 1961.

Parry, Albert. *America Learns Russian.* Syracuse, N.Y.: Syracuse University Press, 1967.

Politzer, Robert L. *Foreign Language Learning: A Linguistic Introduction.* Englewood Cliffs, N.J.: Prentice-Hall, Inc., 1970.

Rivers, Wilga M. *Teaching Foreign Language Skills.* Chicago: The University of Chicago Press, 1968.

Skinner, B. F. *The Technology of Teaching.* New York: Appleton-Century-Crofts, 1968.

Stack, Edward M. *The Language Laboratory and Modern Language Teaching* (revised). New York: Oxford University Press, Inc., 1966.

Valdman, Albert (ed.). *Trends in Language Teaching.* New York: Mc-Graw-Hill Book Company, Inc., 1966.

Chapter 8

Curriculum Change in the Fine and Performing Arts

Since midcentury we have witnessed a remarkable boom in civic-sponsored symphony orchestras, centers for the performing arts, and art galleries and museums—noble proclamations of our devotion to the fine arts. Paradoxically, this seeming cultural renaissance in society has not been accompanied by a comparable surge of activity in the fine-arts curriculum of our secondary schools. Our "pursuit of excellence" in response to the pressures of the cold war has kept the fine arts confined to the domain of the "nonessential" subjects in the high school curriculum.

Of course, a convincing case can be made to show that our civic-sponsored cultural centers are little more than impressive showcases, which serve to display our wares of refinement without changing or even touching our actual life styles. The fine and performing arts seem to be treated as commodities for collection and display—to serve only a narrow segment of the lives of a small proportion of our population. The cities in which our most impressive cultural centers are located remain plagued by every imaginable assault upon our aesthetic senses and physical well-being.

We either tend to regard an aesthetic concept as something amorphous and without value, or as a commodity to be defined and treated in terms of a quantitative value. Like the hero in the fable by Antoine de Saint Exupéry,[1] when somebody says, "I saw a beautiful house today," the likely adult response is: "How much is it worth?" "Where is it located?" "When was it built?" ("How new is it?") "What is the size of the lot?" "How many rooms does it have?" And if one were to inquire about the inhabitants of the house, the questions might well be: "Who lives in it?"

---

[1] Antoine de Saint Exupéry, *The Little Prince* (New York: Harcourt, Brace & World, Inc., 1943), p. 17.

"What does the owner do for a living?" "Is he famous?" It would not occur to us to ask: "Why is the house beautiful?"—or "Are the people who live in the house happy?"

As discussed later in this chapter, we have created a false dichotomy between the utilitarian and the aesthetic. While science and technology have served man in so many countless ways, at times it seems as though we conceive of man as a servant of the machine. In recent years there has been a growing awareness of the intimate connection between aesthetic values and the creation of an environment in harmony with man as a living organism. The arts are indeed the critical element in humanizing our technological age.

Nevertheless, we are a long way from developing a harmonic equilibrium between our technology and our physical and psychic needs. While much can be done in influencing future generations through a reconstructed curriculum, it appears unlikely, if not impossible, for the schools to move in the needed directions in the absence of a societal commitment. As things now stand, the fine and performing arts are not even regarded as essential to general education in the high school. This is not to advocate that the arts be treated in the curriculum in the same manner as English or other so-called academic disciplines. The arts are unique and should not be made imitative of other subjects. Yet we do great damage when we conceive of the arts as nonutilitarian, nonacademic and, therefore, nonessential.

In this chapter we shall explore these and other problems and issues with a view to identifying some needed improvements in the fine and performing arts in our secondary schools. Our major thesis is that the arts are not a curricular extravagance but an essential part of general education in the high school. Furthermore, a reconstruction of the fine-arts curriculum is necessary if it is to exert a positive influence in enriching our life styles.

BACKGROUND FORCES

Our early Colonial schools provided for music instruction, although the activities were limited to the learning of psalms for devotional services. Systematic instruction in art was not introduced until the early nineteenth century and then it was conceived of primarily as part of the necessary social education of women. During this period, music education served our growing nationalism through the singing of folk songs that fostered patriotism.

In the twentieth century the development of the phonograph and radio made possible the teaching of music appreciation. As electives and extracurricular activities gained favor in the secondary school, new opportunities were opened for instruction in instrumental music as well as in a variety of art areas. Nevertheless, music and art were still not recognized as essential subjects for general education in the high school.

From the child-study movement that began in the 1880's, through the progressive-education era of the 1930's and 1940's, the arts gained new recognition in pedagogical literature for their value in providing for creative self-expression. However, this was not an entirely romantic notion concerning the importance of the arts. As the orchestrator of progressive educational theory, Dewey came to grips with questions concerning the function of the arts in the curriculum and their relationships to life. According to Dewey, the arts "are not luxuries of education, but emphatic expressions of that which makes any education worth while." [2]

The False Dichotomy: Cultural Vs. Utilitarian

Although the fine arts occupied an important place in the ancient Greek curriculum, such studies were conceived of as part of the liberal education of freemen, while practical education was deemed appropriate for slaves. During subsequent epochs the fine arts therefore came to be regarded as luxuries or ornamental attributes of the privileged classes and consequently they were treated as nonessential elements of the secondary school curriculum.

In viewing the dichotomy between traditional interpretations of culture and utility in curriculum making, Dewey observed that "only superstition makes us believe that the two are necessarily hostile so that a subject is illiberal because it is useful and cultural because it is useless." [3] Yet this ancient distinction persists to this day, despite the fact that many of the activities that were regarded as narrowly utilitarian and servile in ancient Greece have become matters of scientific and technological application in the modern world. Moreover, as the social uses of such activities are increased and enlarged, according to Dewey, "their liberalizing or 'intellectual' value and their practical value approach the same limit." [4]

This does not mean that the same value must be placed on any form of learning, but rather that our traditional distinctions are no longer valid. Education that is devoid of intellectual and aesthetic experiences cannot be very practical or utilitarian, because intellectuality enables us to transfer and apply knowledge to new situations or conditions, while the aesthetic aspect gives a new and necessary dimension to what we value —whether it be an activity or a product of our labor. And education that is devoid of practical or utilitarian value is limited in its intellectual and

---

2 John Dewey, *Democracy and Education* (New York: The Macmillan Company, 1916), p. 279.

3 *Ibid.*, p. 302.

4 *Ibid.*, p. 303.

aesthetic uses because it lacks the generative force for future learning and for improving our civilization.

Ironically, we often get our wires crossed when attempting to justify and model subject matter according to theoretical as against practical or applied orientations. Thus, where physics was originally introduced into the high school curriculum because of its practical utility, during the curriculum reform movement of the 1960's physical science was redesigned as a high school subject in order to place chief emphasis on the structural principles of the discipline. And where music and art were traditionally recognized for their cultural value, in many high schools and colleges today we find that a student's music education may consist only of training in the skills required to perform in marching bands at football games, while art education is limited to narrow skill development without affecting one's cultural and aesthetic tastes.[5] By separating the theoretical from the applied, the cultural from the utilitarian, or the aesthetic from the practical, we place such artificial constraints on learning that we are left with a curriculum that is a perversion of reality.

The need for curriculum reconstruction takes on a new urgency as our technological productivity makes more leisure time available to virtually all groups in society. No longer can we segment education according to social classes. Moreover, because much of our technological productivity has been allowed to develop largely in the absence of aesthetic and humanizing values, problems that are solved by such productivity are replaced by problems of social disorganization, environmental pollution, and various assaults upon our general well-being. Unless we are able to wed the aesthetic with the utilitarian, the humane with the technological, and the liberal with the practical, our traditional dualism of curriculum will persist and will contribute nothing to social renewal.

Essential Vs. Nonessential in the Curriculum

Cold War Influence.   With our emergence from World War II, leading progressivists had a vision of the school that was very different from what actually emerged. For example, with regard to the arts, a utopian document of the NEA's Educational Policies Commission envisioned the school as a center of artistic interests for the entire community, with the fine arts being integral to the common-learnings or general education program of the high school.[6] In contrast, an influential essentialist document, in proposing a needed curriculum for our secondary schools, made no mention of the fine arts either as an essential part of general education

---

[5] *Ibid.,* p. 302.

[6] Educational Policies Commission, *Education for ALL American Youth—A Further Look* (Washington, D.C.: National Education Association, 1952), pp. 133–135.

or as an important elective option.[7] Science, mathematics, history, English, and foreign languages are regarded in this document as the essentials of the secondary school curriculum, with mathematics and the physical sciences occupying a notable position because "the nation's security has come to depend on Einstein's equation $E = mc^2$." [8] A later publication by the Council for Basic Education, after stating the case for the basic studies in the secondary school, allowed for art and music under the category of "some electives." [9]

Conant's enormously influential report on the American high school did not include the arts in the general education program required of all students, but recommended that "all students should be urged to include art and music in their elective programs." [10] If art and music are of sufficient importance in the education of our high school youth that they be urged to elect these courses, one wonders why Conant did not see fit to include such work in the general education requirements. And in classifying art and music as nonacademic electives, Conant sees these subjects as particularly suited to youngsters who are incapable of doing well in advanced academic areas.[11]

Surely the fine arts should be important to students at all levels of academic ability. But the notion persists that the arts should serve as peripheral subjects, which are to be taken mainly by students who are deemed unsuitable for the academic phase of the curriculum. At the other extreme, we find frantic efforts to promote the development of special courses in the arts for academically talented (not necessarily artistically talented) students on the grounds that the arts have an intellectual worth not unlike that of the recognized academic disciplines.[12] Instead of recognizing the unique and authentic contributions of the arts in the education of all youth, as well as of those who are artistically talented, we either relegate the arts to "frill" status or we seek to justify the place of the arts in the curriculum by making them into paper imitations of the academic disciplines. The cold war pressures of the 1960's resulted in a number of curriculum reports that deliberately ignored the arts,[13, 14]

---

[7] Arthur Bestor, *The Restoration of Learning* (New York: Alfred A. Knopf, Inc., 1955), p. 326.

[8] *Ibid.*, p. 44.

[9] James D. Koerner, *The Case for Basic Education* (Boston: Little, Brown and Company, 1959), p. 209.

[10] James B. Conant, *The American High School Today* (New York: McGraw-Hill Book Company, Inc., 1959), p. 48.

[11] *Ibid.*, p. 94.

[12] William C. Hartshorn, *Music for the Academically Talented Student in the Secondary School* (Washington, D.C.: National Education Association and Music Educators National Conference, 1960).

[13] Robert W. Heath (ed.), *New Curricula* (New York: Harper & Row, Publishers, 1964).

[14] Dorothy M. Fraser, *Current Curriculum Studies in Academic Subjects* (Washington, D.C.: Project on Instruction, National Education Association, 1962).

thereby reinforcing the long-standing notion that the arts are nonessentials in the curriculum.[15]

Elective Status. In interpreting the impact of the Conant report on art education in the high school, an historian notes that Conant's arguments "relegate the arts to the position of attractive subjects that would be most important were not this a time of crisis in the competition of democracy and communist totalitarianism" and consequently "Conant's position is that very little time can be spared for subjects that simply enhance the quality of life." [16]

Making the fine arts an essential part of the general education curriculum of the high school does not require that such studies be allocated an emphasis in time equal to that given the study of English, for example. As discussed later in this chapter, much can be done to provide for systematic experiences in the arts as *performance* as well as the arts as *appreciation* through formal courses and cocurricular activities. Under present conditions the arts are offered as piecemeal electives and as disjointed experiences lumped under extracurricular activities. Teachers of art, music, history, homemaking, and industrial arts tend to go their separate paths at a time when the critical need is to develop coherent programs that will influence the life styles of youth in significant ways.

THE NATIONAL SCENE

Educators have long been aware of our neglect of the fine arts in our high schools; it has, indeed, been fashionable for educators to deplore this situation and to endorse needed changes. For example, a 1962 position paper of the National Association of Secondary School Principals observed that a dichotomy need not exist between the academic studies and the arts, and recommended that while "arts courses have been required only in the junior high school years, . . . systematic contact with the arts needs to be continued for students throughout the years of secondary education." [17] But despite such endorsements, the fine and performing arts have not become part of the general education curriculum of the high school. Unlike the sciences, mathematics, and modern foreign languages—which received enormous support from the federal government as a result of our new national priorities during the cold war—the fine arts remain an orphan of the high school curriculum.

---

15 *Report of the San Francisco Curriculum Survey Committee* (San Francisco: Board of Education, San Francisco Unified School District, 1960).

16 Robert H. Beck, "The Social Background of Art Education," Chapter 1 in National Society for the Study of Education, *Art Education,* Sixty-fourth Yearbook, Part II (Chicago: The University of Chicago Press, 1965), p. 8.

17 "The Arts in the Comprehensive Secondary School," *Bulletin,* National Association of Secondary School Principals, Vol. 46 (September, 1962), p. 7.

Enrollments in the Fine Arts

Curriculum Retrenchment. As discussed earlier, the cold war period witnessed a barrage of attacks on our high schools for allegedly permitting students to devote an excessive portion of their time to nonacademic or "frill" subjects. In 1958 the prestigious Rockefeller Brothers Fund issued a report by its Panel on Education, chaired by John W. Gardner, then president of the Carnegie Corporation, which noted that "we have been extraordinarily tolerant in the matter of electives in the high school." [18] The report went on to recommend that the academic subjects be given the highest priority in the curriculum, particularly science and mathematics, because "the U.S.S.R. has served as a rude stimulus to awaken us to that reality." [19]

In his report on "National Goals for Education," prepared in 1960 for the President's Commission on National Goals, Gardner stressed the importance of reading and writing, mathematics, foreign languages, and social studies, but made no mention of the place of the arts in the curriculum.[20]

National Survey. Although the criticisms directed at the electives gave widespread credence to the notion that secondary school students were spending much of their time on nonessential or "frill" subjects, a national survey conducted by the U.S. Office of Education found that graduates of our public high schools in the class of 1958 had devoted 73 per cent of their studies to academic subjects, while the academically able students had spent 80 per cent of their time in academic work.[21] Seventy-seven per cent of the graduates earned no credits whatsoever in art, while 57 per cent never took a credit course in music during their entire high school careers. Only 5 per cent of the graduates earned more than one credit in music while the figure for art was 3 per cent.[22] In the face of these findings, the report made no mention of the neglect of the fine arts in the curriculum, but concluded, instead, that while "the survey does not indicate that the able pupil shunned academic subjects . . . many of the academically able pupils could have carried heavier [academic] programs." [23]

---

[18] Rockefeller Brothers Fund, *The Pursuit of Excellence: Education and the Future of America* (Garden City, N.Y.: Doubleday & Company, Inc., 1958), p. 26.

[19] *Ibid.,* p. 28.

[20] John W. Gardner, "National Goals in Education" in the Report of the President's Commission on National Goals, *Goals for Americans* (Englewood Cliffs, N.J.: Prentice-Hall, Inc., 1960), pp. 86–88).

[21] Edith S. Greer and Richard M. Harbeck, *What High School Pupils Study* (Washington, D.C.: Office of Education, U.S. Department of Health, Education, and Welfare, 1962), pp. 110–111.

[22] *Ibid.,* p. 72.

[23] *Ibid.,* pp. 119–120.

During the decade of the 1960's, the proportion of high school students enrolled in academic subjects far outstripped the increase in school enrollments, while the fine arts remained badly neglected.[24] Paradoxically, although many of our nation's leaders were proclaiming the importance of the arts in our national life, the arts in the secondary school curriculum continued to suffer from neglect and indifference.

Recent Federal Efforts

U.S. Office of Education.   In response to mounting criticisms leveled at the federal government's policy in supporting only those subjects deemed important to our national defense, the U.S. Office of Education established an Arts and Humanities Program in 1964. Although the financial allocations for this program are minute in comparison to the federal support provided for any of the academic or vocational areas of the curriculum, a number of significant projects have been undertaken in art, music, theater, dance, museum education, and the humanities. However, more than token support will be needed in future years if an important impact is to be made on the curriculum of our secondary schools.

National Endowment for the Arts.   The enactment of the National Foundation on the Arts and the Humanities Act in 1965, creating a National Endowment for the Arts, also served to demonstrate a new federal recognition of the need to support the arts in American life. Except for the support given to the arts for relief purposes during the Depression period, this marked the first venture by the federal government in the area. Since the National Endowment finances a number of systematic educational programs, there is a need to coordinate such efforts more effectively with the Office of Education's Arts and Humanities Program.

Thus far, the National Endowment has had to operate on meager allocations from the federal government and modest contributions from other sources. Although the chairman of the endowment emphasized that, in the national interest, we must give equal consideration to the arts and humanities compared with what we give to science and technology,[25] the federal investment in the endowment in 1970 amounted to only a small fraction of the funds that the National Science Foundation allocated to a single project—Project Mohole—an abortive effort to probe through three miles of the ocean and dig a hole three miles into the earth's crust. It may be naive to expect our nation to support the arts on a level

---

[24] Office of Education, *Digest of Educational Statistics* (Washington, D.C.: U.S. Department of Health, Education, and Welfare, 1969), p. 32.

[25] *National Endowment for the Arts and National Council on the Arts,* Annual Report (Washington, D.C.: U.S. Government Printing Office, 1968), p. 2.

commensurate with the support given science and technology. But the prospects for the development and survival of a culturally rich and rewarding civilization can be measured by the commitment made to the arts.

Public Broadcasting.   Turning to yet another area of federal activity in promoting education in the arts, the Public Broadcasting Act was signed into law by President Lyndon B. Johnson in 1967. This legislation is intended to provide for the production and transmission of noncommercial programs having cultural and educational value. With the failure of commercial broadcasting to meet the public need for artistic programming, Congress created the Corporation for Public Broadcasting to work with our nation's noncommercial stations in developing one or more broadcasting systems to fill a cultural void.

Although the act prohibits federal interference or control, the Corporation for Public Broadcasting is dependent upon federal appropriations. While this may appear to be an unworkable arrangement, the British Broadcasting Corporation has always been able to function with a remarkable degree of autonomy despite the fact that it is supported through a tax on television and radio receivers. But where the BBC is most generously financed, the American Corporation for Public Broadcasting has received only meager allocations from Congress. The BBC, for instance, has supported the world-famous BBC Symphony Orchestra, along with several other orchestras throughout Britain. It also is noted for its opera and theater productions and for its school broadcasts. Public broadcasting in the United States, by contrast, has treated artistic programming as a stepchild. Nevertheless, with the remarkable development of community-sponsored symphony orchestras and cultural centers throughout the United States in recent years, fresh opportunities are unfolding for noncommercial cultural and educational broadcasting. But if public television in the United States is to become a great cultural force comparable to the BBC, public funds will need to be made available on a scale to match the resources of our leading commercial networks.

The Physical Environment of the School

One rarely finds a school building that is an exemplar of man's best architectural creations. Even our so-called functionally designed schools tend to resemble factories for processing or producing material goods. Recent efforts to change the managerial aspects of the curriculum through modular scheduling, nongraded programs, team teaching, large-group instruction, and the utilization of technological devices in teaching have served to reinforce our concept of the school as another industrial enterprise.

While many of us are aware that the physical environment profoundly affects human behavior, we have failed to create schools that represent what is good in our man-created environment. It is not simply a case of economic limitation giving us the schools we have, for one can point to many new facilities that have been constructed at considerable expenditure. As long as we conceive of schooling as a type of industrial processing or as a custodial operation, however, our school facilities will be devoid of beauty.

The modest beginnings on the part of the federal government to stimulate the reconstruction of our communities into model cities presents opportunities for educators and civil leaders to view in a new light the relationship of the school to the community, both in the physical sense and in the sense of contributing to the solution of our most pervasive urban problems. If we expect our schools to play a significant role in cultivating the aesthetic tastes of our younger generation, then we must create physical environments for learning that are aesthetically rewarding.

THE ARTS IN GENERAL EDUCATION: AUTHENTICITY AND UNIQUENESS

Throughout this chapter we have emphasized that the arts have been sadly neglected in meeting the general education needs of students in the high school. Moreover, it is paradoxical that where the arts have been marked by neglect and indifference in the secondary schools, they have managed to occupy a rather fair level of "academic" respectability in our colleges and universities. Is it possible that this contradiction is partially a vestige of the traditional attitude that the arts are the proper province for the higher classes of society? If so, it is time that this dichotomous notion is demolished, for a modern democratic society finds all citizens engaged in labor and leisure. And the traditional distinction between the cultural and utilitarian is no longer valid in a world where aesthetic values play a vital role in controlling the negative forces of science and technology and reshaping these forces so that they are in harmony with man's biological and psychic needs.

Verbal Learning Vs. Performance

Emphasis on the Academic Study of the Arts. As a reaction to the peripheral role accorded the arts in the secondary school curriculum, and in an effort to gain academic respectability for the arts, some educators have proposed that we approach the arts as academic subjects on the same level as science, mathematics, history, and literature, and not as performing experiences.[26] Thus it is proposed that performance or manip-

---

[26] Anthony J. Apicella and Attilio J. Grampa, "The General Truth About General Music," *Music Educators Journal*, Vol. 56 (October, 1969), p. 56.

ulative activities be largely replaced by verbal paths to the understanding and appreciation of the arts during the secondary school years.

> the assumption on the part of most persons that the only way or, at least, the most effective way of becoming conversant with the visual arts is to practice them. This belief engenders an insistence upon studio or manipulative experiences (at the expense of other, primarily verbal, paths to the understanding of art) and results in some art programs which are more time-consuming and less attractive to the academically oriented student than they need be. It might be appropriate to suggest that human growth is characterized, in part, by an increasing ability to think in terms of abstractions. Therefore, the direct-experience approach in learning, which is necessary for younger boys and girls, may be less important to the education of the adolescent. . . . It might, then, be viewed as less appropriate today to insist on manipulative activity to insure accomplishment of the objectives of general education in art. Response to and understanding of the visual arts might be inculcated in the high school primarily by nonmanipulative means, the significant result of which would be a considerable saving of class time.[27]

Many people become appreciators of the arts, and even many of our leading connoisseurs of art or music have gained their status without having to develop the skills necessary for musical performance or for the creation of art works. And where we expect general education to develop the aesthetic tastes of all citizens as consumers of the arts, we do not expect general education to develop all citizens as performers or creators of the arts. But this does not mean that performance or direct experience is unnecessary or of low priority in the education of the adolescent. Education must be concerned with linking performance skills with understandings and appreciations. To hold verbal learning on a higher intellectual plane than performance in the arts is to ignore what the arts really are. In the words of Dewey, "Art denotes a process of doing or making." [28] Of course, doing or making are not educational in the absence of understanding and appreciating. But to divorce education in the arts from doing or making is to deprive the adolescent learner of what may be his only opportunity to see the organic relationship between performance and perception.

Intellectuality and the Adolescent. To hold that the high school should concentrate on nonmanipulative activity in the arts, under the assumption that an adequate foundation of manipulative experience can be provided at the lower levels of schooling,[29] is to assume that adolescence is merely

---

27 Ronald Silverman and Vincent Lanier, "Art for the Adolescent," Chapter VI in National Society for the Study of Education, *Art Education, op. cit.,* p. 121.

28 John Dewey, *Art As Experience* (New York: G. P. Putnam's Sons, 1934), p. 47.

29 Silverman and Lanier, *op. cit.,* p. 121.

a larger extension of childhood. But the work of Piaget and others points clearly to the need to regard adolescence as a genuine state in human development. To separate abstract thinking from performance is to create a duality inimical to education. To embrace the notion that intellectuality is manifest only through verbal signs and words is to divorce schooling from life. As Dewey pointed out, "since words are easily manipulated in mechanical ways, the production of a work of genuine art probably demands more intelligence than does most of the so-called thinking that goes on among those who pride themselves on being 'intellectuals.' " [30]

The arts in the curriculum can enable the adolescent to appreciate the intimate relationship between acts of doing or making and the process of understanding or appreciating. When we limit the study of the arts in the high school to an academic-style course in the humanities, we are not effecting a compromise in the battle of curriculum priorities; instead, we are subordinating the arts to a narrow and artificial level of experience. And we are guilty of similar mischief when we conceive of the arts as mere performance in the absence of the understandings that enhance our perspectives, influence our values, and shape our life styles.

Analytical Study.   Broudy, Smith, and Burnett contend that our secondary schools would be more successful "if the curricular time now given to literature and drawing, art and music can be used for six years of aesthetic education via a study of exemplars . . . styles of life found admirable by the connoisseurs of our culture . . . paintings, musical compositions, poems, dramas, and novels." [31] The goal is to enable the pupil to perceive as the connoisseur perceives.[32] Thus the arts are to be encountered through analytical study rather than through performance. In sharp contrast to this position, many leading art educators see the arts in the secondary school primarily as a means of creative expression.[33]

Emphasis on the history and literature of the arts, and on the development of analytical skills, can lead to fuller perspectives and appreciations of the contribution of the arts to civilization. But such learning experiences are not a substitute for performance and creation in the arts. Actual experience in performance and creation may not be relevant to the expert critic or connoisseur, but this does not mean that such experience is irrelevant to the adolescent.

---

[30] Dewey, *Art As Experience, op. cit.,* p. 46.

[31] Harry S. Broudy, B. Othanel Smith, and Joe R. Burnett, *Democracy and Excellence in American Secondary Education* (Chicago: Rand McNally & Company, 1964), p. 229.

[32] *Ibid.*

[33] Viktor Lowenfeld and W. Lambert Brittain, *Creative and Mental Growth,* 5th ed. (New York: The Macmillan Company, 1970).

The Adolescent and the Subject Matter

Aside from the question of how performance and creation can contribute to appreciation, the assumption that the adolescent should learn to perceive and judge as does the expert critic or connoisseur is open to serious question. Indeed, such an assumption has influenced the curriculum reform movement in the sciences, mathematics, and other disciplines with dubious results. The Brunerian notion that the activity of the schoolboy in a discipline is not different from that of a mature scholar in the forefront of his field must, as we have seen, be challenged on two grounds. In the first place, the adolescent is not a miniature adult and consequently it is doubtful that he can be made to think like the mature scholar. Secondly, even if it were possible to create the adolescent in the image of the mature scholar, this does not, in itself, justify our effort to give priority to such a goal to the neglect of meeting adolescent needs.

It is in the arts, perhaps more than any other area of activity, that the adolescent seeks his own form of identity and expression. Without doubt there can be great value in having adolescents encounter expert exemplars in the arts, but they must encounter these exemplars as adolescents and not as experts. Otherwise, the behavior of the adolescent is imitative rather than authentic. Moreover, the need to utilize expert exemplars in an adolescent's education is matched by the need of the adolescent to express his developing perspectives, references, and tastes in relation to the total scheme of things. To expect the adolescent to exemplify the mature scholar, whether as a nuclear physicist or as an art connoisseur, is to deny the adolescent the right of growth and development.

Yet another point of issue relates to the difference between the art connoisseur as consumer or critic and the artist as creator. The creative artist often distrusts the connoisseur's attempts to reduce a work to verbal explanations and to tell other people what is good or bad in art. Most artists seems to feel that the visual dimension is its own explanation, and that one cannot really reduce the visual arts to verbal descriptions any more than one can convey what music is through words only. The school, in its general education function, must look to the arts as a means of developing adolescent powers of expression as well as appreciation. Such goals are quite different from connoisseurship or professional artistry. Consequently, by recognizing the authenticity of the adolescent experience, the schools can create a unity of expression and appreciation.

Structure of the Disciplines

Inadequate Models. In earlier chapters we have discussed the tendency for curriculum workers in the social studies and English to embrace the notion of "structure" in a manner imitative of the curriculum reform movement in the sciences and mathematics. Some art educators have proposed that the Brunerian concept of structure be applied to art education and that the art student be made to undergo the same processes as the mature artist at work.[34]

As we have just noted, the validity of the assumption that the adolescent and the mature artist are not essentially different in their attitude and activity remains open to serious question. Moreover, to assume that other disciplines can and should serve as models for curriculum construction in the arts carries the real danger that the arts may lose their unique, authentic, and most valuable properties. Just as one cannot define music or the visual arts in verbal terms, one cannot fit the fine arts into the mold of science, or mathematics, or any other academic discipline.

Intellectuality and the Arts. The peripheral status of the arts in the curriculum, and the neglect of the arts in the curriculum reform movement, has caused some educators in the arts to regard the more favored disciplines as promising models. These educators write as though they have been brainwashed into believing that the so-called essential subjects are on a higher and more complete intellectual level than the arts, and that if we are to develop a consistent and logical curriculum in the arts, we will need to find structure by looking to the more intellectual disciplines.

> What is the structure of the visual arts? . . . How is the study of the visual arts similar to and how does it differ from the study of more completely intellectual subjects? These and other relevant questions must be answered satisfactorily before a program that is truly the embodiment of consistency, logic, and significance can be developed for secondary art education.[35]

Dewey observed that "to think effectively in terms of relations of qualities is as severe a demand upon thought as to think in terms of symbols, verbal and mathematical." [36] As an inquirer, discoverer, and performer, the artist is involved in an intellectual and emotional process just as rigorous as that of the scientific inquirer or the creative writer. But this does not mean that curriculum workers in the arts must imitate their colleagues in the scientific, mathematical, and other disciplines. To force the arts into an alien mold is to lose their uniqueness and authenticity. It is one thing to seek interrelationships among the various domains of knowledge for purposes of creating a balanced curriculum in harmony with man as a total being. It is quite another thing to seek to structure

---

[34] Manuel Barkan, "Transition in Art Education," *Art Education,* Vol. 15 (October, 1962), pp. 12–18.

[35] Silverman and Lanier, *op. cit.,* p. 141.

[36] Dewey, *Art As Experience, op. cit.,* p. 46.

the arts in the image of what some art educators self-deprecatingly regard as the "more completely intellectual subjects."

THE ARTS IN GENERAL EDUCATION: BALANCE IN THE CURRICULUM

Although the junior high school has provided opportunities for specialized instruction in art and music in a manner not possible at the elementary level, in many junior high schools pupils must choose between an elective course in either art or music. Or art and music may even be lumped together with other elective offerings and, as a result, the fine arts are not regarded as a necessary part of general education. At the high school level, the fine and performing arts are virtually ignored in the general education and college preparatory phases of the curriculum —with the possible exception of an academic-style humanities course. The present situation calls for a reappraisal of the relationship of the arts to the total school curriculum and the restructuring of the arts as an integrative area of study.

Balance in the Curriculum

As mentioned earlier, the problem of developing balance in the total curriculum in general education is a direct result of a prevailing attitude on the part of the general public and educators who regard the nonacademic subjects as nonessential. And, because of their elective status, offerings in the fine arts are not only exceedingly limited in many schools but suffer from imbalance. Even in the larger comprehensive high schools, where a variety of courses in art and music are available, one is apt to find a lack of sequential coherence in the course offerings. In the visual arts, students may be engaged in too many trivial, imitative, and repetitive projects, while opportunities for significant learning go unexploited. The visual and performing arts need to be more carefully articulated if they are to have a significant impact on the learner.

Too many teachers of art or music either resign themselves to the peripheral status of their subjects, or are content to regard themselves as specialists whose mission it is to concentrate on the special needs of a small segment of the total school population. As a result, such teachers have no interest in developing balanced and viable programs in the arts for purposes of general education.

The Visual Arts in the Curriculum

Offerings for General Education. Offerings applicable to general education in the larger comprehensive high school might include: (1) a basic studio art class giving primary emphasis to manipulative activity in (a) drawing and painting, (b) design—featuring poster work, collage construction, and mosaics, (c) crafts—utilizing a variety of materials including metal, wood, leather, and papier-mâché, (d) sculpture, printmaking, and design, and (e) some treatment of art appreciation through an historical approach; (2) a contemporary survey course, often intended for the terminal student, which may combine manipulative activities as well as reading and visual materials dealing with art (a) in the home, (b) in the community, (c) in communications, and (d) as a vocation; (3) an art history course, often intended for academically oriented students, and dealing with world, American, or western European art; and (4) a humanities course, also geared for the academic student, organized with the intent of interrelating the development of music, literature, dance, theater, and the visual arts in historical and cultural perspective.[37]

Balanced Experiences in the Visual Arts. Earlier in this chapter we discussed the relationship between verbal learning about the arts and actual performance in the educative experience. It is unfortunate that many art classes in our secondary schools consist of little more than manipulative activity through a succession of assigned projects, leaving students without any real understanding and appreciation of the visual arts. The development of artistic attitudes and tastes is neglected in favor of simple production activity. Similarly, the educative experience is out of balance when it is geared primarily to verbal learning. Art education in the secondary school is not intended to create art critics or historians. Art for the adolescent should be as complete an educative experience as possible.

As a reaction to the emphasis on production, and the neglect of meaningful artistic experiences in the secondary school, some art educators have taken the position that "the emphasis in secondary school art be placed upon the study, rather than the practice of art." [38] On the other hand, this should not be taken to mean that the study of art should be patterned after the verbal-learning approaches characteristic of the so-called academic disciplines. In criticizing the overemphasis given to the production of technically acceptable projects in secondary school art programs, Lowenfeld and Brittain contend that "the focus of these programs should clearly be on the process of making art and not on the art itself." [39] Lowenfeld and Brittain see art education in the secondary school as playing a unique role in meeting adolescent needs for self-expression.[40]

---

[37] Silverman and Lanier, *op. cit.*, pp. 122–124.

[38] Howard Conant, *Art Education* (New York: The Center for Applied Research in Education, Inc., 1964), p. 83.

[39] Lowenfeld and Brittain, *op. cit.*, p. 231.

[40] *Ibid.*, p. 233.

A Sample Program. Art educators differ in their opinions on the proportion of time to be devoted to studying about art, and time given to the actual process of producing art. While the following proposed curriculum for all students in grades 7 through 12 is comprehensive and balanced in its representation of content areas, only some 40 per cent of the time is allocated to related studio experiences.

> Grade 7 (125 hours of class study; 75 hours of studio experiences)
> Crafts
> Painting, sculpture, and graphic arts
> Textile and clothing design
>
> Grade 8 (110 hours of class study; 90 hours of studio experiences)
> Graphic arts
> Architecture
> Community planning
> Painting and sculpture
> Commercial design
>
> Grade 9 or 10 (120 hours of class study; 80 hours of studio experiences)
> Photography
> Textile and clothing design
> Industrial design
> Painting, sculpture, and graphic arts
>
> Grade 11 or 12 (120 hours of class study; 80 hours of studio experiences)
> Community planning
> Architecture
> Painting, sculpture, and graphic arts.[41]

However, the real problem is not simply the amount of time to be allocated between verbal experiences and the process of making art, but rather the need to integrate both kinds of activities for authentic learning on the part of the adolescent. Learning is not authentic to the adolescent when it consists of adult-imposed standards and tastes, or when it focuses on studying about art through textbooks, while expressive activity through the making of art is neglected.

More than 90 per cent of our students fail to take a single art course in high school.[42] Although many educators lament the neglect of the arts in general education, little has been done to make a significant place for the arts in this phase of the high school curriculum.

Advanced Courses. At a more specialized or prevocational level, the large comprehensive high school might offer additional courses in commercial art, drawing and painting, graphics, ceramics, sculpture, metalwork and jewelry making, advertising design, fashion design, mosaics,

---

[41] Howard Conant, *op. cit.*, p. 82.
[42] Lowenfeld and Brittain, *op. cit.*, p. 225.

sign painting, photography, interior decorating, stage design, and so on.[43] However, except in the rare instances where specialized high schools prepare students for vocations in the arts, such as New York City's High School of Music and Art and High School of Fashion Design, our high schools do not have the breadth and depth of offerings necessary for vocational preparation. At best, our larger comprehensive high schools, which offer a variety of art courses, provide students with valuable exploratory experiences at the prevocational level.

Music in the Curriculum

Need for Balanced Programs. Our secondary schools have been far more successful in developing programs in instrumental music than in providing for the general education needs of all students. High schools take pride in the technical excellence of their bands and orchestras, which perform not only for the student body but for the community at large. Taking their cue from the colleges, most high schools sponsor marching bands to entertain the spectators at football games. The spectacular development of collegiate football as a commercial enterprise has created a new recognition of the value of the marching band. Many colleges offer scholarships to accomplished high school musicians for the purpose of having them perform in marching bands at collegiate football games and other public functions.

To a lesser extent, it is not uncommon to find in our high schools various choral groups that perform at a high level of competence. As in the case of instrumental music, however, such activity is concentrated on developing the technical skills of only a small segment of the student population.

It must be recognized, however, that the development of a high degree of technical competence in orchestral and choral music can serve as a significant extension of the general education program, and can lead to an avocational or vocational commitment throughout one's lifetime. Participation in music performance groups provides a unique kind of collective experience. The students not only learn to work together in interpreting a composer's creation to an audience, but also are aware that the composition itself has an existence that is subject to continuous interpretation by other performance groups anytime in the future. Such qualities make musical performance a kind of experience that is very different from that gained through participation on the athletic team, for example.

For other students, who are not members of performance groups, there are opportunities to learn to enjoy music through school concerts, which

---

43 Silverman and Lanier, *op. cit.,* p. 125.

can serve an important function in general education. Such students, as well as accomplished musicians, can come to appreciate a wide spectrum of musical exemplars through recordings.

Other General Education Outcomes.   In addition to the outcomes mentioned above, experiences in school music can be designed to contribute to the development of the following specific skills, understandings, and appreciations for purposes of general education:

Skills

1. Listening—ability to recognize the broad melodic and rhythmic contours of musical compositions, the sounds of orchestral instrumental compositions.
2. Singing—ability to carry a part in group singing with confidence and expression.
3. Instrumental—ability to perform, if only at an elementary level, with a percussion instrument, a recorder, or a "social-type" instrument, along with having basic familiarity with the piano keyboard.
4. Musical notation—ability to respond to the musical notation of unison and simple part songs, and follow the scores of instrumental compositions.

Understandings

5. Structure—understanding the component parts of music and the interrelationships of melody, rhythm, harmony, and form; ability to recognize design elements aurally.
6. Historical perspective—understanding of the major historical periods in terms of the styles of musical development, masterpieces of the past and the men who composed them.
7. Relationship between music and other human activities—understanding that the arts have many concepts in common and that they enhance one another.
8. Place of music in contemporary life—understanding the function of music in society.

Attitudes

9. Self-expression—appreciating the uniqueness of music in expressing feelings, whether through actual performance or through listening.
10. Continued learning and appreciation—participating in community musical activities and enjoying a range of musical forms through recordings; keeping informed on developments in the world of music.
11. Taste—making sensitive choices, and evaluating performances with discrimination.[44]

---

[44] Karl D. Ernst and Charles L. Gary (eds.), *Music in General Education* (Washington, D.C.: Music Educators National Conference, 1965), pp. 4–8.

The Music Educators National Conference has identified the following content areas to form the core of experiences in general education for all high school graduates: (1) elements of music, (2) form and design in music, (3) interpretive aspects of music, (4) science of sound, (5) the musical score, (6) historical considerations, (7) music and man, (8) music as a form of expression, (9) types of musical performance, (10) relationship of music to other disciplines in the humanities, and (11) music to-day.[45] This list is not intended as a definitive curriculum, but as an illustrative guide for developing content and activities to meet general education objectives.

Course Offerings and Needs. In addition to classes in instrumental and choral music, many secondary schools offer a course in general music. At the junior high school level, this course may be required of all students as part of the general education sequence. In the senior high school, it is usually offered as an elective. Other nonperformance courses offered as electives in the high school are music history, music literature, and music appreciation. Additional elective specialities include music theory and ensemble classes. A summary of the research on the teaching of music appreciation reveals that very little is known about effective methods for teaching junior and senior high school students or about the music that is most meaningful and appropriate for adolescents of different backgrounds.[46]

At the performance level, secondary schools need to provide for larger time blocks to fit the diverse requirements of musical activities for laboratory purposes. The success of the music education program is dependent also on adequate resources and facilities, including a comprehensive and readily accessible library of recordings, scores, and reading materials, rehearsal and practice rooms, small recital halls, and an aesthetically attractive auditorium-theater.

Teachers must not only have technical competence in their specialties, but must work together in building a comprehensive program of music education that will reach all students. Music should not be regarded as a special area for a limited segment of the school population.

In virtually every generation there is a wide gap between adolescent tastes and expression, and the music of the school. The situation becomes one of adolescent music versus school music. And, all too often, while shunning adolescent interests, school music does not even represent the best musical exemplars of the past and present. A balanced and comprehensive curriculum in music can enable adolescents to gain new under-

---

45 *Ibid.*, p. 16.
46 Erwin H. Schneider, "Music Education" in Robert L. Ebel (ed.), *Encyclopedia of Educational Research,* 4th ed. (New York: The Macmillan Company, 1969), p. 902.

standings and appreciations in a wide variety of musical forms. Like life itself, music has many manifestations and is ever changing.

Other Performing Arts

The theater arts can bring together the activities of drama, music, dance, and the visual arts. In the chapter on English in the curriculum, we noted how the treatment of drama as exclusively a literary experience creates a distorted and misleading notion of the unique role that drama plays in our civilization. For most secondary school students, the only encounter with the theater arts is to attend school productions conducted as cocurricular activities. Such productions commonly are intended to serve as popular entertainment and not as rewarding educative experiences. Although many secondary schools offer drama as an elective, the learning experiences provided through such classes often are devoid of any significant treatment of the contributions of the visual arts and music to the theater. And, all too often, the motion picture as a medium of artistic expression is quite neglected.

Where humanities courses in the high school are intended to provide for integrated learning experiences in the various art forms, the tendency has been to slight the theater arts or to represent them simply as plays to be read. Moreover, the humanities course all too often is organized as an academic-type course for academically talented students and is limited to the analytical study of the arts.

Through the federally sponsored National Council on the Arts and National Endowment for the Arts, a number of programs have been established in several cities to bring secondary school classes to the theater. For most of these adolescents, this is their first experience in attending a professional theater production. In some cases, the theater productions are designed and scheduled to fit into the curriculum of the secondary school. Although these efforts are financed on a modest scale, they give promise of serving as a model for similar programs throughout the nation.

The theater arts can enable adolescents to gain new aesthetic experiences as well as understanding of the role of the theater as a social force. Exemplars of the past and significant contemporary works can serve to expose the learner to a range of experiences that is not provided for in other areas of the curriculum.

While the dance is a vital part of the theater arts, it has been identified most commonly with the physical education program for girls in our secondary schools. Some secondary schools provide instruction in social dancing through coeducational classes, but ballet and modern dance tend to be restricted to girls' physical education programs. Such restriction only serves to reinforce the notion in our society that ballet and modern dance are mainly part of the cultural heritage of females. Through coeducational classes in dance, through the correlation of dance activity in physical education with the curriculum in the fine arts, and through school- and community-sponsored performances, adolescents of both sexes can gain a more sophisticated understanding of the place of dance in our cultural heritage and contemporary life.

The Humanities

The growing role of the humanities in the general education curricula of our colleges and universities has been followed by an increase in the number of humanities courses in the high school. Although the place of the humanities in the secondary school curriculum is discussed in greater detail in our chapter on general education (Chapter 2), some treatment is appropriate here concerning the place of the fine arts and performing arts in the humanities course.

Often taught by a faculty team, the humanities class usually seeks to develop understandings and appreciations concerning the interrelatedness of literature (drama, poetry, novel), fine arts (music, painting, sculpture, architecture, and related arts), dance, history, and philosophy. In some cases, efforts are made to include the historical and philosophical aspects of science and religion in the humanities course.

In an era where the chief emphasis in curriculum reform has been on the separate disciplines, the humanities course represents a significant effort to seek out the interrelatedness of knowledge. Nevertheless, many courses are organized on a multidisciplinary basis and not as an interdisciplinary area of study. Each constituent area of knowledge is treated as almost a mini-course with its own boundaries of separateness. In many cases, the course content is developed historically rather than thematically.

Another problem in the humanities course is the tendency to neglect the arts as performance. For example, plays are studied in their literary form only and consequently students fail to encounter the material in the dramatic theater form for which the work was created. The arts are treated simply as another area of knowledge to be organized into subject matter imitative of the so-called disciplines. Thus, despite the noble objectives often stated for the humanities course, the subject matter often is not made relevant to students and, as a result, exerts little influence on their life styles. As noted earlier in this chapter, the tendency to pattern the humanities course in the high school after its college counterpart has resulted, in many cases, in designing the course for the college-bound and not as an integral part of the general education of all students.

THE CHALLENGE

In establishing our curriculum priorities for the secondary school, we have created many false dichotomies: academic versus nonacademic, essential versus nonessential, practical versus ornamental, social versus aesthetic, and so on. The result has been the relegation of the arts to a frill-like role in the curriculum and to a narrow function in the cocurriculum of the secondary school. Maslow holds that "effective education in music, education in art, education in dancing . . . are so close to our psychological and biological core, so close to . . . biological identity, that rather than think of these courses as a sort of whipped or luxury cream, they must become basic experiences in education." [47]

The answer lies not in simply allocating more time to the arts in the curriculum, although this would be helpful. Recasting the arts to make them fit the image of the verbally oriented academic disciplines would be a perversion of the arts. The need is to reconstruct the arts in the school so that they form a relevant part of the total general education curriculum while at the same time retaining the unique qualities that have made them essential to life. Just as it is impossible to imagine what life would be like without music and the visual arts, it should be impossible for the secondary school to ignore the arts in the education of adolescents. The integrated curriculum, like the integrated individual, is a condition of enhanced identity, not lost identity.

SUMMARY

The arts have long been treated as a stepchild of the high school curriculum. The great curriculum reform movement of the past two decades has been directed at the academic disciplines while the arts, for the most part, have suffered from neglect and indifference. Although many educators have acknowledged that the arts should perform an important general education function in the high school, only a small proportion of our high school students take a course in the arts. The arts are treated as nonacademic, nonessential, ornamental studies.

We are coming to realize, particularly in higher education, that the traditional distinctions between the academic and the nonacademic, the cultural and the utilitarian, the ornamental and the essential, are no longer valid. In the wider society, where the negative forces of science and technology have been allowed to run rampant, we are beginning to discover that our psychic and biological well-being depends greatly on our ability to control and reshape these forces through aesthetic values and commitments. Recent efforts on the part of the federal government in support of the arts in school and society, although relatively insignificant when compared with the support given the sciences, mathematics, and other so-called academic disciplines, should encourage educators to find new recognition for the arts in the curriculum.

---

[47] Abraham Maslow, "Music, Education, and Peak Experiences," in Robert A. Choate (ed.), *Music in American Society,* Documentary Report of the Tanglewood Symposium (Washington, D.C.: Music Educators National Conference, 1968), p. 73.

Unfortunately, many educators see a dichotomy between the analytical study of the arts, and the arts as performance and creation. There are those who seek to gain academic respectability for the arts by recasting them into the image of the traditional academic disciplines. They see the arts in the high school mainly as historical and literary studies, with the goal of developing appreciation and critical skills through verbal expression. On the other hand, there are those who are content to see the arts limited largely to manipulative and performance skills and activities which have little or no connection with aesthetic expression.

To reduce the arts in the high school to cognitive learning activity is to lose the very qualities that make the arts unique as a form of human expression and communication. The same holds true when the arts are reduced to simple manipulative and performance skills. Art is an act of perceiving, valuing, doing, and creating. Unless the adolescent can encounter the arts as authentic expression, he will simply be imitating adult exemplars. Or else the situation will degenerate into one of direct opposition: adolescent tastes and modes of expression versus school-imposed tastes and standards. To impose on the adolescent the judgments, standards, and tastes of the mature scholar or expert is to seek conformity, not growth and development.

Somehow the schools must seek to create a unity of expression and appreciation in the arts. In this way the arts can influence our life styles for the better. But the secondary schools will need to recognize the arts as an integral and essential part of the education of all youth, and not as a frill or luxury item in the curriculum.

PROBLEMS FOR STUDY AND DISCUSSION

1. Do you share the thesis expressed in the quotation below concerning the nature of the adolescent in relation to art experiences in the curriculum? Why or why not?

   It might be appropriate to suggest that human growth is characterized, in part, by an increasing ability to think in terms of abstractions. Therefore, the direct-experience approach in learning, which is necessary for younger boys and girls, may be less important to the education of the adolescent. . . . It might, then, be viewed as less appropriate today to insist on manipulative activity to insure accomplishment of the objectives of general education in art. Response to and understanding of the visual arts might be inculcated in the high school primarily by non-manipulative means, the significant result of which would be a considerable saving of class time. [Ronald Silverman and Vincent Lanier, "Art for the Adolescent," Chapter 6 in National Society for the Study of Education, *Art Education*, Sixty-fourth Yearbook, Part II (Chicago: The University of Chicago Press, 1965), p. 121.]

2. Do you agree or disagree with the following quotation? Why? What are your views regarding the emphasis to be given to performance and creation as compared to the analytical study of the arts in the secondary school curriculum?

> Courses in art that emphasize art criticism and art history fit very well with the image of what is appropriate for the gifted student. In addition, progress in discursively oriented courses can be tested for college entrance in a way that progress in painting or sculpture classes cannot be; thus, programs in art education developed along discursive lines contribute to the "college-needs" of a college-bound population. [Elliot W. Eisner, "American Education and the Future of Art Education," Chapter 13 in National Society for the Study of Education, *Art Education,* Sixty-fourth Yearbook, Part II (Chicago: The University of Chicago Press, 1965), p. 322.]

3. Some art educators regard the academic studies as "more completely intellectual" than the arts. Do you agree with them? Why or why not?

4. John Dewey observed that "hardly a week—certainly not a month—passes that I do not receive a letter, sometimes from a teacher, sometimes from a student, which asks . . . in effect, why teachers and students who wish to do productive work—work productive in experience, intelligence, and interest—should be so hampered and harassed." [John Dewey, and others, *Art and Education,* 2nd ed. (Merion, Pa.: The Barnes Foundation Press, 1947), pp. 7–8.]

   How do you account for the tendency of the schools to divorce verbal learning from direct experience in the arts and other subjects?

5. In 1960, John W. Gardner formulated a program on the "National Goals in Education" for the President's Commission on National Goals [John W. Gardner, "National Goals in Education," in President's Commission on National Goals, *Goals for Americans* (Englewood Cliffs, N.J.: Prentice-Hall, Inc., 1960), pp. 81–100]. In this report, Gardner discussed the importance of reading and writing, mathematics, science, foreign languages, and social studies in the curriculum at the elementary and secondary levels, and how these fields contribute to our national goals. The arts were conspicuously absent from Gardner's statement. How do you account for the fact that many of our national leaders have failed to recognize the importance of the arts in the curriculum?

6. Survey the course offerings in the fine and performing arts in grades 7 through 12 in some nearby schools. Are the students required to take any of these courses, or are the arts offered as electives only? How do the students in the elective arts classes compare in academic ability and vocational plans with other students in these schools?

7. In recent years, many communities have established museums, galleries, and centers for the performing arts on an unprecedented scale. Dewey commented that "these things reflect and establish superior cultural status, while their segregation from the common life reflects the fact that they are not part of a native and spontaneous culture. They are a kind of counterpart of a holier-than-thou attitude. . . ." [John Dewey, *Art As Experience* (New York: G. P. Putnam's Sons, 1934), p. 9.]

To what extent should the secondary school curriculum in the arts be concerned with the common, contemporary culture as compared with the recognized classical works?

SELECTED REFERENCES

Bassett, Richard (ed.). *The Open Eye in Learning: The Role of Art in General Education.* Cambridge, Mass.: The M.I.T. Press, 1969.

Berman, Louise M. (ed.). *The Humanities and the Curriculum.* Washington, D.C.: Association for Supervision and Curriculum Development, National Education Association, 1967.

Bestor, Arthur. *The Restoration of Learning.* New York: Alfred A. Knopf, Inc., 1955.

Broudy, Harry S., B. Othanel Smith, and Joe R. Burnett. *Democracy and Excellence in American Secondary Education.* Chicago: Rand McNally & Company, 1964. Chs. 13, 15.

Choate, Robert A. (ed.). *Music in American Society, Documentary Report of the Tanglewood Symposium.* Washington, D.C.: Music Educators National Conference, 1968.

Conant, Howard. *Art Education.* New York: The Center for Applied Research in Education, Inc., 1964.

Conant, James B. *The American High School Today.* New York: McGraw-Hill Book Company, Inc., 1959.

Conner, Forrest E., and William J. Ellena (eds.). *Curriculum Handbook for School Administrators.* Washington, D.C.: American Association of School Administrators, National Education Association, 1967. Chs. 1, 9.

Dewey, John. *Democracy and Education.* New York: The Macmillan Company, 1916.

———. *Art As Experience.* New York: G. P. Putnam's Sons, 1934.

Dewey, John, and others. *Art and Education,* 2nd ed. Merion, Pa.: The Barnes Foundation Press, 1947.

Educational Policies Commission. *Education for ALL American Youth— A Further Look.* Washington, D.C.: National Education Association, 1952.

Eisner, Elliot W. "Art Education," in Robert L. Ebel (ed.). *Encyclopedia of Educational Research,* 4th ed. New York: The Macmillan Company, 1969, pp. 76–86.

Ernst, Karl D., and Charles L. Gary (eds.). *Music in General Education.* Washington, D.C.: Music Educators National Conference, 1965.

Getzels, Jacob, and Philip Jackson. *Creativity and Intelligence.* New York: John Wiley & Sons, Inc., 1962.

Hausman, Jerome. "Research on Teaching the Visual Arts," Chapter 22 in N. L. Gage (ed.). *Handbook of Research on Teaching.* Chicago: Rand McNally & Company, 1963.

Kaplan, Max. *Foundations and Frontiers of Music Education.* New York: Holt, Rinehart and Winston, Inc., 1966.

Lowenfeld, Viktor, and W. Lambert Brittain. *Creative and Mental Growth,* 5th ed. New York: The Macmillan Company, 1970.

McLuhan, Marshall. *Understanding Media: The Extensions of Man.* New York: McGraw-Hill Book Company, Inc., 1964.

National Society for the Study of Education. *Basic Concepts in Music Education,* Fifty-seventh Yearbook, Part I. Chicago: The University of Chicago Press, 1958.

————. *Art Education,* Sixty-fourth Yearbook, Part II. Chicago: The University of Chicago Press, 1965.

Schneider, Erwin H. "Music Education," in Robert L. Ebel (ed.). *Encyclopedia of Educational Research,* 4th ed. New York: The Macmillan Company, 1969, pp. 895–907.

Smith, Ralph A. (ed.). *Aesthetics and Criticism in Art Education.* Chicago: Rand McNally & Company, 1966.

Sur, William R., and Charles F. Schuller. *Music Education for Teenagers,* 2nd ed. New York: Harper & Row, Publishers, 1966.

Chapter 9

Curriculum Change in Physical Education, Health, and Recreation

With the exception of English, physical education is the most commonly required subject at each of the grade levels in our secondary schools. Yet the current history of the field of physical education is marked by serious differences of opinion regarding goals, functions, program content, and emphasis in the total school curriculum. The relationship of health education, interschool athletics, and intramural sports to the total program in physical education continues to be a source of conflict and confusion.

Most statements on the goals of secondary education appearing in the twentieth century make notable mention of the importance of fostering good health practices and developing the physical well-being of pupils. Professionals in the field of physical education have responded by claiming that physical education can contribute to a great variety of significant attributes and outcomes: character and sportsmanship, civic responsibility, physical fitness, health knowledge and habits, self-discipline, lifelong recreational skills and interests, aesthetic development, leadership, cooperativeness, wholesome competitiveness, and so on. Nevertheless, many programs suffer from a lack of adequate time and resources for the average student, failure to provide activities that will lead to lifelong recreational pursuits, excessive time devoted to monotonous physical drills which lead to negative attitudes on the part of learners toward physical education, inadequate individual and small-group instruction, and overemphasis on varsity sports.

While it is easy to lay the blame for such shortcomings on physical educators, at times of crisis we find our national leaders either stressing physical fitness as the only important concern of the physical education program of our schools or, at the other extreme, emphasizing cognitive development in certain specialized disciplines as the source of our salvation while according physical education "frill" status in the curriculum. Many of our most severe critics of interschool athletic programs are professors at universities that are ever alert in recruiting star high school athletes for commercial exploitation. Within the school itself, the administration may be tempted to favor the varsity athletic program for its contribution to good public relations while the rest of the program in physical education is largely ignored or neglected. Rewards are bestowed on winning coaches and not on effective teachers.

In recent years, there has been a growing awareness of the need to build balanced and meaningful programs of physical and health education in our secondary schools. In many communities, the schools no longer can avoid the topics of sex and drugs in society. Growing numbers of parents are demanding that the schools come to grips with questions that were once left to the home and the streets. Such demands require not only that the program content in health education be changed, but that new and more effective curricular relationships be developed among the areas of health education, biology, social studies, and homemaking. Never before has the need been greater for recognizing the essential role and relationship of physical and health education in the total program of general education in the secondary school. We can, in fact, no longer conceive of physical and health education as entities largely separated from the academic and other phases of the curriculum.

TWENTIETH-CENTURY DEVELOPMENTS

With the opening of the twentieth century, physical education in American secondary schools was limited largely to calisthenics and gymnastics patterned after European practices. Such activities required only a modest investment in facilities and equipment and were promoted as a means of developing physical fitness. Little, if any, attention was given to adolescent interests and health needs. A survey of public high schools in 1910 revealed that more than 95 per cent of these schools did not have a teacher in charge of a physical education department.[1] As we entered World War I, only a small proportion of secondary schools had gymnasium facilities and qualified teachers of physical education; medical examinations were rarely provided, and the common practice was to allocate two periods per week for dull and repetitive physical exercise described by an educator of that day as "little more than a pretense of education." [2]

---

[1] Alexander Inglis, *The Principles of Secondary Education*, 6th ed. (Boston: Houghton Mifflin Company, 1918), p. 641.

[2] *Ibid.*, p. 642.

National Needs and Physical Fitness

With one third of the conscripts in World War I being rejected for military service, the schools were accused of failing to provide for the physical fitness needs of our nation. While the schools could hardly be blamed for many of the physical ailments—such as heart disease, eyesight deficiencies, flat feet, mental retardation, or tuberculosis—the schools, nevertheless, bore the brunt of the criticism. State after state soon passed laws making physical education mandatory in our schools. Although the war emergency can be credited with promoting the recognition of the need for physical education, the emphasis was given mainly to the physical fitness aspect.

Soon after our entry into World War II, military leaders again attacked the schools for the rejection of one third of our total manpower of draft age. At the War Fitness Conference in 1943, a military leader attacked the physical education programs in our high schools as a "miserable failure" and attributed the unnecessary loss of American lives to school programs that were concerned with play instead of the development of physical fitness and stamina.[3] Many high school athletic fields began to resemble military obstacle courses during this period. With hundreds of thousands of young women serving in the armed services in World War II, and with millions of women engaged in occupations previously limited to men, the stress on physical fitness also influenced the physical education programs for girls in our nation's high schools. The developing comprehensiveness of the curriculum in physical education between World War I and II was forced to give way to the narrow function of achieving physical fitness at a time of national crisis.

Changing Conception of Man

The progressive education movement caused educators to see the human organism in a new light. When Dewey attacked the fallacy in the traditional conception of man as "an isolation of mind from activity involving physical conditions, bodily organs, material appliances, and natural objects," [4] many educators began to recognize the fallacy of separating mind from body. The emerging progressive literature on curriculum pointed to the inseparability of the cognitive processes from attitudes, emotions, physical well-being, and behavior. The conception of man as

---

3 Theodore P. Bank, "Physical Fitness from the Standpoint of the Army," *Proceedings, National War Fitness Conference* (Washington, D.C.: U.S. Government Printing Office, 1943), p. 29.

4 John Dewey, *Democracy and Education* (New York: The Macmillan Company, 1916), p. 377.

a unity called for a more comprehensive and unified curriculum. The legitimate place of health and recreation began to be recognized in physical education. In the words of Dewey:

> Recreation, as the word indicates, is recuperation of energy. No demand of human nature is more urgent or less to be escaped. The idea that the need can be suppressed is absolutely fallacious, and the Puritanic tradition which disallows the need has entailed an enormous crop of evils. If education does not afford opportunity for wholesome recreation and train capacity for seeking and finding it, the suppressed instincts find all sorts of illicit outlets. . . . Education has no more serious responsibility than making adequate provision for enjoyment of recreative leisure; not only for the sake of immediate health, but still more if possible for the sake of its lasting effect upon habits of mind.[5]

In refuting the ancient dualism between mind and body, Dewey also attacked the "social ruptures of continuity . . . such as that of labor and leisure, practical and intellectual activity, man and nature, individuality and association, culture and vocation." [6] The changing conception of man clearly called for a comprehensive curriculum that would serve the learner as a total being. The recognition of this essential unity came to be reflected in many statements on educational ends and means. For example, the Harvard Report of 1945 pointed to the necessity for the secondary school to be concerned with developing integrated and sound human beings through programs that foster not only intellectual development but the physical and mental health of pupils. Accordingly, "the human body must be healthy, fit for work, able to carry out the purposes of the mind." [7]

Changing Social Forces and Conditions

The elimination of child labor, the advent of compulsory education, the impact of science and technology on industrial productivity, the demands of the working classes for a more equitable share in the fruits of their labors—all called for a reconstruction of education to meet the requirements of a reconstructed society in twentieth-century America. The increase in leisure time for the masses was accompanied by a growing recognition of the school's legitimate role in developing the interests and abilities of youth to make worthy use of leisure time. For example, a midcentury statement by the NEA's Educational Policy Commission included in a list of ten "imperative needs of youth" the "need to de-

---

5 Dewey, *ibid.*, pp. 240–241.

6 *Ibid.*, p. 377.

7 Report of the Harvard Committee, *General Education in a Free Society* (Cambridge, Mass.: Harvard University Press, 1945), p. 168.

velop and maintain good health and physical fitness" and the "need to be able to use . . . leisure time well and to budget it wisely, balancing activities that yield satisfactions to the individual with those that are socially useful." [8]

Schramm's study of the television viewing habits of children and youth, conducted a decade ago, found that youngsters were devoting approximately one sixth of their waking hours to watching television.[9] On a year-round basis, this amounts to more time than is spent in school. No evidence has been presented since Schramm's research that shows any significant changes in the time devoted to TV viewing by children and youth. President Kennedy cited both television and the motion picture for inducing physical passivity among youth and adults, and blamed these media for contributing to the poor physical condition of our population.[10] Some critics of television observe that the medium "keeps young people from engaging in the physical activities and outdoor exercise which doctors and physical educators agree are desirable." [11] Moreover, television has been attacked for promoting spectator sports and the passive act of sitting.

> Sports used to be something wholesome that people did. Now it is something they watch. It now means passivity. . . . This tendency to keep viewers immobilized, as receptors of commercials, is particularly unfavorable for young children, who need activity for growing and learning. Simply sitting, for hours on end, is likely to have many adverse effects on young people aside from what they view during those hours. Other countries have limited the hours of television to permit more physical activity, yet United States broadcast leadership shows no evidence of changing its practices.[12]

Lifelong Needs. Studies of how adults spend their leisure time reveal that direct participation in physical recreational activity represents only a very minute fraction of the time devoted to vicarious participation in sporting events through television viewing and direct attendance.[13] Such findings point to the need for physical education programs in our schools to give concerted attention to activities that are likely to be continued into adulthood. Traditional programs, giving emphasis to dull

[8] Educational Policies Commission, *Education for ALL American Youth—A Further Look* (Washington, D.C.: National Education Association, 1952), p. 216.

[9] Wilbur Schramm, Jack Lyle, and Edwin B. Parker, *Television in the Lives of Our Children* (Stanford, Calif.: Stanford University Press, 1961).

[10] Harry J. Skornia, *Television and Society* (New York: McGraw-Hill Book Company, Inc., 1965), p. 164.

[11] *Ibid.*

[12] *Ibid.*, p. 165.

[13] Wynn F. Updike and Perry B. Johnson, *Principles of Modern Physical Education, Health, and Recreation* (New York: Holt, Rinehart and Winston, Inc., 1970), pp. 462–463.

physical drills and regimentation, create negative attitudes toward physical education, while gang-type sports have little carry-over into adult recreational practices other than possibly contributing to spectator interests.

This does not imply that spectating at sports events is, in itself, an undesirable activity. Anyone who maintains that the act of spectating is undesirable would have to condemn audiences at concerts, operas, and ballets. But what makes sports spectating undesirable is the enormous imbalance of leisure time devoted to it in proportion to direct participation in sports activities that actually contribute to our physical and psychical well-being.

Relationship to General Education and Social Problems.   The changing conception of man, the universalization of secondary schooling, the growing population mobility, and the increasing recognition of the importance of health in a modern technological society placed new demands on the function of the school in relation to the family and the community. Even the relatively conservative Harvard Report of 1945 stressed the legitimate function of the secondary school in providing for health instruction as an integral part of general education wherever the home is inadequate for such learnings.

> . . . the role of the school in the development of health may be decisive. Although the first responsibility in this matter rests with the family and community, in some places the schools must assume the task of giving direct instruction in health, personal or civic. For many young people the elementary facts about diet, rest, exercise, drugs, and disease will have to be learned away from home if they are to be learned at all. Such instruction may make the difference between a debilitated and a healthy community. The subject may take time from other pursuits of more central intellectual importance. But no educational or social system is sound unless it rests on solid physical foundations.[14]

Yet the cold war epoch that was to follow gave priority to the academically talented student and those academic pursuits deemed essential for our military and world-leadership needs. Forgotten for a time were the needs of the disadvantaged, as well as the personal and social health needs of all youth. We were unable to see the crises and disasters that lay ahead in our urban areas. Not until the late 1960's would our society come to look to the schools for help in stemming the adolescent drug epidemic and in providing programs in sex education for youth in a society of changing mores.

---

[14] Report of the Harvard Committee, *op. cit.,* pp. 174–175.

The Cold War Epoch

We have already discussed how, during times of war crises, the social objectives of physical education give way to the objective of physical fitness. In the wake of the cold war and the Korean conflict, the U.S. Office of Education and the American Association for Health, Physical Education, and Recreation (AAHPER) jointly sponsored the National Conference for the Mobilization of Education held in 1950 in Washington, D.C. As the result of the conference, a set of physical fitness standards for high school youth was prepared by the AAHPER Armed Forces Committee in cooperation with military authorities, and a Committee on Education for National Defense was designated. A subcommittee on physical education recommended that the schools emphasize activities designed to develop physical fitness and skills in self-protection and survival.

Fitness as a Recurrent Objective.   Physical fitness problems among members of the armed forces led to research, which in 1952 produced the Kraus-Weber Minimum Muscular Fitness Test. As discussed in earlier chapters, the decades of the 1950's and 1960's were marked by an unprecedented interest on the part of our educators and national leaders in comparing educational achievement in the United States with performance in other nations. In the same vein, a popular activity on the part of physical fitness researchers was to conduct standard comparative performance measurements of American and foreign children and youth. The finding that European children outperformed American children in the Kraus-Weber Test led President Eisenhower to establish the President's Council on Youth Fitness in 1956. It should be noted that the sample of American children was limited to states along the Atlantic seaboard and that the Kraus-Weber Test is an assessment of muscular fitness and not health. Moreover, where programs in European schools tended to stress fitness exercises, the American schools were favoring sports activities. Nevertheless, the findings of the Kraus-Weber Test comparisons, widely publicized in the American press, were reported to have "shocked" Eisenhower.[15]

Neglect of Health Needs.   Immediately following the establishment of the President's Council on Youth Fitness, the AAHPER moved to sponsor a nationwide test of school children and youth, resulting in the publication of the *Youth Fitness Manual* in 1958. A rash of new studies followed in which the AAHPER Youth Fitness Test and the Kraus-Weber Test were used in comparing performance standards of American young-

---

[15] Updike and Johnson, *op. cit.,* p. 28.

sters with those of other nations. One such study even showed that Pakistani school children outscored American youngsters,[16] but no mention was made of the fact that Americans enjoy better health and longer life expectancy than Pakistanis—although comparative data on health and life expectancy reveal that the United States lags behind the Scandinavian and northern European nations.[17] Nevertheless, the superior health and life-expectancy data for these latter nations in comparison to the United States cannot be attributed to their school programs of physical education, as these nations have medical-care programs that reach all citizens. Furthermore, these nations have virtually eliminated poverty and they have significantly lower rates of infant mortality than the United States.

The essential point is that, during the crisis of the cold war, the type of research undertaken in physical education and the interpretations of such research reflected a new urgency for fitness as the key to our nation's world-leadership role. Studies revealed that Americans boys and girls were deficient in arm and shoulder-girdle strength as measured through pull-ups. These findings were compared with fitness standards for our armed forces. National norms were established for various fitness measures on the AAHPER Youth Fitness Test. The avid interest of President Kennedy in physical fitness gave impetus to a national fitness program for the elementary and secondary schools. In addition to promoting fitness-test activities in the schools, the President's Council on Youth Fitness and the AAHPER recommended that the junior and senior high schools offer a regular class period daily for physical education.

The new obsession with fitness not only served to de-emphasize the social and recreational goals of our physical education programs, but largely ignored the urgent need for diagnostic, preventive, and remedial work connected with the general health problems of children and youth. None of the professional organizations raised objections to this narrow conception of physical education. On the contrary, they joined in promoting fitness as the prime and urgent goal.

New Curriculum Priorities

With the advent of the space age, new priorities were established in the curriculum. The cry now was for brain power—with science and mathematics receiving the lion's share of federal funding for curriculum reform and emphasis. Contrary to our historical experience with military

---

16 M. S. Kelliher, "A Report of the Kraus-Weber Test in East Pakistan," *Research Quarterly,* Vol. 31 (March, 1960).

17 *Demographic Yearbook* (New York: United Nations, Department of Economic and Social Affairs, 1969).

crises and the resultant emphasis on fitness, physical education and sports activities in the schools were now regarded in many quarters as curriculum frills. Ironically, it was one of our military leaders who, as a leading cold war and space age critic of American education, advocated that we de-emphasize body power in favor of brain power. According to Admiral Rickover, "The consequence of technological progress is that man must use his mind more and his body less. We still think in terms of a more primitive era; we overvalue physical prowess and undervalue intellectual competence." [18] Rickover went on to observe that "Sputnik may well be the catalyst which brings about drastic and long-overdue reforms in utilizing the nation's intellectual resources." [19] The concept of physical fitness as a commodity to be developed for national purposes was now replaced by the concept of mind power to be used for the same ends. Once again, mind was to be conceived as separate from body in the new urgency to develop and utilize our nation's intellectual resources.

Emphasis on Intellectual Resources. Where physical fitness traditionally was regarded as essential to our nation's defense, the National Defense Education Act of 1958 made no provision for physical education. Instead, NDEA focused on the discovery and development of our intellectual resources through the support of counseling and guidance programs in our schools, and curriculum improvement in areas deemed essential to our world-leadership role (science, mathematics, and modern foreign languages).

The highly influential Conant report of 1959 offered no specific recommendations concerning the nature and quality of the physical education program other than stressing the importance of organizing the school day into at least six periods "in addition to the required physical education and driver education which in many states occupy at least a period each day. . . . With a six-period day, one period of which is taken up by physical education, the academically talented student cannot elect the wide academic program recommended." [20] In acknowledging the practice, if not the requirement, in many states of providing a daily period in physical education, Conant's concern was to organize the school day into a sufficient number of periods to allow the academically talented student to pursue the wide academic program that Conant deemed appropriate. In a later report on the junior high school, Conant recommended that instruction in physical education be scheduled regularly each week in

[18] Hyman G. Rickover, *Education and Freedom* (New York: E. P. Dutton & Co., Inc., 1959), p. 17.
[19] *Ibid.,* p. 158.
[20] James B. Conant, *The American High School Today* (New York: McGraw-Hill Book Company, 1959), pp. 64–65.

grades 7 and 8, but observed that, for the warmer regions of our nation, "one can question whether in such areas the gymnasium is a necessity for satisfactory instruction." [21]

Although the Harvard Report of 1945, commissioned by Conant as President of Harvard University, included physical education as part of general education in our secondary schools, Conant chose not to categorize physical education with general education in his 1959 report on the high school. Conant's conception of general education was limited to those academic courses required of all students for high school graduation. And he made no mention of health education and recreation as essential aspects of the program in physical education.

Neglect and De-emphasis of Physical Education.
A number of reports began to appear recommending that less emphasis be given to physical education in our schools. For example, the San Francisco Curriculum Survey Committee, composed of liberal arts professors from Stanford University and the University of California at Berkeley, recommended that "physical education should be reduced to two or three times a week [and] . . . that a forceful attempt be made to change the present State requirement of five periods." [22]

The curriculum reform movement of the late 1950's and the decade of the 1960's eventually was extended to include a number of academic disciplines other than the sciences, mathematics, and modern foreign languages. However, the areas of physical education, health, and recreation were kept out of the mainstream of the reform movement during this period. Thus, in the report of the 1961 National Conference on Curriculum Experimentation, no mention was made of curriculum developments in physical education, health, or recreation. [23] Similarly, a 1964 review of the new curriculum projects had nothing to report in physical education and related areas. [24] Goodlad's review of curriculum projects, prepared for the Ford Foundation in 1966, made only brief mention of one project in health education, the School Health Education Study, supported through private funds and designed for grades K through 12. [25] Goodlad acknowledged the low status of health education in the school curriculum. He noted that health has never been a clearly defined study

21 James B. Conant, *Education in the Junior High School Years* (Princeton, N.J.: Educational Testing Service, 1960), p. 31.

22 *Report of the San Francisco Curriculum Survey Committee* (San Francisco: Board of Education, 1960), p. 12.

23 Paul C. Rosenbloom and Paul C. Hillestad (eds.), *Modern Viewpoints in the Curriculum* (New York: McGraw-Hill Book Company, 1964).

24 Robert W. Heath (ed.), *New Curricula* (New York: Harper & Row, Publishers, 1964).

25 John I. Goodlad, *The Changing School Curriculum* (New York: The Fund for the Advancement of Education, 1966), pp. 85–87.

in the schools, being considered a part of science in the elementary grades, and combined with physical education in the high school, where it "becomes the subject of discussion chiefly when inclement weather disrupts outdoor activities." [26]

Another matter that demands attention is the assumption on the part of physical educators that programs in physical education cannot be conducted successfully unless a class period is required daily of every student. Under such circumstances, students are left with little time for actual engagement in physical education activities, when so much of the class period is devoted to the changing of clothes, the taking of showers, and the performing of warm-up exercises. A promising solution is to provide larger modules or blocks of time for classes in physical education and to schedule such classes three days per week instead of five. Properly supervised, intramural athletics could also be scheduled so as to create a balanced program of physical activity throughout each week of the school year.

More attention also needs to be given to adapted or remedial programs for the physically handicapped youngster. Relatively few teachers have adequate training and interest in adapted physical education. As a consequence, schools sometimes exempt handicapped youngsters from physical education when these youngsters could derive incalculable benefit from adapted work.

CHANGING GOALS AND FUNCTIONS

We have seen how various societal pressures have influenced the goals and functions of physical education. Although the changing concept of man during the twentieth century led many educators to conceive of physical education as necessary for "complete living," at different times the goals and functions of physical education have been narrowed and pushed to the point of imbalance. In one epoch we are threatened with losing the cold war unless we are made physically fit. In another epoch, physical education is regarded as a curriculum "frill" which detracts from the goal of the school in developing our intellectual resources in the cold war era of science and technology. How to provide balanced and coherent programs in physical education to meet the developmental needs of youth and remain consistent with the ideals of a democratic society should be the major concern of physical educators. To regard the human organism as a machine to be honed for nationalistic purposes not only undermines the precepts of democracy but violates much of what we know about the nature of the human organism.

---

[26] *Ibid.*, p. 85.

Developmental Tasks and Physical Education

The theory of developmental tasks, advanced by Havighurst,[27] has particular relevance for those who see physical education as education for "complete living." The goal is the integrative development of the individual as a "whole" person in society. Learning experiences provided through the program in physical education presumably should be designed to foster healthful psycho-social-biological development. For the adolescent, this would include such vital developmental tasks as accepting one's physique and using the body effectively, achieving a masculine or feminine social role, achieving new and more mature relations with age-mates of both sexes, desiring and achieving socially responsible behavior, acquiring a set of values and an ethical system as a guide to behavior, and developing the intellectual skills and concepts necessary for civic competence.

Thus the goal of physical fitness is organic health, and not merely muscular strength. If the physical fitness activities engaged in at school are boring and distasteful to the adolescent, the program is self-defeating. Through the physical education program, adolescents can learn to appreciate the normality of variability and, consequently, can learn to accept and use their bodies effectively. Selected coeducational activities can help adolescents in achieving new and more mature relations with age-mates of both sexes, and in achieving a masculine or feminine role. Group activities, including team sports, can be designed and administered to emphasize socially responsible behavior, while contributing to the acquisition of desired values and an ethical system as a guide to behavior. And, if physical education is to be concerned with the integrated human being, it must contribute to the development of intellectual skills and understandings for personal and civic competence.

In too many physical education programs, the atmosphere is authoritarian or quasimilitary. Such an atmosphere, coupled with activities centered around mob drills and monotonous fitness exercises, results in negative attitudes toward physical education and serves to undermine the democratic goals that are espoused by the profession. Too many authoritarian societies have used physical education to serve nationalistic needs rather than personal and adolescent-group needs of a developmental nature. Our own society in recent years has too often been prone to apply pressures on the schools under conditions of national crisis. The result is that democratizing goals and adolescent needs are forgotten in the process.

Moreover, as discussed later in this chapter, a wide variety of learning activities in physical education, health, and recreation can contribute

---

[27] Robert J. Havighurst, *Development Tasks and Adolescence* (New York: Longmans, Green & Co., 1952).

significantly to the development of thinking skills and the attainment of new understandings and appreciations. But many problems will need to be solved if the physical education programs in our schools are to meet these important needs.

The Problem of Definition

For many years, a number of theorists in the field of physical education have contended that the rejection of the body-mind dualism and the conception of man as a unified organism require that physical education be renamed and redefined. In 1940, one writer proposed that this term be abandoned in favor of *sports education,* because human conduct cannot be separated into physical, mental, and social categories.[28] The question of nomenclature and definition has been a persistent one, and the theorists differ as to what must be done. For example, a contemporary theorist offers this criticism in proposing that the term *kinesiology* (the study of movement) be used.

> The concept of the totality and integrated nature of the human being negates the notion that education is a fractionated process of *mental* education on the one hand and *physical* education on the other. Education is concerned with the whole being and consists of learning modes that are based upon the interrelated cognitive, affective, and motor behaviors of man. There just cannot be a process called *physical education!* . . . Thus the term physical education should be discarded so that confusion will not be perpetuated and views of the field will not be too constricted.
>
> . . . I am reluctant to suggest a new name, but to be consistent with my beliefs and logical in their interpretation, I am forced to offer one: *kinesiology.*[29]

In each case, the change of nomenclature also calls for a change in the focus and content of the curriculum. Perhaps the real issue is the nature of the curriculum and not the label ascribed to the profession. After all, one could offer an identical argument against using the term *mental health,* because one's mental health cannot really be separated from one's general physical well-being. Indeed, authorities in the field of mental health embrace this unitary concept of the human organism. Yet use of the term *mental health* does not invalidate the work of theorists and practitioners in this field. The term simply denotes an area of focus in relation to other areas of human well-being, and consequently it serves a useful purpose. In view of the many serious problems in curriculum imbalance

---

[28] Seward C. Staley, *The Curriculum in Sports* (Champaign, Ill.: Stipes Publishing Company, 1940), p. 105.

[29] Marlin M. Mackenzie, *Toward a New Curriculum in Physical Education* (New York: McGraw-Hill Book Company, Inc., 1969), p. 9.

and fragmentation in physical education, it would seem that physical educators should give first priority to re-examining the curriculum while being less concerned with an appropriately prestigious label for the profession.

The Problem of Curriculum Imbalance and Fragmentation

Earlier in this chapter we discussed how pressures are exerted on the schools to embrace narrow goals in times of national crises—such as the emphasis given to physical fitness for military preparedness, or the de-emphasis given to physical education in favor of cognitive development for the nuclear and space-age era. The adolescent drug epidemic and our changing sexual mores have placed new demands on the schools to solve emerging social problems as we entered the decade of the 1970's. And the exploding interest in spectator sports on the part of the general public has produced added pressures on the schools to field winning varsity teams.

Need for Relationship and Coherence in the Total Curriculum. Added to these problems is the fragmented relationship among physical education, health education, and recreation in the curriculum. Furthermore, in many secondary schools, physical education is treated as a curriculum requirement that is separate from general education. The consequence is that no effort is made to correlate or integrate the treatment of topics that are common to several subject fields. For example, the study of problems of drug addiction or sex may occur in classes in health education, biology, and social studies, without any attempt on the part of teachers to develop the subject matter into a coherent framework. Yet another example is the place of dance in the curriculum. While dance activities are confined mainly to the field of physical education, the study of dance as an art form presents important implications for the curriculum areas of music, theater, and the humanities. In most secondary schools where some efforts are made to provide for ballet and modern dance, the activities are either limited to girls' physical education or to cocurricular programs. Coeducational dance activities within the framework of the curriculum in physical education can help adolescents not only in gaining new cultural appreciations, but in such developmental tasks as learning to accept and use their bodies effectively, achieving new and more mature relations with age-mates of both sexes, and achieving a masculine or feminine role.

Need for Relationship and Coherence in Physical Education. Turning again to the relationship among physical education, health education, and recreation, we find some educators who maintain that the rationales and functions for each of these areas are essentially different.[30] Thus, some authorities contend, for example, that health and physical education be taught as separate subjects, because "each has a unique contribution to make to the educational program: the two subjects have different content, different methodology, different problems, and different organizational relationships; are taught in different environments; and require different sets of competencies and skills from the teacher." [31] However, the authors fail to discuss the problem of how the study of health education as a separate course would relate to the treatment of health topics in other courses in the secondary school curriculum, such as biology, social studies, homemaking, and physical education. Also, to separate health objectives from physical fitness and recreation is ridiculous. This does not mean that these areas should be regarded as synonymous. But they do share closely related objectives and consequently should not be treated as fragmented and isolated subject matters. Yet there are specialists who insist on curriculum separateness and hold that the "time allotment for health education or health science should be in keeping with other essential subject fields in the curriculum." [32]

As knowledge becomes increasingly specialized, the specialists demand that their particular domains of knowledge be identified as separate and essential subjects in the curriculum of the secondary school. Ironically, the widely accepted premise that the learner be treated as an integrated being is contradicted by proposals that call for the strict separation of health education from physical education, recreation, and other subjects in the curriculum.

The Problem of Focus on Curriculum Content

Closely related to the problems just discussed is the matter of curriculum focus. We have also noted that some educators maintain that the many disparate elements in physical education, health education, and recreation require that we scrap our present approach and replace it with a singular unifying subject matter of *kinesics,* with kinesiology serving as the new name for physical education.[33] The entire curriculum in physical education would then be focused on the singular and unifying study of human movement. It is contended that such a focus would bring the

---

[30] *Ibid.,* p. 7.

[31] Edward B. Johns and Marion B. Pollack, "Health Education," Chapter 5 in Forrest E. Conner and William J. Ellena (eds.), *Curriculum Handbook for School Administrators* (Washington, D.C.: American Association of School Administrators, 1967), p. 109.

[32] *Ibid.*

[33] Mackenzie, *op. cit.,* p. 10.

field of physical education into the mainstream of curriculum reform through an emphasis on the structure of a unified body of knowledge or discipline, as proposed by Bruner.[34]

> If we are to survive as an effective, contributing, educational agency, we must accept the obligation to become experts in the unique subject matter of our profession: *human physical activity* in all of its ramifications and implications. The current emphasis is on determining the logical boundaries for the discipline. Although agreement has not been reached on details, it seems evident that our profession is moving rapidly toward defining its overall concern in terms of "man in motion." [35]

Structure and Specialization.   Not only are there many unanswered questions concerning the validity of the notion of structure for an area as broad as physical education, not to mention the more specialized areas of knowledge or disciplines, but kinesics represents a specialized perspective of man. Consequently, it becomes another specialized subject in the curriculum. Thus we find proposals that not only call for the replacement of physical education with kinesiology, but that require that kinesiology be offered as a discipline entirely apart from other areas normally treated in the broad field of physical education. A 1967 curriculum publication of the American Association of School Administrators presents physical education and health education in separate and unrelated chapters, and treats physical education only as the study of "the discipline of human movement." [36]

Kinesiology represents a legitimate attempt to understand important aspects of human behavior. In recent years, there has been a growing body of literature in this field. With regard to subject matter content, one proposal identifies seven major classifications for the study of human movement: (1) movement forms (descriptions of sports and dances, strategies of competition, instruments and surroundings); (2) mechanical principles of movement (isometric and isotonic contractions; gravity, inertia, force, and leverage; positioning and movement for specific tasks); (3) structure and function of the moving human organism (anatomy, physiology, environmental conditions); (4) movement and the person (personality, group dynamics, aesthetics, nonverbal communication); (5) learning how to move (motor learning); (6) movement and health; and (7) movement and meaning (interpretations of movement).[37]

---

34 *Ibid.*, pp. xi, 59–60.

35 Updike and Johnson, *op. cit.*, p. 22.

36 Camille Brown and Rosalind Cassidy, "Physical Education," Chapter 10 in *Curriculum Handbook for School Administrators, op. cit.*, p. 206.

37 Mackenzie, *op. cit.*, p. 17.

Eclectic Nature of Physical Education. Kinesiology can offer adolescents many valuable insights concerning all aspects of human movement, including various biomechanical aspects of sports, dance, and psychomotor learning. But the notion that kinesiology is the singular and unifying solution to the problem of defining and selecting appropriate subject matter in the eclectic field of physical education needs to be explored more critically. As an effort to intellectualize the curriculum in physical education, it may be superimposing a type of academic discipline on a field that was conceived to provide adolescents with relief from the overly verbalized academic curriculum and its instruments of talk, chalk, and textbook. Surely certain aspects of kinesiology have a legitimate place in the curriculum, but to reduce physical education to another academicism in the secondary school is likely to lead to more problems than solutions.

CONTEMPORARY SOCIAL PROBLEMS AND THE CURRICULUM

The emergence of serious social problems invariably results in new pressures on the schools to provide systematic instruction for the prevention and treatment of these problems. The inability of the family and various nonschool agencies to solve these problems places the school in the position of being open to criticism for ignoring the needs of youth and society or of attempting to do too much in the name of education. In 1902 Dewey observed that various agencies of social control—the home, the church, and other forms of constituted authority—were losing their effectiveness and that other agencies, namely the schools, will be called upon to repair the loss.

> There has come a relaxation on the bonds of social discipline and control. I suppose none of us would be willing to believe that the movement away from dogmatism and fixed authority was anything but a movement in the right direction. . . . We may feel sure that in time independent judgment, with the individual freedom and responsibility that go with it, will more than make good the temporary losses. But meantime there is a temporary loss. Parental authority has much less influence in controlling the conduct of children. . . . The church . . . finds its grasp slowly slipping away from it. We might as well frankly recognize that many of the old agencies for moralizing mankind, and of keeping them living decent, respectable and orderly lives are losing in efficiency—particularly, those agencies which rested for their force upon custom, tradition, and unquestioning acceptance. It is impossible for a society to remain purely a passive spectator in the midst of such a scene. It must search for other agencies with which it may repair the loss, and which the former methods are failing to secure. Here, too, it is not enough for society to confine its work to children. However much they

may need the disciplinary training of a widened and enlightened education, the older generation needs it also.[38]

As we entered the 1970's, renewed demands were being made on the schools to solve a variety of exploding social problems. The 1950's and 1960's had been largely a period in which the crises of the cold war and the space age created a new priority for curriculum development in certain academic disciplines. The narrowing of the curriculum focus was accompanied by pressures to eliminate some of the broader social functions of the school—functions which had emerged during the progressive education era of the 1930's and 1940's. But this retrenchment proved to be largely a temporary measure. Not only have high school and college students of the 1960's and 1970's been clamoring for curriculum relevance, but certain societal agencies are increasingly demanding that our educational institutions grapple directly with many exploding social problems.

In the area of health education, two illustrative social problems of contemporary urgency are drugs and sex education. Yet both of these problems can and should be treated in other areas of the curriculum, such as biology and the social studies, as well as in health education. However, as pointed out earlier in this chapter, relatively little effort has been made to bring about the needed correlation or integration of the curriculum.

Health Education and Narcotics

Over the years, many efforts have been made to identify the areas to be included in the curriculum of health education. A 1948 joint report of the NEA and AMA failed to include such areas as tobacco, drugs, sex education, and consumer health education in a list of twelve areas of health education.[39] Even as recently as 1964, a national study of health education failed to identify drugs as a problem area requiring emphasis in the curriculum, although the study recommended the inclusion of the following: alcohol, community health, consumer health, environmental hazards (safety), health careers, international health, nutrition and weight control, sex education and family life, veneral disease, and smoking.[40]

Until recently, the use of narcotics was regarded mainly as a problem concentrated in the nonwhite populations of our urban ghettos. However,

---

38 John Dewey, "The School as a Social Center," in National Education Association *Proceedings* (Chicago: The University of Chicago Press, 1902), pp. 377–378.

39 Report of the Joint Committee of the National Education Association and the American Medical Association (Washington, D.C.: National Education Association, 1948), pp. 237–238.

40 Elena M. Sliepcevich, *Summary Report of a Nationwide Study of Health Instruction in the Public Schools* (Washington, D.C.: School Health Education Study, 1964), pp. 38–39.

it is now recognized as a problem among college and school youth from a wide range of socioeconomic backgrounds. Nevertheless, the rates of addiction and fatalities continue to be highest in the disadvantaged populations of our major cities. In 1970 the use of narcotics among school children and youth reached such acute proportions in New York City that the mayor described the schools of his city as "the training ground for the next generation of addicts," and announced that a drug-education program was being instituted in the city's schools.[41] Although the problem did not begin in the schools, the schools were expected to help solve the problem. Another report revealed that narcotics addiction was found to be the leading cause of death in the fourteen-to-thirty-five age group in New York City, with the rate of narcotics fatalities among teenagers having increased more than 700 per cent over a three-year period.[42]

Course Proliferation. Citing various surveys, which revealed that one third of the students in New Jersey high schools have smoked marijuana at least once, the governor of that state called for legislation requiring a course in drug abuse for every new teacher, and that a course dealing with this problem be made mandatory in all public secondary schools.[43]

There is no limit to the number of courses that can be added to the requirements of the secondary school curriculum as a response to social problems and crises. To prevent course proliferation, it would be desirable to incorporate the treatment of such problems as narcotics within the existing curriculum framework. Thus, the problem of narcotics could be included as part of a problem-centered core curriculum, as well as in the health education course, the biology course, and in the social studies program. But there is a critical need to correlate or integrate the material so that comprehensive treatment is provided without unnecessary duplication. And the instruction must be made realistic rather than moralistic if it is to do more than simply conform to state requirements.

The Discipline-Centered Curriculum. While we have noted that the problem of narcotics is relevant to the subject of biology, as well as to health education and the social studies, the discipline-centered curriculum projects in biology and the social studies have tended to ignore this topic. Of the three versions of the Biological Sciences Curriculum Study (BSCS), only the Yellow version makes some mention of narcotics—and this is limited to three brief sentences in a textbook of 840 pages.[44] Even the efforts to produce integrated and problem-centered or issue-centered pro-

---

41 *The New York Times* (February 8, 1970), p. 1.

42 *The New York Times* (February 22, 1970), p. 37.

43 *The New York Times* (April 28, 1970), p. 33.

44 Biological Sciences Curriculum Study, *Biological Science: An Inquiry into Life,* 2nd ed. (New York: Harcourt, Brace & World, 1968), pp. 452, 662.

grams in the social studies often ignore the important and highly contro-versial problem of narcotics.[45]

The report of a national seminar on "High School Students and Drugs," sponsored by the Kettering Foundation's Institute for Develop-ment of Educational Activities (IDEA)—an organization whose major concern until now has been the promotion of educational efficiency through management and technology—recommended that NSF sponsor several national drug-abuse curricula similar to the cold war inspired projects in the sciences and mathematics.[46] It is unfortunate that a crisis syndrome is required for marshaling the financial resources and expertise needed to support curriculum change. Under such circumstances, instead of effecting changes coherently through various areas of the curriculum, the tendency is to impose a series of specialized super-courses on an al-ready proliferated curriculum. Furthermore, until now, the National Science Foundation's interests in the curriculum have focused mainly on discipline-centered projects for the development of budding scientists, mathematicians, and technologists. Drug abuse is not centered in any discipline. It is a social problem that has relevance for many curriculum fields, and must be treated in the curriculum in an integrated and coherent way.

Sex Education

Although public and professional opinion is overwhelmingly in favor of sex education in the schools, many conservative groups have fought to keep sex education out of the schools. In addition to the various conserva-tive lay organizations, opposition to sex education in the schools has been voiced over the years by essentialists, such as Arthur Bestor, who have argued that sex education is the responsibility of the home.

> Much of the cant about education for "home and family living" is a disguised way of saying that the school must take the responsibility for things that the family today is supposedly failing to do. If family life is in a parlous state, that is a national calamity. But it does not mean that we can or should reproduce its intimacies in the schoolroom. Even if it were true, for example, that parents are not giving adequate sex instruction to their children (and I suspect that they are giving it more fully and explicitly than in any earlier period), does anyone seriously expect an embarrassed schoolteacher to explain the physiology of human reproduction to boys and girls in public, and to use franker and more explicit terms than their parents are willing to employ in private? [47]

45 Donald W. Oliver and James P. Shaver, *Teaching Public Issues in the High School* (Boston: Houghton Mifflin Company, 1966).

46 Report of the National Seminar, *High School Students and Drugs* (Dayton, Ohio: Institute for Development of Educational Activities, Inc., 1970).

47 Arthur Bestor, *The Restoration of Learning* (New York: Alfred A. Knopf, Inc., 1956), p. 119.

But the problem of global overpopulation, the rise in illegitimate births and venereal disease among teenagers, and the growing divorce rates have become matters of social concern that cannot be limited to the privacy of the family. Scientists have warned that the world's ecological balance is threatened by the exploding human population.

Turning again to adolescent problems, New York City's Board of Education reported an increase of 100 per cent in pregnancies among unmarried schoolgirls in grades 7 through 12 during the 1960's, and recommended that the city provide funds for the establishment of special school centers for the thousands of youngsters who are found to be pregnant each year.[48]

Like Bestor, many educational critics have confused reproduction education with sex education. Although reproduction has been treated as a topic for many years in secondary school courses in general science and biology, the systematic teaching of sex education has been another matter. On the whole, the schools have avoided any systematic effort to counteract the bombardment of negative influences from our culture. But such avoidance does not prevent sex education from occurring, whether in desirable or undesirable forms, beginning with the earliest stages of childhood.

A number of secondary schools have attempted to integrate sex education into the curriculum in health education, with some success. Nevertheless, the health educator should also work closely with teachers of biology, general science, homemaking, social studies, physical education, and any other area of the curriculum where sex education has relevance. The preparation of competent teachers is a serious challenge. An Arthur Bestor may find the subject of sex education embarrassing, but this does not mean that competent professionals cannot be made available to provide needed instruction in the physical, psychological, social, and ethical aspects of human sexuality.

Other Areas of Health Education

The rise in alcoholism, the relationship of cigarette smoking to cancer and circulatory diseases, and the problem of inadequate nutrition have all become matters of national concern. The result is that the schools are no longer able to ignore these and other health problems of society. Through health education and other subjects in the curriculum, the secondary schools are expected to provide some systematic instruction in various aspects of personal and social health needs.

However, it is no longer realistic to provide for book learning on health in the absence of actual diagnostic and corrective health measures. Comprehensive and periodic medical and dental examinations along with prompt referral and follow-up must be provided for all children and

---

[48] *The New York Times* (February 18, 1970), p. 50.

youth. If other agencies of society do not meet these needs, the schools will be called upon to do so simply because they, more than any other institution of society, reach virtually all children and youth.

Health and Learning. Yet, as recently as 1967, the prevailing attitude of the American Medical Association, as expressed in the inaugural address of its president, was that the medical profession must oppose the concept that health care is "a right rather than a privilege." [49] This position is indefensible when one considers that personal physical and mental health have an important bearing on learning and that an individual's health status can seriously affect the health of the group of which he is a member. Furthermore, the child and adolescent are particularly vulnerable to health problems because they are in the formative stages of development and because their position in society leaves them without the power to exercise any direct choice in their medical and dental care.

Mental Health. Another area of increasing concern in society and school is the problem of mental health. Although topics concerning the emotional adjustment of adolescents are normally discussed in health education classes, the promotion of good mental health should be a total school function. Classroom teachers in all subject fields must be sensitive to the adjustment needs of adolescents. Teachers can contribute a great deal toward fostering good mental health, though more teachers need to recognize the degree to which mental health problems impair learning. The schools need to provide effective counseling programs and psychological services so that teachers are assured of competent follow-up of all referrals.

A review of the studies on mental disorders finds that "approximately 10 per cent of our public school children are mental health problems." [50] Some mental health experts see the schools as the logical focus for a national program of mental health because the schools provide access to virtually all children and youth, there is a high incidence of mental health problems in this age group, and early diagnosis and treatment enhance the possibilities for success. However, others hold that "the primary and distinctive function of the school in our society is not to promote mental health and personality development but to foster intellectual growth and the assimilation of knowledge." [51] But to raise an issue as to whether intellectual development or mental health should be the prime focus of schooling is simply creating a straw man. Because mental health has

---

[49] *The New York Times* (June 26, 1967), p. 13.

[50] Eli M. Bower, "Mental Health," in Robert L. Ebel (ed.), *Encyclopedia of Educational Research,* 4th ed. (New York: The Macmillan Company, 1969), p. 817.

[51] David P. Ausubel, *Educational Psychology: A Cognitive View* (New York: Holt, Rinehart and Winston, Inc., 1968), p. 411.

important bearings on cognitive development and academic success, the schools cannot ignore psychological problems that interfere with learning. Nor can the schools perform their educational functions effectively if, unwittingly or otherwise, they make unproductive and unrealistic demands on adolescents. According to Bower, "Competence in meeting the demands of school probably supersedes other factors affecting mental health." [52] Even in higher education we find increasing concern and effort to provide diagnostic and therapeutic services for troubled students. If such services are deemed necessary for college students, it makes no sense to ignore the needs of secondary school youngsters. Moreover, by taking preventative and constructive measures at the earlier stages of human development, the chances for success are enhanced considerably.

Safety Education

Accidents are the leading cause of death in the period from early childhood to age thirty-seven and, consequently, the schools have been expected to provide instruction in safety.[53] Safety education takes place in a wide variety of school activities, whether in the laboratory, gymnasium, industrial-arts or homemaking class. Although some secondary schools offer a separate course in safety, the problem of accident prevention is relevant to so many areas of the curriculum that it is unrealistic to compartmentalize the treatment of safety within a single course.

Driver Education. The automobile has become such a central part of American life and has been such a compelling attraction to adolescents that most of our larger high schools offer course work in driver and traffic-safety education including at least thirty hours of classroom instruction plus laboratory or practice-driving lessons. The National Study of Secondary School Evaluation identifies the following elements to be included in driver education in addition to laboratory instruction: driver behavior and physical characteristics (reaction time, vision and perception, effects of alcohol and drugs), rules of the road, physical principles in relation to the automobile, good pedestrian practices, attitudes, and automobile maintenance.[54]

An increasing number of high schools are arranging for commercial instructors to provide for the on-the-road training, while teachers are in charge of the classroom phase of the program. Although the connection between driver education in the high school and the reduction of auto-

[52] Bower, *op. cit.,* p. 821.

[53] Norman Key, "Safety Education," Chapter II in *Curriculum Handbook for Administrators, op. cit.,* p. 227.

[54] National Study of Secondary School Evaluation, *Evaluative Criteria,* 4th ed. (Washington, D.C.: American Council on Education, 1969), p. 89.

mobile accidents has been difficult to establish scientifically, many insurance companies offer a lower rate to adolescent drivers who have successfully completed a driver-education course in high school.

Criticisms. Essentialist critics of our secondary schools frequently point to driver education as a curriculum frill that should be provided outside the school. In his Pulitzer Prize-winning work, Hofstadter criticized the new ("life-adjustment") educators for the range and content of the courses offered by the schools where "it is deemed important that the pupil learn, not chemistry, but the testing of detergents; not physics, but how to drive and service a car; not history, but the operation of the local gas works; not biology, but the way to the zoo." [55] Although such accusations are overdrawn to the extent of foolishness, they have exerted considerable influence among academicians who view with suspicion or disdain any attempt on the part of the school to deal with problems of personal and social utility. Whatever the pros and cons, however, the schools have simply reacted to the demands and pressures of society in instituting courses that attempt to deal with pervading social problems —from automobile slaughter to drug abuse.

Intramural Sports

A great deal has been written about the need to develop program balance in our high schools in physical education, interscholastic athletics, and intramural sports. Where interscholastic athletics are limited to our most talented athletes, intramural sports are intended to provide opportunities for direct participation on the part of the total student body.

However, in too many schools, the varsity program receives first priority in financial support, professional staffing, and availability of physical facilities and other resources. Moreover, few intramural programs encompass a sufficient variety of activities to enhance lifelong recreational interests of a wholesome nature. Most intramural programs are limited to some touch football, basketball, softball, volleyball, and soccer. As in the case of the program in physical education, opportunities are rarely provided for individual, dual, or small-group activities, which are more likely to be carried into adulthood—such as swimming, tennis, or golfing.

Unless the varsity and intramural activities are carefully related to the total instructional program in physical education, the present state of chaotic imbalance will persist and the needs of most of our students will continue to be ignored. Our schools must do more than pay lip service to student participation and to meeting the need for developing wholesome lifelong recreational interests, skills, and commitments.

[55] Richard Hofstadter, *Anti-intellectualism in American Life* (New York: Alfred A. Knopf, Inc., 1963), p. 356.

Overemphasis on Interscholastic Sports

The growing interest in spectator sports and the overemphasis on varsity athletics in the high school were discussed briefly at the opening of this chapter. Veblen observed that "the relation of football to physical culture is much the same as that of the bull-fight to agriculture." [56] Yet, as Veblen pointed out before the turn of the century, those who seek to justify large-scale athletic contests under school and college sponsorship invariably claim that such activities are invaluable for developing the contestant's character and physique while strengthening the spirit of the community.[57] Historically, similar advantages have been attributed to war, though it must be acknowledged that sports are infinitely safer for all concerned.

Varsity athletics have served as a reasonably healthful (or harmless) outlet for some of our predatory impulses, though in recent years the massive demonstrations and riots in our schools and colleges have coupled the need for fulfilling the atavistic impulses with the need for ideological protest. Neither the sports contest nor the panty raid could claim the function of ideological expression and fulfillment. Obviously, our educational institutions and units of government much prefer the less disturbing and highly regulated sports activities to these other forms of massive social demonstration.

College Influences. Many colleges and universities also find the particular sports of football and basketball financially lucrative while, at the same time, such sports activities serve as professional or vocational preparation for our more precocious and aspiring athletes who are bent on sports careers. By the same token, the high schools serve as the training grounds for collegiate athletics. Our precocious athletes in high school find themselves bombarded by the colleges with athletic scholarship offers of bewildering temptation. The competition for athletic talent by the colleges has become so vigorous that various regulatory or "fair-trade" agreements have been established. Academicians in the universities who view with snobbish disdain the overemphasis on varsity athletics in the high schools would do well to examine the climate and mechanisms in higher educational institutions and in society which create such overemphasis.

Community Relations. Although it can be argued convincingly that interscholastic sports provide special opportunities for developing the talents of precocious athletes, enormous benefits are to be reaped in improved school-community relations. Many schools have equipped their

---

[56] Thorstein Veblen, *The Theory of the Leisure Class* (New York: The Macmillan Company, 1899), p. 261.
[57] *Ibid.*

football fields with lights and conduct their basketball games at night when community attendance is likely to be greater. It is clear that varsity athletics serve the demands of the adult community at least as much as they serve the needs of the gifted athlete, though it must also be conceded that these contests perform a useful function in developing school spirit and in detracting the spectator student from other mischief. The important role of interscholastic athletics as an expression of community spirit is cited by Coleman:

> Communities, like schools without interscholastic games, have few common goals. They fight no wars, seldom engage in community rallies, and are rarely faced with such crises as floods or tornadoes that can engender a communal spirit and make members feel close to one another by creating collective goals. One of the few mechanisms by means of which this can occur is that of games or contests between communities. Sometimes these games are between professional teams representing the communities. More often, they are high school games, and these contests serve the purpose admirably. The community supports the team, and the team rewards the community when it wins. The team is a community enterprise; its successes are shared by the community, and its losses mourned in concert.[58]

Is it any wonder, then, that communities will invest far more in athletic facilities for team sports in the high schools than in school libraries?

Democratization. Another important aspect of varsity athletics, often overlooked by critics, is their democratizing influence in bringing together students of varied socioeconomic backgrounds and academic abilities. Students of relatively low academic achievement and socioeconomic background can gain high status and recognition in the school and community through outstanding performance in varsity athletics. Although the programs in physical education and intramural athletics also serve to break down the barriers created in the academic phases of the curriculum through ability grouping and tracking, varsity athletics are unmatched by any other program or function of the school for building the status of adolescent boys. And, as Coleman observes, "If it were not for interscholastic athletics or something like it, the rebellion against school, the rate of dropout, and the delinquency of boys might be far worse than they presently are." [59]

Relationship to the Academic Studies. How to create enthusiasm for academic activity comparable to that shown for athletics has been a matter of concern of many educators. Coleman notes that one of the problems lies

---

[58] James S. Coleman, *Adolescents and the Schools* (New York: Basic Books, Inc., 1965), p. 50.
[59] *Ibid.,* p. 45.

in the fact that where varsity athletics represent cohesive group effort, academic studies are predicated on divisive interpersonal competition. He proposes that we revise our emphasis on interpersonal competition and pressures for grades by stressing group projects, contests, and games of an intellectual or academic nature both within the school and between schools.[60] To some extent, this has been attempted through science projects and fairs, debating teams, music competitions, and public-speaking contests—although not on a scale envisioned by Coleman.

Undoubtedly, curriculum workers would benefit greatly by studying such possibilities. Nevertheless, where play and athletic games appear to be natural expressions of our atavistic impulses, bookish learning is an entirely different form of human behavior. The book and the pigskin are both symbolic of the school, but this is where their resemblance ends.

SUMMARY

Although physical education has become a universal requirement in the secondary school, there is much confusion and conflict of opinion regarding the goals, functions, program content, and relationship of this field to the general education curriculum. The problem of imbalance and lack of coherence among physical education, health education, and athletics requires concerted attention. The curriculum goals in physical education are ambitiously comprehensive and include biological, social, cultural, cognitive, affective, and aesthetic needs. Yet the problem of imbalance and disjointedness in the program of study and activity has served to undermine such comprehensive objectives.

Too many programs fail to provide learning activities for the development of lifelong recreational interests, skills, and commitments. Inadequate attention is given to individual and small-group instruction to meet the variable needs of the normal adolescent and the adapted needs of the physically handicapped youngster. The national concern for physical fitness has led to a distorted emphasis on tests of muscular strength and monotonous physical drills, which produces negative attitudes on the part of adolescents toward physical education. Moreover, physical fitness has not been linked successfully in the curriculum with health needs. Very often fitness and health are treated as virtually separate areas of the curriculum. And our schools have neglected to meet the health needs of developing adolescents through diagnostic, remedial, and preventive medical services.

The curriculum in health education has not been adequately supported to meet the changing problems and dislocations in society. Many parents and political leaders are demanding that the schools assume a responsibility for sex education and provide instruction on drug abuse. Since the

---

[60] *Ibid.,* pp. 84–85.

new curricula in biology are discipline-centered rather than problem-centered, virtually no attention is given to the personal and social dangers of narcotics. And, instead of sex education, we have reproduction education in these biology courses. Similar omissions and inadequacies are found in the discipline-centered curricula in the social studies. The growing demands for the study of these social problems require a careful reappraisal, not only of the curriculum in health education, but of the relationship of health education to all other areas of the school curriculum.

If we are to deal effectively with these and other problems of adolescence and society, we must not conceive of physical and health education as areas that are entirely separated from the academic phases of the school curriculum. The solution is not to make physical and health education imitative of the discipline-centered approaches in certain academic studies. Imitative intellectuality will not meet these important health and life needs. Instead, the curriculum in health and physical education must deal authentically with learning problems, while functioning in concert with other relevant studies in the school. Those who propose that the total curriculum in physical education be reconstructed to focus on the specialized area of kinesiology, or the study of human movement, must take care that they are not merely substituting another academicism for physical education. While the study of human movement can make important contributions to our understanding of the human organism, the goals and functions of physical education must be comprehensive rather than discipline-centered if the personal and social needs of the developing adolescent are to be dealt with effectively.

Relatively little effort has been made to analyze the validity of the grade placement of activities and studies in physical education and health in accordance with the psychomotor, affective, and cognitive development of adolescents. In addition, little attention has been given to the need for developing coeducational classes for appropriate activities in physical and health education.

Many programs suffer from a lack of adequate resources and facilities for the average student while, at the same time, the program of varsity sports is very well endowed to develop the talents of the precocious athlete. The blame does not rest entirely with physical educators. Powerful community influences create an imbalance of priorities. And the commercial exploitation of varsity athletics in colleges and universities serves as a poor model for our high schools.

Physical education and recreation have an advantage over other areas of the school curriculum in being closely tied to the life impulses of the normal adolescent. Academicians have often envied the enthusiasm that adolescents display when engaged in sports. Whether such enthusiasm can become manifest in the academic phases of the curriculum through applications of game theory and team projects remains to be seen. But, in any case, physical educators would do well to capitalize on the natural propensities and concerns of adolescents.

PROBLEMS FOR STUDY AND DISCUSSION

1. Coleman observes that "athletics is wholly outside the focus of attention of many educators in schools of education, for whom curriculum variations have overriding importance. Yet athletics is central to the attention of adolescents, far more so than curriculum variations. And, despite educators' professional disinterest, athletics is an activity promoted by the schools themselves—not an outside interest like cars and dates." [James C. Coleman, *Adolescents and the Schools* (New York: Basic Books, Inc., 1965), p. 45.] How do you account for this seeming inconsistency and paradox?

2. Do you believe that it is possible to engender enthusiasm for academic studies comparable to that displayed by adolescents for sports by adapting certain team and project competitions as proposed by Coleman? Why or why not?

3. How do you account for the failure of the new high school biology (BSCS) and many of the curriculum reform projects in the social studies to deal with the problems of drug abuse and sex education? What should be the relationship among health education, general science, biology, the social studies, homemaking, and other subjects in dealing with these and other health problems affecting adolescents and society?

4. Do you agree with Bestor that sex education is strictly a family responsibility and has no place in the school? Why or why not? [Arthur Bestor, *The Restoration of Learning* (New York: Alfred A. Knopf, Inc., 1956), p. 119.]

5. What is your opinion of this position? "Imparting health knowledge is the primary responsibility of health educators—not of physical educators." [James A. Baley and David A. Field, *Physical Education and the Physical Educator* (Boston: Allyn and Bacon, Inc., 1970), p. 3.]

6. Dewey emphasized that "education has no more serious responsibility than making adequate provision for enjoyment of recreative leisure; not only for the sake of immediate health, but still more if possible for the sake of its lasting effect upon habits of mind." [John Dewey, *Democracy and Education* (New York: The Macmillan Company, 1916), p. 241.] How might recreative leisure contribute significantly to "habits of mind" or cognitive development?

7. How might the curriculum in physical education and recreation make a more significant contribution to lifelong recreational interests of a wholesome nature?

8. Various presidents of the United States have promoted physical fitness as the primary goal of physical education in our schools. Do you see any limitations in such emphasis? Explain.

9. In contrast to the land-grant universities of the West, which recognized the importance of coeducation from their inception, many of the Ivy League colleges did not discover the value of coeducation until the late 1960's and early 1970's. In addition to instituting coeducational classes in the academic studies, a number of these colleges have developed coeducational classes in areas of physical education. What should be the nature and extent of coeducational classes in physical education and health education in the secondary school?

SELECTED REFERENCES

American Educational Research Association. "Mental and Physical Health," *Review of Educational Research,* Vol. 38 (December, 1968).

Baley, James A., and David A. Field. *Physical Education and the Physical Educator.* Boston: Allyn and Bacon, Inc., 1970.

Beisser, Arnold R. *The Madness in Sports.* New York: Appleton-Century-Crofts, 1967.

Coleman, James S. *Adolescents and the Schools.* New York: Basic Books, Inc., 1965.

Conant, James B. *The American High School Today.* New York: McGraw-Hill Book Company, Inc., 1959.

Conner, Forrest E., and William J. Ellena (eds.). *Curriculum Handbook for School Administrators.* Washington, D.C.: American Association of School Administrators, 1967. Chs. 5, 10, 11.

Daughtrey, Greyson. *Methods in Physical Education and Health for Secondary Schools.* Philadelphia: W. B. Saunders Company, 1967.

Educational Policies Commission. *Education for ALL American Youth— A Further Look.* Washington, D.C.: National Education Association, 1952.

Hackensmith, C. W. *History of Physical Education.* New York: Harper & Row, Publishers, 1966.

Havighurst, Robert J. *Developmental Tasks and Education.* New York: Longmans, Green & Co., 1952.

Kozman, Hilda C., Rosalind Cassidy, and Chester O. Jackson. *Methods in Physical Education,* 4th ed. Dubuque, Iowa: William C. Brown Company, 1967.

Locke, Lawrence F. *Research in Physical Education: A Critical View.* New York: Teachers College Press, 1969.

Mackenzie, Marlin M. *Toward a New Curriculum in Physical Education.* New York: McGraw-Hill Book Company, Inc., 1969.

Mayshark, Cyrus. "Health Education" in Robert L. Ebel (ed.). *Encyclopedia of Educational Research,* 4th ed. New York: The Macmillan Company, 1969, pp. 579–589.

Montoye, Henry J., and David A. Cunningham. "Physical Education," in Robert L. Ebel (ed.). *Encyclopedia of Educational Research,* 4th ed. New York: The Macmillan Company, 1969, pp. 963–973.

Mosston, Muska. *Teaching Physical Education.* Columbus, Ohio: Charles E. Merrill Books, Inc., 1966.

Skornia, Harry J. *Television and Society.* New York: McGraw-Hill Book Company, Inc., 1965. Ch. 7.

Updike, Wynn F., and Perry B. Johnson. *Principles of Modern Physical Education, Health, and Recreation.* New York: Holt, Rinehart and Winston, Inc., 1970.

Veblen, Thorstein. *The Theory of the Leisure Class.* New York: The Macmillan Company, 1899.

Chapter 10

Curriculum Change in Vocational and Industrial Arts Education

"By a peculiar superstition," wrote Dewey, "education which has to do chiefly with preparation for the pursuit of conspicuous idleness, for teaching, and for literary callings, and for leadership, has been regarded as nonvocational and even as peculiarly cultural." [1]

A strange dualism persists to this day between the liberal (academic) studies and the practical (vocational) studies. While this dualism had its origin in ancient Greece, where cultural or liberal education was the province of the free man and practical training was relegated to the slave, many of our intelligentsia deprecate the vocational studies even in a society where virtually all men, regardless of social status, are part of the workaday world.

Oddly, this ancient dualism has faded away in our colleges and universities, where it is perfectly respectable for a student to receive vocational preparation as an aspiring physicist, engineer, economist, accountant, and so on. For such students, the high school will have no difficulty in prescribing the necessary courses for college entrance. But a majority of our youth do not go on to college. And relatively few high schools offer the courses of study that will enable these youth to enter gainful careers upon graduation. It is ironic, and perhaps hypocritical, that vocational education should be accepted and even esteemed in our colleges and universities, and regarded as odious by so many of our intelligentsia when it is offered in the high schools. They see vocational education in the high school as encroaching upon the academic studies. They argue that our technology is changing so rapidly that any vocational training in high school will

---

[1] John Dewey, *Democracy and Education* (New York: The Macmillan Company, 1916), p. 365.

eventually lead to unemployment. They contend that the high schools should concentrate on the academic studies while leaving occupational training to business and industry for those youth who do not go on to higher education. They hold that vocational education in the high school is anti-intellectual and smacks of "life-adjustment" education.

But neither these arguments nor the academic curricula in the high school have solved the problem of youth unemployment. It is easy for the college educated to see their own education as "liberal," while denigrating as narrowly vocational any type of career preparation that terminates in high school. Dewey observed that "many a teacher and author writes and argues in behalf of a cultural and humane education against the encroachments of a specialized practical education, without recognizing that his own education, which he calls liberal, has been mainly training for his own particular calling. He has simply got into the habit of regarding his own business as essentially cultural and of overlooking the cultural possibilities of other employments." [2]

THE COMPREHENSIVE HIGH SCHOOL AND VOCATIONAL EDUCATION

The comprehensive high school is a uniquely American invention. Conceived to serve all the youth of all the people through diversified curricula, the comprehensive high school has been looked upon as the embodiment of the ideals of American democracy. It has also been looked upon as an unworkable institution. There are those who would prefer to have us adopt a dual system of secondary schooling with separate academic and vocational schools. There are others who see the secondary school as an exclusively academic institution with no place for vocational studies.

During the past quarter of a century, the comprehensive high school has been severely attacked and vigorously defended. While it has not always lived up to the ideals for which it has been lauded, it has somehow managed to survive.

The Midcentury Vision of Comprehensive Secondary Schooling

During World War II and the years immediately following, considerable attention was given to the function of the comprehensive school in extending educational opportunity and in strengthening our democracy. Various documents appeared that examined the relationship between general and vocational education and looked with great optimism to the future of the comprehensive high school. Here was an institution that

---

[2] *Ibid.*, p. 366.

could play a vital role in building a spirit of social interdependence, not division, from our nation's great diversity.

The Harvard Report.   Prepared by a committee of the Harvard faculty during World War II, the Harvard Report concluded that "the aim of education should be to prepare an individual to become an expert both in some particular vocation or art and in the general art of the free man and the citizen. Thus the two kinds of education once given separately to different social classes must be given together to all alike." [3]

The Harvard Report went on to recommend that, for students who do not continue their formal schooling beyond high school, approximately one third of the time could be devoted to vocational education. And, regardless of the point at which one terminates his education, he should receive the necessary specialized or vocational education so that he is equipped for life.[4]

The Progressivist Vision.   The progressive document *Education for ALL American Youth,* prepared by the NEA's Educational Policies Commission in 1944 and revised in 1952, envisioned a comprehensive high school in which vocational education would prepare youth who are not going on to college for successful entry into the work life of society.[5] Vocational preparation would occupy one sixth of the student's program in grade 10, and one third in grades 11 and 12. Supervised work experience would be an integral part of the program to enable the student to become gainfully employed upon completing high school. The community college would offer, among other studies, education for technical and semiprofessional occupations through both formal studies and supervised work experience. Part-time and evening classes would be offered to out-of-school youth to serve their special interests and to further improve their vocational competencies. The vocational programs would be sufficiently flexible and of such a quality as to minimize the possibilities of technological unemployment. Through effective counseling, and through a comprehensive curriculum in the high school grades, the door to higher education would always be open to students with changing aspirations and rising levels of academic achievement. Although every high school would be comprehensive, in the larger communities the various high schools would divide their specialized vocational offerings and would be open to any student regardless of his place of residence.

Education for ALL American Youth came under severe attack for its

---

[3] Report of the Harvard Committee, *General Education in a Free Society* (Cambridge, Mass.: Harvard University Press, 1945), p. 54.

[4] *Ibid.,* p. 102.

[5] Educational Policies Commission, *Education for ALL American Youth—A Further Look* (Washington, D.C.: National Education Association, 1952), pp. 65–81, 264–287.

vocational-utilitarian-egalitarian bent, its rejection of the traditional aristocracy of subjects, and its broadly based curriculum goals formulated on the needs of youth. It was labeled as an anti-intellectual document of the "life-adjustment" movement.[6] Its utopian-progressivist flavor made it vulnerable to criticism in an era when our national priorities were undergoing drastic change. At midcentury, the Soviet threat had ushered in a new era—the pursuit of academic excellence. Forgotten for the time being were the legions of school dropouts and unemployed youth.

Survival of the Comprehensive High School

The pursuit of academic excellence to meet our new national needs was accompanied by an unprecedented surge of interest in European educational systems. Many critics of American education advocated that we eliminate the comprehensive high school and adopt the specialized academic high school characteristic of European nations. One of the most severe and influential critics, Admiral Hyman G. Rickover, contended that the comprehensive secondary school is unworkable.

> The comprehensive secondary school is a uniquely American institution, an outgrowth of the post-Jacksonian upsurge of democracy. It is the concrete expression of an ideal of one free school attended by all American children, rich and poor, native and foreign-born, of one faith or another—all growing up together, learning to get along with each other, absorbing democratic habits and ideals as by osmosis. This ideal runs smack into the incontrovertible fact that children are unequally endowed with intelligence and determination and that it is impossible to educate the slow, average, and fast learners together if by educating we mean development of the capacity to think, to understand, and to make wise decisions.[7]

Rickover's criticisms came at a time when some of our leading scientists were advocating in testimony before congressional committees that those who are not academically talented be eliminated from further schooling as early as the sixth grade.[8]

Defense of the Comprehensive High School.   But the forces and influences were not completely one-sided. Conant's report on the American high school, commissioned by the Carnegie Corporation, vigorously de-

---

[6] Richard Hofstadter, *Anti-intellectualism in American Life* (New York: Alfred A. Knopf, Inc., 1963), p. 353.

[7] Hyman G. Rickover, *Education and Freedom* (New York: E. P. Dutton & Co., Inc., 1959), p. 134.

[8] Hearings before the Committee on Labor and Public Welfare, United States Senate, Eighty-fifth Congress, *Science and Education for National Defense* (Washington, D.C.: U.S. Government Printing Office, 1958), pp. 36–84.

fended the comprehensive high school and the place in the curriculum of diversified programs for the development of marketable skills.[9] As an answer to the critics who were maintaining that academic excellence is not possible in a school that seeks to serve all the youth of all the people, Conant arranged to have aptitude and achievement-test batteries administered to students in selected academic high schools and comprehensive high schools. The academic high schools were noted for their record of excellence in preparing a large proportion of students for college. The comprehensive high schools selected by Conant were those in which a majority of the student population terminated their full-time education at graduation. These comprehensive high schools were adjudged to be comprehensive because they provided (1) a general education for all students, (2) vocational programs for those who need to begin work immediately upon graduation, and (3) academic programs for those whose vocational goals require a college education. After controlling for differences in aptitude, the tests revealed no important differences in the achievement of students enrolled in the two different types of schools, although the students in one of the comprehensive high schools outscored the students in all of the academic high schools.

In undertaking the study, Conant had noted that "the comprehensive high school is characteristic of our society and further that it has come into being because of our economic history and our devotion to the ideals of equality of opportunity and equality of status." [10] He reasoned that if there are comprehensive high schools that are providing highly satisfactory programs of general education, vocational education, and college-preparatory studies, then no radical change in the structure of American public secondary education would be necessary. From his data, Conant concluded, "I am convinced American secondary education can be made satisfactory without any radical changes in the basic pattern." [11]

Vocational Education.   Many aspects of Conant's report were conservative, particularly his recommendations concerning the general education phases of the curriculum, which were mainly a listing of standard Carnegie units in academic subjects. Although he recommended a system of ability grouping, he stressed that students must not be labeled or tracked as "college preparatory," "vocational," or "commercial," and that programs should be individualized to allow students to shift from a vocational sequence to an academic sequence and vice versa. Regarding diversified programs for the development of marketable skills, Conant made these recommendations:

---

9 James B. Conant, *The American High School Today* (New York: McGraw-Hill Book Company, Inc., 1959).

10 *Ibid.*, p. 8.

11 *Ibid.*, p. 96.

Programs should be available for girls interested in developing skills in typing, clerical machines, home economics. . . . Distributive education should be available if the retail shops in the community can be persuaded to provide suitable openings. If the community is rural, vocational agriculture should be included. For boys, depending on the community, trade and industrial programs should be available. Half a day is required in the eleventh and twelfth grades for this vocational work. In each specialized trade, there should be an advisory committee composed of representatives of management and labor. Federal money is available for these programs.

The school administration should constantly assess the employment situation in those trades included in the vocational programs. . . . In some communities, advanced programs of a technical nature should be developed.[12]

Although Conant recommended that the students enrolled in vocational programs should not be isolated from other students, he could only point to the homeroom, student activities, and a heterogeneously grouped course in the twelfth grade on American problems or government as the means through which students of different abilities, achievement levels, and educational goals would be grouped together intentionally.

Despite the many conservative qualities of Conant's report, it was enormously influential in its defense of the comprehensive high school and vocational education. Except for this, the report bore little resemblance to the progressivist document, *Education for ALL American Youth —A Further Look,* prepared by the NEA's Educational Policies Commission in 1952 under Conant's chairmanship. But Conant's 1959 report on the American high school was prepared at a time when, in the eyes of many critics, the paramount task of the schools was to serve the national interest.

Continued Criticism. Attacks on the comprehensive high schools continued into the decade of the 1960's. For example, Rickover persisted in maintaining that the institution of comprehensive secondary schooling is inefficient and wasteful of our intellectual talent and that we must follow the European model.

One cannot argue the issue of comprehensive schooling versus separate secondary education on a philosophical basis. But one can argue it on the basis whether the country really has a choice as between efficient education—that is separate schools above the elementary level—and pure "democratic" education which insists on the inefficient, time-wasting comprehensive school. In my opinion, we no longer have that choice. We must opt for efficiency.

---

12 *Ibid.,* p. 52.

. . . We need merely to look at Europe to see that she does this better than we. The only sensible thing is to follow suit.[13]

While the attacks on the comprehensive high school continued into the 1960's, they attracted less attention and appeared less convincing for a number of reasons. The enormous federal support of curriculum reform projects in the sciences and mathematics gave assurance that our nation's intellectual resources were being exploited most adequately within our existing educational structure. The public was convinced through our mass media that the new mathematics in the third grade was well beyond the comprehension of most adults. The crisis syndrome of the cold war could not be maintained indefinitely and, consequently, the cold war became a normal condition of life. If the highly propagandized missile gap was not a fabrication, at least our leaders gave ample demonstration that we had come to surpass the Soviets in this competition. Under such circumstances, the argument that we must adopt the European educational structure became less convincing. Some European nations, in efforts to democratize their own educational systems, were adopting the American-style comprehensive secondary school. Nevertheless, vocational education continued to come under attack as the disciplinarity principle dominated the new curriculum reform movement.

INDUSTRIAL ARTS IN THE COMPREHENSIVE SECONDARY SCHOOL

Many people erroneously think of the industrial arts and "shop courses" as being synonomous with vocational education. While various aspects of the industrial arts are related to many vocational curricula, industrial-arts programs are designed to serve the purposes of general education, exploratory education, and prevocational education. Junior high schools typically require all seventh- or eighth-grade boys to take at least one course in the industrial arts. Industrial arts courses also are typically offered as electives for boys and girls in junior and senior high schools.

Although courses in industrial arts have become well established among the elective offerings in the secondary school curriculum, there has been considerable misunderstanding and debate over the value of the industrial arts. The essentialists have attacked the industrial arts as "frills." Too many high schools, lacking programs in vocational education, have assigned students to various shop classes where, at best, they can gain some prevocational learning experiences. But the industrial arts should not be expected to perform a vocational education function. Yet another prob-

---

[13] Hyman G Rickover, *American Education—A National Failure* (New York: E. P. Dutton & Co., Inc., 1963), p. 89.

lem is that our schools very often fail to provide the up-to-date facilities and resources required for modern programs of industrial arts.

Curriculum Objectives

Some of the objectives of industrial arts are to (1) explore industry and industrial civilization in terms of organization, raw materials, processes and operations, products, and occupations; (2) develop avocational and recreational interests and skills of a productive nature; (3) gain an appreciation for good craftsmanship and design, both in the products of modern industry and in artifacts from the material cultures of the past; (4) gain an understanding of consumer affairs and problems, and how to select, purchase, use, and maintain the products of industry intelligently; (5) develop an understanding and appreciation of some of the basic processes of industry; (6) develop skills in using basic materials, tools, and machinery—including problem-solving skills relative to materials and processes; (7) provide opportunity for creative expression and the development of talents in using industrial materials; and (8) develop habits of safety and knowledge of safety practices.[14]

In summary, industrial arts can be defined as the study of tools, materials, processes, products, occupations, and related problems of industrial society. It encompasses experiences in design and drafting, graphic arts, wood, metals, ceramics, plastics, electronics, and industrial processes.

Rationale

The Harvard Report made this case for the industrial arts in general education more than a quarter of a century ago:

> Such experience is important for the general education of all. Most students who expect to go to college are now offered an almost wholly verbal type of preparatory training, while hand training and the direct manipulation of objects are mainly reserved for the vocational fields. This is a serious mistake. . . . The direct contact with materials, the manipulation of simple tools, the capacity to create by hand from a concept in the mind—all these are indispensable aspects of the education of everyone.[15]

In the section of the Harvard Report dealing with "Science and Mathematics," the relevance of the industrial arts for students planning on scientific and technological careers was stressed:

---

[14] See Gordon O. Wilber and Norman C. Pendered, *Industrial Arts in General Education* (Scranton, Pa.: International Textbook Company, 1967), p. 53.

[15] Report of the Harvard Committee, *op. cit.*, p. 175.

For those who intend to go into scientific or technological work, it has special relevance. The manipulation of objects, the use of tools, and the construction of simple apparatus all are required for entry into the world of experimentation. Even the pure mathematician is greatly aided by shop experience; the forms, contours, and interrelations of three-dimensional objects provide a stimulus and satisfaction not to be achieved altogether within the limits of plane diagrams. The lack of shop training is at present a most serious deterrent to entry into all types of technological work and to college and postgraduate training in science, medicine, and engineering.[16]

Of course, there are many other kinds of learnings that can take place through the curriculum in industrial arts. Students can learn to appreciate, through direct experience, the revolution that has taken place as man left the era of handicraft and entered the age of technology. They can learn how our society can no longer rely on an apprenticeship system in preparing persons for skilled occupations. As Veblen observed early in this century, "this commonplace information that is requisite to any of the skilled occupations can no longer be acquired in the mere workaday routine of industry, but is to be had only at the cost of deliberate application with the help of the schools." [17]

Students in industrial-arts classes also can learn of some of the problems that have been created by technology. Although activities and projects in industrial-arts classes all too often are routine and trivial, this need not be the case. When individual and group projects are stimulating and challenging, they engage youngsters in the act of thought and in the realization of a total process. As Dewey emphasized,

> It has an end in view; results are to be accomplished. Hence it appeals to thought; it demands that an idea of an end be steadily maintained, so that activity cannot be either routine or capricious. Since the movement of activity must be progressive, leading from one stage to another, observation and ingenuity are required at each stage to overcome obstacles and to discover and readapt means of execution.[18]

Problem of Low Priority in the Curriculum

Rickover has attacked the industrial arts by referring to this area of the curriculum as "manual training" and as a "know-how" subject. According to Rickover, "The educational process for all children must be one of absorbing knowledge to the limit of their capacity . . . know-how subjects have little effect on the mind itself, and it is with the mind that the

---

16 *Ibid.,* p. 160.

17 Thorstein Veblen, *The Instinct of Workmanship* (New York: The Macmillan Company, 1914), pp. 307–308.

18 Dewey, *op. cit.,* p. 361.

school must solely concern itself. The poorer a child's natural endowments the more he needs to have his mind trained." [19]

We need not go into the fallacy of the notion that the mind is like a sponge. Nor is it necessary to attack the premise that the cognitive processes can be treated apart from the affective processes in human thinking and behavior. Few educators hold such views today. But the belief that "know-how" and application are necessarily divorced from understanding and interpretation is shared by too many educators.

In their curriculum design for secondary education, Broudy, Smith, and Burnett have proposed a secondary school curriculum that has no place for the industrial arts, as commonly taught for purposes of general education.[20] They contend that, as the skills of using basic tools can be picked up by trial and error and do-it-yourself kits, the industrial arts should be limited to the understandings of the technological processes underlying our culture. The emphasis is on interpretive, not applicative knowledge. And activities connected with the making of objects are eliminated. Moreover, instead of being identified as industrial arts, such book work would come under a group of social science disciplines.

There are many benefits to be derived from correlating, fusing, and integrating subject matters but in this case there is no mention of where mathematics and science would fit in. After all, there are scientific and mathematical skills and understandings in the industrial arts. Furthermore, the notion that, for purposes of general education, we should limit the study of the industrial arts to interpretive rather than applicative knowledge only serves to reinforce the age-old shibboleth of knowing versus doing. An artificial dichotomy is created and, as a result, whatever is learned lacks relevance and authenticity.

ANTIVOCATIONALISM AND THE ACADEMIC PRIORITIES

"It is a strange state of affairs in an industrial democracy," noted the Harvard report, "when those very subjects are held in disrepute which are at the heart of the national economy and those students by implication condemned who will become its operators. The question to which no adequate answer has as yet been found is, then, how to endue all subjects in the modern high school, and the teachers of these, with a respect commensurate to their equally necessary part in American life." [21]

This "strange state of affairs" was only to become even more strange as a result of the new curriculum priorities of the cold war era. Such

---

19 Rickover, *Education and Freedom, op. cit.,* p. 133.

20 Harry S. Broudy, B. Othanel Smith, and Joe R. Burnett, *Democracy and Excellence in American Secondary Education* (Chicago: Rand McNally & Company, 1964), pp. 181–182, 265.

21 Report of the Harvard Committee, *op. cit.,* pp. 27–28.

subjects as science, mathematics, and foreign languages, once justified for their powers in developing the intellectual as opposed to the utilitarian skills, gained priority for their newly recognized instrumental value in meeting our nation's cold war needs.

The Essentials and Intellective Power

Traditionally, the essentialists have disparaged the vocational subjects for their narrow utilitarian motive. They have contended that the schools should confine their offerings to the basic or essential disciplines, because these are concerned with the development of our intellective powers. Writing for the Council on Basic Education at the height of the cold war era, Clifton Fadiman argued that "other subjects may seem transiently attractive or of obvious utility. . . . Yet we cannot afford to be seduced by such 'subjects.' Hard though it may be, we must jettison them in favor of the basic subject matters. And there is no time for an eclectic mixture; only a few years are available . . . to educate the rationale soul." [22]

According to Bestor, liberal education is "essentially the communication of intellectual power." [23] In his proposal for the restoration of learning in our high schools, Bestor held that "vocational courses would carry no academic credit, and would not in general be open to students under the age of seventeen." [24] However, he failed to discuss the implications of such restrictions for the great numbers of our youth who do not continue their schooling beyond the age of seventeen.

In holding that the essential subjects or disciplines cultivate the powers of the intellect, the essentialists have labeled the vocational studies as narrowly utilitarian and anti-intellectual. Consequently, the essentialists see the comprehensive curriculum being marked by an intellectual-utilitarian duality that deters the school from its paramount task of cultivating the intellect.

The Essentials Become Utilitarian

Where our nation's need for food, fiber, and technically trained manpower during the emergency conditions of World World I led to the first federal legislation in support of vocational education at the high school level (Smith-Hughes Act of 1917), the crises of the cold war in the nuclear and space age led to the federal support of curriculum reform in the academic fields of science, mathematics, and modern foreign languages.

---

[22] Clifton Fadiman, in James D. Koerner (ed.), *The Case for Basic Education* (Boston: Little, Brown and Company, 1959), pp. 7–8.

[23] Arthur Bestor, *The Restoration of Learning* (New York: Alfred A. Knopf, Inc., 1956), p. 35.

[24] *Ibid.*, p. 326.

Thus, in the second half of the twentieth century, certain so-called cultural subjects came to be justified for their contribution to our nation's technological, military, and political leadership in a divided world. No longer was it necessary to justify these subjects solely because of their alleged powers of developing the intellect. In an era of world crisis, these subjects were recognized for their urgent utilitarian value. Where in one era our federal government looked to vocational education to meet the needs of a nation in crisis, in another era of crisis it looked to the academic essentials of science, mathematics, and modern foreign languages.

Although the intellectual-utilitarian duality had traditionally been a fundamental issue in the rationale of essentialism, the impact of the cold war in the nuclear and space age found the essentialists eagerly embracing the very utilitarian motive which they had previously held in utter contempt. Now they contended that if the United States was to regain its technological, military, and political leadership in the world, utmost priority would have to be given to the academic disciplines, particularly the sciences, mathematics, and modern foreign languages. Ignoring the vocationalism of the Soviet schools, Bestor argued that "we have wasted an appalling part of the time of our young people on trivialities. The Russians have had sense enough not to do so. That's why the first satellite bears the label 'Made in Russia.'" [25] Bestor went on to condemn the federal support of vocational programs and advocated that the federal government subsidize science and mathematics instead.

> Under the Smith-Hughes Act and certain other ones, it (the Federal Government) has made grants for agricultural education, home economics and similar subjects in the schools. In my opinion, this was exactly the wrong direction for federal support to take. . . . What they seem to be reluctant to do is furnish enough money for basic education. I think the Federal Government's role ought to be to subsidize instruction in fundamental fields such as science and mathematics.[26]

Thus the disciplines once considered to be essential for developing the intellective powers came to be regarded by the essentialists as valuable for their instrumental power of meeting our nation's scientific, technological, and military priorities.

Antivocationalism and the Argument of Obsolescence

As discussed in Chapter 2, the focus on disciplinarity in the new wave of curriculum reform, which began in the mid-1950's and extended through the decade of the 1970's, led some educational theorists to hold

---

25 Arthur Bestor, "What Went Wrong With U.S. Schools," interview in *U.S. News & World Report*, Vol. 54 (January 24, 1958), p. 69.

26 *Ibid.*, p. 75.

that the curriculum should have no place for any studies that are based only on the nature, needs, and interests of the learner and that do not belong within the structure of the disciplines.[27] Such a position obviously precludes any place for vocational education in the curriculum. Although many educators do not hold that disciplinarity is the only valid basis for curriculum construction, they nevertheless oppose vocational education in the high school on other grounds. Probably the argument most commonly leveled against vocational studies is that they train adolescents in skills that rapidly become obsolete.

> Such programs, even though they train the students to operate some of the most sophisticated electronic hardware on the present-day market, may well be preparing a wave of school graduates for technological unemployment ten or fifteen years after graduation, because the emphasis is upon merely the gross elements which are mainly of momentary significance.[28]

The authors of the above quotation go on to recommend that vocational preparation be postponed to the postsecondary years "if we wish to provide a maximum of choice and mobility to the student in his life, and if we wish to avoid the specificity in vocational training which too often ends in early technological unemployment."[29] The curriculum of the secondary school is seen by these educators as being properly concentrated on and limited to a reorganization of academic studies for purposes of general education. They are joined by others who contend that "the survival of the concept of 'vocation' during this period of rapid technological change and subsequent job obsolescence is doubtful."[30]

Another educator states the case against vocational education by fabricating a case history of a young lady, Susie, who enters an office career after graduating from junior college where she devoted a third of her time to business studies.[31] She is highly successful in her career, but eventually marries and later leaves her job to raise a family. After thirteen years as a full-time homemaker, she seeks office employment only to find that her skills in typing, stenography, bookkeeping, and other office practices have become totally obsolete. The author then argues that had Susie devoted her high school and college studies to subjects that cultivated her powers of abstract reasoning, instead of business studies, she would not have faced the problem of technological obsolescence.

---

27 Philip H. Phenix, "The Disciplines As Curriculum Content" in A. Harry Passow (ed.), *Curriculum Crossroads* (New York: Teachers' College Press, 1962), p. 64.

28 Broudy, Smith, and Burnett, *op. cit.*, p. 16.

29 *Ibid.*, p. 36.

30 Arthur R. King, Jr., and John A. Brownell, *The Curriculum and the Disciplines of Knowledge* (New York: John Wiley & Sons, Inc., 1966), p. 4.

31 James E. Russell, *Change and Challenge in American Education* (Boston: Houghton Mifflin Company, 1965), pp. 8–14.

She needed to be able to use her powers of abstract thought—and these were undeveloped. She aimed at things she could see and understand: marriage, job, home. She neglected a longer look, which, if taken, would have told her that as her world changed it would be up to her to "see" the changes and to change with them.

. . . There may have been a time when a person could learn a trade while young and then by practicing it be an effective and contributing person for life. . . . That time has gone.[32]

Now there is just enough truth in the argument of technological obsolescence to convince many that vocational education is outmoded because it prepares one in skills that are temporal and restrictive in an age of accelerating change. But suppose Susie had been educated and employed as a chemist, physicist, physician, or economist. Would she be better equipped to return to her career after thirteen years of failing to keep abreast of the developments in her occupation? More than likely she would have even less of a chance of re-entry to her occupation under such circumstances. Nor can we assume that any of the liberal arts would have had more lasting value for Susie. For example, had Susie majored in mathematics or a foreign language in college—two favorite essentialist subjects—and then had she failed to use her knowledge and skills for thirteen years, undoubtedly she would find herself in the same boat. Imagine what would happen to someone who stopped using his native language for thirteen years! The point is that whatever is learned must be used continuously in a variety of life situations if it is to stay alive. Whether one is a machinist or a linguist, one must keep up with new developments and changing conditions.

Vocational education in the high school or community college need not be more delimiting and vulnerable to scientific, technological, or social change than any other kind of specialized education. Many a Ph.D. in medieval history or Elizabethan literature finds that the only place where his specialized training is marketable is in college teaching, and even here he may well be regarded as a glut on the market.

General education is not only important for effective citizenship in a free society; it is essential to virtually any kind of specialized education and occupational preparation. But unless one is to join the leisure class, or the ranks of the unemployed, or unless one is to take a menial job requiring skills of no consequence, specialized and vocational education are also necessary for a place in the life stream of society. Typist-stenographers, machinists, chefs, welders, farmers, and salesmen have been less vulnerable to changing times than the Latinists and philologists. The farmer who was vocationally well-equipped was able to capitalize on the twentieth-century revolution in agricultural production. If vocational

---

[32] *Ibid.,* p. 23.

education is broad, rich, and relevant, and if the individual finds his chosen work challenging and rewarding, and if he is impelled to keep up with changing conditions, neither he nor his education are likely to become irrelevant.

Except in times of economic depression, the problem of unemployment has been confined largely to those who are unskilled. As discussed later in this chapter, our high school programs of vocational education have not reached a sufficient proportion of our youth. And there are many aspects of these programs that are in need of improvement. But the essentialist argument that vocational education is obsolete because of accelerating technological change is based on the assumption that vocational education equips one with the narrowest of skills and, like Latin, is static. This is not the kind of occupational preparation that vocational educators are advocating. A person who is well equipped vocationally is able to adapt to technological change. People do not become obsolete because of machines, but because other people have left them ill prepared for change.

ACHIEVEMENTS AND FAILURES

In 1961, at the request of President Kennedy, the Secretary of Health, Education, and Welfare appointed a panel to review and evaluate the nation's vocational education effort in the light of the technological changes taking place in society. Despite the federal support of a variety of vocational education programs at the high school level, there was a growing army of out-of-school youth who had not been served by these programs and who were unemployed. In 1961 Conant described the situation in our large cities as "social dynamite." [33] At a time of unprecedented prosperity, our nation had not solved the problem of poverty and unemployment. This also was a time when the priority of the school was curriculum reform in the academic disciplines, with a special focus on the development of our academically talented youth.

Federal Efforts in Vocational Education (1917 to 1962)

The role of the federal government in supporting vocational education can be traced to the Morrill Act of 1862, signed by President Lincoln, which provided for the establishment of the land-grant colleges of agriculture and the mechanic arts—later to become our great state universities. But it was not until World War I that the federal government moved to support vocational education of less-than-college grade. Through the

---

[33] James B. Conant, *Slum and Suburbs* (New York: McGraw-Hill Book Company, Inc., 1961), p. 2.

Smith-Hughes Act of 1917, signed by President Wilson, federal funds were made available to prepare persons over fourteen years of age for careers in agriculture, home economics, trades, and industries. These programs typically were administered as an integral part of our public secondary schools. A number of subsequent acts provided funds for the expansion of these programs. Distributive education (retailing, wholesaling, transporting, storing, advertising, and so on) was added with the passage of the George-Deen Act, signed by President Roosevelt in 1936.

During the Depression years, some of the nonschool federal agencies, such as the Works Progress Administration and the Civilian Conservation Corps, offered some classes of a vocational nature for out-of-school youth. However, youth education was not a principal function of these emergency agencies, and consequently the quality of the programs suffered from the temporary and emergency character of the sponsoring agencies. The National Youth Administration, organized in 1935, provided part-time employment to help students to remain in school, while also providing work for out-of-school youth.

The National Defense Training Program was established in 1940 to prepare workers for the defense industries of World War II. Through this program, many high schools conducted day classes for in-school youth and evening classes to train defense workers.

The Servicemen's Readjustment Act of 1944, popularly known as the G.I. Bill of Rights, enabled veterans of World War II to continue their education. Although this legislation proved to be a giant step in opening the doors of higher education to an unprecedented proportion of our population, almost 4 million veterans also enrolled in educational programs below college level. One year after the end of World War II, President Truman signed the George-Barden Act, which provided significant increases in appropriations for vocational education of less-than-college grade in agriculture, home economics, trades and industries, and distributive occupations. Through this legislation, funds also were authorized for vocational guidance.

Although the National Defense Education Act (NDEA) of 1958 was aimed primarily at improving instruction in science, mathematics, and modern foreign languages in public elementary and secondary schools, and for the improvement of guidance and testing programs in the schools, Title VIII of NDEA amended the George-Barden Act so as to provide funds for the training of highly skilled technicians in fields deemed necessary for national defense.

Other federal legislation included the Area Redevelopment Act (1961) to provide vocational training for unemployed persons in economically distressed areas, and the Manpower Development and Training Act (1962) for vocational training and basic skill development in connection with unemployment problems.

Impact of Federal Programs to 1962

Despite the host of federal laws passed in support of vocational education at the secondary school level from World War I to 1962, most of the legislation was essentially an extension of the original provisions of the Smith-Hughes Act of 1917. Moreover, the legislation following the Smith-Hughes Act tended to be categorical rather than comprehensive. It was more of a series of responses to emergencies rather than a concerted approach toward improving the curriculum of the high school.

Yet the students enrolled in these federally supported programs were, on the whole, remarkably well served. After having reviewed the impact of the various National Vocational Education Acts at the request of President Kennedy, the Panel of Consultants on Vocational Education reached the conclusion "that graduates of high school vocational education programs are less likely to be unemployed than other high school graduates, that vocational education graduates do in fact work in the occupations for which they prepare, and that vocational education increases their subsequent earnings." [34]

But the panel also found that these programs were available only in a small proportion of high schools and were reaching only a minute fraction of the student population. For example, only 13 per cent of the fifteen to nineteen-year-old age group were enrolled in federally supported programs of vocational education, and most of these students were in home-economics education. Only 2 per cent were in trade and industrial education, and a mere 0.3 per cent were enrolled in distributive education. The panel also found that the vocational education programs were not preparing our youth for a sufficient variety of career choices, that services to the student population in our largest cities is meager, and that there is a critical need for technical education after high school. Rural high schools were found to be paying insufficient attention to the vocational needs of the large number of youth who must migrate to urban areas to obtain employment. The panel noted that cooperative (school-work) programs of vocational education appeared to offer a promising opportunity for helping solve the dropout problem, but few schools offered such programs.

Concerning the categorical and emergency character of federal legislation over a period of almost half a century, the panel reached this conclusion:

> Investment in vocational education is today grossly incommensurate with the national interest and Federal responsibilities. . . .
> The legislative patchwork of the past will not suffice. . . . Despite

---

[34] Report of the Panel of Consultants on Vocational Education, *Education for a Changing World of Work* (Washington, D.C.: U.S. Government Printing Office, 1963), p. xvi.

the administrative downgrading at the Federal level and the increased complexity of its statutory framework, vocational education has made outstanding contributions during and following two World Wars and in some heavy economic weather. But adding successive legislative "patches" to meet every ill wind which blows across our land is both poor long-range planning and evidence of little faith in the local-State-Federal partnership at the heart of our political system. Unification of Federal legislation for vocational education to provide a broad and flexible foundation for the future is now long overdue.[35]

Finally, the panel warned of the "social dynamite" being created in our central cities when youngsters, denied vocational education and employment opportunity, drop out of high school and become prime candidates for street-corner standing and delinquency. "Not only is the individual's economic and social stability at stake," declared the panel, "but also the economic, social, and political stability of large population centers." [36]

The Vocational Education Act of 1963

Signed into law by President Johnson, the Vocational Education Act of 1963 represented the first major revamping of vocational education in almost a half century of federal participation in the secondary level of schooling. Like the Vocational Education Act of 1917 (Smith-Hughes), which grew out of a comprehensive study of national needs by a federal commission, the 1963 law came into being as a result of the report of the Panel of Consultants on Vocational Education.

The Vocational Educational Act of 1963 provided for the (1) expansion of existing programs; (2) elimination of the categorical restrictions of previous legislation to allow the redirection of funds for career preparation in tune with the realities of the labor market; (3) development of programs to serve urban youth through instruction in semiskilled occupations as well as in skilled employment; (4) expansion of area vocational schools and work-study programs; and (5) establishment of experimental four-year residential schools. Broadening the definitions of the old vocational categories, the 1963 legislation allowed vocational education in agriculture to include agriculture-related occupations, and home economics was expanded to include a wide range of employment careers. And, for the first time, office occupations education also has been greatly expanded. Thus the new legislation gave promise of extending the opportunity of vocational education to a far larger proportion of our youth.

In addition to its greater flexibility in program definition and allocation of funds, the 1963 act places greater responsibility on the states and

---

[35] *Ibid.,* pp. 213–214.
[36] *Ibid.,* p. 229.

local communities for curriculum development to meet the urgent problems of our times. But despite the new and needed directions in vocational education made possible by the 1963 legislation, a number of curricular and social problems and issues remain unresolved. These are discussed throughout much of the remainder of this chapter.

The Changing Curriculum

By eliminating categorical restrictions, the Vocational Education Act of 1963 has opened the way to the development of new courses to meet changes in the labor market and to provide education for new careers in our changing economy. Recognizing that vocational programs and success in so many occupations require a reasonable level of competency in language and mathematical skills, as well as in applied science, the new legislation allows schools to design integrated programs of vocational and general education, provided that the students are enrolled in genuine vocational programs. This flexible feature may be of particular benefit to disadvantaged youngsters who previously had been denied opportunities in vocational education because they were deficient in basic skills. The new legislation also allows the curriculum to be designed for occupational or career clusters, rather than being narrowly focused on specific occupations or jobs that restrict employment and career opportunities.

Agricultural Education.   Scientific and technological advancements have created a revolution in agricultural production in the United States. Although the increased efficiency in production has been accompanied by a sharp decline in our farm population, the occupation of farming requires more specialized education at higher levels than ever before in our history. Moreover, these developments have been accompanied by a vast expansion of agri-business and other allied careers.

As a result of the Vocational Education Act of 1963, the high school curriculum in vocational agriculture, grades 9–12, has been expanded to include preparation for these allied careers (agricultural mechanization, supply, processing, ornamental horticulture, and others). Students in production agriculture engage in an approved farming program under the supervision of the teacher of vocational agriculture. An increasing proportion of high school students of vocational agriculture are going on to college. Opportunities for continuing education are also provided through postsecondary and adult classes conducted through the high school program of vocational agriculture. In response to the many career opportunities in ornamental horticulture in our cities, an increasing number of urban high schools have instituted programs of vocational agriculture to prepare youngsters for these careers.

Distributive Education. In addition to new course offerings to prepare students for the expanding careers in distribution and marketing, this program has been made available to high school students beginning in the tenth grade. Cooperative work experience is an important part of the curriculum, although many schools are using directed observation, case analyses, and individualized projects. Postsecondary programs have increased markedly through the high schools, community colleges, and four-year colleges. An increasing number of high schools have developed cross-vocational or multiple-field programs combining distributive education with agri-business or trades and industries.

Health Occupations Education. With the expansion of federal programs in health and welfare, an acute shortage of qualified health workers has developed. Although the enrollment in vocational health programs in our high schools is small, it is growing rapidly as more employers are looking to the schools as a source of new personnel for expanding health programs. Most of the high school students enrolled in the vocational health-occupations curriculum are preparing for careers as practical nurses. Their preparation extends from grade 12 into a post-high school year, leading to a certificate in practical nursing as well as a high school diploma. However, there is a trend toward developing a comprehensive curriculum to prepare youth for a wide range of health careers, including nurse's aides, medical record clerks, medical office assistants, and others. New types of programs need to be developed for entry-level employment allowing for career advancement through continued specialized training. Postsecondary curriculum offerings are being expanded in community colleges to prepare registered nurses, dental hygienists, X-ray technicians, and other health personnel.

Home Economics Education. Where the traditional program of vocational home economics education was limited to homemaking, the new emphasis is on career preparation in such occupational areas as (1) food management, production, and services; (2) child-care services; (3) institutional and home management; (4) clothing management, production, and services; and (5) home furnishings, equipment, and services. The emphasis on occupational preparation has necessitated major changes in the home economics curriculum of the high school. Enrollments have increased significantly as a result of these new programs in the high schools. Expansion also has taken place at the postsecondary level, particularly in the community colleges. Increasing attention is being given to reaching youth and adults in our urban centers, particularly the disadvantaged. For many students, the program has been designed to provide training for the dual role of homemaking and wage earning.

Office Occupations Education. Vocational education in office occupations has dramatically transformed the traditional high school offerings from a group of isolated business subjects into a viable curriculum including cooperative work experience, block-time classes for laboratory work, and simulated office experience. The vocational program in office occupations has expanded rapidly at the secondary, postsecondary, and adult levels. Many schools have developed comprehensive curricula in business data processing and computing occupations, in addition to the usual stenographic-secretarial, bookkeeping, and accounting course offerings. The cooperative work-experience program has enabled a very high proportion of students to be placed in full-time positions that are closely related to their educational programs.

Trades and Industrial Education. In addition to expanding and modernizing the traditional offerings in construction and machine trades, the vocational program in trades and industrial education has been extended to include maintenance and repair specialities. The curriculum in trades and industrial education has undergone considerable change to prepare youth for new occupations emerging from technological change. At the postsecondary level, opportunities are being provided to prepare for supervisory and middle-management careers. Facilities and equipment are being modernized in the schools and community colleges to strengthen the various programs. Efforts have been made to expand and improve the cooperative work-experience programs, and to meet the special needs of adults. The most successful programs are characterized by a high degree of cooperation among the professional staffs and leaders in business, industry, labor, and other agencies.

Technical Education. There has been a growing trend toward developing programs of technical education that extend from high school through two years of postsecondary preparation. A major problem has been recruiting students who have the capability and desire to pursue studies that are no less demanding than many baccalaureate programs. Efforts are being undertaken to develop pretechnical programs to enable underprepared students with potential to meet the stringent requirements of technical programs of community colleges, technical institutes, and area vocational schools. The need for technical workers has grown enormously as a result of the great advances in science and technology. However, many youths who qualify for programs in technical education are understandably attracted to baccalaureate programs.

Changing Educational Priorities

Quite suddenly, the drive to develop an academic elite is no longer our nation's first educational priority. Somehow, this goal has lost its ring of urgency, and a new urgency has taken its place. We have come to realize that a large proportion of our youth has been denied a productive place in our society. Even among some of those who have most enjoyed the fruits of the national drive to develop our academic talent for the space age, we find a new concern for reallocating our educational priorities.

> For a favored sixth of the youth of this country, the educational system represents a pathway to a successful career. The remaining five-sixths are not so fortunate, and many find that their training has prepared them for nothing. Today skilled labor is in short supply. It is often necessary to wait weeks for services such as automobile repairs. Nevertheless, many young people are unemployed. . . .
>
> As a nation we have been preoccupied with fostering excellence of a limited group while neglecting the overwhelming majority of our youth. . . . Moreover, there have been many curriculum reform efforts benefiting college-bound students while vocational curricula have been little improved. One of our greatest mistakes has been to accord special prestige to a college degree while displaying indifference toward quality in craftsmanship. We reward verbal skill and abstract reasoning and deny dignity to manual workers.
>
> . . . In our society there is little place for the man or woman who has no special skill. If our increasingly technological society is not to deteriorate, we must find means of helping the young find useful roles whatever their particular aptitudes.[37]

This editorial in one of our leading scientific journals goes on to support the new federal programs in vocational education. It does not advocate the creation of jobs to keep youth out of trouble or to alleviate our social conscience. The argument is simply that by neglecting the majority of our youth while fostering excellence of a limited group, our technological society cannot function effectively. To wait weeks for the repair of one's automobile or household plumbing is particularly vexing in a society that sends astronauts to the moon.

A national business magazine, which in an earlier era had concentrated on the development of our scientific talent, saw fit to publish the text of a report of the U.S. Advisory Council on Vocational Education, which stressed that by neglecting vocational education our society is paying the price of crime and violence.

> The violence that racks our cities has roots in unemployment and unequal opportunity. Those who have no jobs in an affluent community lash out in anger and frustration. Young men and women who cannot qualify for decent jobs distrust the society which reared them. Dissidents speak with the voice of rebellion; campus and inner-city revolt reaches into our schools. Our nation seethes.

---

[37] Philip H. Abelson, "Toward Better Vocational Education," Editorial, *Science*, Vol. 161 (August 16, 1968), p. 635.

Racial unrest, violence and the unemployment of youth have their roots in inadequate education. Each year the ranks of the school drop-outs increase by three quarters of a million young men and women. They enter the job market without the skills and attitudes employers require. They and . . . the graduates of our high schools who are inadequately trained for anything are tragic evidence of the present inadequacy of our educational system. . . .

The costs, the blighted lives, the discontent, the violence and the threat of revolution are needless. . . .

At the very heart of our problem is a national attitude that says vocational education is designed for somebody else's children. This attitude is shared by businessmen, labor leaders, administrators, teachers, parents, students. We are all guilty. We have promoted the idea that the only good education is an education capped by four years of college. This idea, transmitted by our values, our aspirations and our silent support, is snobbish, undemocratic and a revelation of why schools fail so many students.

The attitude infects the Federal Government, which invests $14 in the nation's universities for every $1 it invests in the nation's vocational-education programs. . . . It infects school districts, which concentrate on college-preparatory and general programs in reckless disregard of the fact that for 60 per cent of our young people, high school is still the only transition to the world of work. . . .

We recommend that the Federal Government immediately exercise its leadership and allocate more of its funds to cure our country of our national sin of intellectual snobbery.[38]

The many years of neglecting to relate education to the life needs of a large proportion of our adolescents has produced another crisis situation. Emphasis must be given not merely to emergency measures, but to making education really relevant so that all youth have the opportunity for a recognized place in society. When the school and society deny youth the opportunity to fulfill their developmental tasks, grave social consequences are to be expected. For example, by denying our young people the opportunity of preparing for an occupation, we are also denying them such normal tasks of development as achieving assurance of economic independence, desiring and achieving socially responsible behavior, developing a socially acceptable set of values and an ethical system as a guide to behavior, achieving new and more mature relations with age-mates and adults, achieving a masculine or feminine role, developing intellectual skills necessary for civic competence, and preparing for marriage and family life.[39]

---

38 "Too Much Stress on College—An Official Report," *U.S. News & World Report,* Vol. 67 (October 13, 1969), pp. 45–46.

39 See Robert J. Havighurst, *Developmental Tasks and Education* (New York: Longmans, Green & Co., 1952).

NONSCHOOL EDUCATIONAL PROGRAMS AND THE WAR ON POVERTY

"I see one-third of a nation ill-housed, ill-clad, ill-nourished," declared President Roosevelt in a speech to the nation during the Great Depression. In presenting his War on Poverty measure to Congress in 1964, President Johnson noted, "There are millions of Americans—one fifth of our people—who have not shared in the abundance which has been granted to most of us, and on whom the gates of opportunity have been closed."

But the essential difference between the Great Depression and the 1960's was not the proportion of our population in poverty, but the fact that poverty, so highly visible and so much a part of our social awareness during the Depression years, had been largely removed from our social conscience during an era of prosperity.

Economic Opportunity Act of 1964

Known as the War-on-Poverty Bill, the Economic Opportunity Act of 1964 allocated almost one billion dollars to fight poverty mainly through education. However, the various educational programs provided through this measure were to be administered through a new agency—the Office of Economic Opportunity (OEO). As in the case of various emergency educational measures of the Great Depression, the U.S. Office of Education was bypassed and a new federal agency was created.

Jobs Corps. An important provision for vocational education was found in Title I, which called for the establishment of the Job Corps to provide job training in residential centers for thousands of out-of-school and unemployed youth. Funds also were allocated for work-study and part-time employment to enable needy students to continue their schooling. The Urban and Rural Community Action Programs under Title II included funds for job training, vocational rehabilitation and adult basic education.

Hundreds of Job Corps centers were established throughout the nation, many under contract with industry. However, students who completed the program satisfactorily were not guaranteed job placement. The program made no provision for cooperative on-the-job training. Many of the contracting industries were criticized for participating in the program solely from a profit motive. Staffs were hastily assembled to administer the centers and there was an acknowledged shortage of qualified professional educators. Many centers were criticized for their quasimilitary climate. A number of centers for males were located on abandoned military bases, hundreds of miles from the youngsters' homes.

A 1969 study, ordered by Congress, reviewed the entire War-on-Poverty effort and found that "corps trainees did little better in the labor market than poor youths without such training." [40] The devastating findings resulted in the relocation of a number of centers and some curtailment and modification of the program, which had enrolled an average of approximately one hundred thousand youths during the first five years of operation at an expenditure of some one billion dollars. But, measured in other terms, this huge expenditure just about matched the federal allocations for the blueprint design of a commercial supersonic jet aircraft—a vehicle yet to be produced.

Neighborhood Youth Corps. Another OEO program is the Neighborhood Youth Corps, which provides summer and part-time employment for disadvantaged high school youth. For youth who do not return to school, full-time employment may be provided through public service jobs, or they may enter a work-training program in industry sponsored by the corps. However, the major effort of the Neighborhood Youth Corps has not been vocational education, but to engage disadvantaged youth in productive activity while helping them remain in school. The summer-employment function of the corps has been primarily that of keeping disadvantaged youngsters "off the streets." As the corps is administered independently of the schools, no concerted effort has been made to relate the school studies to the job experiences in the community.

Upward Bound. Project Upward Bound, established by the OEO in 1966 to motivate and prepare disadvantaged high school youth for college, was transferred to the U.S. Office of Education in 1969. Undoubtedly, Upward Bound has enabled thousands of disadvantaged youngsters to succeed in school and college. However, the program has been administered through the colleges and has had little influence in changing the curricula of our secondary schools. The program is largely concentrated on an intensive in-residence summer program on college campuses. While controlled research has not been undertaken nationally to evaluate the effects of Upward Bound, such research has been conducted in connection with one of the leading Upward Bound projects. The results revealed that when disadvantaged high school youth are in an academic-year program that is designed to develop their potential for college through curricular redesign, tutoring, and other supportive services, participation in Upward Bound had no incremental effect on their academic achievement.[41, 42] In

40 *The New York Times* (March 19, 1969), p. 1.

41 Daniel Tanner and Genaro Lachica, *Discovering and Developing the College Potential of Disadvantaged High School Youth* (New York: The City University of New York, 1967), pp. 104–113.

42 Lawrence Brody, Beatrice Harris, and Genaro Lachica, *Discovering and Developing the College Potential of Disadvantaged High School Youth* (New York: The City University of New York, 1969), pp. 78–81.

other words, the youngsters who were enrolled in the special academic-year program provided by the schools, but were not in Upward Bound, performed as well academically as those youngsters who participated both in the special academic-year program and in Upward Bound. From these findings it can be inferred that Upward Bound is not necessary when the college preparatory curriculum of the high school is effectively reconstructed for disadvantaged youth.

It should also be pointed out that Upward Bound has been concentrated nationally on preparing youth for careers that require four years of college. Insufficient emphasis has been given to career preparation through the community colleges.

The Problem of Fragmentation of Effort and Responsibility

The future of the Office of Economic Opportunity is uncertain. However, it may be useful to examine some of the strategies and assumptions underlying many of the educational efforts of the OEO in relation to the operations of other federal agencies and the functions of our schools. The strategy of completely bypassing the schools in establishing the OEO and in implementing its various educational programs appeared to stem from the belief that the educational system had failed our disadvantaged youth and, therefore, an anti-Establishment approach would be necessary to solve the crisis. Undergirding this notion was the conviction that business and industry would readily provide the know-how and commitment. But business and industry were not equipped to solve a problem that was not really a result of technological unemployment, but a consequence of many years of social neglect and misguided national priorities.

While the separation from the schools of the various educational programs of the OEO was deliberately intended to free the OEO to develop new and creative approaches toward solving the problem of youth unemployment, the results have been disappointing. Ironically, similar disappointments resulted during the Great Depression, when many emergency agencies of the federal government took on systematic programs of education for which the schools were intended.

As long as our nation continues to act on education through fragmented programs and specialized agencies in a spirit of "temporary emergency," more efforts will be expended in treating problems than in their prevention. Furthermore, as a special poverty agency, the OEO has given the impression of being a vehicle of national philanthropy for the purpose of alleviating the conscience of a guilt-ridden society.

The Radical Critics

A number of critics of our educational system have attracted attention during the late 1960's with their radical proposals for abolishing compulsory education and allowing adolescents to make their own arrangements for self-education, or to learn through apprenticeships, while being supported with federal stipends. Goodman puts it this way:

> On the whole, the education must be voluntary rather than compulsory, for no growth to freedom occurs except by intrinsic motivation. . . . We must diminish rather than expand the present monolithic school system. I would suggest that, on the model of the GI Bill, we experiment, giving the school money directly to the high school age adolescents, for any plausible self-chosen educational proposals, such as purposeful travel or individual enterprise.[43]

Thus Goodman's vision of the federal government paying students to drop out of high school so that they may engage in any plausible self-chosen educational venture presents a romanticized picture of adolescence and society. Moreover, where the G.I. Bill paved the way for millions of exservicemen to return to school, Goodman's proposal would tend to support a new exodus from school. In primitive societies and in the pretechnological era it was possible for young people to find their way into the social order without formal schooling. The very problem of youth unemployment in the latter half of the twentieth century is a result of the inability of our technological system to find places for adolescents who are lacking in general education and who are without marketable skills. Goodman has great faith in apprenticeships and informal, self-chosen activities rather than formal schooling for many of our adolescents:

> very many of the young would get a better education and grow up more usefully to themselves and society if the school money were used for real apprenticeships, or even if they were given the money to follow their own interests, ambitions, or even fancies, rather than penning them for lengthening years in increasingly regimented institutions; anyway, many young people could enter many professions without most of the schooling if we changed the rules for licensing and hiring.[44]

Friedenberg has made similar proposals to abolish compulsory education in the belief that our youth should be "left to work out their own arrangements to meet their own needs with the assurance of a reasonable level of state support." [45]

However, technological society creates increasing demands for competency. Altruistic arrangements can only go so far if they are not to become demeaning and if they are not to lead to dead ends. And the apprenticeship system has lost much of its viability because we are no

---

43 Paul Goodman, *Compulsory Mis-education* (New York: Horizon Press, 1964), p. 76.

44 Paul Goodman, *Like a Conquered Province* (New York: Random House, 1967), pp. 15–16.

45 Edgar Z. Friedenberg, *Coming of Age in America* (New York: Vintage Books, Alfred A. Knopf and Random House, Inc., 1967), pp. 250–251.

longer living in an age when "training necessary to a mastery of any one of the crafts lay within so narrow a range that what was needful could all be acquired by hearsay and as an incident to the discipline of apprenticeship." [46] Dewey also noted that "while the intellectual *possibilities* of industry have multiplied, industrial conditions tend to make industry, for the great masses, less of an educative resource than it was in the days of hand production for local markets. The burden of realizing the intellectual possibilities inhering in work is thus thrown back on the school." [47]

It would appear, then, that the most constructive and promising solution is not in a return to apprenticeships, but to develop cooperative work-experience programs integral to the curricula in trades and industries, technical occupations, distributive occupations, office occupations, and so on. The school would be responsible for seeing to it that the work experiences are educational. Students could be rotated in certain work assignments, thereby exploring a range of vocational opportunities and gaining an understanding and perspective of the larger processes and organizational arrangements in given industries and business. Such understandings and perspectives often are denied many workers today. Education need not "become an instrument of perpetuating unchanged the existing industrial order of society, instead of operating as a means of its transformation." [48]

Cooperative work-experience programs should lead directly to gainful employment for those students who desire to enter the world of work. The programs should be sufficiently flexible to enable students to explore career alternatives, to change their goals, and to find new opportunities for educational and career success. Our programs of vocational education have not exploited the many promising opportunities of cooperative work-experience.

PROBLEMS AND PROSPECTS

"Besides general schooling," wrote Gunnar Myrdal, "America needs very much greater efforts in the field of vocational training. Training for work has never been made a regular part of the American educational system. A new philosophy is also needed." [49]

Despite the long history of federal support of vocational education in our secondary schools, the various programs have been treated as ancillary to the academic curriculum and, in many cases, have been regarded as inferior studies for inferior students. Many educators look upon voca-

---

46 Veblen, *op. cit.,* p. 308.

47 Dewey, *op. cit.,* p. 367.

48 *Ibid.,* p. 369.

49 Gunnar Myrdal, *Challenge to Affluence* (New York: Vintage Books, Alfred A. Knopf and Random House, Inc., 1965), p. 33.

tional education as a form of class discrimination. Yet they show little concern for the millions of youth who leave school for futures marked by the uncertainties of unemployment, unskilled jobs, and no opportunity for continuing education. Moreover, as discussed earlier, the federal programs in vocational education have served only a very small fraction of our youth.

Impact of the Vocational Education Act of 1963

Follow-up studies of persons who completed the formal day-school programs of vocational education at the secondary and postsecondary levels reveal an unemployment rate of less than 5 per cent. In comparison, the national rate of unemployment for the sixteen to nineteen-year-old age group has averaged more than 14 per cent, while the figure for nonwhite teenagers has been around 27 per cent.[50] Where enrollments in vocational-technical programs at the secondary school level totaled slightly over 2 million in 1964, it had risen to approximately 5 million in 1970. Nevertheless, with only a small proportion of our nation's youth being served by these programs, coupled with difficulties in the national employment picture through the recession of 1970, the rate of youth unemployment nationally has remained at such high levels as to constitute a crisis situation.

A study of the effect of federally supported vocational education programs in secondary schools in nine cities of varying size revealed that while a reasonably high proportion of graduates were being placed in occupations for which they were prepared, the small enrollments in these programs failed to make an impact on the manpower needs of the communities.[51]

In the Coleman study we find that almost half of the secondary school principals reported that no vocational program was offered by their schools. Twelfth-graders were asked, "Would you have enrolled in a vocational (job training) program if one that interested you were offered in your high school?" In response to this question, 13 per cent reported that they were already enrolled in such a program, while 44 per cent replied affirmatively and 44 per cent negatively. However, 67 per cent of the Negro students in the South, and 53 per cent of the Negro students elsewhere in the nation responded affirmatively to this question.[52]

---

[50] Office of Education, *Vocational & Technical Education* (Washington, D.C.: U.S. Government Printing Office, 1969), p. 9.

[51] Jacob J. Kaufman, Carl J. Schaefer, and others, *The Role of the Secondary Schools in the Preparation of Youth for Employment* (University Park, Pa.: The Pennsylvania State University, 1967).

[52] James S. Coleman, *Equality of Educational Opportunity* (Washington, D.C.: U.S. Government Printing Office, 1966), p. 545.

Although the Vocational Education Act of 1963 has led to dramatic enrollment increases in vocational programs at the high school level, the large majority of adolescents who could benefit from such programs are yet to be reached. Many people have come to think of vocational education as terminal training for a dead-end job. In actuality, it is the school dropout and the individual without marketable skills who are most vulnerable to dead ends and unemployment. "Vocational training, like education in general," noted Myrdal, "must help young people to move horizontally to other occupations, and vertically to higher responsibilities, as future opportunities may occur."[53]

The Problem of Social Separation

At the beginning of this chapter we discussed the democratizing influence of the comprehensive high school. Unfortunately, in many comprehensive high schools with highly heterogeneous student populations, the separation of students into vocational, college preparatory, and general tracks or streams has served to accentuate social-class and racial differences and to isolate students from one another. Moreover, it has created a built-in rigidity that prevents or inhibits students from changing their programs and goals, and makes it difficult for them to develop flexible programs of study. But such practices are not an inherent feature of the comprehensive high school. Tracking or streaming appears to serve as an administrative convenience more than anything else.

Curriculum Prestige and Priority.   There has also been a tendency to favor the college preparatory program in the comprehensive high school. Not only does this program enjoy the highest prestige, but it has received the highest priority in the national curriculum reform movement for almost two decades. In addition, school administrators are well aware of the implications that College Board Examinations, National Merit Scholarship tests, and the National Assessment of Educational Progress will have for their clientele. As a result of the various mechanisms for isolating the vocational student, and giving priority to the college-bound student and the academic phase of the curriculum, it is not surprising to find academic teachers opposed to the expansion of vocational education. And it is not surprising to find academic teachers "looking down on" the vocational students while these students, in turn, are made to feel "looked down upon." [54]

However, it should be stressed again that these undesirable outcomes are the result of practices, or malpractices, in schools where vocational

53 Myrdal, *op. cit.,* p. 33.
54 Kaufman, Schaefer, and others, *op. cit.,* pp. 12–17.

education is given low priority and where students with different educational goals and backgrounds are isolated by tracking systems. Fortunately, there are many comprehensive high schools with heterogeneous student populations where the programs in vocational education receive strong support and enjoy a high degree of prestige to match their success. Even during the height of the cold war era, Conant was able to find such schools.[55]

The Area Vocational School.   Now that a new era in developing flexible programs of vocational education is on the horizon as a result of the Vocational Education Act of 1963, the comprehensive high school should be making giant steps toward realizing its obligation of serving all the youth of all the people. But in recent years, area vocational schools are being established throughout the various states. The area schools (those serving students from more than one school district), originally conceived of to prepare highly skilled technicians, are a product of Title VIII of the National Defense Education Act.

Are such specialized single-purpose institutions necessary? It has already been demonstrated in many sections of the nation, such as California, that specialized educational programs can be developed in comprehensive community colleges. While there are those who contend that the single-purpose school is more economical, this does not necessarily make it more effective from an educational standpoint. The wisdom of establishing such single-purpose institutions is open to serious question in view of the resultant educational and social isolation. Moreover, the comprehensive community college is far more flexible in allowing students to change curricula and in extending educational opportunity to the university.

Additional funds for area vocational schools have been made available through the Vocational Education Act of 1963. This legislation allows the states to establish area schools in a variety of patterns. In some cases, students bused from several surrounding high schools spend part of each day in the area vocational school. In other cases, students from several districts are enrolled full-time in these specialized schools. The area vocational schools also provide programs for postsecondary students, out-of-school youth, and adults.

It has been observed that "the development of area vocational schools tends to establish more firmly a division of our youth along class lines." [56] Coleman found that minority students who are disadvantaged, and who attend schools where they are in contact with students very much like themselves, have a poorer self-image and show lower achievement levels

---

[55] Conant, *The American High School Today, op. cit.*

[56] Carl J. Schaefer and Jacob J. Kaufman, *Occupational Education for Massachusetts* (Boston: Advisory Council on Education, 1968), p. 16.

than those who attend schools with heterogeneous student populations.[57] Coleman also found that variations in educational resources do not compensate for social and racial isolation. In many of our larger cities having vocational high schools it has been found that such schools serve to isolate students racially and socioeconomically.

Potential of the Comprehensive High School. It would appear, then, that a far more desirable alternative to the area vocational school would be to designate a comprehensive high school as an area vocational center to serve more than one district. The remarkable trend toward school district reorganization makes this a viable alternative in many areas. In our larger cities, different specialized vocational programs could be established in various comprehensive high schools, and students could be assigned to a given comprehensive high school according to their particular areas of need for vocational education. This would seem to be an educationally effective and economically sound approach to meeting the specialized educational needs of youth in a comprehensive high school setting.

Too many educators and educational critics have come to look upon student heterogeneity and curriculum diversity in the secondary school as a weakness rather than a strength. Even in many of our elitist institutions of higher education, there is a growing recognition of the educational powers which can be awakened when, in the words of a college president, we have "a good mixture of city boys and country boys, rich boys and poor boys, bright boys and average boys, athletes and physically handicapped, Americans and foreigners, boys of all races, of all faiths and even of no faith." [58]

Our people have long been committed to supporting educational institutions that seek to meet the diversified needs of a heterogeneous population under "one roof." The comprehensive high school, in principle, and often in function, has been the most promising of these institutions.

SUMMARY

One of the great ironies of our times is that vocational education has managed to gain a recognized place in our colleges and universities, while the struggle to make it an integral part of the high school curriculum continues. Many college educators, who do not challenge the place of vocational curricula in the universities, regard such studies as inferior and even anti-intellectual when offered in the high schools.

The pursuit of academic excellence and the curriculum reform empha-

---

[57] Coleman, *op. cit.*, pp. 21–23.
[58] *The New York Times* (June 4, 1970), p. 35.

sis in the academic disciplines received such high priority during the 1950's and 1960's that little was done to reconstruct the curricula in vocational education at the secondary level. The emphasis was on the exploitation of our academically talented students, while the needs and talents of the majority of our youth who do not continue their education beyond high school were largely ignored.

Our nation now is coming to recognize that the educational needs and talents of all its youth must be fulfilled if society is to function effectively. The dangerous consequence of denying our youth a constructive place in the life stream of society has become clearly evident. But instead of patchwork adjustments and assorted emergency projects, we will need concerted efforts to reconstruct the vocational curricula of our high schools and to make education for productive careers available to all. Through comprehensive programs of vocational education, students can prepare themselves for careers rather than merely for jobs. Such programs can be made flexible to allow for changing interests and aspirations, educationally and vocationally. Cooperative work-experience programs can be made an integral part of the high school curriculum, thereby making education relevant to the world of work.

But education, to paraphrase Dewey, should not be merely an instrument of perpetuating the existing industrial and social order, but of bringing about its improvement.

PROBLEMS FOR STUDY AND DISCUSSION

1. In stating the case for vocational education, Dewey warned that "there is danger that vocational education will be interpreted in theory and practice as trade education: as a means of securing technical efficiency in specialized future pursuits. Education would then become an instrument of perpetuating unchanged the existing industrial order of society, instead of operating as a means of its transformation." [John Dewey, *Democracy and Education* (New York: The Macmillan Company, 1916), p. 369.]

   In view of the current changes taking place in vocational education, what can the schools do to avoid such a narrow interpretation of the function of vocational education?

2. The National Advisory Council on Vocational Education states the case for vocational education as a means of solving the problem of violence and revolt that stems from youth unemployment. The editor of a leading scientific journal supports vocational education because skilled labor is in short supply, as witnessed by the fact that it sometimes takes weeks for services such as automobile repairs, and we must not allow our technological society to deteriorate.

From the standpoint of adolescent development, what arguments can you offer in favor of vocational education in the curriculum of the secondary school?

3. At one point in our contemporary history, proponents of vocational education were attacked as anti-intellectuals and labeled as "life-adjustment educators." [Richard Hofstadter, *Anti-intellectualism in American Life* (New York: Alfred A. Knopf, Inc., 1963), Ch. 13.]

   More recently, the schools have been criticized for neglecting vocational education and promoting academic snobbery. How have various social and political forces influenced the secondary school curriculum in recent history? Give some specific examples.

4. How do you account for the high status enjoyed by vocational and technical curricula in our colleges and universities, while such curricula traditionally have been given low status and low priority in the high school?

5. The Vocational Education Act of 1963 provides for the establishment of specialized, single-purpose area vocational schools. What are the pros and cons of such schools in comparison to comprehensive high schools? This legislation also provides for the establishment of residential vocational schools, particularly for disadvantaged youth from urban areas who have dropped out of school or who are unemployed. What educational issues do you see in connection with such residential schools?

6. What should be the relationship between the high schools and the community colleges in providing for vocational and technical education?

SELECTED REFERENCES

American Educational Research Association. "Vocational, Technical, and Practical Arts Education." *Review of Educational Research,* Vol. 38 (October, 1968).

Barlow, Melvin L. *History of Industrial Education in the United States.* Peoria, Ill.: Charles A. Bennett Co., Inc., 1967.

Bestor, Arthur. *The Restoration of Learning.* New York: Alfred A. Knopf, Inc., 1956.

Broudy, Harry S., B. Othanel Smith, and Joe R. Burnett. *Democracy and Excellence in American Secondary Education.* Chicago: Rand McNally & Company, 1964.

Coleman, James S. *Equality of Educational Opportunity.* Washington, D.C.: U.S. Government Printing Office, 1966.

Conant, James B. *The American High School Today.* New York: McGraw-Hill Book Company, Inc., 1959.

————. *Slums and Suburbs.* New York: McGraw-Hill Book Company, Inc., 1961.

Cremin, Lawrence A. *The Transformation of the School.* New York: Alfred A. Knopf, Inc., 1961.

Dewey, John. *Democracy and Education.* New York: The Macmillan Company, 1916.

Educational Policies Commission. *Education for ALL American Youth— A Further Look.* Washington, D.C.: National Education Association, 1952.

Ellul, Jacques. *The Technological Society.* New York: Alfred A. Knopf, Inc., 1964.

Galbraith, John Kenneth. *The New Industrial State.* Boston: Houghton Mifflin Company, 1967. Chs. 32, 33.

Giachino, J. W., and Ralph O. Gallington. *Course Construction in Industrial Arts, Vocational and Technical Education,* 3rd ed. Chicago: American Technical Society, 1967.

Goodman, Paul. *Compulsory Mis-education.* New York: Horizon Press, 1964.

Hall, Richard H. *Occupations and the Social Structure.* Englewood Cliffs, N.J.: Prentice-Hall, Inc., 1969.

Hofstadter, Richard. *Anti-intellectualism in American Life.* New York: Alfred A. Knopf, Inc., 1963.

Kerner, Otto (chairman). *Report of the National Advisory Commission on Civil Disorders.* Washington, D.C.: U.S. Government Printing Office, 1968.

King, Arthur R., Jr., and John A. Brownell. *The Curriculum and the Disciplines of Knowledge.* New York: John Wiley & Sons, Inc., 1966.

Lecht, Leonard. *Manpower Needs for National Goals in the 1970's.* New York: Frederick A. Praeger, Publishers, 1969.

National Society for the Study of Education. *Vocational Education.* Sixty-fourth Yearbook, Part I. Chicago: The University of Chicago Press, 1965.

Office of Education. *Vocational and Technical Education.* Washington, D.C.: U.S. Government Printing Office, 1970.

Report of the Harvard Committee. *General Education in a Free Society.* Cambridge, Mass.: Harvard University Press, 1945.

Rhodes, James A. *Alternative to a Decadent Society.* Indianapolis: Howard W. Sams & Co., 1969.

Roberts, Roy. *Vocational and Practical Arts Education,* 2nd ed. New York: Harper & Row, Publishers, 1965.

Rickover, Hyman G. *American Education—A National Failure.* New York: E. P. Dutton & Co., Inc., 1963. Chs. 12, 13, 14.

Tanner, Daniel. *Schools for Youth—Change and Challenge in Secondary Education.* New York: The Macmillan Company, 1965. Ch. 9.

U.S. Advisory Council on Vocational Education. *Vocational Education: The Bridge Between Man and His Work.* Washington, D.C.: U.S. Government Printing Office, 1968.

Veblen, Thorstein. *The Instinct of Workmanship.* New York: The Macmillan Company, 1914.

Wilber, Gordon O., and Norman C. Pendered. *Industrial Arts in General Education.* Scranton, Pa.: International Textbook Company, 1967.

Wolfbein, Seymour. *Education and Training for Full Employment.* New York: Columbia University Press, 1967.

Part III

Patterns and Prospects

In everything which has to do with the shaping
and expression of thought and feeling,
"the letter killeth; the spirit giveth life."
And if the models we put before them have no spirit
our students' progress must be slight.

—REPORT OF THE HARVARD COMMITTEE

Chapter 11

Innovation and Curriculum Improvement

"Education which is not modern," wrote Whitehead, "shares the fate of all organic things which are kept too long." [1] But mere change and innovation do not necessarily make education modern. Change and innovation must be directed at curriculum improvement. All too often innovations have been treated as ends, not means. Innovations, not the learner and the curriculum, become the points of focus. Organizational and operational elements of the school are altered or changed without improving learning outcomes. Innovations are institutionalized without changing the institution.

Throughout this book, we have examined critically various major efforts in curriculum reform and improvement. Because the curriculum reform movement has been concentrated on the separate disciplines and fields of knowledge, curriculum improvement, in the eyes of many teachers, administrators, and parents, is simply a matter of adopting one or more of the new curriculum packages. The curriculum of the school and the school as an institution of learning have not been treated as a unity. The outcomes of a change in one area are rarely studied in terms of the effects on other areas. The learner often is unable to find coherence and synthesis in a curriculum and in an organization that is fragmented and compartmentalized.

Innovations directed at the organization and management of the instructional program and the utilization of new media tend to be characterized by disjointedness. The lack of coordination often is complicated by the practice of adopting certain instructional innovations to improve

---

[1] Alfred North Whitehead, *The Aims of Education* (New York: The Macmillan Company, 1929), p. 117.

administrative efficiency and not to improve the teaching-learning process. In this chapter various innovations in the organization and management of the instructional program are examined critically in terms of effecting needed improvements in the total school curriculum.

CURRICULUM IMPROVEMENT

If innovations are intended to result in curriculum improvement, they must be designed to improve the planned learning activities sponsored by the school. And they should be coordinated with all other innovations that are aimed at curriculum improvement. As we have pointed out, not only are many new practices adopted and administered disjointedly, but they are often used for purposes other than the improvement of the teaching-learning process.

Aims and Functions

Modular-flexible scheduling, team teaching, large-group instruction, independent study, technical devices, and physical facilities frequently are designed for improving the efficiency of staff utilization rather than for improving the quality of the learning experiences. Yet such innovations often are promoted under the expectation that they will automatically bring about marked improvements in the quality of teaching and learning. A school may adopt a particular curriculum package and may institute modular-flexible scheduling for very different purposes. Moreover, when innovations are disjointed, and when they are instituted for entirely different objectives, educators must take care that such innovations do not operate at cross purposes.

As an illustration, suppose that a school has adopted a program of independent study in which students are stimulated to undertake a great deal of individualized library work. The school then introduces programmed instruction during the time allocated for independent study. Both the independent study program and the programmed instruction were originally intended to provide for individualized learning, and both innovations were introduced for the purpose of improving the learning activities sponsored by the school. Yet the disjointedness of the two innovations may produce unanticipated conflicts. Because of the way in which the programmed instruction is administered, the students may find themselves devoting less time to reading library books and spending more time on standardized learning activity.

Other innovations are commonly promoted and adopted without giving adequate attention to the problem of changing the style of teaching so that the quality of learning is improved. For example, instead of utilizing television to do what the good teacher cannot do, we use it to do what the good teacher can do. The result is that the medium is used as an automation device which presents information to students in a manner remarkably similar to that of the lecturing teacher in the conventional classroom. Then we find negligible differences in learning outcomes when such uses of television are compared with conventional teaching as measured by paper-and-pencil tests. The usual conclusion is that students learn just as much from television as they do from conventional classroom situations and, therefore, television can be used in place of the teacher. In this respect, television is regarded as an automation device in the production process of schooling. Adopting an innovation for the purpose of eliminating the need for additional staff may be perfectly legitimate as a managerial efficiency measure. But it has little or nothing to do with curriculum improvement. Therefore, such measures should not be promoted under the guise that they will improve the quality of teaching and learning.

Definition of Curriculum

The concept of curriculum has undergone considerable change. Doll notes that it has changed from the "content of courses of study and lists of subjects and courses to all the experiences which are offered to learners under the auspices or direction of the school." [2] The problem with Doll's broad definition is that it would include even the unplanned experiences, such as whatever might occur on the school bus or elsewhere. Alexander and Saylor also define curriculum as "all learning opportunities provided by the school." [3] Here again, the definition is so broad that it would include many unanticipated and even undesirable learnings. For example, in recent years certain slum schools have been found to serve as centers in which students learn how to use narcotics and to engage in various other illegal activity. The suburban school and college may also serve as centers in which students learn to use narcotics and to become involved in actions that are neither approved by the school nor by society.

In noting that the very breadth of such definitions makes them nonfunctional, Taba conceives of curriculum as "a plan for learning." [4] However, a plan for learning can also be a lesson plan or a unit plan. One can hardly conceive of a lesson plan or a unit plan as constituting the curriculum of the school. Furthermore, this definition fails to differentiate between the curriculum of a school and that of a nonschool educative agency.

---

[2] Ronald C. Doll, *Curriculum Improvement* (Boston: Allyn and Bacon, Inc., 1970), p. 21.

[3] J. Galen Saylor and William M. Alexander, *Curriculum Planning for Modern Schools* (New York: Holt, Rinehart and Winston, Inc., 1966), p. 5.

[4] Hilda Taba, *Curriculum Development: Theory and Practice* (New York: Harcourt, Brace & World, Inc., 1962), p. 11.

For our purposes, then, a curriculum consists of the *planned learning activities sponsored by the school.*

Curriculum Change

The process of curriculum development, according to Taba, includes the following steps: (1) diagnosis of needs, (2) formulation of objectives, (3) selection of content, (4) organization of content, (5) selection of learning experiences, (6) organization of learning experiences, and (7) determination of what to evaluate and of the ways and means of evaluation.[5] These steps are similar to Tyler's questions in developing a curriculum,[6] discussed in Chapter 2.

Such a schema of steps or questions is invaluable in the process of curriculum development. As emphasized throughout this text, the major efforts toward curriculum reform in recent years have been directed at the separate domains of knowledge without giving adequate attention to the necessary interrelationships between and among these domains. In following a schema for curriculum development, it is important that each area of subject matter is treated in relationship to the total curriculum of the school. Otherwise, the curriculum is in danger of becoming fragmented, unbalanced, and even in conflict with the needs of the learner and the broader goals of the school.

Similarly, we have noted in earlier chapters how many innovations in the organization and operation of learning activities are undertaken piecemeal and without being directly related to the educational objectives of the school. If managerial innovations are directed at functions other than the planned learning activities of the school, then they are not likely to lead to curriculum improvement.

Dynamics of Curriculum Change. In their efforts to improve the school curriculum, educators need to understand the dynamics of the various forces at work. Many texts on curriculum development focus on educators as the principal source of curriculum change. Throughout this book, however, we have stressed how such change is brought about through various sources and means, including federal legislation and the foundation which provide funds for the engagement of university academicians who collaborate in developing curriculum packages to be adopted by schools throughout the nation.

Mackenzie has analyzed the curriculum change process in the cultural context consisting of (1) internal and external participants, (2) their sources of power and methods of influence, (3) the several phases in the

---

[5] *Ibid.*, p. 12.

[6] Ralph W. Tyler, *Basic Principles of Curriculum and Instruction* (Chicago: The University of Chicago Press, 1950), pp. 1–2.

process of change and the ways in which the participants relate to the change process, and (4) the ways in which the determiners, as the focal points of the change effort, are affected.[7] The focal points for such change are teachers, students, subject matter, materials and facilities, and time.[8] Mackenzie's schema is presented in Table 11-1.

An Illustrative Case. At one point in time we might find Admiral Rickover and Professor Bestor advocating a national testing program to assess educational achievement. Neither advocate is supported by any formal agency, public or private. However, Rickover's reputation with nuclear-powered submarines and Bestor's position as a university historian make available to them the mass media for communication with the public, professional educators, and legislators at all levels of government. The crisis of the cold war and the missile gap serves to create an urgent climate for change. At a subsequent stage, two of the leading private foundations (Carnegie and Ford) cooperate to provide funds and machinery for instituting a program of National Assessment of Educational Progress. The foundations engage a prestigious and competent educator, Ralph W. Tyler, to head up the total effort. Recognizing the difficulty in instituting such a program nationally when education is legally decentralized, the foundations turn to a quasipublic agency of their own creation, the Education Commission of the States, to gain the cooperation of the various states and to coordinate the total effort politically. Advocates of the program, despite initial opposition, eventually are successful in their efforts to gain the endorsement of the American Association of School Administrators. At various stages, advocates of National Assessment of Educational Progress seek federal funds for their foundation-supported venture. Not long after the former president of the Carnegie Corporation resigns as Secretary of the U.S. Department of Health, Education, and Welfare, the Office of Education joins the Carnegie Corporation and the Ford Foundation in funding the National Assessment of Educational Progress. Soon the project is officially launched, and teachers and students are affected, directly or indirectly.

This brief synopsis of a particular project is presented as an illustration of the evolvement in the relationships among participants in educational change, and the influences exerted on the determiners of the curriculum. The extent to which the National Assessment of Educational Progress will actually bring about curriculum change has been hotly debated. Nevertheless, the National Assessment of Educational Progress cannot be interpreted apart from the curriculum objectives of our schools.

---

[7] Gordon N. Mackenzie, "Curricular Change: Participants, Power, and Processes," Chapter 17 in Matthew B. Miles (ed.), *Innovation in Education* (New York: Teachers College Press, 1964), pp. 399–424.

[8] *Ibid.*, p. 402.

Table 11-1. Curriculum Change: Participants, Power, and Processes

Cultural Context

Participants in curricular change ⟶	Having control of certain sources of power and methods of influence ⟶	Proceed through various phases in a process ⟶	To influence the determiners of the curriculum
Internal participants: Students Teachers Principals Supervisors Superintendents Boards of education Citizens in local communities State legislatures State departments of education State and federal courts External participants: Noneducationists Foundations Academicians Business and industry Educationists National government	Advocacy and communication Prestige Competence Money or goods Legal authority Policy, precedent, custom Cooperation and collaboration	Initiated by internal or external participation: Criticism Proposal of changes Development and clarification of proposals for change Evaluation, review and reformulation of proposals Comparison of proposals Initiated by internal participants: Action on proposals Implementation of action decisions	Teachers Students Subject matter Methods Materials and facilities Time

Source: Gordon N. Mackenzie, "Curricular Change: Participants, Power, and Processes," Chapter 17 in Matthew B. Miles (ed.), Innovation in Education (New York: Teachers College Press, 1964), p. 401.

While the analysis of curriculum change in this text is not intended to focus on the actual change processes, participants, and determiners per se, the author has identified some of these sources in order to enable the reader to better understand the complex forces at work.

Other Analyses of Educational Change Processes

Many attempts have been made to analyze the change processes in education. An interesting and useful analysis, developed by Guba and Clark, consists of the following major processes:

Research
Development
   Invention
   Design
Diffusion
   Dissemination
   Demonstration
Adoption
   Trial
   Installation
   Institutionalization.[9]

The processes identified by Guba and Clark are remarkably similar to those connected with production agriculture where (1) basic research is conducted by agricultural scientists at the land-grant university; (2) research findings are tested and developed in the field through the agricultural experiment station; (3) outcomes of the field tests which give promise of improved agricultural practice are diffused through actual demonstrations in the field, and proven practices are disseminated through consultation with the county agricultural agent, the teacher of vocational agriculture, bulletins, films, conferences, short courses, institutes, radio, television, and other media and communication channels; and (4) approved practices are tried out by farmers and, if successful, are adopted and become part of the on-going process of farming. Continuous evaluation, modification, and feedback are ensured through the farmer's contact with the local agricultural agent, teacher of vocational agriculture, and land-grant university. Obviously, these four processes are oversimplified and do not account for the powerful influences of peer leadership, agricultural cooperatives and other farmer organizations, and commercial agricultural enterprises. Recognizing the power of peer-leader-

---

[9] Egon G. Guba and David L. Clark, "Methodological Strategies for Educational Change." Paper presented to the Conference on Strategies for Educational Change (Washington, D.C.: November 8–10, 1965).

ship influence, concerted efforts are made by the county agricultural agent and land-grant university to work closely with influential farmers, through direct consultation and local demonstration activities.

Figure 11-1 presents a considerable elaboration of Guba and Clark's schema, incorporating some ideas of Mackenzie,[10] concerning certain major processes related to curriculum change. The model in Figure 11-1 is hypothetical and is not intended to include the various agents or actors in the change process, or the important sociopolitical-economic forces which influence decision making, as these are represented in Mackenzie's schema already presented in Table 11-1.

As shown in Figure 11-1, the first major process is research involving theory and the testing of theory through experimentation. The second process is that of development, which involves invention, design, and application. Diffusion is identified as the third process, which includes the dissemination of innovative ideas and the demonstration of new practices in the field. Fourth is the process of assessment, through which the practitioner compares the innovative ideas and practices against existing practices and makes his interpretations. The fifth process is adoption and adaptation, in which the practitioner installs the new practice and subjects it to trial while adapting it to his own local circumstances. Sixth is the process of reassessment, where the innovation is revised and adjusted under local operational conditions. Legitimation is the seventh process, in which the innovation acquires acceptance on the part of both the practitioner and a significant proportion of his peers. Finally, the eighth process, institutionalization, involves sufficient commitment by the practitioner and his peers that the innovation has replaced the old practice and, in so doing, becomes a common practice in its own right.

Through each process, the innovation must be continuously evaluated and modified, and there must be continuous feedback, if the original basic research is to lead to sound application and operation in the field.

Some final words of caution are in order concerning the schematic representation in Figure 11-1. The processes are not necessarily in a consecutive or hierarchical order. Frequently, a particular innovation may be returned to the research and development stages where it is further modified before reaching the field. Moreover, some of the processes often occur simultaneously. In addition, the eventual legitimation and institutionalization of the innovative practice, as mentioned earlier, may depend not only on its proven validity and reliability, but on social, political, and economic factors.

---

[10] See Gordon N. Mackenzie, "Why a Strategy for Planned Curricular Innovation?" Chapter 1 in Marcella R. Lawler (ed.), *Strategies for Planned Curricular Innovation* (New York: Teachers College Press, 1970), p. 10.

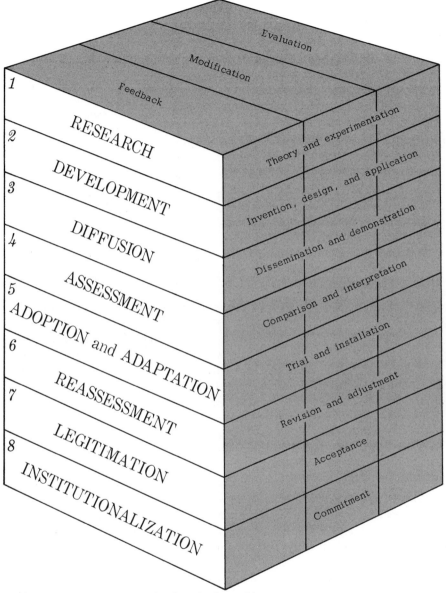

Figure 11-1. Processes in Curriculum Change

Research and Developmental Centers and Regional Educational Laboratories

As a result of the growing recognition that there are wide gaps in the processes through which educational research and development lead to improved practices, the Research and Development Center Program was established in 1963 under the Cooperative Research Program of the U.S. Office of Education. A number of Research and Development Centers have been established at various universities to conduct research on a wide variety of educational problems, to explore various intervention strategies, and to test findings under laboratory and field conditions.

As a further effort to bridge the gap between basic research and improved practice, Regional Educational Laboratories were established through Title IV of the Elementary and Secondary Education Act of 1965. The laboratories are intended to further develop, disseminate, and adapt the findings of the R & D Centers to the particular conditions of the various regions. And the laboratories are expected to work closely with state departments of education, school districts, and community agencies in further developing innovations, demonstrating improved practices, subjecting innovations and practices to field tests, and disseminating needed information. While they are independent of the universities, the laboratories tend to work closely with university scholars on the development of new practices.

The R & D Centers and the Regional Educational Laboratories were established with the intention that they would emulate the successes of the agricultural experiment stations and the Cooperative Extension Service in linking the processes between research and practice. However, where these agricultural agencies have developed highly comprehensive programs, the activities of the R & D Centers and the Regional Educational Laboratories have been largely specialized and piecemeal. For example, one laboratory might be working on the technology of instruction for disadvantaged children while another is developing microteaching packages for the training of teachers in the techniques of verbal reinforcement.

Moreover, there has been some confusion in differentiating the functions of the R & D Centers and those of the Regional Educational Laboratories. And, unlike the above-mentioned agricultural agencies, which are integral to the public land-grant universities, some of the R & D Centers are located at private universities having a limited commitment to serving the people at large. Nor are all of the Regional Laboratories bona fide public agencies. For example, the Education Development Center is a private nonprofit corporation.

The failure to develop and promote innovations and new packages in terms of the total equilibrium of the school curriculum continues to be a most serious problem. Until the Research and Development Centers and the Regional Educational Laboratories focus on the larger problem of total curriculum design and equilibrium, they are not likely to accomplish their mission.

The Need for Total Curriculum Design and Equilibrium

A major thesis of this book is that planned curriculum change should be instituted in relationship to the total design of the curriculum. Furthermore, as discussed throughout this text, many of the new curriculum packages have been developed, endorsed, and promoted without being subjected to independent and rigorous experimentation and evaluation. Relatively few of these packages have undergone the processes represented in the model shown in Figure 11-1. Notable exceptions are the University of Illinois Committee on School Mathematics and the Harvard Social Studies Project. The Biological Sciences Curriculum Study also should be cited for rejecting the dogmatic notion that there exists a singular approach to subject matter and organization which is valid everywhere. Instead, alternative approaches have been developed and subjected to continuous evaluation and modification.

In too many instances, those responsible for developing the new curriculum packages have promoted their works through testimonials rather than through experimentation. And they have often been all too eager to capitalize on a political climate that, for almost two decades, caused school administrators to look for instant answers to curriculum improvement under conditions of emergency and crisis. Too many school administrators have been willing, if not anxious, to adopt new curriculum packages and innovations as a means of demonstrating to their constituencies and peers that their schools are keeping abreast of the times. Rarely have they examined these packages and innovations in terms of learning outcomes. And rarely have they considered the total equilibrium of the school curriculum in their adoption of these changes.

Emphasized in virtually every chapter of this text is the neglect of the total curriculum design during the late 1950's and the decade of the 1960's, when reform efforts were concentrated on the individual disciplines and subject fields. Although this problem is discussed in detail in Chapter 2, a concluding statement is in order in this final chapter.

New Demands and Developments.   In recent years, our nation has witnessed a growing social consciousness, particularly among the new generations of college and high school youth. They have demanded that their studies be made relevant to their own personal-social problems and those of contemporary society. While it may be too early to assess the full effects of these developments on the curriculum, there is reason for considerable optimism.

First, in response to the social and political crises of our times, there appears to be a growing recognition of the need in curriculum development to take into account the problems of contemporary society, and the problems and needs of the learner. In this connection, educators are becoming increasingly aware of the limitations and inadequacies of the scholar-specialist as the single determining source of educational objectives and subject matter. Moreover, the scholar-specialists themselves are taking cognizance of the need to make their disciplines relevant to the contemporary problems of society and to the learner as a citizen of society.

Second, an increasing proportion of secondary school educators and university scholars are becoming aware of the need to develop interdisciplinary and problem-focused studies if the curriculum is to be made relevant to the life of the learner. And where most of the curriculum reform efforts of the 1950's and 1960's stressed disciplinarity as opposed to application, a number of newer projects are designed to relate theoretical knowledge to practical application.

Third, virtually all of the desirable features of the discipline-centered curriculum reforms are being applied to these newer problem-centered and interdisciplinary approaches to curriculum construction. Among these desirable features are: the emphasis on more open-ended learning in opposition to the memorization and regurgitation of subject matter; the use of multimedia approaches to teaching and learning; the organization of subject matter according to meaningful concepts, generalizations, and principles as opposed to encyclopedic approaches; and a project approach is being employed in marshaling a wide variety of resources toward a concerted goal.

And, fourth, a new partnership may be emerging in which scholar-specialists not only are working with each other in developing cross-disciplinary, interdisciplinary, and problem-centered courses, but are working with teacher educators, curriculum generalists, and educational psychologists in an effort to improve the effectiveness of the teaching-learning process.

Focus on Design and Equilibrium.   Nevertheless, the larger problem of total curriculum design and equilibrium remains sadly neglected. For almost two decades this larger problem has been put aside as educators responded to other priorities.

Now, and in the years immediately ahead, educators will need to develop a new equilibrium in the curriculum among (1) studies that are discipline-centered; (2) studies that are cross-disciplinary, multidisciplinary, and interdisciplinary within given fields of knowledge—such as the sciences taken as a whole, or the social studies taken as a whole; (3) studies that are cross-disciplinary, multidisciplinary, and interdisciplinary—involving two or more different fields of knowledge and their component disciplines—such as mathematics and science, or history, sociology, and literature; (4) studies that are focused on pervading personal and societal problems without being limited to any given area of organized subject matter; (5) prevocational and vocational studies; and (6) independent learning experiences, both in school and out of school.

How these different types of studies are to be interrelated for purposes of general education will require enormous attention and effort. But in view of the growing social consciousness, an awareness of the limitations of our past approaches to curriculum construction, and the need to make education relevant to the life of our times, educators will no longer be able to ignore the need to focus on the design of the total curriculum and its equilibrium in instituting innovations.

The remainder of this chapter examines critically several of the major recent innovations in the organization and operation of learning activities in the school, with the primary focus on assessing these innovations in terms of their possible contribution toward curriculum improvement.

MODULAR-FLEXIBLE SCHEDULING

Throughout the 1950's and 1960's, the Ford Foundation and the Carnegie Corporation provided considerable financial support for projects designed to improve the efficiency of American public education. The adoption of new managerial techniques, the utilization of the new technology, the differentiation of staffing functions, and the assessment of achievement through national testing programs were some of the areas of activity promoted by the Ford Foundation and the Carnegie Corporation during this period.

A Comprehensive Proposal

Under the auspices of the Ford Foundation, a comprehensive proposal for the reorganization of the secondary school was developed at Stanford University's School of Education.[11] The proposal called for the adoption of a modular-flexible schedule having the following features: (1) classes in each subject will vary in size and will include large-group instruction, small-group instruction, independent and individualized study, and laboratory instruction; (2) length of class meeting and the number and spacing of classes will vary according to the nature of the subject, the type of instruction, and the level of ability and interest of pupils; (3) differentiated staffing will be provided, consisting of teams made up of senior teachers, staff teachers, beginning teachers, interns, teaching assistants, technical assistants, clerical assistants, and resource personnel; (4) students will be grouped, subject by subject, according to their achievement, ability, and interests; and (5) considerable use of the new technology will be made.

---

[11] Robert N. Bush and Dwight W. Allen, *A New Design for High School Education* (New York: McGraw-Hill Book Company, Inc., 1964).

The basic premise of the proposal for modular-flexible scheduling is that "the entire curriculum can be thought of as an *area* to be scheduled." [12] This definition reflects the concept of the school as an educational engineering enterprise. "The curriculum, conceived as an area to be scheduled, is made up of subparts called modular units which are derived from units of time, units of class size, and units of course structure." [13]

Thus the day's schedule might consist of 16 modules of 30 minutes each. As many as 300 students might meet together for three half-hour time modules of large-group instruction. The group of 300 students might then be subdivided into four classes of 75 students for another time period, followed by further subdivision into groups of 15 for a given time period of small-group instruction and, finally, the students would be scheduled for independent or individualized study. Each student's schedule would vary daily, but would repeat itself weekly.

Evaluation and Implications

In the conventional secondary school, students follow an identical schedule of classes each day throughout the semester, and each class consists of approximately 30 students and one teacher scheduled daily for some 50 minutes. Modular-flexible scheduling is intended to break this lockstep by allowing schools to alter the size of the classes and to vary the time period for each class session in accordance with the kind of learning activity taking place.

Obviously, teachers must adapt their methods according to the size of the instructional group. Thus, a large-group activity might consist of a lecture, television lesson, or motion picture. The small-class group might involve discussion of the material presented in the large-group session. Time for independent and individualized study allows students to work on their own in the school library or learning-resource center where they might also be engaged in programmed instruction.

Problem of Rigidity. Although the proposals for modular-flexible scheduling are advanced on the premise that this system allows for greater flexibility in teaching and learning activities in comparison to conventional school schedules, it is possible to make certain adjustments to allow for team teaching, combined classes, and independent study, even in the conventional situation. Moreover, an examination of a sample schedule for a given student in a modular-flexible program reveals a new kind of schedule rigidity. Let us look at a sample schedule for a given student in grade 7 on a Monday, as illustrated in the proposal by

---

[12] *Ibid.*, p. 21.
[13] *Ibid.*, p. 24.

Bush and Allen, and presented in Table 11-2. It is important to note that Table 11-2 presents a schedule for one day of the week and that each day's schedule is different. Nevertheless, this will give the reader an idea of what a day in the life of a student might be like under a modular-flexible schedule. Each module in Table 11-2 is 30 minutes in length, and the Roman numerals denote the particular achievement level of the class grouping.

Table 11-2. Sample Schedule for a Seventh-Grade Student on a Given Day

Number of Modules (30 mins.)	Class
1	Independent study or other activity
1	Guidance (large group)
1	Science IV (large group)
2	Social Studies I (small group)
2	English Lab III
1	Mathematics IV (large group)
1	Physical Education II (large group)
1	Lunch
1	Foreign Language Lab III
2	Independent or individualized study
3	Arts I (large group)

Source: *Adapted from Robert N. Bush and Dwight W. Allen,* A New Design for High School Education *(New York: McGraw-Hill Book Company, Inc., 1964), p. 180.*

Although the schedule varies each day of the week, it is repeated identically in a weekly cycle. Thus, as shown in Table 11-2, the student will begin each Monday with a single module of individual study, followed by a single module of large-group guidance, and so on. The rigidity of the schedule becomes readily apparent. Moreover, one is inclined to wonder whether much can be accomplished in a mere 30-minute class session in physical education or independent study. After allowing for time to pass to and from classes, the length of the module is reduced further. When two modules are combined, the time block approximates that of the conventional class period, while three modules constitute 90 minutes minus the time required for passing between classes.

Emphasis on Staff Utilization.   Of course, the modular-flexible schedule can be modified further so that it allows for larger time blocks. However, when various proposals for modular-flexible scheduling are examined carefully, the chief emphasis appears to be on the more efficient utilization of physical facilities and deployment of pupil and teacher personnel in the process known as schooling. Relatively little attention is given to the ways in which teachers should alter their methods and utilize more appropriate learning resources for curriculum improvement. The detailed emphasis given to staff differentiation in the proposal by Bush and Allen led one reviewer to observe that "Bush and Allen recommend a hierarchy that makes the German General Staff by comparison seem like an anarchist's club." [14]

The Bush and Allen proposal draws heavily on the earlier work of Trump and Baynham, also supported by the Ford Foundation, under the auspices of the National Association of Secondary School Principals.[15] A statement on the cover of the Trump and Baynham proposal bears this message: "How your tax dollar can go further"—indicating that the focus on change is also on improving the managerial efficiency of the educational enterprise. Neither of the two proposals presents research data concerning the improvement of learning outcomes as a result of modular-flexible scheduling.

Curriculum Improvement. As emphasized early in this chapter, when innovations are designed for purposes other than the improvement of teaching and learning, the outcome is not likely to be curriculum improvement. Although modular-flexible scheduling has been promoted as a system for improving the curriculum, the actual proposals appear to be concerned mainly with problems of logistics in processing students and utilizing teachers and facilities in an economically efficient system. Recent reports indicate that modular-flexible scheduling has many inflexible features and the system may simply result in a reallocation of time in which traditional teaching takes place.[16] Hopefully, the time will come when a school devises a modular-flexible schedule with the primary focus on the improvement of teaching and learning.

THE NONGRADED SECONDARY SCHOOL

While nongrading is most often found in the primary level of elementary schooling, a few secondary schools in recent years have abandoned the conventional grade-level designations to allow students to enroll in courses and advance in accordance with their individual capa-

---

14 John F. Warner, "The Changing Shape of Contemporary Education," *Teachers College Record*, Vol. 66 (May, 1965), p. 763.

15 J. Lloyd Trump and Dorsey Baynham, *Guide to Better Schools: Focus on Change* (Chicago: Rand McNally & Company, 1961).

16 Juanita Wilmoth and Willard Ehn, "The Inflexibility of Modular Flexible Scheduling," *Educational Leadership*, Vol. 27 (April, 1970), pp. 727–731.

bilities. Where most secondary schools attempt to adjust for differences in aptitude and achievement through various class groupings within grades, as proposed by Conant,[17] the nongraded approach provides for multi-age groupings without regard to grade levels. Because the nongraded approach allows each student to advance in his studies at his own rate, it is sometimes referred to as a "continuous progress" plan.

Rationale

Although the common practice is to classify students by grade level, achievement variability is such that a large proportion of students are performing at levels which do not fit their grade-level designations. For example, it has been found that in English and social studies, about 30 per cent of the students in grade 9 exceed the average student's performance in grade 12.[18]

While ability grouping is the usual method of attempting to reduce variability, such grouping often fails to produce the "homogeneity" that is claimed for it. Furthermore, the research on the effects of ability grouping on student achievement reveals no clear and consistent patterns.[19] Possible reasons for the failure of ability grouping to be associated with higher achievement are that: (1) teachers fail to differentiate their methods and materials in accordance with the nature and needs of the group; (2) disadvantaged youngsters who are segregated in low-ability classes are denied the benefits of stimulation that accrue from being associated with youngsters of different backgrounds; on the other hand, the achievement of youngsters from educationally supportive families does not seem to be affected by school grouping; [20] (3) students in low-ability classes suffer from a self-fulfilling prophecy through which they and their teachers have low-achievement expectations that are allowed to come true; [21] and (4) the correlation between standardized measures of aptitude and actual school achievement is very low.

Ability grouping also fails to overcome the limitations inherent in a system whereby courses, like students, are classified according to grade levels. And since nonpromotion has been shown to have negative affects on achievement, it is contended that grade-level designations might well

---

[17] James B. Conant, *The American High School Today* (New York: McGraw-Hill Book Company, Inc., 1959), pp. 49–50.

[18] Marion F. Shaycoft, *The High School Years: Growth in Cognitive Skills* (Pittsburgh: American Institute for Research and the University of Pittsburgh, 1967).

[19] Glen Heathers, "Grouping," in Robert L. Ebel (ed.), *Encyclopedia of Educational Research*, 4th ed. (New York: The Macmillan Company, 1969), p. 565.

[20] James S. Coleman, *Equality of Educational Opportunity* (Washington, D.C.: U.S. Government Printing Office, 1966), p. 22.

[21] Robert Rosenthal and Lenore Jacobson, *Pygmalion in the Classroom* (New York: Holt, Rinehart and Winston, Inc., 1968).

be eliminated.[22] Proponents of the nongraded secondary school claim that able students can advance in the curriculum according to their achievement while the less able are not obliged to advance until they are ready.

Evaluation and Implications

Although the proponents of nongraded secondary schools make many enthusiastic claims for this system of organization, no research has been offered to support their claims.[23] The program advanced by Brown at Melbourne High School in Florida utilizes national standardized achievement tests in the placement and advancement of students.[24] Yet test experts acknowledge that standardized test scores are poor predictors of achievement. For example, the highest multiple correlations between test scores and freshman college grades run betwen .50 and .60,[25] making any prediction only from 25 to 36 per cent better than chance. Such tests do not measure a student's powers of motivation in applying himself to longer term tasks. Consequently, they should not be used as a sole or even major criterion for student placement. Such misuses of standardized tests, reported by Brown, are not characteristic of practices in nongraded schools, however.

In classifying students according to test scores, Brown notes that a "student may remain in a lower phase indefinitely." [26] This obviously prevents him from taking many courses, since he is stuck with those courses open only to "lower-phase" students. Since the content of many secondary school subjects is not always arranged according to levels of progression in cognitive difficulty, the practice of locking students out of such courses on the basis of a single criterion measure is indefensible. For example, a class in English composition and one on the contemporary American novel are focused on two different kinds of learning experiences. The same is true of a course in U.S. history and one in the problems of democracy. Consequently, unless it can be demonstrated that there is a progression of levels of cognitive difficulty in a sequence of courses, students should not be prevented from taking these courses. This applies to any system of school organization, whether graded or nongraded.

---

22 NEA Project on Instruction, *Schools for the Sixties* (New York: McGraw-Hill Book Company, Inc., 1963), p. 76.

23 Heathers, *op. cit.*, pp. 563–574.

24 B. Frank Brown, *The Nongraded High School* (Englewood Cliffs, N.J.: Prentice-Hall, Inc., 1963).

25 Henry S. Dyer, "Admissions—College and University," in *Encyclopedia of Educational Research, op. cit.*, p. 38.

26 *Brown, op. cit.*, p. 49.

Although proponents of the nongraded school contend that it serves to reduce the stigma of being a slow learner, no research studies are available that compare this problem in graded schools as against nongraded schools. In many graded secondary schools, an effort is made to advance students by chronological age as well as by achievement, while making adjustments for levels of achievement in certain subjects through grouping practices. In addition, there is a process of self-selection or natural selection, in which students in conventionally graded high schools are allowed to schedule courses according to their interests, goals, and levels of achievement. Thus the course in chemistry may enroll mainly college-bound juniors and seniors, while a required course in American problems may be taken by all seniors regardless of their educational and occupational goals or achievement levels.

Nongraded approaches should allow for greater flexibility in teaching-learning practices and in curriculum design. Students are not well served when a new set of locksteps is substituted for the old. The comprehensive secondary school should be a place where students from different walks of life and with different aspirations and aptitudes find opportunities for success.

TECHNOLOGY AND THE CLASSROOM

Technology in education, as in society, is a process through which planned objectives are carried out. Thus, modular-flexible scheduling is one organizational schema of educational technology. The textbook, motion picture, teaching machine, and computer are technological devices. Nevertheless, there is an essential difference between technology as an industrial process and as an educational process. It may seem trite to point out that where the product of the industrial process is an inanimate object, the product of education is a human being. Yet, as we shall see, many educational technologists seem to lose sight of this difference as they seek to use the devices of technology for educational automation. But before discussing the implications of such efforts, let us examine the uses of the medium of television in instruction.

Promises and Pitfalls in ITV

The early efforts to promote television as a medium for systematic instruction found it being described as "the most powerful medium of communication yet devised by man." [27] This may indeed be the case, judging by the enormous amount of time devoted to watching television

---

[27] Ford Foundation, *Teaching by Television* (New York: The Ford Foundation, 1959), p. 2.

at home and by the studies that reveal that television is regarded as the most credible source of news.[28]

Yet, in terms of the typical classroom, television has not yet been discovered. Throughout the 1950's, the Ford Foundation was the main source of support for instructional television (ITV) in our schools and colleges. But the Ford Foundation's purpose in promoting systematic instruction via television was chiefly to demonstrate its efficacy as an automation device to solve the teacher shortage in the face of exploding enrollments. Consequently, instead of being directed at bringing new dimensions to classroom teaching and learning, ITV was used primarily as a surrogate teacher. The instructional methodology employed in most television courses tended to closely resemble the traditional classroom teacher, who spends most of his time telling and explaining the material to his students. Under such circumstances, the several hundred studies comparing ITV courses with conventional classroom instruction tended to reveal no significant differences. As a result of the dull repertoire of television teaching, high school and college students often expressed negative attitudes toward the medium.

Despite the growing federal support of instructional and educational television through the National Defense Education Act (1958), the Educational TV Facilities Act (1962), the Higher Education Facilities Act (1963), the Elementary and Secondary Education Act (1965), and the Public Broadcasting Act (1967), there are no signs of an impending revolution in teaching via television.

Uses and Abuses.   After having promoted ITV as an automation device for more than a decade, a former officer of the Ford Foundation identified "two prime causes for instructional television's limited acceptance: the quality of the transmitted instruction, and the way it is used in the classroom." [29] He then went on to acknowledge that television had served largely as a conveyor of conventional modes of instruction and that, as a result, there had been widespread disenchantment with the mediocre level of teaching via television.

In the same report, Murphy and Gross review the history of a widely publicized Ford Foundation project in which television was used for large-class instruction to effect economies in teaching personnel in a county-wide school system. The authors conclude that "by magnifying and extending mediocrity, television may actually lower instructional quality instead of raising it." [30] After six years of large-group TV instruc-

---

28 Burns W. Roper, *A Ten-Year View of Public Attitudes Toward Television and Other Mass Media, 1959–1968* (New York: Television Information Office, 1969).

29 Alvin C. Eurich, Preface in Judith Murphy and Ronald Gross, *Learning by Television* (New York: The Ford Foundation, 1966), p. 6.

30 *Ibid.,* p. 44.

tion in this school system, public opinion became aroused and a Quality Education Committee was formed in 1963. Consultants brought in to study the situation recommended that large-class instruction be abandoned and that the quality of the programming be improved.

During the early part of 1961, the author of this text had read a glowing account of this project by the Ford Foundation and paid a visit to a high school in this system to observe how large-group ITV was being used successfully. The author then wrote this account of his observations:

> I recently visited a high school where large groups of students were being instructed in US history via television. The setting was a large auditorium where television receivers were scattered among 550 students. A head teacher and three assistants supervised the class. As the television lesson began, I took a seat among the students. I was surprised to find that although neither I nor the students in my immediate vicinity could see the screen with any reasonable degree of clarity (both the distance and angle of the television receiver were unsatisfactory), no complaints were registered by the students. As I looked about, I was even more surprised to find that most of the students around me were not even attempting to look at the television receiver. They simply were listening to the television teacher and dutifully writing in their notebooks. The television teacher was merely a "talking face" to these students, and once they had seen his face, it was only necessary to listen to the lecture and take conventional notes. Following the telecast, the head teacher made a few points about the lesson and raised some factual questions which were answered by individual students via a roving microphone carried by one of the assistant teachers. Needless to say, no class discussion was possible in such a large group. The culminating activity was a reading assignment in the textbook. The head teacher later told me that the students were required to keep notebooks to insure, among other things, their attentiveness to the TV lessons.[31]

The author went on to note that the great potential of television was in its use for providing learning experiences beyond whatever is possible in the conventional classroom.

> It is clearly time that we regard instructional television as more than a way of extending technologically our conventional teachers and their teaching practices. Instead, we need to determine the differences in learning experiences which the medium of television can effect beyond whatever is possible in the usual classroom setting. Vice versa, we need to find out what learning values can be derived through a classroom setting in which direct interaction between teacher and learner and among peer learners is facilitated. This would necessitate the development of far more sophisticated instruments of evaluation. Instead of

---

[31] Daniel Tanner, "Television and Learning," *Teachers College Record*, Vol. 65 (December, 1963), pp. 243–244.

measuring only verbal and skill criteria in learning, we would need to assess visual and behavioral dimensions in the teaching-learning process. . . .

The special characteristics of television need to be more fully understood. Its directness, immediacy, and visual eclecticism are not embodied in any other medium. Such attributes make television a unique medium for instruction.

We need to break away from the notion that we must avoid those parameters for which numerical values are not immediately applicable. There are many qualitative dimensions of learning for which numerical values cannot be assigned. But this does not mean that we should constrict our instructional efforts and research to quantifiable elements only. For example, we know that patterns of human behavior are frequently developed through emulation of a human model—a parent, a teacher, a peer. An accomplished person may credit his creative performance to the inspiration of a teacher, a literary source, or some other experience. It would be useful to know whether such emulation, for example, is facilitated (or possible at all) through television.[32]

Expanded Vision and Curriculum Improvement. Throughout this chapter we have emphasized how so many innovations are adopted for purposes of administrative efficiency and not for curriculum improvement. Yet, somehow, the sponsors of such innovations often express disappointment when the evaluation reveals that no improvement in learning outcomes can be demonstrated. The history of instructional television in school and college is a case in point. In the few instances where television has been used to do what the good teacher cannot do, the results have been gratifying. Many of our medical schools and some law schools are using the medium for expanded vision. Closed-circuit TV is used for studying surgical techniques and for viewing courtroom procedures. The British Broadcasting Corporation (BBC) has capitalized on the unique qualities of the medium to provide dramatizations and documentary lessons for classroom inquiry into social problems and national and international affairs.

If ITV is to find a significant place in the mainstream of American education, we shall have to capitalize on the unique attributes of the medium. High-quality programming will necessitate centralized resources and the marshaling of talent comparable to what the BBC has been doing for the British School Broadcasting Council for more than a decade. New breakthroughs are on the horizon, in which classroom receivers will be equipped with automatic recording, storing, and playback devices. But the key to curriculum improvement will be in the quality of the programming as well as in the way it is used in the classroom.

---

[32] *Ibid.*, p. 247.

The Human Learner and the Machine Teacher

Supported primarily through federal funds and grants from the Ford Foundation, Carnegie Corporation, and Kettering Foundation, programmed instruction and computer-assisted instruction gained a considerable following during the decade of the 1960's. The revolution in instruction that television had failed to usher in could now be sought through other devices of technology.

Chief theoretician of programmed instruction is the behaviorist B. F. Skinner of Harvard. Since the early 1950's, Skinner has predicted that his theory of operant conditioning would lead to a veritable revolution in shaping human behavior through programmed instruction and teaching machines. But in seeking to establish his case, Skinner fails to distinguish between the role of the human teacher and the role of the machine teacher.

> The application of operant conditioning to education is simple and direct. Teaching is the arrangement of contingencies of reinforcement under which students learn. They learn without teaching in their natural environments, but teachers arrange special contingencies which expedite learning, hastening the appearance of behavior which would otherwise be acquired slowly or making sure of the appearance of behavior which might otherwise never occur.
>
> A teaching machine is simply any device which arranges contingencies of reinforcement.[33]

Need for Human Interaction.   The only role left for the human teacher, if Skinner's views are to be taken seriously, is that of managing the machines that arrange the contingencies of reinforcement for the learners. Yet our common sense tells us that how we learn and what we learn must somehow enable us to function more effectively with other human beings in society. Skinner's conception of teaching and the role of the teaching machine appears to eliminate the need for human interaction. The learner is simply conditioned to interact with his machine under a system managed by somebody who is still called a teacher. Nevertheless, we know that most complex forms of learned behavior, such as speech, are developed through social interaction. The kinds of learning that are most effectively developed through human interaction are virtually ignored by Skinner and other proponents of operant conditioning.

The behaviorists who see programmed instruction as the chief mode of teaching and learning ignore the considerable body of research that shows that mere verbal learning does not lead automatically to changes in social behavior. Such change is most successfully developed through

---

[33] B. F. Skinner, *The Technology of Teaching* (New York: Appleton-Century-Crofts, 1968), pp. 64–65.

human interaction. The isolated nature of automated instruction ignores the interpersonal aspects of learning. Children and adolescents develop their codes of behavior, vocational aspirations, and role expectations through emulation of the human model—the parent, the teacher, the peer, and others. The developmental tasks and psychobiological needs of children and youth are virtually ignored in operant conditioning. Machines cannot serve as ideals toward which humans aspire. What human would want to be like a machine?

Diversity of Learning Experiences. Many educational technologists are so obsessed with promoting their own creations that they fail to see the limitations of their theories and devices in the educative process. For example, while it is entirely possible to program all of the essential elements of *Huckleberry Finn* or *Doctor Zhivago* into a teaching machine or into a computer for instructional purposes, the nature of the learning experience derived from such programming cannot in any way be regarded as a substitute for the reading of a novel. Yet it might be possible to demonstrate that computer-assisted instruction imparts more information in far less time than that which can be derived from actually reading the novel. The point is that the two kinds of learning experiences bear no resemblance to each other. This applies to many activities that transcend the limitations of programmed instruction, computer-assisted instruction, and operant conditioning. Enjoying a novel, writing a theme, or engaging in group discussion are some such learning experiences.

Uniformity and Conformity. Where Skinner's technology of teaching is limited to convergent types of thinking, humans require divergent modes of thinking in expressing their individuality and in contributing to social change and social betterment.

The claim is made that programmed instruction is an individualized approach to education. But the only individualized feature of programmed instruction is that it controls the material presented to the learner in accordance with the learner's rate of correct responses. Branching programs provide for some differences in repertoire when students give incorrect responses, but these differences are decidedly limited. Successful achievement through programmed instruction requires absolute uniformity of interpretation and response on the part of the learner. Consequently, programmed instruction is not designed for individualized education, but represents a mass standardization of curriculum and instruction.

Even the conventional textbook does not require the uniformity and conformity of learning that are essential in the programmed text or in other devices for programmed instruction. Where the teaching machine atomizes and predigests the subject matter for the student, leaving little latitude for individual interpretation, the typical textbook requires the student to sort out relevant material and make his own analysis and synthesis of the subject matter. This does not imply that the learning process must be made as difficult as possible for the student. But the process of inquiring into complex representations of knowledge, such as through textbooks, documents, literary sources, and other reading material requires skills and presents opportunities for developing modes of inquiry which are fundamentally different from what is required in programmed instruction. In programmed instruction, the learner cannot develop a style of inquiry of his own.

Research on Programmed Instruction and Operant Conditioning

The most common finding from the hundreds of studies on programmed instruction is that there are no significant differences in achievement when comparisons are made between conventional learning materials and various different forms of programming.[34] In such studies we must recognize that the students engaged in programmed learning are being fed constantly with the "right" answers. If students were fed the "right" answers when working with conventional materials, one wonders what the comparisons might reveal. Yet there undoubtedly is value to be derived from a process, however "inefficient," that allows the student to develop his own styles of analyzing and synthesizing the subject matter from a variety of reading material.

Thus far, most of the evidence used to support the theory of operant conditioning is derived from observations of laboratory animals and limited work with individual humans. But there is no experimental evidence in classrooms that shows that programmed learning should be based only upon operant conditioning. Of course, it has been demonstrated that humans, as well as lower animals, do learn through operant conditioning. Young humans are sufficiently intelligent and adaptable so that they can readily demonstrate their ability to learn like rats or pigeons, if this is what is expected of them. And while some forms of human behavior are indeed learned through conditioning, this does not mean that all forms of human behavior are learned in this manner. The same is probably the case for the rat or pigeon who is sufficiently intelligent to meet the terms of the behaviorist. After all, if the poor animal is to get his food pellet and avoid starvation in his cage, he is going to push the buttons, press the levers, stand on his head, and do whatever else is animally possible despite the abnormality of the behavior.

---

[34] Lawrence M. Stolurow, "Programmed Instruction," *Encyclopedia of Educational Research, op. cit.*, p. 1020.

Computer-Assisted Instruction

The unbridled enthusiasm once expressed for television and mechanical devices for the improvement of learning has now been transferred to computer-assisted instruction (CAI). The computer's memory is used to process and react to student responses through the electric typewriter, which also serves as an input device for the student. In addition, various audiovisual media can be controlled through the computer program, making the system considerably more flexible than the programmed textbook or teaching machine. Nevertheless, the learner's styles of response are completely under the control of the computer program.

Goodlad sees a new era on the horizon in which human-to-human instruction is superseded by the computer.

> The era that is in full bloom and about to fade is human-to-human instruction. . . . The era of instruction that will supersede the era of human-based instruction is that of man-machine interaction. We might not like that, but the signs are clear. The instructional era that is now on the horizon is man-machine interaction. The problem is not whether or not we like it, but what we are going to do about it. The machine is, of course, the computer. We have lived in the shadow of the computer long enough now, but used it so little in instructional affairs that we may be inclined to believe that its future and our own are going to be very far apart. Nothing could be farther from the truth. The computer will march relentlessly into our instructional lives.[35]

Goodlad goes on to predict the eventual demise of the school as each home is connected to a community learning center which is equipped with a computer-controlled videotape, microfiche, and record library and is hooked up with state and national television networks.

Goodlad is not alone in his vision of the future. In a publication celebrating the centennial of the U.S. Office of Education, this vision of education in 1997 was presented:

> The learning console at which Johnny Brook spends much of his time in Concenter 417 appears to be an enclosed desk with a television set and a typewriter built into it. He starts his lesson by inserting his aluminum identification plate into the console demand-slot. Within a few seconds, the screen projects a problem in mathematics. Johnny recognizes it: he had the same problem at the end of yesterday's lesson. He picks up his electronic stylus and writes the answer on his response slate; . . . it has several hundred thousand tiny pores that receive impulses from the stylus and translate handwriting to machine language.
>
> A voice from the speaker in the console congratulates Johnny on getting the right answer, then urges "Now try this one" as the screen

---

35 John I. Goodlad, *The Future of Learning and Teaching* (Washington, D.C.: National Education Association, 1968), pp. 9, 11.

projects a new problem. If he gets a wrong answer, the screen projects the same kind of problem a different way; if Johnny gets three wrong in a row, a soft tone rings in Betty Raschke's lapel alarm and brings her into his console.

Dr. Raschke, the concenter monitor, isn't the only person keeping track of Johnny's progress. His console and concenter . . . are connected to the Educational Resource Center downtown. There, the record of Johnny's progress that has been tabulated by computers is combed by a team of psychologists, programmers, expert teachers [sic] of everything from arithmetic to zoology, remedial specialists, and guidance counselors.

. . . The Brook family has two learning consoles at home. . . . In Johnny's world, education never stops; learning is a year-round, lifelong process.[36]

Obviously, the job of Dr. Raschke and her team is to determine, by remote control, what is wrong with Johnny—not what is wrong with the system. We can only hope that Johnny's eventual success with the machine does not cause him to want to be like his machine when he grows up.

Goodlad takes us quite a bit further in his view of the future of education and mankind, by pointing to the promising possibilities for the production (sic) of different kinds of human beings than those we now have, through the uses of chemicals, drugs, electric currents, and eugenics.

The first educational question will not be what knowledge is of most worth, but what kinds of human beings we wish to produce. The possibilities defy our imagination. The nerve cells of the brain, far more than muscles or organs, are highly sensitive to small electric currents, to a variety of chemicals, and to changes in blood supply and its accompanying nourishment . . . behavior can be manipulated by applying electrical currents to regions of the brain. Experiments are now underway with drugs and brain extracts designed to enhance human learning or memory. . . . We may not like it, but it's here—the means of drastically altering the course of human development through artificial insemination, chemical treatment, and electronic manipulation.[37]

Our purpose is not to explore the full implications of such a vision (or nightmare), but one is compelled to recall the vision of the Thousand-Year Reich. Human variability, individuality, and dissent have kept us from disaster. Jacques Ellul, the French sociologist, observes that as the human brain is made to conform to the much more advanced brain of the machine, even the intelligentsia will not be a conscience for man,

---

[36] U.S. Office of Education, *OE 100—Highlighting the Progress of American Education* (Washington, D.C.: U.S. Government Printing Office, 1967).

[37] Goodlad, *op. cit.*, pp. 22–23.

but will become "the servants, the most conformist imaginable, of the instruments of technique. . . . And education will no longer be an unpredictable and exciting adventure in human enlightenment, but an exercise in conformity and an apprenticeship to whatever gadgetry is useful in a technical world." [38]

It is ironic that the devices and systems of technology, which give promise of freeing man to become more human, also portend a danger of diminishing our humanity. In education, we have made the error of seeking to use the devices and systems of technology to restrict our notions of human behavior. We become less tolerant of ambiguity, digression, divergence, and expressions of feeling—all characteristically human qualities.

The new technology can be used in education to provide learning experiences that are not otherwise possible, to reduce or eliminate many repetitive and unproductive tasks, and to free teachers and learners to devote more time to learning activities that are characteristically human.

In their admiration for the precision of the machine, some educational technologists propose schemes whereby machine operations become the model for the learning behavior of the student. The episode goes something like this: The machine is programmed by a human to generate a message for the learner. The learner responds to the machine with a message, right or wrong, which is anticipated by the machine. If the learner's rseponse is in error, the machine transmits another message until the learner's response satisfies the machine. The machine generates another message and the learner, in turn, generates a response for each message. The success of the machine is measured by its ability to create the learner in its own image.

"Render unto man the things which are man's and unto the computer the things which are the computer's," wrote Norbert Wiener, the father of cybernetics.[39] Some day man may succeed in transforming himself into an organism that is almost as infallible as his most perfected machine. The new man may not have to eat, sleep, study, play, or have sexual intercourse. But he will then be more like a machine than a member of *Homo sapiens*. When this happens, the next step, which may prove to be impossible, will be to re-create *Homo sapiens*.

Such visions of the future may make us more tolerant and appreciative of our present-day weaknesses and inefficiencies in education. We may even come to cherish these weaknesses and inefficiencies because they are so characteristically human.

---

[38] Jacques Ellul, *The Technological Society* (New York: Vintage Books, Alfred A. Knopf and Random House, Inc., 1954), p. 349.

[39] Norbert Wiener, *God and Golem, Inc.* (Cambridge, Mass.: The M.I.T. Press, 1964), p. 73.

SUMMARY

Processes in curriculum change include (1) research, (2) development, (3) diffusion, (4) assessment, (5) adoption and adaptation, (6) reassessment, (7) legitimation, and (8) institutionalization. The eventual legitimation and institutionalization of a given educational innovation may be more dependent on social, political, and economic factors than on its proven validity and reliability in effecting needed improvements in the educational system. Relatively few of the new curriculum packages have been subjected to independent and rigorous experimentation and evaluation.

During the past two decades of curriculum reform, little attention has been given to the design of the total curriculum. In seeking equilibrium, educators need to develop patterns of relationships in the curriculum among (1) studies that are discipline-centered; (2) studies that are cross-disciplinary, multidisciplinary, and interdisciplinary within given fields of knowledge—such as the sciences taken as a whole, or the social sciences taken as a whole; (3) studies that are cross-disciplinary, multidisciplinary, and interdisciplinary—involving two or more different fields of knowledge—such as mathematics and science, or history, sociology, and literature; (4) studies that are focused on pervading personal and societal problems without being limited to any given area of organized subject matter; (5) prevocational and vocational studies; and (6) independent learning experiences, both in school and out of school.

Many innovations in education have been aimed at goals other than the improvement of the curriculum. As a consequence, they effect no improvement in learning outcomes. Instead of using the new media to convey new learning experiences and to improve the quality of our conventional messages, we often find that these devices are used to increase the efficiency of transmitting our old messages. Perhaps this is because the people who have elected educational technology as a career have nothing else to communicate. Perhaps this is also because those who exert the greatest influence for change in the institution of schooling have regarded education as not unlike a factory process where efficiency is gauged by maximizing outputs in relation to inputs.

Too often innovations are conceived and adopted as entities and not as relations. Instead of curriculum development, we have curriculum packages and new technological devices which are plugged into separate slots in the schooling process.

In their eager promotion of the new devices, the educational technologists have failed to distinguish between the functions of the human teacher and those of the machine teacher. Some of the technologists see no essential differences between the two, except to point out that technological devices are far more precise and efficient in the messages they convey and in their capacity to evoke predictable and measurable responses on the part of the learner. Thus the human teacher is regarded as primarily a manager of a machine-student learning system.

While it is conceivable that programmed instruction and computer-assisted instruction can be utilized for developing a wide range of cognitive styles, much of the effort to date has been directed at fairly concentrated learning skills. The potentiality of the new technology lies in (1) freeing the teacher and student from certain types of repetitive and tedious drill; (2) providing learning experiences that are otherwise not possible within the time-and-space limitations of the classroom and school; and (3) freeing the teacher and students to develop important learning outcomes that are uniquely derived from human interaction.

Programmed instruction and computer-assisted instruction need not be limited to an operant-conditioning rationale. Instructional television need not be a "talking face" in place of the live teacher. Modular-flexible scheduling, team teaching, pupil grouping, and so on, need not be merely techniques of managerial efficiency. The key focus of educational innovation should be the improvement of teaching and learning. The new technology should challenge educators to "render unto humans the things which are human."

PROBLEMS FOR STUDY AND DISCUSSION

1. Skinner contends that "in the long run a technology of teaching helps most by increasing the teacher's productivity. It simply permits him to teach more—more of a given subject, in more subjects, and to more students. . . . A technology of teaching by its very nature maximizes the teacher's achievement. The whole establishment gains." [B. F. Skinner, *The Technology of Teaching* (New York: Appleton-Century-Crofts, 1968), p. 258.]

   In an advanced system of educational technology, what changes in the function of the human teacher, other than those mentioned by Skinner, do you see taking place?

2. The claim is made that programmed instruction and computer-assisted instruction provide for the individualization of learning. What is meant by the individualization of learning in this context? Do you see any contradictions in the claim that these devices and methods provide for individualized learning?

3. It is claimed that by using explicit, quantifiable behavioral objectives—those that "describe without ambiguity the nature of learner behavior or product to be measured"—educators will find themselves entering "an era which promises to yield fantastic improvements in the quality of instruction." [W. James Popham, and others, *Instruc-*

tional Objectives (Chicago: Rand McNally & Company, 1969), pp. 33, 35.]

On the other hand, it is observed that "behavioral objectives with a strong taste of the explicit, the quantitative, and the measurable account for but a small fraction of the many effects we expect of schooling." [Anthony G. Oettinger, *Run, Computer, Run* (Cambridge, Mass.: Harvard University Press, 1969), p. 221.]

What are some of the effects we expect from schooling which cannot be measured in terms of behavioral objectives? Should the schools continue to seek effects that cannot be quantified and measured? Why or why not?

4. The development of the motion picture and television was accompanied by predictions of a revolution in instruction. Such a revolution has failed to materialize. How do you account for this failure? Today, with the advent of computer-assisted instruction, once again an educational revolution is predicted. Are any parallels to be drawn or lessons to be learned from the earlier failures in applying the new media to education? Explain.

5. Jacques Ellul contends that the new technology, especially television, is destructive of personality and human relations:

> Men become accustomed to listening to machines and talking to machines. . . . No more face-to-face encounters, no more dialogue . . . man finds refuge in the lap of technique, which envelops him in solitude and at the same time reassures him with all its hoaxes. Television, because of its power of fascination and its capacity of visual and auditory penetration, is probably the technical instrument which is most destructive of personality and human relations. [Jacques Ellul, *The Technological Society* (New York: Vintage Books, Alfred A. Knopf and Random House, Inc., 1964), pp. 379–380.]

What implications does Ellul's thesis have for the new educational technology?

6. What are your views concerning Goodlad's vision of the future of education and mankind, as expressed in the two quotations in this chapter?

7. Near the close of this chapter is a description of education in the year 1997 as predicted in a federal publication celebrating the centennial of the U.S. Office of Education. What is your reaction to this image of the future?

8. During the curriculum reform movement of the late 1950's and the decade of the 1960's, little attention was given to the design of the total school curriculum. How do you account for this neglect?

SELECTED REFERENCES

American Library Association and National Education Association. *Standards for School Media Programs.* Chicago: American Library Association, 1969.

Bent, Rudyard K., Henry H. Kronenberg, and Charles C. Broadman. *Principles of Secondary Education,* 6th ed. New York: McGraw-Hill Book Company, Inc., 1970. Chs. 18, 19.

Bush, Robert N., and Dwight W. Allen. *A New Design for High School Education.* New York: McGraw-Hill Book Company, Inc., 1964.

Crary, Ryland W. *Humanizing the School.* New York: Alfred A. Knopf, Inc., 1969.

Doll, Ronald C. *Curriculum Improvement.* Boston: Allyn and Bacon, Inc., 1970.

Ellul, Jacques. *The Technological Society.* New York: Vintage Books, Alfred A. Knopf and Random House, Inc., 1954.

Goodlad, John I. *The Future of Learning and Teaching.* Washington, D.C.: National Education Association, 1968.

Koestler, Arthur. *The Ghost in the Machine.* New York: The Macmillan Company, 1967.

Lawler, Marcella R. (ed.). *Strategies for Planned Curricular Innovation.* New York: Teachers College Press, 1970.

Miles, Matthew B. (ed.). *Innovations in Education.* New York: Teachers College Press, 1964.

Morphet, Edgar L., and Charles O. Ryan (eds.). *Planning and Effecting Needed Changes in Education.* Designing Education for the Future, No. 3. New York: Citation Press, 1967.

Murphy, Judith, and Ronald Gross. *Learning by Television.* New York: The Ford Foundation, 1966.

National Society for the Study of Education. *Programmed Instruction.* Sixty-sixth Yearbook, Part II. Chicago: The University of Chicago Press, 1967.

Oettinger, Anthony G. *Run, Computer, Run.* Cambridge, Mass.: Harvard University Press, 1969.

Popham, W. James, Elliot W. Eisner, Howard J. Sullivan, and Louise L. Tyler. *Instructional Objectives.* Chicago: Rand McNally & Company, 1969.

Saettler, Paul. *A History of Instructional Technology.* New York: McGraw-Hill Book Company, Inc., 1968.

Saylor, J. Galen, and William M. Alexander. *Curriculum Planning for Modern Schools.* New York: Holt, Rinehart and Winston, Inc., 1966.

Skinner, B. F. *Walden Two.* New York: The Macmillan Company, 1948.

———. *The Technology of Teaching.* New York: Appleton-Century-Crofts, 1968.

Smith, Karl U., and Margaret F. Smith. *Cybernetic Principles of Learning and Educational Design.* New York: Holt, Rinehart and Winston, Inc., 1966.

Taba, Hilda. *Curriculum Development: Theory and Practice.* New York: Harcourt, Brace & World, Inc., 1962.

Tanner, Daniel. *Schools for Youth: Change and Challenge in Secondary Education.* New York: The Macmillan Company, 1965. Ch. 10.

Trump, J. Lloyd, and Dorsey Baynham. *Guide to Better Schools: Focus on Change.* Chicago: Rand McNally & Company, 1961.

Trump, J. Lloyd, and Delmas F. Miller. *Secondary School Improvement.* Boston: Allyn and Bacon, Inc., 1968. Chs. 17–30.

Tyler, Ralph W. *Basic Principles of Curriculum and Instruction.* Chicago: The University of Chicago Press, 1950.

Wiener, Norbert, *The Human Use of Human Beings,* 2nd ed. New York: Anchor Books, Doubleday & Company, Inc., 1954.

———. *God and Golem, Inc.* Cambridge, Mass.: The M.I.T. Press, 1964.

Witt, Paul W. F. (ed.). *Technology and the Curriculum.* New York: Teachers College Press, 1968.

Author Index

Subject Index

English *(cont.)*
new media in, 251, 253, 265
problem of identity of, 214
problem of priorities in, 247–248
progressive educational influences on, 222, 227, 230–231, 235, 254
relationships of, with other subjects, 215–218, 227, 229, 230, 233–235, 242
remedial, 231
as required subject, 215, 232
research on teaching of, 256–265
"revolution" in, 219, 220, 226
search for sequential curriculum in, 238–239, 241, 255
semantics and, 219–220
as separate subject matters, 57, 214–219, 254, 258
skill-emphasis in, 217, 229, 230, 234
social problems and, 235
speech and, 251–252, 259
strategy for curriculum development in, 246–247
tripartite model of, 216, 220, 239, 242, 261
unitary approach to, 254–255
See also Grammar; Literature
English composition, 227–228, 244–245, 251–252, 261
articulation of, with other subjects, 228
assessment of performance in, 240, 244, 251
assignments and teacher load in, 228, 232–233, 263
essentialist influences on, 227–228
evaluation of, by lay readers, 244, 263
neglect of, 261
progressive educational influences on, 227
English Program of the U.S. Office of Education, 213, 236–237, 246
Enrichment studies, 65
Essentialism, 15
Essentialists, 53, 66, 183, 227–228, 231–232, 235
English curriculum and, 224, 227–228, 231–232
foreign languages and, 271–272
social studies curriculum and, 178–180
study of personal and social problems and, 352, 356
vocational education and, 374–378
Essentials *vs.* "nonessentials," 66, 309–312, 377–378
European education, 67, 141–151
dual system of, 143–144, 145, 147–148, 365, 367, 369–370
See also Comparative education

Examinations, "external"
influence of, on curriculum, 254, 256
Exemplars, 58–59, 317–318
Experimental schools, 51, 79
Experimentalism, 5, 49. *See also* Progressive education; Progressivism
Experimentalists, 55, 104
Exploratory studies, 63, 64. *See also* Electives

Fine and performing arts, the
academic ability and, 310
in academic studies, 311–313, 315–316, 320, 327, 328–329
academically talented and, 310, 330
authenticity and uniqueness of, 315–319, 328, 329
as cocurricular activities, 323, 326, 328
cold war influences on, 309–312
Conant's recommendations on, 310–311
criterion of disciplinarity in, 43
criticism and connoisseurship *vs.* creation and performance in, 317–318, 330
cultural *vs.* utilitarian dichotomy in, 308–309, 315
curriculum reform in, 315–330
enrollment in, 312–313
essentialist influences on, 309–310
federal support of, 313–314, 326, 328
as "frill" subjects, 310, 312, 328
general education and, 307, 309–311, 315–316, 320–330
humanities and, 317, 320, 321, 326, 327
intellectuality and, 316–317, 319–320, 330
need for coherent programs of, 311, 320–322
neglect of, 312–313, 315, 319, 322, 328, 330
as nonacademic electives, 59, 310–311, 320
as "nonessential" subjects, 306, 309–312, 320, 328
place of, in the total curriculum, 320, 328
prevocational studies in, 322–323
progressive educational influences on, 308, 309
search for disciplinarity and structure in, 319
verbal learning *vs.* performance in, 315–317, 321–322, 328, 329–330
See also Dance; Theatre arts; Visual arts
Ford Foundation, 88, 238, 407, 415, 418, 422–423, 425
Foreign language learning, and cognitive code-learning theory, 286, 297